Frontiers in Economic History

Economic historians have contributed to the development of economics in a variety of ways, combining theory with quantitative methods, constructing new databases, promoting interdisciplinary approaches to historical topics, and using history as a lens to examine the long-term development of the economy. Frontiers in Economic History publishes manuscripts that push the frontiers of research in economic history in order to better explain past economic experiences and to understand how, why and when economic change occurs. Books in this series will highlight the value of economic history in shedding light on the ways in which economic factors influence growth as well as social and political developments. This series aims to establish a new standard of quality in the field while offering a global discussion forum toward a unified approach in the social sciences.

More information about this series at http://www.springer.com/series/16567

Stefanos Gimatzidis · Reinhard Jung
Editors

The Critique of Archaeological Economy

Springer

Editors
Stefanos Gimatzidis
Austrian Archaeological Institute
Vienna, Austria

Reinhard Jung
Austrian Archaeological Institute
Vienna, Austria

ISSN 2662-9771 ISSN 2662-978X (electronic)
Frontiers in Economic History
ISBN 978-3-030-72538-9 ISBN 978-3-030-72539-6 (eBook)
https://doi.org/10.1007/978-3-030-72539-6

This Springer imprint is published by the registered company Springer Nature Switzerland AG
The registered company address is: Gewerbestrasse 11, 6330 Cham, Switzerland

Contents

1 **An Introduction to the Critique of Archaeological Economy** 1
Reinhard Jung and Stefanos Gimatzidis

2 **Writing the Deep History of Human Economy** 19
Randall H. McGuire

3 **Wealth, Women's Labour, and Forms of Value: Thinking from the Study of Ancestral Central America** 35
Rosemary A. Joyce

4 **"The Economy Has No Surplus": Harry W. Pearson's Contribution Revisited, 60 Years Later** 55
Svend Hansen

5 **Crafting Values in Chalcolithic Cyprus and Anatolia** 71
Bleda S. Düring

6 **The Bornhöck Burial Mound and the Political Economy of an Únětice Ruler** 85
Roberto Risch, Harald Meller, Selina Delgado-Raack, and Torsten Schunke

7 **Property and Markets: The Uses of Land in Pharaonic Egypt Beyond Redistributive and Neoliberal Approaches** 117
Juan Carlos Moreno García

8 **Uneven and Combined: Product Exchange in the Mediterranean (3rd to 2nd Millennium BCE)** 139
Reinhard Jung

9 **Tripod Dedication: Gift and Commodity Exchange in Ancient Greece** 163
Stefanos Gimatzidis

10 Happily Connected? The Interconnectivity Paradigm and the Debate About the Ancient Economy 183
Jan Paul Crielaard

11 Aegean Transport Amphoras (Sixth to First Centuries BCE): Exploring Social Tension in a Path Dependency Model 205
Mark L. Lawall

12 Modelling Trade in Athenian Pottery in the Archaic and Classical Period 223
Robin Osborne

Chapter 1
An Introduction to the Critique of Archaeological Economy

Reinhard Jung and Stefanos Gimatzidis

Abstract This book studies past economics from anthropological, archaeological, historical and sociological perspectives. By analyzing archeological and other evidence, it examines economic behavior and institutions in ancient societies. Adopting an interdisciplinary perspective, it critically discusses dominant economic models that have influenced the study of past economic relations in various disciplines, while at the same time highlighting alternative theoretical trajectories. In this regard, the book's goal is not only to test theoretical models under scrutiny, but also to present evidence against the rationalization of past economic behavior according to the rules of modern markets. The contributing authors cover various topics, such as concepts of commodity and value, trade in the classical Greek world, and management of economic affluence.

This book presents a collection of papers by scholars of different disciplines and theoretical orientations, who discuss recent developments in the reconstruction of past economies through anthropological, historical and archaeological perspectives. The starting point for this critical discussion was a turn in archaeological theory and interpretive practice during recent decades towards economic models regulated by individual agency. A single and isolated individual driven by their economic agency has emerged in modernity in an imaginary free market and accordingly defined archaeological theory and interpretative praxis. Social anthropological research has been showing since the nineteenth century that such "Robinsonades" lack foundations in pre-capitalist societies. Instead, they represent projections of contemporary economic role models into the remotest past. Furthermore, certain current perceptions of the singular individual and eternal market forces are more or less unconsciously inspired by the hegemonic neoliberal economic discourse of our time.

R. Jung (✉) · S. Gimatzidis
Austrian Archaeological Institute, Austrian Academy of Sciences, Vienna, Austria
e-mail: Reinhard.Jung@oeaw.ac.at

S. Gimatzidis
e-mail: stefanos.gimatzidis@oeaw.ac.at

S. Gimatzidis and R. Jung (eds.), *The Critique of Archaeological Economy*,
Frontiers in Economic History,
https://doi.org/10.1007/978-3-030-72539-6_1

Archaeological studies of past economic systems require a critical study of historical and archaeological data through an anthropologically informed theoretical approach and testing of the results in the field. The quality of a model is evaluated against its ability to explain a specific historical situation, the residue of which is archaeological evidence in context. The evidence, in turn, offers the tools for testing—rejecting or adjusting—the model.

Archaeological theory in the western world often seems to have overwhelmingly favoured a neoliberal positivism in the interpretation of past economic relations. In the first half of the twentieth century, cultural historical approaches projected modern economic models into the past through a rather formalist perspective; processual archaeology attempted to quantify these relations; finally, post-processual critique emphasized the role of the individual in shaping ancient economic patterns. Archaeological theorizing is a reflection of advances in sociology and philosophy but also of socio-political transformations making, therefore, interpretation of the past vulnerable to manipulation, especially when economic relations are at stake. Economics of the past have been studied through several different theoretical approaches not only in accordance with the respective socio-political background of the observer, but also depending on the *Zeitgeist*. There are only a few academic fields, where interpretation depends so heavily on ideology and the theoretical methods engaged, as economic studies of the past.

We therefore understand that the discussion regarding past and modern economic relations will never be exhausted because it is both historically and socially contingent. This book appears in the midst of a series of crises that have shaken the foundations of the world economy and, consequently, the historical conceptualization of modern economic models. The main question that inevitably arises concerns the current role of archaeology after its emergence in the modern period as a colonialist and nationalist device, or an expression of the noble spirit of upper class humanists, and the subsequent—often-disoriented—critique in the postmodern era. If archaeology has a social role today, this is portrayed by personal and collective visions and anticipations that are embedded in social experience. Denouncing archaeology's embeddedness in social matters (cf. Papadopoulos & Urton, 2012: 20) does not serve any alleged objectification in the reconstruction of economic and social relations, but rather obscures the motives of the historiographer or observer. Archaeology and anthropology may present a tool kit for explaining the domination of certain economic models over others, the class, gender or ideological determinants in the definition of modes of production and thus assume an active social role—every time through a different historical and social perspective. In this sense, the present volume is inevitably different in the conceptualization and reconstruction of past economic relations from earlier works treating the same topic. Furthermore, it presents a conscious effort to raise awareness about social needs and expectations, also in fields dedicated to the study of the past.

A constant challenge in archaeological interpretation is that of becoming aware of several points of critique and reasserting them in analytical praxis. One of such points that is selectively treated in this introduction is the notion of commodity, which has undergone several re-definitions since its introduction from a production-oriented perspective in the nineteenth century. Another critical issue is the social conditioning of property in past economies, which have been historically shaped through continuous transformations. Relations among cultural phenomena can reflect, and more often, conceal or fetishize the economic behaviour of social groups with distinct interests that historically defined and transformed concepts such as commodity and property. Human agency is socio-historically embedded, which means that individuals can become active social performers, yet under the restriction of certain conditions. These conditions may emerge independently of human will, but they are always subject to transformation by means of conscious human (re)action.

The Conceptualization of Commodity in the Exploration of Past Economies

The definition of commodity has been a central issue in Marxist discourse and formed the basis of the critique of political economy. It was Georg Wilhelm Hegel who suggested that a product becomes a commodity in private exchange and implied its use- and exchange-value that was subsequently elaborated by Karl Marx (Hegel, 2019; Marx, 1962 [1867]: 49–98; https://www.marxists.org/archive/marx/works/1867-c1/ch01.htm). The latter developed further the labour theory of value in accordance with Adam Smith's definition of labour as "the real measure of the exchangeable value of all commodities" (Smith, 1976 [1776]: 47). Marx explained the generation of "surplus value" by means of "unpaid" labour as a result of the commodity character of labour power itself, which was of crucial importance in his definition of accumulation of capital (Marx, 1962 [1867]: 331–340). This implies the production of commodities above subsidence needs and as such it found application in economic studies, often deprived of its political connotations.

The commodity has usually been perceived according to the Marxian definition as a notion deriving from and applying to modern capitalist markets. Marx, however, held that the commodity was also a phenomenon of "an earlier date in history, though not in the same predominating and characteristic manner as nowadays (Marx, 1962 [1867]: 97)". What makes the difference in this ambiguous definition of the role of commodities are apparently the modes of production that significantly differed in modern and pre-modern societies. The Marxian approach to the dual character of the commodity, as characterized by use and exchange value, presupposed a ruling class that appropriates the surplus product generated by others. Commodity exchange was a mechanism to achieve this. Such economic systems, characterized by marked inequality, could not have been accommodated outside hierarchically organized societies.

The exploration that began a long time ago of the modes of exchange, with a focus on gift and barter, was a substantial contribution of anthropology to the understanding of pre-modern economic transactions. Social-cultural anthropologists from the 1980s onwards attempted to overcome complications in the conceptualization of commodity by depriving this notion of its production properties and defining it merely as a product of exchange and consumption (Appadurai, 1986; Miller, 1995). These developments in anthropological theory had some impact on archaeological thought (Mullins, 2011). Consumption was soon established as a conceptual framework in the Mediterranean and elsewhere, where anthropologists and archaeologists focused on the use value of commodities and downplayed not only modes of production but also the economy of exchange (Dietler, 2005, 2010). All this started, according to Graeber (2001: 26, 30), when post-structuralism urged the "shatter[ing of] totalities", took individual agents as constructs of the fields they were playing on, and finally "opened up another space into which the maximalizing individual could crawl". At the same time "contemporary neo-conservative forces have rewarded postmodernism (and its post-processual archaeological manifestation of archaeology) because of its relativism and nihilism", according to Bruce Trigger quoted by Randall McGuire (2006: 70).

That the value of commodities derives from labour tends to be forgotten or obscured, according to Karl Marx, when the products are detached from their place of origin and circulate in the market. This is at the core of his concept of "commodity fetish" (Marx, 2009 [1866]: 59–61). Karl Polanyi (1944, 1957) argued that market behaviour was mainly a modern state phenomenon and that we can barely talk about an "economy" as a rationally governed and organized institution in past societies. Polanyi's famous economy was embedded in and ruled by social institutions whose choices were not always rational.

A common question asked not only by economic historians such as Polanyi but also by anthropologists concerns the conditions under which a market economy appeared for the first time. According to Polanyi governed market economies are recent constructs of modernity. In the past, social institutions posed restrictions of several kinds on economic exchanges, and defined economic behaviour not only in the despotic oriental states during the Bronze Age but also in the Greek and Roman world. Moses Finley (1973), who followed the conceptual footsteps of Polanyi, acknowledged the performance of private transactions in the Near East, Greece and Rome, but still regarded the dominant economic models in antiquity as socially embedded and static, at least until the later phases of ancient Greek history. According to the Anglo-American ancient historian, these were mainly agricultural economies with limited surplus production and restricted transactions. Nevertheless, these economic systems allegedly experienced transformations such as the introduction of gift exchange in the Homeric period, which may have prepared the ground for a new commodity-centred economy in the Mediterranean.

Already prior to Polanyi and Finley, the French sociologist Marcel Mauss had begun analysing modes of exchange and obligation that defined social and economic relations in "pre-modern" societies, from the Indian and Pacific oceans to the American Northwest. After commenting on several reciprocal mechanisms and the spiritual connotations of giving, accepting and repaying gifts, and after analysing their role in the emergence and maintenance of social ties and the definition of structures and rights, he turned his attention to early historical societies. The aim of that comparative study in his most influential essay *Le don* (The Gift) was to explore "a stage of social evolution" since "institutions of this type are a step in the development of our own economic forms, and serve as a historical explanation of features of our own society" (Mauss, 1966 [1925]: 46). After discussing a number of case studies of the Roman period, Mauss (1966 [1925]: 52) came to the conclusion that "it was precisely the Romans and Greeks, who possibly following the Northern and Western Semites, drew the distinction between personal rights and real rights, separated purchases from gifts and exchanges…passed beyond the excessively hazardous, costly and elaborate gift economy, which was…incompatible with the development of the market, trade and production, and, in a word, uneconomic". This was what Pierre Bourdieu (1977 [1972]: 172) called a transition from a "good-faith" to an "undisguised self-interest economy".

Property and Social Relations of Power

The exchange of commodities presupposes a state of ownership. The free labourer, for instance, owns his labour power and sells it to the owner of the means of production (e.g. a factory) for a defined time span, during which he then works for that factory owner. The goods produced during that time span are the property of the factory owner. These property relations in capitalist production are quite clear-cut (even if fetishized), while defining property in many pre-capitalist societies poses considerable problems. Especially in archaeology this is a most challenging endeavour because property is a juridical category. Archaeologists seek support from and cooperation with other disciplines for unravelling the historical dimension of property.

Although in this volume we are not dealing with the Palaeolithic period, it is important to note at the outset that the human claim to property is a historical and not a natural phenomenon (see especially McGuire, in the present volume). For the greatest period of human existence, the survival of the small and vulnerable groups (extended families), who lived by hunting and gathering their food, depended on sharing what they appropriated from nature. Hunter-gatherers of the modern age entertain food sharing alliances spanning vast territories, which provides security in times of need. Failing to share resources would endanger the group, so generosity is valued, while greed is discouraged and ridiculed. While clothing, tools and weapons, and ornaments are personal possessions, sanctions are imposed on those who try to accumulate even such personal possessions (Woodburn, 1982; Flannery & Marcus, 2012: 23–39). Anthropological studies focusing on isolated hunter-gatherer communities revealed these common characteristics of social behaviour, the ultimate purpose of which is the elimination of status and inequality. They have thus disproven the infamous economic "Robinsonades"—hypotheses speculating about primordial individual claims to land and resources and their treatment as commodities (Marx, 1962 [1867]: 90 n. 29). Marshall Sahlins famously spoke of the original affluent society, characterized by limited needs but also by a quite limited amount of time dedicated to work for survival (Sahlins, 1972 [2017]: 1–37).

Agrarian societies turned the rules of free access to natural resources upside down by limiting that access to specific groups of people through the definition of property that was then defined by laws (unwritten or written), fortified by coercion and enshrined by ideology (Flannery & Marcus, 2012; cf. Hansen in the present volume). Like the general concept of property, so its various forms appear as historical inventions created by specific societies according to their economic needs and social relations.

Besides the personal belongings mentioned above, property concepts came to be applied to the means of production (implements/tools and land, the latter being the most important means of production in pre-industrial societies), to consumables and dwellings. The question arises, if and to what extent the producers owned their products and which groups of people became excluded from ownership. Moreover, in many past societies and even up to the present day, property rights may also include the working people themselves, degrading them to the status of slaves (Zeuske, 2013) or semi-free people of various kinds (Luraghi & Alcock, 2003).

Since its emergence, the state guaranteed the endurance of an established mode of production characterized by opposing classes, which was possible most importantly due to the power (and regularly the monopoly) of its political institutions to enforce coercion. However, as the appropriation of surplus in the hands of a dominant minority causes social tension and ultimately conflict, state authorities early on tried to present themselves as a balancing factor attenuating the consequences of such uneven distribution of property and power. "I did not deliver the orphan up to the rich man; I did not deliver the widow up to the mighty man; I did not deliver the man of [only] one shekel up to the man of one mina… I installed justice in the land," said king Ur-Nammu in the oldest known law code at the end of the 3rd millennium BCE (Neumann, 1989: 101).

Although even simple tools were not necessarily the property of craftspeople, but might have been made available by state administrations for specific tasks, especially in public works (Palaima, 2015: 629–633), the ways in which land was classified as property form a basic criterion for the differentiation among various economic systems. Land could be collective or private property and access to it may have been restricted depending on gender or age. Furthermore, property of land (and its size) was bound to membership in a political collective, e.g. in Archaic and Classical Athens and Sparta (Finley, 1973: 48, 95; Demandt, 1995: 143–144, 200–203). Plots might be fenced, even named as specific property, one of the earliest cases for the latter practice being the labels of agricultural domains controlled by the ruler buried in the Naqada IIIA2 tomb U-j at Abydos around 3200 BCE (Dreyer, 1998). Products may also have been marked and inscribed with names or symbols indicating their producers, while the material properties of the containers and closing devices such as sealings may confer information on the location of the estate (e.g. Bavay, 2015). Marks, inscriptions and the like would then enable an assessment of the juridical status of plots via archaeological finds. Usually, however, the prospects of direct archaeological verification of property rights on land are rather limited. Other economic regimes may consist of landholding without proper ownership. In those cases, the right of cultivation and cropping may have been coupled with obligations to *corvée* or payment of rents. The archaeological differentiation between landownership and other types of tenure may prove a difficult or impossible task without written sources (and sometimes even with those written sources, cf. Moreno García in the present volume). The possibility to inherit land, to mortgage and especially to sell it would indicate true private property.

Another way to elucidate property regimes in a past society is to investigate the evidence of storage facilities, their distribution, capacities and especially accessibility as well as their contents (thus including archaeobotanic and archaeozoological research). In terms of capacity, one may ask if products stored in a house can be classified as evidence for subsistence production (Chayanov, 1966) or as surplus. Household archaeology seeks to identify a residence group with shared tasks in production or, in short, an economic entity. Such a household does not necessarily coincide with a single house structure nor with a kinship group (Johnston & Gonlin, 1998) that may have formed a political unit and determined inheritance of property according to the social norms of a given society. Testing hypotheses about lineage and kinship groups using only archaeological means is impossible, but archaeometric investigations based on aDNA can, in certain cases, provide hard evidence on kinship relations—provided a sufficiently large section of the community received a formal inhumation burial and that the soil conditions favour the preservation of aDNA (e.g. Alt et al., 2014).

Of critical relevance for the economic classification of a society is the question which social groups can appropriate (agricultural) surplus. The way surplus is stored can provide important information in that regard. Is it centrally stored or in a dispersed way; is access to storage facilities restricted (spatially or by closing devices, perhaps including sealing practices); are there administrative control mechanisms for the regulation of delivery and withdrawal and how did those work? To answer such questions—or better, to draw reliable conclusions, representative areas of settlements need to be investigated through excavation, while survey as well as excavation data should provide evidence about possible settlement hierarchies.

Property regulations are the juridical expression of the existing relations of production. However, different kinds of property, such as collective and private, landholding and landownership, *latifundia* tilled by slaves and smallholdings worked by free peasants, etc. coexisted in many past societies. This leads to further questions. Is it possible to determine if one type of relations of production was dominant? Are the coexisting relations of production the result of preceding socio-economic experiences with enduring implications, or does one type replace the other?

A growing interest in the coexistence of different relations of production has certainly provoked in-depth research in recent years. Following, for instance, the reconstruction of the modes of production in Mesopotamia and the Bronze Age eastern Mediterranean after the substantivist/formalist debate and the conceptualization of a binary model (palatial vs. non-palatial) centred on the ruler (royal property) and the villages (communal and private property), respectively (Zaccagnini, 1981; Halstead, 1992; Buccellati, 1996), more recent approaches stress the more complex and at the same time denser entanglement that different relations of production had with each other in those societies (McGeough, 2007: 350–361; Shelmerdine, 2013; Nakassis, 2013).

Humans produce property through labour in the framework of their social relations under given historical conditions. They distribute the products of their work and consume them, and they can exchange part of the surplus product against others. Products transferred in trade amphorae could be marked in various ways in order to express the role of producers, land owners or political authorities. Such marks may have reflected relations of power of all agents participating in production and exchange (Lawall, in the present volume).

As a result of the socially uneven distribution of goods in most societies, property can also be appropriated by force by means of theft, piracy or war including enslavement of captives, a practice possibly used as a threat by rulers in order to appropriate labour (Bernbeck, 2019). In trade, property can be accumulated by cheating and overreaching. In addition, someone's property can be seized by others as an effect of the failure to repay a debt, which in many ancient societies could include the possibility that the debtor became the property of someone else—the well-known phenomenon of debt slavery (Zurbach, 2017).

Property laws regulate the appropriation of nature by humans in specific social relationships. There is admittedly a general historical tendency of private property to extend its sphere at the expense of other forms of property (Hudson, 1996)—which at least during the last 500 years happens on a global scale. In the most recent stage of capitalist production, private property laws (patents, intellectual property rights) become increasingly applied to immaterial products and to natural living organisms, their genetic codes and the knowledge about those organisms preserved by oral history—even when they are not genetically engineered products and have been used by humans for hundreds of years (e.g. Pearson, 2013; Sezneva & Chauvin, 2014). Such practice of course serves to preserve and secure their commodity character, but legal and other enforcement strategies such as terminator genes in genetically manipulated seeds lead to increasing costs for preventing that these commodities will be (self-)reproduced at the expense of the extraction of surplus value. At the same time, agricultural surplus is destroyed at a large scale in certain countries of the European Union to prevent unwanted market fluctuations and imbalances. These recent developments show at the same time the historical limits of private property and the commodity form itself. "Today, the very swelling of juridical and technological measures developed to stabilize content and limit the satisfaction of needs, their rising economic cost and the surging amount of collective social energy they require to waste, may thus similarly speak for the impending obsolescence of the commodity form: not so much its actual social decline as the increasingly blatant historical inadequacy of its forcibly prolonged maintenance" (Sezneva & Chauvin, 2014: 150).

In general, the historical tendency of enforcing private property laws and regulations globally onto nature was of course never a linear and continuous process, nor was there any lack of resistance against it by those who were becoming expropriated either from their collective property or from free access to resources.

Finally, in many societies, we are witnessing a growing awareness of how property regimes, and the way modern capitalist economies appropriate nature to the benefit of a tiny minority, have the effect of ruining the resources of the vast majority—in the last consequence the living conditions of all of humanity (WMO, 2020). This makes it not only an interesting task, but a necessary one to investigate the historical genesis and development of all forms of property and the ways they shaped human life.

Contributions to the Critique of Archaeological Economy

The papers in this book undertake a critical discussion of dominant theoretical models that have been applied to the study of past economic relations during the last two centuries, and consider alternative theoretical trajectories. These are conceived against the background of recent developments in the capitalist world system such as the current enduring crisis. They are further tested on the grounds of well-documented archaeological and historical contexts. Economic behaviour is conceptualized as the diachronically changing relations of production, distribution and consumption. The intention is not always to test the theoretical models under scrutiny, but rather to present evidence against the rationalization of past economic behaviour according to the rules of modern markets.

The History of Archaeological Thought was illustrated in the seminal study of Bruce Trigger (2006) for the most part as a reflection of Modernity. As such it has always been subject to its historical and cultural context and apt to embrace theoretical advances in other disciplines such as philosophy, sociology, economics and science. Some of the most influential theories that shaped archaeological thought throughout the twentieth century and continue to do so derive from Marxism. Randall H. McGuire comments in his paper on the various perceptions and applications of Marxism in the understanding of social and economic structuring, and argues that a Relational Dialectical Marxism still provides an apt theoretical framework for the analysis of past social relations. McGuire has previously discussed in a critical manner post-modernist theories and approaches that found their way into archaeology. In this paper, he does more than that. The confrontation with the "new shiny theory" of New-Materialism that is appropriated by the Symmetrical Archaeology current presents an opportunity to elucidate the Hegelian concept of Relational Dialectic. Recent critique from a New-Materialist perspective against "Marxist archaeology" is unsustainable because it downplays and oversimplifies the variability of Marxist approaches to the exploration of the past. The glorification of the Thing and its agency by New-Materialism and the perception of humans, animals and things as equal agents in an imagined flat ontology by Symmetrical Archaeology are critiqued for having misconceived the substance of historical disciplines—that is to understand processes of social change. This task is instead achieved through a Relational Dialectic, an effective tool for the exploration of interactions between human and non-human actors. Last but not least, McGuire addresses the role of archaeology in the current world as a social discipline, an issue that is rarely treated by historical disciplines.

"The economy" of past societies used earlier to be perceived as a male domain, where female agency found a place usually in the form of either slave or domestic labour. Women were accordingly reduced to commodified labouring bodies in the reconstruction of the modes of production and exchange. The socio-economic roles ascribed to women were those of wives, concubines and most usually child bearers. Disciplines with a historical record, such as classical archaeology, attributed to women distinctive social roles such as princesses or priestesses that were, however, always dependent on some male-constructed hierarchy. Rosemary Joyce shows that similar trends persist in recent and modern studies, and argues that a requirement for any analysis of past economic relations is the prior definition of what is really "economic". She undertakes this endeavour through the examination of her case studies in ancient Mexico and Central America, with the aim of elucidating concealed forms of female economic agency. The labour of women is usually treated as "household" activities and by this means alienated from "real" economy. By exploring the modes of production of cloth and cacao, which were used as value standards for tribute payments so that their exchange consequently defined social hierarchies, Joyce highlights a special role of females in the economic relations of their societies. Although these goods were produced by women in the so-called "household" sphere, their economic implications had major effects on the structuring of their societies. Nevertheless, certain finds indicate that these goods were not produced in common domestic but special elite contexts. A key point in understanding the use value of cloth and cacao is their embeddedness in social relations that reserved a special social status for women.

Polanyi's school certainly has had a lasting impact on the anthropological and historical disciplines, as Svend Hansen demonstrates in his contribution. He is inspired by a re-reading of "The economy has no surplus" by Harry W. Pearson, a close collaborator of Karl Polanyi and editor of his works. Hansen engages with the debate regarding the interpretation of surplus production and its emergence in human societies. The scholars investigating the "zen way" of "affluent" (Sahlins) hunter-gatherer societies stressed the advantages of less work expenditure, more leisure time coupled with a generally low living standard and a presumably lower percentage of hunger in the earth's population compared to today. However, it is clear that industrial civilization will not be discarded—as Polanyi had aptly formulated in 1947. In the tradition of enlightenment, Marx and later Polanyi and the substantivists emphasized the social embeddedness of economy and the evolutionary consequences a surplus product has had for human history. Pearson's point in 1957 was to insist that the amount of surplus is always relative to the needs of a specific society, i.e. not determined by biological needs. Therefore, there can be no absolute surplus as economic liberalism would have it. However, his critique stressed the evolutionary viewpoint on surplus, its enhancement and growth, while Marxist scholars insisted that surplus itself was not the problem, but instead the struggle over its distribution. Against this background, Hansen evaluates the results of recent research on the Neolithic period, stressing instances of inequality and vertical control mechanisms in societies evolving in the northern Fertile Crescent, as well as in south-eastern Europe, relatively early in the respective paths of Neolithic economy. He concludes that the concept of "affluent society" does not hold for many of these developments. Referring to Pearson's point that surplus does not simply emerge, but results from decision-making in society, Hansen at the end invites us to search for that first moment of that (political) decision to organize surplus production among the egalitarian societies.

Investigating possible concepts of value that existed in past societies that were still largely egalitarian is a difficult task and therefore rarely embarked upon. Bleda S. Düring looks into production and exchange of Chalcolithic societies by applying a "regime of value" approach sensu Appadurai. He focuses on stone figurine production in Asia Minor during the middle of the 5th millennium BCE (Kilia figurines) and on Cyprus in the second half of the 4th millennium BCE (cruciform figurines)—unrelated to each other, but exhibiting some common traits, which he explores. As such regimes of value are culturally specific, he investigates the stone statuettes in terms of technological and stylistic characteristics that are common in all the regions in which they appear, in order to identify what made them desirable and valuable to their users. In the case of Kilia figurines, the marble they were made of was not an exotic raw material, but attention should be paid to both the stylistic standardization and the craftsmanship, because the round, protruding heads in particular must have been difficult to make. The Cypriot figurines made of pikrolite from the Troodos Mountains also exhibit a marked stylistic standardization. Again, the material was common, but the challenge consisted in shaping the figurines. Here, it proved difficult to cut the cruciform shape from a kind of stone that only occurs in a small amount, in veins penetrating a different rock ground. In both cases, Düring argues, the figurines had evolved from earlier stone-working traditions, and were part of a widespread craft tradition. In addition, they were highly stylized and thus related to iconic images; they therefore potentially functioned as indicators of membership in a certain collective. He does not try to pinpoint a specific value or meaning, but reflects that these figurines could have served in the negotiation of identities and, through their exchange, stand at the beginning of subsequent developments of exchange networks.

Given the lack of written sources, the earliest stages of the emergence of states can be apprehended only with great difficulty, when the study's focus is placed on political institutions and jurisdiction. Another approach, namely the investigation of the economic structures underlying the formation of political institutions, may be more promising. The group from Barcelona (Roberto Risch and Selina Delgado-Raack) and Halle (Harald Meller and Torsten Schunke) investigates the economy of the earliest case of a stratified society characterized by marked social inequality in central Europe, the so-called Circum-Harz group of the Central German Únětice Culture (Early Bronze Age, c. 2200–1600 BCE). In earlier papers, Meller has proposed the interpretation of that society as a state maintaining a permanent army (with a hierarchical significance of different weapon types) and other dependent specialists not employed in agriculture. In this contribution, for the first time, a group of scholars investigates the economic basis of that society. They refer to the more than 70 macrolithic tools used as fill material in the construction of the Bornhöck burial mound, which is the largest Early Bronze Age mound in Central Europe and dates to the second half of the nineteenth century BCE. Most importantly, the grinding slabs from the innermost stone core convey important information about economy, as they clearly differ in size and utility from the (smaller) grinding stones of contemporary longhouses, the typical settlement dwellings of the Únětice Culture. Due to their size, those grinding slabs should have been used by pairs of cooperating hard-working persons, were intended for a higher productive capacity than the grinders from the settlements, and were unrelated to the domestic sphere. From the concentration of these specialized grinding slabs in the mound, the authors draw conclusions regarding the person buried there. They infer a centralized organization of an important part of the agricultural production and a control of that agricultural surplus product by the ruling social group. Regarding the question as to who would have needed those food supplies, they propose an army serving the ruler buried underneath the Bornhöck.

Pharaonic Egypt provides scholars with a totally different kaleidoscope of source material—both archaeological and textual, which is of course partly due to the very favourable preservation conditions offered by the desert climate. Nevertheless, the reconstruction of an encompassing picture of Egyptian economy and society in the three millennia BCE continues to provoke lively debates. Juan Carlos Moreno García challenges the classic description of Pharaonic economy as purely centralized and redistributive in the Polanyian sense. While acknowledging recent critiques of neo-institutionalism, he finds usefulness in these approaches especially for investigating the role that private property of land, markets and rational economic behaviour had throughout Egyptian history. He focuses on those actors who, according to inscriptions and papyri, did display individual initiative motivated by economic gain, especially wealthy landholders, who constituted a tiny minority of Pharaonic society since the Old Kingdom of the 3rd millennium BCE. Often the sources do not allow the determination whether these were private landowners, rather than holders of land that belonged to a particular institution (such as a temple). While the pursuit of individual economic interest was hampered by the social environment of family, fellow citizens and patronage networks, Moreno García is able to show how kings could favour them to counter opposing interests of powerful families. Crisis situations—such as the end of the monarchy in the late 3rd millennium—also offered occasions for privatization seized by wealthy individuals, who exploited the poverty and indebtedness of other social groups. However, the diachronic evaluation of the manifold (yet imbalanced with regard to certain sectors of the economy) written sources lead him to the conclusion that individualist economic strategies were mostly carried out inside the institutions of the Pharaonic state such as temples, crown lands and royal grants of fields. They had little impact outside of these, and thus neither destabilized those institutions nor led to the establishment of a sizable real estate market.

In recent years, the societies of the Mediterranean Bronze Age, with their wide array of archaeological evidence complemented by limited written sources, have stimulated a growing number of scholars to turn to modernist approaches to their economies. As a response, Reinhard Jung chose to investigate goods exchange and trade in the Mediterranean Bronze Age with a classical Marxist approach; he applies the commodity criteria as defined by Marx to different kinds of products exchanged from the 3rd to the end of the 2nd millennium BCE. A commodity is a useful thing produced in order to be exchanged against other commodities on the basis of their exchange values. While the commodity character of products is characteristic of capitalist production, typically also including labour power (as a commodity), commodity production did exist in many pre-capitalist societies, as Marx had already noted. As exchange relations become more regular and take on a greater (quantative) importance, the quantities of products that are exchanged will increasingly come to depend on production factors. Their exchange value, as defined by the necessary production time (on average in society), will then become important and distinct from their value in consumption (use value). As this development typically appears first in exchange relations between societies, the examples discussed by Jung refer to metal export from Cyprus and Mycenaean pottery export from Greece among others. Written sources of different Mesopotamian and eastern Mediterranean societies reveal that the respective temple and palace bureaucracies were well aware of the socially necessary labour time that went into the production of goods, including the subsistence goods necessary for maintaining the work force (and thus determining the value of labour). However, the fixation of a general, socially accepted value equivalent, typically expressed in quantities of precious metals, occurred only in the societies of Mesopotamia, Asia Minor, Egypt and the Levant, but not in Mycenaean Greece nor in Bronze Age Italy. The exchange relationships between different Mediterranean societies involved products which fulfil the criteria of commodities to various degrees, while the process of commodification seems to have started earlier in the east and progressed towards the west. Under specific circumstances, these exchange relations led to a rapid acceleration of socio-economic transformations in certain societies (uneven and combined development).

The emergence of the formal market has been a focal topic in studies of past economic relations. Earlier discussions about the social conditions that favoured its appearance were conducted in the framework of the dichotomy between formalists and substantivists that was introduced by Karl Polanyi in his opus magnum *The Great Transformation*. This dualistic opposition—between views perceiving economic relations either through the perspective of an allegedly inherent economic maximization principle and rational economic thinking or as "embedded" in social institutions—was rejected by David Graeber (2001) and other anthropologists. Commodity is a term that commonly appears in the anthropological and archaeological debate about modes of exchange. This notion was used by Karl Marx to describe objects produced to be sold in a market. Commodities were thus predominantly thought to represent a feature of market economy, in contrast to earlier gift economies (to the latter usually belong all forms of exchange that do not aim at economic maximization). Anthropological analyses of the modes of exchange or the process of "commodification" in the past demonstrate, nevertheless, that (the same) objects can at the same time be exchanged either as gifts or commodities depending on their circulation between different social spheres. This view is exemplified in Stefanos Gimatzidis' paper through the examination of the exchange of bronze tripods, a historically and archaeologically documented cultural phenomenon in Homeric and Classical Greece. A major archaeological manifestation of this practice is the massive deposition of tripods in Greek sanctuaries. This was previously understood as a ritual practice or as a material expression of social antagonisms through the dedication of precious artefacts by peers. Gimatzidis instead recognises major economic implications in this practice, whose primary and main outcome was wealth accumulation. It is argued that tripods were exchanged not only as gifts but also as commodities through a ritual system of wealth redistribution.

Connectedness is an issue commonly treated in archaeological and historical disciplines. The notion of connectivity and its economic implications attracted particular attention in Mediterranean archaeology after the publication of Peregrine Horden and Nicholas Purcell's *The Corrupting Sea*. In his paper, Jan Paul Crielaard demonstrates how the new conceptualization of this notion challenges earlier models that understood past economic and social relations through a fragmentation or a centre-periphery perspective. Crielaard focuses on the examination of the agents who formed the connecting tissue of the exchange network in the maritime landscape of the Mediterranean that has been usually understood as an entity. He stresses the role of cabotage in economic interrelations and explores the input of small traders in the free movement of goods. The major objective of this paper is to show that connectivity is not an all-applicable norm that a priori characterizes all cultural entities through time, and in fact several social, political and cultural restrictions existed. The same micro-regions experienced different forms of connectivity through time, which accordingly defined their social and economic relations. In other words, there may have been several different economic models shaping variable social behaviours and creating unequal social relations during the same period in different regions. The region of Karystia in the southern part of the island of Euboea is examined as a case study exemplifying the variable forms of economic development and interconnectedness in its Aegean setting through time.

Transport jars of specific types that were produced for exchange of agricultural goods in the eastern Mediterranean, the Aegean and, over the course of time, in many other regions all over the Mediterranean became the hallmark of maritime economic transactions through a standardization process in their modes of production and exchange. The study of Aegean transport amphoras, which from a certain point of time onwards were furnished with stamps, has become a distinct discipline known as amphorology. Mark Lawall, who has extensively explored several economic and social aspects of this topic, presents a new approach in his paper through the notion of Path Dependency and its conceptualisation by the new institutional economist Douglass North. This relates to the power of experience and previous practices that shape "paths" of economic behaviour. Lawall's endeavour is, nonetheless, not to demonstrate the consistency of allegedly pre-determined economic structures but to explore social tensions in the inconsistencies of established patterns. A definition of the modes of technology transfer is a requirement in understanding the spatial organization of pottery production. Shifting consistencies and inconsistences in the amphora types and their geography, as well as their stamped impressions bearing personal names and symbols, are taken as evidence indicating the state's—successful or unsuccessful—participation in their production and exchange. The purpose was to ease tensions among the social agents involved in these economic transactions, who were elite landowners, city-assigned fabricants and workers.

The exchange of archaic and classical Attic pottery overseas has been a focal topic in the studies of the ancient economy. This is due to its high representation in almost every context in the Mediterranean and the Black Sea, its variable types and figurative decoration, the relevant textual evidence and finally its alleged artistic quality. Attic pottery has been treated several times in the past by Robin Osborne, who in his contribution to this book takes a holistic approach to its production, exchange and consumption and presents in an almost narrative way variable aspects of its trade pattern overseas. Osborne's starting point is that Greek pots were certainly not carried as ship ballast, as has been previously claimed. He argues instead that their use and exchange value, and consequently circulation, were regulated, among other factors, also by distributors. The supplying system of certain cultural contexts with certain Attic pottery types is examined in juxtaposition to the formation of temporal patterns in this pottery's distribution. A thought-provoking reconstruction of the scale of production is argued by means of the reproduction of the same decorative scenes with minor variabilities, which are ascribed to individual artistic agency. Osborne concludes that trends in Attic ceramic shape and decoration types were defined by painters' tastes and were primarily shaped in the Athenian society they were part of. Additionally, Attic potters obtained a worldview through middlemen, a reciprocal relation that further affected the selection of types and decoration. It was therefore this kind of cultural interaction between producers and consumers, but also the agency of image which was at least partly driven by merchants, that shaped the patterns of Attic pottery exchange overseas. All these factors defined a special trend of pottery consumption outside the Aegean that can be compared to the appropriation of other aspects of Greek culture.

The idea for this book goes back to a symposium which we organized at the Austrian Academy of Sciences in Vienna from the 13 to 15 June 2018 with the title "The Critique of Archaeological Economy". We wish to express our gratitude to the Academy for financially supporting this symposium and the Viennese academic and non-academic public that attended it for its feedback. We also thank Annalisa Rumolo for manifold help during this event and Lia Ludwikowski for her efforts in the preparation of this volume.

References

Alt, K. W., Knipper, C., Peters, D., Müller, W., Maurer, A.-F., Kollig, I., Nicklisch, N., Müller, C., Karimnia, S., Brandt, G., Roth, C., Rosner, M., Mende, B., Schöne, B. R., Vida, T., & von Freeden, U. 2014. Lombards on the move—An integrative study of the Migration Period cemetery at Szólád, Hungary. *PLoS One, 9*(11), e110793. https://doi.org/10.1371/journal.pone.0110793.

Appadurai, A. (1986). Introduction: Commodities and the politics of value. In A. Appadurai (Ed.), *The social life of things: Commodities in cultural perspective* (pp. 3–63). Cambridge University Press.

Bavay, L. (2015). Canaanite jars and jar sealings from Deir el-Medina: Scattered evidence of Egypt's economic relations with the levant during the New Kingdom. In B. Eder & R. Pruzsinszky (Eds.), *Policies of exchange: Political systems and modes of interaction in the Aegean and the Near East*

in the 2nd millennium B.C.E. Proceedings of the International Symposium at the University of Freiburg, Institute for Archaeological Studies, 30 May–2 June 2012, (pp. 129–140). OREA 2. Austrian Academy of Sciences Press.
Bernbeck, R. (2019). Monumental negligence: The difference between working and alienated labor. In F. Buccellati, S. Hangeneuer, S. van der Heyden, & F. Levenson (Eds.), *Size matters—Understanding monumentality across ancient civilizations* (pp. 133–155). Histoire 146. transcript.
Bourdieu, P. (1977 [1972]). *Outline of a theory of practice*. Cambridge University Press [Esquisse d'une théorie de la pratique. Précédé de trois études d'ethnologie kabyle. Librairie Droz].
Buccellati, G. (1996). The role of socio-political factors in the emergence of "public" and "private" domains in early Mesopotamia. In M. Hudson & B. A. Levine (Eds.), *Privatization in the ancient Near East and Classical World: A colloquium held at New York University, 17–18 November 1994*, (pp. 129–147). Peabody Museum Bulletin 5. Peabody Museum of Archaeology and Ethnology, Harvard University.
Chayanov, A. V. (1966). *The theory of peasant economy*. The American Economic Association.
Demandt, A. (1995). *Antike Staatsformen. Eine vergleichende Verfassungsgeschichte der Alten Welt*. Akademie-Verlag.
Dietler, M. (2005). *Consumption and colonial encounters in the Rhône Basin of France: A study of Early Iron Age political economy*. CNRS.
Dietler, M. (2010). Consumption. In D. Hicks & M. C. Beaudry (Eds.), *The Oxford handbook of material culture studies* (pp. 207–226). Oxford University Press.
Dreyer, G. (1998). *Umm el-Qaab I: Das prädynastische Königsgrab U-j und seine frühen Schriftzeugnisse*. Archäologische Veröffentlichungen, Deutsches Archäologisches Institut, Abteilung Kairo 86. Philip von Zabern.
Finley, M. I. (1973). *The ancient economy*. University of California Press.
Flannery, K., & Marcus, J. (2012). *The creation of inequality: How our prehistoric ancestors set the stage for monarchy, slavery and empire*. Harvard University Press.
Graeber, D. (2001). *Toward an anthropological theory of value: The false coin of our own dreams*. Palgrave.
Halstead, P. (1992). The Mycenaean palatial economy: Making the most of the gaps in the evidence. *Proceedings of the Cambridge Philological Society, 38*, 57–86.
Hegel, G. W. F. (2019). *The collected works of Georg Wilhelm Friedrich Hegel: Phenomenology of mind, philosophy of mind, Hegel's aesthetics, the criticism of Hegel's work and hegelianism* by Schopenhauer, Nietzsche (J. B. Baillie, W. Wallace, S. W. Dyde, F. P. B. Osmaston, J. Sibree, E. Haldane, & E. Brown Speirs, Trans.). e-artnow.
Hudson, M. (1996). The dynamics of privatization, from the Bronze Age to the present. In M. Hudson & B. A. Levine (Eds.), *Privatization in the ancient Near East and Classical World: A colloquium held at New York University, 17–18 November 1994*, (pp. 33–57). Peabody Museum Bulletin 5. Peabody Museum of Archaeology and Ethnology, Harvard University.
Johnston, K. J., & Gonlin, N. (1998). What do houses mean? Approaches to the analysis of Classic Maya commoner residences. In S. D. Houston (Ed.), *Function and meaning in Classic Maya architecture* (pp. 141–185). Dumbarton Oaks Research Library and Collection Washington, DC.
Luraghi, N., & Alcock, S. E. (Eds.). (2003). *Helots and their masters in Laconia and Messenia: Histories, ideologies, structures*. Center for Hellenic Studies, Harvard University Press.
Marx, K. (2009 [1866]). *Das Kapital 1.1. Resultate des unmittelbaren Produktionsprozesses. Sechstes Kapitel des ersten Bandes des „Kapitals" (Entwurf)*. Dietz Verlag.
Marx, K. (1962 [1867]). *Das Kapital. Kritik der politischen Ökonomie. Erster Band: Der Produktionsprozeß des Kapitals*. Marx Engels Werke 23. Dietz Verlag.
Mauss, M. (1966 [1925]). *The gift*. Cohen & West LTD [Essai sur le don. Forme et raison de l'échange dans les sociétés archaïques, in L'année sociologique 1, 1923–24 [1925], 30–186].
McGeough, K. M. (2007). *Exchange relationships at Ugarit*. Ancient Near Eastern Studies Supplement 26. Peeters.

McGuire, R. H. (2006). Marx, childe and trigger. In R. F. Williamson & M. S. Bisson (Eds.), *The archaeology of Bruce Trigger: Theoretical empiricism* (pp. 61–79). McGill-Queen's University Press.
Miller, D. (1995). *Acknowledging consumption: A review of new studies*. Routledge.
Mullins, P. R. (2011). The archaeology of consumption. *Annual Review of Anthropology, 40,* 133–144. https://doi.org/10.1146/annurev-anthro-081309-145746.
Nakassis, D. (2013). *Individuals and society in Mycenaean Pylos*. Mnemosyne Supplement 358. Brill.
Neumann, H. (1989). Entwicklungen im Recht. In H. Klengel (Ed.), *Kulturgeschichte des alten Vorderasien* (pp. 100–105). Veröffentlichungen des Zentralinstituts für Alte Geschichte und Archäologie der Akademie der Wissenschaften der DDR 18. Akademie-Verlag.
Palaima, T. (2015). The Mycenaean mobilization of labor in agriculture and building projects: Institutions, individuals, compensation and status in the Linear B tablets. In P. Steinkeller & M. Hudson (Eds.), *Labor in the ancient world: A colloquium held at Hirschbach (Saxony), April 2005* (pp. 617–648). International Scholars Conference on Ancient Near Eastern Economies 5. Islet.
Papadopoulos, J. K., & Urton, G. (2012). Introduction: The construction of value in the ancient world. In J. K. Papadopoulos & G. Urton (Eds.), *The construction of value in the ancient world* (pp. 1–47). Cotsen advanced seminar series, 5. Cotsen Institute of Archaeology Press.
Pearson, T. W. (2013). "Life is not for sale!": Confronting free trade and intellectual property in Costa Rica. *American Anthropologist, 115,* 58–71.
Polanyi, K. (1944). *The great transformation*. Rinehart.
Polanyi, K. (1957). The economy as an instituted process. In K. Polanyi, C. M. Arensberg, & H. W. Pearson (Eds.), *Trade and market in the early empires* (pp. 243–270). The Free Press.
Sahlins, M. (1972 [2017]). *Stone Age economics*. Routledge.
Sezneva, O., & Chauvin, S. (2014). Has capitalism gone virtual? Content containment and the obsolescence of the commodity. *Critical Historical Studies, 1,* 125–150.
Shelmerdine, C. W. (2013). Crafts, specialists, and markets in Mycenaean Greece: Economic interplay among households and states. *American Journal of Archaeology, 117*(3), 447–452.
Smith, A. (1976 [1776]). *An inquiry into the nature and causes of the wealth of nations*. Oxford University Press.
Trigger, B. G. (2006). *A history of archaeological thought* (2nd ed.). Cambridge University Press.
WMO. (2020). *WMO statement on the state of global climate in 2019. WMO-Nr. 1248*. World Meteorological Organization. https://library.wmo.int/doc_num.php?explnum_id=10211.
Woodburn, J. (1982). Egalitarian societies. *Man* N.S. 17: 431–451.
Zaccagnini, C. (1981). Modo di produzione asiatico e Vicino Oriente antico. *Dialoghi di Archeologia, 3,* 3–65.
Zeuske, M. (2013). *Handbuch Geschichte der Sklaverei. Eine Globalgeschichte von den Anfängen bis zur Gegenwart*. De Gruyter.
Zurbach, J. (2017). *Les hommes, la terre et la dette en Grèce c. 1400–c. 500 a.C.* Scripta Antiqua 95. Ausonius éditions.

Chapter 2
Writing the Deep History of Human Economy

Randall H. McGuire

Abstract In archaeology, a New Materialism has developed. Archaeological promoters of this theory reject Marxism out of hand. These archaeologists equate the relational dialectic with oppositional thinking and declare Marxism as dead. A refutation of the New Materialism's critique of the dialectic leaves open the question of why archaeologists should embrace Marxism, which is a theory of Capitalism, to archaeologically study the deep history of human economy? My simple answer is twofold: (1) if we wish to transform capitalism we must demonstrate that people created Capitalism in the past and that people can therefore transform it for the future, and (2) Marxism offers archaeologists an intellectual tool kit to study the ancient past.

Archaeologists have always recognized that we live in a world that entails never-ending and diverse interactions between people and things. Most commonly archaeologists have used things to try and understand people. Lately, bright new theories/philosophies have enticed many Anglophone archaeologists to embrace forms of Neo-Materialism that take the material seriously, often more seriously than the human. These philosophies advocate for thing power (Bennett, 2010), Object Oriented Ontology (Morton, 2017: 12), Assemblage Theory (DeLanda, 2016), and Thing Theory (Brown, 2003). To clear space for the Neo-Materialism these philosophers reject the timeworn Marxist Historical Materialism. They declare Marx *ist tot*. Within archaeology we see this Neo-Materialism most adamantly expressed in the Symmetrical Archaeology.

I will focus on archaeological applications of Neo-Materialism most especially those under the heading of the Symmetrical Archaeology. I will argue that archaeologists who dismiss Marxism provide a weak alternative in Neo-Materialism. This alternative maintains the status quo of Capitalism, limits our ability to critique Capitalism, and weakens our capacity to proffer alternative to it. Their dismissal of Marxism springs from a profound misreading that oversimplifies the various interpretations

R. H. McGuire (✉)
Binghamton University, Binghamton, NY, USA
e-mail: rmcguire@binghamton.edu

S. Gimatzidis and R. Jung (eds.), *The Critique of Archaeological Economy*, Frontiers in Economic History,
https://doi.org/10.1007/978-3-030-72539-6_2

of Marx and that more importantly misrepresent the relational or Hegelian dialectic that underlies most Marxist theory in U.S. archaeology. A Relational or Hegelian Marxism provides a profound way to write the deep history of human economy.

Before getting to the meat of things, I want to position myself and my ideas. First, I am an archaeologist not a philosopher. I will be engaging with philosophy, but my goal is to comment on archaeology and not the philosophers that archaeologists interpret. Second, my own philosophical understandings derive principally from left-wing Anglophone thinkers such as Bertell Ollman (2003), Angela Davis (2015), Roy Bhaskar (2013), David Harvey (2019), bell hooks (2000), Terry Eagleton (2016), Vine Deloria Jr. (1997) Heidi Hartman (1981), and Raj Patel and Jason W. Moore (2017). Third, I will of course, speak of French and German philosophers (including Karl Marx) but I have only read them in translation. Fourth, I am an U.S. archaeologist who works in Latin America. I participate in Hispanic theoretical archaeology. What I present here is very much an American perspective, American in the broadest sense of all the Americas. Finally, I have published two books that provide much more in-depth presentations of my reading of Marx and my praxis of applying it in archaeology (McGuire, 1992, 2008).

Relational Marxism

Marxism originated with the ideas of Karl Marx and has matured, developed, and grown for more than 100 years. Like other grand theories of humankind and society it has come to include a great variety of different viewpoints, drawn understandings from other theories, and inspired persons outside of the tradition. Also, like other grand theories, people have bent and hammered it into an instrument for pernicious purposes.

Interpretations of Marx

Marxism starts with the ideas of Marx. Marx pondered the fundamental issues of social life in order to formulate a critical theory of Capitalism. He did this in tentative, dynamic, and often paradoxical ways. Marxism ultimately relies on a radical concept of history. For Marx, history fashioned the stage for social action but people created history. The creation of history involves culture, identity, and interpretation and thus affords the opportunity for people to come to a critical awareness of their own social actions that leads to Praxis. Marxists take an anti-reductionist holistic approach to the study of humanity's history. They reject the idea that scholars should divide real life to parts (culture, economy, politics, society, or history) and that they should particularize different theories to explain these parts. The logic of the dialectic directs us to research society as an interconnected whole.

Marx did not leave us Marxism. The term was unknown during his lifetime. Over more than a century, Western Marxists have developed, differentiated, and diversified their scholarship. They did not create a single, unified, doctrinaire, theory of society that advocates can simply hitch to our empirical cart or that critics can simply dismiss in a few pithy sentences. Instead Western Marxists have created a tradition of thought, a philosophy, a mode of theoretical creation that has and will generate many theories.

Scholars have developed Marxist archaeologies in many parts of the world including the former Soviet Union, Europe, China, Latin America, North America, and Japan. Many communist states transformed Marxism, including archaeology, into little more than an ideology to legitimate the exercise of political power. Ideology lacks the tension between knowledge, critique, and action. Without this tension, Marxism became totalitarian party communism and a source of alienation, domination, exploitation, and oppression that used archaeology to justify the state (Klejn, 1991: 70; 1993; Trigger, 1995: 326). Western archaeologists rejected party communism. Many adopted a traditional or classical Marxism that uses Engels' (1927) dialectics of nature. These include scholars such as V. Gordon Childe (1956, 1989), Bruce Trigger (1995, 2003), Antonio Gilman (1998), Thomas Patterson (2003), and the Hispanic Arqueología Social (Lumbreras, 1974; Vargas & Sanoja, 1999; Lull et al., 1990; Lull & Micó, 2011; Bate, 1998; Tantaleán, 2016). Others developed a critical archaeology that draws on French Structural Marxism, the Frankfurt School, and Gramci (Leone, 2005; Shackel, 2000). In North America, many researchers, including myself, embraced a Hegelian or Relational Marxism (McGuire, 2008; Wurst, 2002). These Western Marxist archaeologies form a continuum of interrelated positions and ideas that range from the more scientific Classical Marxism to the more humanistic Relational Marxism.

Critiques of Marxist approaches to archaeology rarely attempt to understand the range and depth of positions that different Western approaches embody. This is especially the case for Neo-Materialist critics (Harris & Cipolla, 2017). Rather than doing the hard study required for nuanced understandings, they cherry pick ideas from the complex range of Marxist thought. They then use the oversimplification that they have produced to reject "Marxist" Archaeology.

Differences in the concept and use of the dialectic distinguish different approaches to Marxism in general and in archaeology. Party communism makes the dialectic a deterministic and teleological tool. Western Marxism dismisses the communist position as not dialectical and as vulgar materialism (McGuire, 1992: 91–99). French Structural Marxism replaces the dialectic with structuralism. Engels' (1927) *Dialectics of Nature* parallel much thought in complex adaptive systems theory or Chaos theory (Woods & Grant, 2015). The perspective that I take is the relational dialectic of Hegel as interpreted by Bertell Ollman (2003).

Hegelian Relational Dialectic

Relational Dialectical thinking starts with social relations and not with social categories or the classification of concrete entities (such as classes, the economy, modes of production). These entities are just appearances. A complex web of dialectically related social relations creates society. A web of intricate interconnections creates any given unit through its relationship to other entities. Masters do not exist without slaves nor slaves without masters. The underlying social relationship of slavery creates both master and slave. The unity of opposites recognizes that each social unit necessitates the existence of its opposite and of the social relationship that creates them both.

A relational dialectic does not assume that the entities that make up the social whole will fit peacefully together. They might fit, but the dynamics of change do not spring from functional relations. Rather, relational contradictions inherent in the unity of opposites drive change. Thus, slavery creates both the master and the slave. For one to exist so too must the other, yet as opposites they are inherently in conflict. Each has conflicting interests and a dissimilar lived experience in a shared history. These relations do not simply change quantitatively or qualitatively. Quantitative changes can lead to qualitative transformations, and qualitative transformation inevitably indicates a quantitative change. Struggles that spring from relational contradictions may result in quantitative changes in those relations that build to a qualitative transformation. Rebellion by slaves may lead the masters to enforce harsher and harsher discipline, thereby heightening resistance until people overthrow slavery. The social relations that spring from such a qualitative change remake the old with the addition of the new.

A Relational Dialectic does not predict or explain social transformation (Ollman, 2003: 12). It is both a way of observing the world, and a method of investigation. Explaining social change requires the dialectical analysis of historically grounded social relations and contradictions. A scholar uses the Relational Dialectic as a method to detect these asymmetries. A successful dialectical view of the world has utility. It helps archaeologists to choose important problems and steers them to the empirical observations needed to evaluate those problems. It provides a framework for assessing empirical observations that help scholars to build knowledge, make critique, and act in the world.

A Relational Marxism creates praxis (McGuire, 2008). Praxis is theoretically informed action. Praxis springs from the realization that people make the social world in their lived experience and that they can also subvert and alter that world. Successful praxis necessitates that people know the world, critique the world, and take action in the world. Action deprived of correct knowledge of the world will fail but simple empiricism does not yield useful knowledge. Archaeologists construct knowledge in a complex dialectic between the reality that they examine, the methods that they employ, and the consciousness that they bring to that examination. They need to be self-reflexive and critical about how reality and their consciousness affect their enquiries and knowledge construction. If archaeologists do not critique the ethics, politics, epistemology, and reality behind their knowledge, then their actions in the world will be defective and their action may result in unforeseen, detrimental, and/or counterproductive consequences. Critique lacking knowledge creates self-delusion and critique lacking action leads to nihilism and despair.

Now that I have positioned myself, the reader might ask "why do archaeologists need to consider Marxism?" Communism has diminished as a political force in the world and the major Communist nations (Russia and China) have adopted nineteenth century style Capitalisms without twentieth century liberal reforms. Doing archaeology is more and more about toys (drones, lidar, 3D printers, GPS etc.). Many "scientific" archaeologists have little interest in theory they just want to play with their toys. At the end of the twentieth century, Post-Modern archaeologist rejected the totalizing framework of Marxism. In the twenty-first century, a new materialism has appeared, and many archaeologists have eagerly adopted it and rejected Marxism (Harris & Cipolla, 2017). I will argue that despite these factors, a Relational Marxism still provides an insightful way to write the deep history of human economy and to relate that history to modern praxis.

Neo-Materialism

Why should archaeologists use Marxism when we can play with bright and shiny neo-materialisms? Newfangled bright and shiny things have attracted many theoretical archaeologists especially the Post-Modernist, British scholars such as Ian Hodder (2012) and Michael Shanks who introduced Post Modernism to archaeology. They declare that Marxism is timeworn and exhausted. These new bright shiny things involve a diversity of approaches that scholars have variously branded "post-humanism," "Object Agency," "Thing Theory," and the "New Materialism." One of Neo-Materialism's most prominent advocates, Jane Bennett (2010: xvi) questions: "Why did Marx come to stand for materialism?"

I am not a philosopher and I am not qualified to fully engage with the nuances or variants of Neo-Materialism. I am an archaeologist. As an archaeologist, I will critique the concepts that Symmetrical Archaeologists have adopted from Neo-Materialism and their rejection of a Relational Marxism. I write to debate archaeology not philosophy. The faults and errors that I find are the sins of archaeologists not necessarily the philosophers that they read.

Neo-Materialism ascends from the ruins of Post-Modernism. It seeks to replace discourse and the linguistic turn with the material. Bill Brown (2003) describes Thing Theory to examine object–culture relations in literature. Bennett (2010) advocates for thing power, that is taking the material seriously. Timothy Morton (2017) offers an Object-oriented Ontology that does not privilege the human over nonhuman things. Many archaeologists have also read Manuel DeLanda's (2016) assemblage theory's bottom-up framework that emphasizes fluidity, exchangeability, and multiple functionalities in the analysis of social complexity.

These perspectives share important commonalities, most significantly that scholars should examine things, objects in their own right and not merely as a way of understanding the human. They define humans, non-humans, and material things as actants, that is active agents in cultural change and diversity. This broad concept of actant and agency depends upon a denial of dualisms such as culture/nature, animate/inanimate, thinking/being, subject/object, and human/animal. Putting all things on the same plain requires a rejection of anthropocentric approaches that sets humans at the center of our analysis. Finally, they shift the focus on epistemology (how humans know the world) to stress in its place ontology (the nature of being in the world).

There is a lot that I approve of in Neo-Materialism and their argument to take things seriously seduces archaeologists. Giving priority to the study of the material in its own right spotlights the stuff that archaeologists dig up, examine, and study. This priority makes things the objects of our study and not just a lesser means to access human agency and cultural change. Concepts such as "assemblage" embrace archaeological logic and I have even heard some advocates attribute archaeology as one origin point for the concept. Generally, when reading Neo-Materialism I generally go yes, yes, yes until I reach a point where I can only go no, no, no, or maybe hell no. That point occurs when the Neo-Materialists equate things with people and ignore human suffering.

Symmetrical Archaeology

We should not be surprised that archaeologists have been inspired in various ways by these approaches. This inspiration manifests in the Symmetrical Archaeology and in the work of its principle advocates Michael Shanks (Olsen et al., 2012), Bijorn Olsen (2010), Christopher Witmore (2014), and Þóra Pétursdóttir (2017). Symmetrical archaeology springs from a critique of postmodern archaeology. Symmetrical archaeologists accused Post Modernism of being preoccupied with the individual and the socio-cultural and of forgetting the 'thingly component' of the past. They objected to Post Modernism's asymmetrical relationship between people and things, that favored the human over the thingly.

These archaeologists makes the relationship between people and things symmetrical. They want to study non-humans most specifically things not merely as useful stuff or as objects that humans fill with meaning, symbols, and identities but rather as active agents or actants. They reject the idea of human exceptionalism as "foolishness." They dismiss putting humans at the center of everything, and reject Anthroporcentric approaches. Symmetrical archaeology generates a flat ontology that places things, animals, and humans on the same plain (Olsen & Witmore, 2015). They admit the possibility of highlighting the human, but they begin their analysis with no assumptions about the priority of people.

Dualism and the Dialectic

The polemic of symmetrical archaeologists discards any dualism. Dualisms prioritize Western Ontology and in doing so obscure other non-Western Ontologies. They reject the essentialism of Dualisms. They assume that every entity holds characteristics (an essence) that create its identity and function in contrast to the essence of another entity. Dualisms do not always define the same oppositions. They worry that dualisms enact groupings that may or may not exist and that may or may not be valuable to analysis. This polemic paradoxically depends upon a dualism between Cartesian (dualistic) thought and relational (non-dualistic) thinking.

Symmetrical archaeologists (Harris & Cipolla, 2017) base their denunciation of Marxism in large part on this disdain for dualism. They reject Marxism out of hand by cherry picking from Mark Leone's Marxist studies of representation and presenting Leone's critical archaeology as the whole of Marxism. They also use a shallow misreading of the dialectic as a straw dog.

They reject the dialectic as imperfectly relational or as a type of dualism. They find Daniel Miller's (2012) dialectical research on materiality inadequately relational. They profoundly misread the unity of opposites in a Marxist dialectic as a dualism. They do not even consider the Hegelian relational dialectic that I will argue is a more powerful tool than the relational empiricism that they embrace.

Calling the dialectic a dualism miscomprehends the core concept of the unity of opposites. The dialectical opposites do not have essences that define them. Rather, an underlying social relationship generates the social entities and changes in that relationship alter the entities. Polemical descriptions of the dialectic focus on two opposites to simplify the concept. But in actual historical cases, the underlying relationships are intricate, multifractionated and not simply dualistic. In the U.S. south, the underlying relationship of antebellum slavery created the master and the slave in Alabama, but it also created the overseer, the cotton merchant in Charleston and the textile workers in Manchester, England. A slave rebellion that disrupted the production of cotton or a strike that stopped the looms could have transformed the whole intricate web of relations that form the mode of production.

To dismiss the active and relational character of the dialectic, critics define a tripartite dialectic of thesis, anti-thesis, and synthesis (Harris & Cipolla, 2017: 91). This frequently used definition is not relational (it is dualistic) because it is mechanical and because it leads to closure (synthesis). The triad does not reflect a relational Hegelian dialectic or Marx's use of the dialectic (Mueller, 1958). The thesis, antithesis, synthesis triad originates with Emanuel Kant and his students (McFarland, 2002). Kant defined thesis and antithesis and later his student Johann Gottlieb Fichte followed this dyad with synthesis to create the tripartite dialectic. In a single passage, Hegel references Kant's use of thesis and anti-thesis but he does not accept Kant's definition of the dialectic or use the term "synthesis" (Kaufmann, 1966). Marx never referenced or used the tripartite dialectic. He used a relational Hegelian dialectic (Ollman, 2003). Equating the tripartite dialectic with Hegel and Marx result from inept readings of Hegel (or no reading at all). In archaeology, this misreading allows critics to mischaracterize all concepts of the dialectic as dualisms and to dismiss out of hand the relational dialectic used by many Anglophone, Marxist archaeologists. These critics do not realize that the relational dialectic resolves the dualism Symmetrical Archaeology creates between Cartesian vs Relational thinking.

History

Symmetrical Archaeology scorns political economy as much as it disdains dualities. Political Economy is the core of Historical Materialism. Just as with the dialectic there are many interpretations of Historical Materialism, but all approaches focus on human societies and historical transformation. Historical materialism theorizes that the material means and relations that humans use collectively to produce the necessities of life drives developments and transformations in human society. Marxist Archaeologists study things and materiality to understand how human societies change. Symmetrical Archaeologists study objects and materiality to comprehend things in their own right.

This difference represents an essential divide between Marxist and Symmetrical Archaeologies and creates a basic disparity in how each archaeology studies history. Both archaeologies empirically examine material remains. Symmetrical Archaeology, however, does not use this study to interpret social change. These archaeologists argue that we must thoroughly understand thing history before we can study cultural change. Symmetrical Archaeologists research the history of things (artifact biographies) from their raw materials, to their manufacture, to their uses, and finally to their disposal and decay. To fully understand artifact biographies, symmetrical studies also contemplate the shifting relations that these things enter into with other things, humans, and animals. This is history as exhaustive, never ending description.

Andreassen et al. (2010) studied an abandoned Soviet artic mining town called Pyramiden. The authors reference but they do not investigate the economic, political, social, and cultural processes that created the mines and that led to their expiry. They ignore political economy. Instead, they write a descriptive history of buildings and things and of their post human decay. They illustrate the study with stunning artistic photographs that aestheticizes the abandonment and decay to produce ruins porn. After viewing this study, I realized that my meager skills as a photographer prevent me from ever being a Symmetrical Archaeologist.

Symmetrical Ontology

Ruins porn beguiles the observer with rotting things and human absence. This absence echoes Symmetrical Archaeology's denunciation of an anthropocentric archaeology. Symmetry springs from a flat ontology that presupposes humans, animals, and things have the same nature of being in the world.

To the contrary, Marxist Archaeologists assert that people, animals, and things have unique ontologies. In *Capital*, Marx (1906: 198) compares bees and humans based on the absence or presence of consciousness:

> A spider conducts operations that resemble those of a weaver, and a bee puts to shame many an architect in the construction of her cells. But what distinguishes the worst architect from the best of bees is this, that the architect raises his structure in imagination before he erects it in reality.

Marxist archaeologists have pointed out that things do not suffer as humans do (Bernbeck, 2018). Things do not feel physical pain, anguish, loss, exhaustion, agony, or fear. They do not shiver in the snow or burn in the sun. If you prick things, they do not bleed. If you tickle them, they do not laugh.

The cultural anthropologist Tim Ingold (2011: 172–188) compares a tree and a house. He begins by rejecting the oppositions of nature and culture and natural organism vs cultural design. He points to many parallels between trees and houses. Both trees and houses are lived in. DNA does not simply determine the form of the tree but instead the tree's form develops through being in the world. Similarly, a house does not emerge as a final static thing but rather as a material process built by the people and animals that inhabit it. Both trees and houses develop from the relational meshwork of people, animals, plants, materials, weather, etc. He concludes that the difference between tree and house is not natural organism vs cultural design but rather in the degree of human engagement. He argues that this proves that trees and houses exist in the same ontological realm.

Ingold's arguments significantly develop a relational understanding of trees or houses but things and people do not have to exist on the same ontological plain for us to understand them relationally. Ingold's similarities do not alter the truth of Marx's contrast between bees and architects. His observation about the differences being in the degree of human engagement is insightful but it does not validate the absence of ontological difference. Trees may also vary in their degree of human involvement. For instance, a topiary has a high degree of human involvement and a pine tree in the forest has less human involvement. But to understand the difference between a topiary and a forest pine we must discuss human consciousness, concepts of aesthetics, and even class relations, aspects of being human in the world but not aspects of being thingly in the world.

Þóra Pétursdóttir (2017) studies "drift matter" (marine debris) that washes up along the coastlines of northern Norway and Iceland. This material drifts and amasses in the intertidal zones of these countries. Drift matter is a resource for humans who walk the beach or it can be a global environmental problem of great concern. Pétursdóttir insightfully discusses how drift matter exposes both opportunities and barriers for an Anthropocene Archaeology. She discusses how the physical and ideological climate change of the Anthropocene will affect the craft of archaeology and how can archaeology meaningfully address the challenges of the Anthropocene. She seeks to take drift matter seriously as actant things that exist out of hand, in a post-human space.

Tragically, in the world today, post-human material actants are not the only things washing up on beaches. Over the last decade, thousands of people have drowned in the Mediterranean Sea fleeing war, violence, poverty, oppression, and exploitation. We all remember the tragic photograph of twenty-seven-months-old Alan Kurdi's body washed up on a Turkish beach (Kurdi, 2018). If we accept a flat ontology, a symmetrical archaeology that eschews an anthropocentric approach, then we must initially treat drift matter and the body of a child homogeneously. Olsen and Witmore (2015) argue that ontology should be flat only in the first instance possibly allowing us in the next instance to recognize the humanity and tragedy of a dead child on the beach. For me, there is no instance in which I can accept a symmetrical ontology that would equate drift matter and a dead child.

Yet at least some Symmetrical Archaeologists do liken the being of things with human suffering. These archaeologists claim that we should give more attention to exploited things than to humans. Harris and Cipolla (2017: 185) write; "So following this logic, rather than freeing people from the tyranny of colonialism, it is things themselves that need our assistance." Olsen (2003: 100) argues; "Archaeologists should unite in the defense of things, a defense of those subaltern members of the collective that have been silenced and 'othered' by the imperialist social and humanistic discourses." This equation of human exploitation and suffering with the being of things is the moment when I go hell no. In a brilliant critique of the Symmetrical Archaeology, Severn Fowles (2016) argues that in the second half of the twentieth century non-Western peoples resisted being subjects of Western research. Their resistance interrupted Western scholarship and led some anthropologists and related scholars to study non-human objects as quasi-human subjects. It is easier to research things rather than people because things do not talk back (yet another ontological difference).

Praxis is the most essential difference between a Relational Marxist Archaeology and the Symmetrical Archaeology. Praxis is conscious theoretically based human action that comes from knowing the world, critiquing the world, and acting in the world. To engage in Praxis, we need to understand the relations and entanglements that people enter with each other, animals, things, and plants. A relational dialectic offers a method to diagnose and investigate the active role of non-human things. But if we wish to design, facilitate, or participate in transformative change we must study the relationship of these non-human actants to conscious, purposive human agency.

Why Marxism?

Marxism is first and foremost a Praxis that seeks to know capitalism, critique capitalism (and itself), and transform capitalism. Despite the critique of Neo-Materialism and others, Marxism remains a viable, profound approach to archaeology. This leaves the central question of this symposium why should we apply Marxism to the deep past? I offer two answers to this question: (1) If we wish to transform Capitalism we must demonstrate that alternatives to Capitalism existed in the past and that we can therefore create alternatives in the future, and (2) Marxism offers archaeologists an intellectual tool kit that they can use to understand non-Capitalist economies.

Capitalism as a Product of History

The most basic and blatant lie of Capitalism is that the relations of Capitalism spring from human nature. Capitalist maintains that private property, individualism, profit, wage labor, voluntary exchange, a price system, competitive markets, and economic maximization are inherent in the human condition. Based on this claim, supporters argue that Capitalism does not have a history. If the key features of Capitalism do not have a history of development, then they cannot be changed. If human hands and minds did not create Capitalism, then human hands and minds cannot transform it into something else.

Marx and Engels studied "primitive" societies to expose the blatant lie. Friedrich Engels (1972) published *The Origins of the Family, Private Property and the State* and a short work called "The Part Played by Labor in the Transition from Ape to Man." *The Origins of the Family, Private Property and the State* used contemporary Social Evolutionary theory and classical sources to discuss the origins and processes of development for the key features of Capitalism. In the shorter work Engels argues that labor shapes human's relation to nature interdependently with human social relations. The Ethnological Notebooks in the Grundrisse contain most of Marx's (1974) unpublished notes and observations on pre-capitalist modes of production. Marx and Engels studied non-capitalist modes of production to demonstrate that the relations of Capitalism had a history. Human hands and minds had made Capitalism and they could therefore transform it.

Karl Polanyi (2001) critiqued the universality of Capitalist Market Society in his seminal work *The Great Transformation: The Political and Economic Origins of Our Time.* He showed that wage labor, voluntary exchange, a price system, competitive markets, and economic maximization were not universal characteristics of human economies but rather products of the development of market societies. He contrasted the market economy driven by scarcity, individual desires, and economic maximization with gift and redistributive economies where the economy was embedded in social and cultural relations. Formalist critics of Polanyi argued that scarcity and economic maximization existed in all societies while Substantivists supported Polanyi's position that these things only became important when historical processes disembedded the economy from the social. Much more recently David Graeber (2001) accepts that scarcity and economic maximization result from historic development, but he rejects the dualistic opposition of formalist and substantivist. He instead seeks to understand how peoples in different times and contexts found meaning in their actions.

Marxism as an Intellectual Tool Kit

Marxism is a rich conceptual source of models and theories for the study of cultural change. Many others considering the conditions of economic development of their own times have interpreted anew Marx's basic—and often somewhat ambiguous—observations (Foster, 2016; Patel & Moore, 2017). This fruitful tradition of scholarship has produced a copious body of theories, concepts, ideas, and insights on human history (Chapman, 2003; Cobb, 2000; Earle & Spriggs, 2015; McGuire & Saitta, 1996; Trigger, 2003). Marx's focus on the role of socially constituted labor in the production and reproduction of real life—and his realization that these social relations are objectified in various ways, including through material culture—is compatible with the craft of archaeology (Shanks & McGuire, 1996). Thus, the archaeologist V. Gordon Childe (1944: 1) noted that material culture reflects and participates in the social relations that produce it and that we can therefore study these social relations using material culture.

The key instrument in the Marxist tool kit is the method of class analysis. Marx's analysis focused on the relations between classes and class factions. Complex relations between material conditions, consciousness, and social agency create classes and class fractions. Class analysis starts with real individuals, their actions, and the material (economic) conditions under which they live/lived, both the conditions that they inherited from the past and the conditions that they create/created through their actions. A dialectical archaeology should start and end with the real lived experience of people and seek an understanding of how people transformed that experience and that experience transformed people.

Marx developed class analysis to study Capitalism. He did not develop it to explain all human history. Cultural anthropologists working at the end of the twentieth century demonstrated that a Marxist class analysis could be applied to any social groups that have common interests and consciousness (Bloch, 1985: 162–163). Any group of individuals who share a common identity, and mutual interests can form a group consciousness to engage in social agency. This demonstration extended class analysis into pre-class societies. It also opened the door for complex analyses that include gender, race, ethnicity, sexuality, and age as well as classes and class factions.

For example, if scholars accept either a totalitarian notion of Marxism (class is the root of all exploitation) or a totalitarian notion of Feminism (gender is the root of all exploitation), then Marxism and Feminism must be at odds. The Feminist ideas of intersectionality and of entry point, however, offers an alternative to these totalitarian ideas (Wylie, 1991). If we are to take diversity and the complexity of oppression seriously, then we must recognize that oppression derives from the intersectionality of many relationships including those of gender, class, race, sexuality, and ethnicity (Battle-Baptiste, 2011). Each of these provides an entry point to the study of social relations and of oppression. Marxists will enter the study of the social world with the analysis of class and from this entry point examine the intersectionalities between class, gender, race, sexuality, and ethnicity in the construction of oppression. Feminists will begin their analysis with gender. As long as Feminists seek a radical transformation of gender relations that must also address class, race, sexuality, and ethnicity (hooks, 2000) and Marxists recognize that relations of class also must involve relations of gender, race, sexuality, and ethnicity than the two approaches can be compatible and complementary.

Even though every new shiny theory wants to dismiss Marxism out of hand, Marx *lebt*. Archaeological advocates for a New Materialism dismiss Marxism. They do this by distorting the relational dialectic as oppositional thinking. They provide a weak alternative in Neo-Materialism. This alternative maintains the status quo of Capitalism, limits our ability to critique Capitalism, and weakens our capacity to proffer alternative to it. A relational dialectical Marxism still provides a profound way to address the deep history of human economy. It confronts the lie that Capitalism results from an unchanging human nature. It demonstrates that human hands and minds built Capitalism and thus, human hands and minds may transform Capitalism.

References

Andreassen, E., Bjerck, H., & Olsen, B. (2010). *Persistent memories: Pyramiden—A Soviet mining town in the High Arctic*. Tapir Academic Press.

Bate, F. (1998). *El Proceso de Investigación en Arqueología*. Crítica.

Battle-Baptiste, W. (2011). *Black feminist archaeology*. Left Coast Press.

Bennett, J. (2010). *Vibrant matter: A political ecology of things*. Duke University Press.

Bernbeck, R. (2018). Intrusions—On the relations of materiality and suffering. In K. Kaniuth, D. Lau, & D. Wicke (Eds.), *Übergangszeiten. Altorientalische Studien für Reinhard Dittmann anlässlich seines 65. Geburtstags*. Zaphon.

Bhaskar, R. (2013). *Critical realism in a Nutshell: A brief introduction to critical realism*. Routledge.

Bloch, M. (1985). *Marxism and anthropology*. Oxford University Press.

Brown, B. (2003). *A sense of things: The object matter of American literature*. University of Chicago Press.

Chapman, R. (2003). *Archaeologies of complexity*. Routledge.

Childe, V. G. (1944). *Progress and archaeology*. Cobbett.

Childe, V. G. (1956). *Society and knowledge: The growth of human traditions*. Harpur.

Childe, V. G. (1989). Retrospect. In G. Daniel, & C. Chippendale (Eds.), *The Pastmasters: Eleven modern pioneers of archaeology* (pp. 10–19). Thames and Hudson.

Cobb, C. R. (2000). *From Quarry to Cornfield: The political economy of Mississippian hoe production*. University of Alabama Press.

Davis, A. B. (2015). *Freedom is a constant struggle*. Haymarket Books.

DeLanda, M. (2016). *Assemblage theory*. University of Edinburg Press.

Deloria, V. J. (1997). *Red Earth, White Lies: Native Americans and the myth of scientific fact*. Fulcrum Publishing.

Eagleton, T. (2016). *Materialism*. Yale University Press.

Earle, T., & Spriggs, M. (2015). Political economy in prehistory: A Marxist approach to pacific sequences. *Current Anthropology, 56*(4), 515–544.

Engels, F. (1927). *The dialectics of nature*. Foreign Language Publishers (first published 1883).

Engels, F. (1972). *The origins of the family private property and the state*. International Publishers (first published 1884).

Foster, J. B. (2016). Marxism in the anthropocene: Dialectical rifts on the left. *International Critical Thought, 6*(3), 393–421.

Fowles, S. (2016). The perfect subject (Postcolonial Object Studies). *Journal of Material Culture, 21*(1), 9–27.
Gilman, A. (1998). The Communist Manifesto 150 years later. *Antiquity, 72,* 910–913.
Graeber, D. (2001). *Toward an anthropological theory of value: The false coin of our own dreams.* Palgrave.
Harris, O. J. T., & Cipolla, C. N. (2017). *Archaeological theory in the new millennium: Introducing current perspectives.* Routledge.
Hartmann, H. (1981). The unhappy marriage of Marxism and Feminism: Towards a more progressive union. In L. Sargent (Ed.), *Women and revolution: A discussion of the unhappy marriage of Marxism and Feminism* (pp. 1–42). South End Press.
Harvey, D. (2019). *Abstract from the concrete.* Sternberg Press.
Hodder, I. (2012). *Entangled: An archaeology of the relationships between humans and things.* Wiley-Blackwell.
hooks, b. (2000). *Feminism is for everybody.* South End Press.
Ingold, T. (2011). *The perception of the environment.* Routledge.
Kaufmann, W. (1966). *Hegel: A reinterpretation.* New York (NY): Anchor Books.
Klejn, L. S. (1991). A Russian lesson for theoretical archaeology: A reply. *Fennoscandia Archaeologica, 8,* 67–71.
Klejn, L. S. (1993). *La arqueología soviética: historia y teoría de una escuela desconocida.* Crítica.
Kurdi, T. (2018). *The boy on the beach: My family's escape from Syria and our hope for a new home.* Simon and Schuster.
Leone, M. B. (2005). *The archaeology of liberty in an American capital: Excavations in Annapolis.* University of California Press.
Lull, V., & Micó, R. (2011). *Archaeology of the origin of the state: The theories.* Oxford University Press.
Lull, V., Micó, R., Montón, S., & Picazo, Y. M. (1990). La arqueología entre la insoportable levedad y la voluntad de poder. *Archivo de Prehistoria Levantina, 20,* 461–474.
Lumbreras, L. G. (1974). *La arqueología como ciencia social.* Ediciones Histar.
Marx, K. (1906). *Capital: A critique of political economy.* The Modern Library (Originally Published 1867).
Marx, K. (1974). *The ethnological notebooks of Karl Marx.* Van Gorcum.
McFarland, T. (2002). Prolegomena. In *Opus Maximum* (S. T. Coleridge). Princeton University Press.
McGuire, R. H. (1992). *A Marxist archaeology.* Academic Press.
McGuire, R. H. (2008). *Archaeology as political action.* University of California Press.
McGuire, R. H., & Saitta, D. J. (1996). Although they have petty captains, they obey them badly: The dialectics of Prehispanic Western Pueblo social organization. *American Antiquity, 61,* 197–216.
Miller, D. (2012). *Consumption and its consequences.* Polity.
Morton, T. (2017). *Humankind: Solidarity with non-human people.* Verso.
Mueller, G. (1958). The Hegel legend of "thesis-antithesis-synthesis. *Journal of the History of Ideas, 19*(4), 411–414.
Ollman, B. (2003). *Dance of the dialectic: Steps in Marx's method.* Urbana-Champagne, University of Illinois Press.
Olsen, B. (2003). Material culture after text: Re-membering things. *Norwegian Archaeological Review, 36*(3), 87–104.
Olsen, B. (2010). *In defense of things: Archaeology and the ontology of objects.* AltaMira Press.
Olsen, B., Shanks, M., Webmore, T., & Witmore, C. (2012). *Archaeology: The discipline of things.* University of California Press.
Olsen, B., & Witmore, C. (2015). Archaeology, symmetry and the ontology of things: A response to critics. *Archaeological Dialogues, 22*(2), 187–197.
Patel, R., & Moore, J. W. (2017). *A history of the world in seven cheap things: A guide to capitalism, nature, and the future of the planet.* University of California Press.
Patterson, T. (2003). *Marx's ghost: Conversations with archaeologists.* Berg.

Polanyi, K. (2001). *The great transformation: The political and economic origins of our time* (2nd ed.). Beacon Press.
Shackel, P. A. (2000). *Archaeology and created memory: Public history in a national park*. Kluwer Academic/Plenum Publishers.
Shanks, M., & McGuire, R. H. (1996). The craft of archaeology. *American Antiquity, 61*(1), 75–88.
Pétursdóttir, Þ. (2017). Climate change? Archaeology and anthropocene. *Archaeological Dialogues, 24*(2), 175–205.
Tantaleán, H. (2016). *Peruvian archaeology: A critical history*. Routledge.
Trigger, B. (1995). Archaeology and the integrated circus. *Critique of Anthropology, 15*(4), 319–335.
Trigger, B. (2003). *Understanding early civilizations: A comparative study*. Cambridge University Press.
Vargas, I., & Sanoja, M. (1999). Archaeology as a social science: Its expression in Latin America. In G. G. Politis & B. Alberti (Eds.), *Archaeology in Latin America* (pp. 59–75). Routledge.
Witmore, C. (2014). Archaeology and the new materialisms. *Journal of Contemporary Archaeology, 1*(2), 203–246.
Woods, A., & Grant, T. (2015). *Reason in revolt: Marxist philosophy and modern science*. Wellred Publications.
Wurst, L. (2002). "For the means of your subsistence... Look under god to your own industry and frugality": Life and labor in Gerrit Smith's Peterboro. *International Journal of Historical Archaeology, 6*(3), 159–172.
Wylie, A. (1991). Gender theory and the archaeological record: Why is there no archaeology of gender? In J. Gero & M. Conkey (Eds.), *Engendering archaeology* (pp. 31–56). Basil Blackwell.

Chapter 3
Wealth, Women's Labour, and Forms of Value: Thinking from the Study of Ancestral Central America

Rosemary A. Joyce

Abstract A turn to the archaeologically documented past as a source of data for generalizing models explaining the roots of contemporary economic reality can involve treating pasts that were shaped under far different social conditions as equivalent to the contemporary world of nation states and global economies. Using case studies from ancient Mexico and Central America, I examine two sources of incommensurability that should be taken into account in any attempt to think from the past of economic relations to the present. The first is how labour is conceived of, counted, and understood in different situations. As feminist scholars of the contemporary economy have long noted, large areas of economic activity by women are routinely excluded in modern analyses, based on a tacit distinction between household labour (viewed as intimate, domestic, and ruled only by naturalized relations of sex and age) and extra-domestic labour. For the societies of ancient Central America, such a division simply did not exist. Accordingly, the standards of value and exchange that emerged in such societies were entangled in social relations that need to be accounted for before these societies are used as evidence for long-term human economic patterns.

Reconsideration of the "deep past" of contemporary socioeconomic relations is enjoying a remarkable moment of public attention: whether the massive reconsideration of debt by David Graeber (2014), James Scott's somewhat more limited discussion of changes to what he thought he knew about the emergence of urbanism in Mesopotamia (Scott, 2017), or the universalizing of modern measures of economic inequality by the team of archaeologists led by Timothy Kohler and Michael Smith (Kohler & Smith, 2018), authors aiming at transdisciplinary or even popular audiences are returning to archaeological data to trace genealogies for the contemporary situation in which we find ourselves.

However, in the process, these works can be insufficiently critical of the terms of intellectual conceptualization under which archaeological reports—often treated as

R. A. Joyce (✉)
Department of Anthropology, University of California, Berkeley, USA
e-mail: rajoyce@berkeley.edu

S. Gimatzidis and R. Jung (eds.), *The Critique of Archaeological Economy*, Frontiers in Economic History,
https://doi.org/10.1007/978-3-030-72539-6_3

"data" for these projects—were formed. In this paper, I seek to contribute to a critique of the way archaeologists, and hence others relying on archaeological information, understand and thus characterize activities and relations as "economic". It is not an accident that I put understanding before characterization here. I argue that before archaeologists ever create observations treated by themselves or others as "data", they have already formed ideas of what is observable, how the observable can and should be measured, and often even what the explanatory variables will be.

In the remainder of this chapter, I will do three things. First, I will consider how certain understandings are tacitly employed, even in relatively sophisticated contemporary work, that equate women's activities in something called "the household" with a non-economic sector. Second, using material from Mexico and Central America, I will show that the distinction between the "household" and a presumed political or public economic sector does not hold up. Finally, I will link these observations to writing by feminist and Marxist-Feminist critics of standard economic models. While my case studies come from a specific region, I argue that the critique I am presenting offers insights for many other instances where an initial division between public and private, economy and household, is relied on by archaeologists or those using the information archaeologists generate.

In speaking about "women" in this paper, I am not ignoring the actual complexity of past gender relations whose appreciation is one of the central developments in contemporary archaeology. This includes research that treats assumptions of binary heterosexuality as historically contingent, demands attention to intersectionality between gender and other dimensions of social position, and thus resists collapsing people into two simple categories of men and women (Joyce, 2001b, 2008). It is remarkable how little impact this work on gender and sexuality in the past has had on recent literature on ancient economies. In most works I would include under this rubric, even when the society at issue is one where researchers have demonstrated through deep and sustained analysis that it makes no sense to talk about a unified category of "women" juxtaposed to an equally unified category of "men", precisely such a dichotomy is usually employed. As a beginning point, however, it is helpful to see how recent works have treated women as an aggregate subject, and even if they have, in models of ancient economies. My case study then considers a situation where economic relations surrounding the main standards of value implicate gendered labour, at least of women of certain classes, in ways that make considering gendered subjectivity indispensable for understanding the production of economic value. In my conclusion, I will return to this point, suggesting that more critical archaeology of the economy is advanced by more critical archaeology of gender.

How Models of the Ancient Economy Treat Women

To begin, let us examine how authors expressly addressing economic relations in the past, and in particular, relations of economic inequality, treat women as individualized embodied persons whose life chances are coordinated because of their similar biology. A simple experiment consists of attending to the way scholars index gender, sex, or women in the newly visible works dedicated to economic relations in the deep past. Often, the answer is that these dimensions of social difference are not explicitly addressed.

For example, James C. Scott, in *Against the Grain: A Deep History of the Earliest States* (2017), does not include gender or sex as index terms. In his retelling of the history of the state in Mesopotamia, women appear *only* as a subentry under slavery and slaves ("women as"). The majority of in-text discussions having to do with women are indexed under terms that relate to women as reproductive bodies: fertility, menopause, maternal mortality, ovulation, and puberty. These two lines of discussion, women as enslaved, and women as reproductive bodies, are intimately related by a running argument that states relied on "unfree labor" that led to "attention to 'husbanding' the subject population, including women, as a form of wealth, like livestock, in which fertility and high rates of reproduction were encouraged" (Scott, 2017: 29). Scott draws out the equation of women with livestock in a section called "Speculation on Human Parallels" where he seeks to extend information about changes non-human animals experience with domestication to humans, specifically women, in early sedentary societies. Generalizing from bioarchaeological study of skeletal remains from Abu Hureya he writes:

> Women in grain villages had characteristic bent-under toes and deformed knees that came from long hours kneeling and rocking back and forth grinding grain. It was a small but telling way that new subsistence routines– what today would be called a repetitive stress injury– shaped our bodies to new purposes, much as the work animals domesticated later– cattle, horses, and donkeys–bore skeletal signatures of their work routines. (Scott, 2017: 83)

While offered as part of a general discussion of "self-domestication" of the human species, the slippage here is telling: it is women's bodies that are domesticated, and specifically, the signs of their work grinding grain that makes women equivalent to "animals domesticated later". Men do not appear in these passages as domesticated animals, even though bioarchaeologists document alterations to labouring bodies of various sexes from their work regimes (Agarwal et al., 2015; Bolger, 2010).

That this is not simply oversight is underlined by the subsequent discussion in a section titled "A Note on Fertility and Population". Here, ignoring decades of critique by archaeologists, Scott uses selected studies of contemporary hunter-gatherers as a proxy for historic populations, to argue that "the burden of a much shorter spacing of children…is much reduced" in sedentary populations, while "the greater value of the children as a labor force in agriculture is enhanced" (Scott, 2017: 114). From this, he projects a raft of apparently inevitable changes to women's reproductive biology caused by sedentism, including earlier menstruation, ovulation (encouraged, he says, by a high carbohydrate diet), and extension of "a woman's reproductive life". In two short pages Scott returns to one of the enduring tropes about women in the past, that all women in the past were primarily valued socially for their reproductive potential and histories. This is an assumption that quite notably has been troubled by actual research on the varied histories of gendered and reproductive lives evident in bioarchaeology of early farming communities. These studies demonstrate variation between settlements, most not showing the patterns Scott emphasizes. Bolger (2010: 511–512) contrasts observations from Abu Hureya with the results of studies at other sites, including Çatalhöyük, where bioarchaeological differences were not marked between men and women (Agarwal et al., 2015).

Women come in for the most extended discussion in a chapter called "Population Control: Bondage and War". Women, in Scott's understanding, are mainly valuable as sources of additional labouring bodies. This is made explicit in a section of this chapter called "Slavery as 'Human Resources' Strategy". Here we are told that

> women and children were particularly prized as slaves. Women were often taken into local households as wives, concubines, or servants, and children were likely to be quickly assimilated, though at an inferior status. Within a generation or two they and their progeny were likely to have been incorporated into the local society... Women captives were at least as important for their reproductive services as for their labor. Given the problems of infant and maternal mortality in the early state and the need of both the patriarchal family and the state for agrarian labor, women captives were a demographic dividend. Their reproduction may have played a major role in alleviating the otherwise unhealthy effects of concentration... Here I cannot resist the obvious parallel with the domestication of livestock, which requires taking control over their reproduction... women slaves of reproductive age were prized in large part as breeders because of their contribution to the early state's manpower machine. (Scott, 2017: 168–169)

Shortly after this, Scott provides a discussion of male slaves who, he informs us, were employed "outside the households", away from the centre of urbanism, in "the most brutal and dangerous work" of mining, quarrying, and other manly tasks (Scott, 2017: 169–170). Women, it would seem, are natural sex slaves and "breeders", while male labouring bodies are naturalized as brute force.

It is worth noting that both primary and secondary sources cited in the same chapter are inconsistent with this uniform treatment of women as a group, and inconsistent with treating the population as divided into a group of men and a corresponding group of women. One poetic text cited, for example, mentions the experiences of three different female subjects: "the slave woman", "her mistress", and "the widow" (Scott, 2017: 164). As serious scholarship on gender in ancient Mesopotamia affirms, there was not a single categorical status for women (Bahrani, 2001; McCorriston, 1997; Wright, 1996). Free or unfree, unmarried, married, or widowed, member of a wealthy family, a ruling family, or a temple community, women's experiences were varied and their roles in production, distribution, and consumption of goods were varied as well.

These highly stereotyped assumptions—most offered with little or no reliance on cited sources, which often are dismissed as understating the oppressive conditions Scott projects onto ancient Mesopotamia—culminate in a final summary of the argument:

> In wars for captives, the strong preference for women of reproductive age reflects an interest at least as much in their reproductive services as in their labor. It would be instructive, but alas impossible, to know, in the light of the epidemiological challenges of early state centers, the importance of slave women's reproduction to the demographic stability and growth of the state. The domestication of non-slave women in the early grain state may also be seen in the same light. A combination of property in land, the patriarchal family, the division of

> labor within the domus, and the state's overriding interest in maximizing its population has the effect of domesticating women's reproduction in general. (Scott, 2017: 181)

Scott, of course, is not an archaeologist; as a historical researcher crossing the boundary between political science and anthropology, he privileges written records over other forms of evidence. He characterizes many aspects of the past whose story he is telling as lacking evidence, including such topics as the "collapse of states", "hunting and gathering", "nomadism", and "resettlement" (in Mesopotamia, specifically, but generalized as a global strategy of states)—all in fact areas in which archaeological research is relatively robust.

So it is worth examining an approach to related issues by archaeologists. *Ten Thousand Years of Inequality*, edited by Timothy Kohler and Michael Smith, has a similar synthetic aim, a broader global scope, and an explicit model of how economic wealth differentials can be assessed in the past directly from material remains, not just texts. They frame their core question as understanding the "growth of wealth disparities, including their connection to the development of domesticated plants and animals and to increases in sociopolitical scale" (Kohler et al., 2017: 619).

As with Scott's book, the published volume that summarizes this project does not include gender or sex as index terms. Similar conclusions about women as contributors to economic life in the transition to agriculture reappear, although not with the absolute equation of women and domesticated animals. An index term for "women, mobility and health of", leads to an introductory discussion about the origins of social inequality (Smith et al., 2018: 9). Here, we are told that "in areas where farming developed during the Holocene" (as well as areas where sedentary life was possible without farming) "reduced mobility improved women's energy balance and decreased interbirth spacing". In the concluding chapter, women reappear in the guise of mothers, freed by use of cow and goat milk to "wean their children and resume bearing earlier" (Kohler et al., 2018: 307).

While gender doesn't appear as an index term, it does figure in the discussion of inequality in a chapter on Mesopotamia, as a variable that would have been useful if burial remains had been identified by sex (Stone, 2018). With this exception, the book treats its subject—household level wealth differences—without explicit consideration of the varying positions of men and women. Implicitly, women appear as parents of children who may inherit their position and receive "high parental investment" (Smith et al., 2018: 11, 21). We are told that "households or families go through a developmental cycle" that includes "child bearing and rearing", implying the presence if not the agency of female parents (Peterson & Drennan, 2018: 47). While offering a much more grounded empirical discussion than Scott, the participants in this project depart from some of the same assumptions Scott employs: that women are primarily active as embodied sources of children, always encompassed by a family structure in which the active political (and thus economic) agency is implicitly that of men.

The contributors to this project use a metric based on the GINI coefficient, widely used in contemporary economic analyses as a measure of inequality in income distribution. Because there is no easy way to measure income archaeologically across cultures, they developed a proxy based on house structures to measure a different economic dimension, household wealth, distinguishing "embodied, relational and material aspects of wealth" that do not necessarily co-vary (Kohler et al., 2017: 619).

As a result, this analysis cannot easily address gender-based variation, because the wealth being measured is held by an aggregate group that merges men and women. Nor would an attempt to calculate something closer to the contemporary GINI coefficients assessing income distribution be much more likely to help. Economic activity that is not formally registered as producing income is excluded from calculations of the GINI coefficient. While normally exemplified as represented by income derived from the informal economy of barter, illicit trade, and payment for services outside legal recording, this also includes one startlingly large sector of every contemporary economy: the unpaid, unreported work that is put into maintaining residential life at the scale of the household. As noted by feminist analysts, this includes the largely unwaged labour of women bound to households through social ties rather than by paid employment, work done by women involving structural maintenance (including cleaning), provisioning of residents (shopping, cooking, sewing), and care of others (including childcare and eldercare) (Hoyman, 1987). This labour effectively has no value in contemporary economic analysis. Merging men and women together in GINI coefficient equivalents based on treating house structures as reservoirs of wealth does not correct for the exclusion of this constant maintenance labour from formal consideration, while leaving the account of the ancient economy troubled by the same issues feminist scholars have criticized in analyses of contemporary economies.

When women appear in these new deep histories, they are most often seen in surprisingly uniform ways. Unenslaved women are presented as maintaining a sector of social life that is not seen as central to something called "the economy". When they are recognized as part of the economy, it is normally either as adjuncts to male-ordered economic processes, or even as objectified labouring bodies, perhaps even normative subjects of chattel slavery. Yet even in the societies under examination by the authors of such deep histories, the claim that women play a role in the economy only as tools for the agency of men is questionable.

A common tendency is to treat as exceptions those women who form part of political leadership, or who are recorded as independently owning property. Repeatedly, we are told that these women only have this kind of economic agency because of something unique that happened: the end of a marriage endowing legal independence and control over an estate, or inheritance of a position and estate as a sole heir; although the same unique things seem to happen quite often.

More troubling than this kind of exceptionalism, in which individual women count as quasi-men, is a systematic and usually inexplicit assumption that women's efforts were normally not recognized to their credit. Here, I want to turn to *Maidens, Meal and Money*, which is perhaps one of the clearest classic ethnographic statements of this (Meillassoux, 1981). Women, we are told, are significant to "the economy" both as the ultimate origin of new labouring bodies (that is, children—incidentally rendering all women heteronormative) and as a force of labouring bodies themselves—but whose labour is seen as just support for everyday life of the family, accruing credit only to the head of the family (rendering all families as patriarchal structures exploiting women as a class, and young men as a temporary category).

In the archaeology of Mesoamerica, this kind of thinking leads to claims that even documented production by women of textiles that formed the key political valuable, standard of exchange, and medium of political tribute in hierarchical political organizations produced no value for, and no social credit to, the women whose work was required to make these pieces of cloth. What I want to do in the next section of this paper is use the Mesoamerican case to begin to rethink how we might avoid the naturalizations of heteronormativity, individuality, patriarchy, and labour alienation that can be treated as givens if they are not explicitly questioned.

Making an Ancestral Economy in Mexico and Central America

Much of Mexico, all of Guatemala and Belize, and parts of Honduras and El Salvador are usually discussed by archaeologists as a single culture area, Mesoamerica (Joyce, 2004). To the extent that this formulation is defensible, it reflects histories that resulted in a linked network of politically administered societies that were incorporated into the Spanish colonial empire in the sixteenth century. Anthropologists who defined the Mesoamerican Cultural Area stressed a core of shared values, embodied in cultural practices including the use of interlocking calendar systems; a vision of cosmic order in which humans occupy a middle world between upper and lower worlds; and religious beliefs and practices in which forces of nature, sometimes anthropomorphized, and ancestral beings were engaged with by human specialists. As defined, all the societies that were recognized as Mesoamerican were primarily reliant on agriculture, with the northern boundary of the network set to coincide with the appearance in northern Mexico of mobile societies in which gathering and hunting were more important, coinciding with the edge of more arid environments. The southern boundary of the network was, in contrast, less about environmental and subsistence differences, and more concerned with political structure, with state-level, highly centralized hierarchical societies a hallmark of "Mesoamerica" and absent from its southern neighbours, conceived of as classic examples of chiefdom society.

Mesoamerica as defined encompassed a high diversity of spoken languages, with a few language groups being entirely, or almost entirely, contained within its loose borders. This included the Maya languages of Guatemala and Belize, and adjacent Mexico, El Salvador, and Honduras, and the language families of the Gulf of Mexico, Isthmus of Tehuantepec, and Valley of Oaxaca. Ancestral versions of these languages were recorded using writing systems that ranged from the fully phonetic Maya script to more ideographic scripts used elsewhere, all unified by employing a base-20 number system expressed using at most three signs (for zero, one, and five), especially to record calendrical dates in a calendar of common structure. Linguists note that contemporary languages spoken in this region share features as a result of intensive historic interactions, not simply inherited from a common ancestral language.

For my purposes, one of the most significant things about the network of societies glossed as "Mesoamerican" is their long-term use of a small number of items as valuables, fostered by and fostering the integration of relations recognized by analysts as an economy (Joyce, 2000). Some scholars have even employed Immanuel Wallerstein's world-systems theory as a model for Mesoamerica (Blanton & Feinman, 1984; Smith & Berdan, 2000). World-systems theory is seen as particularly useful at the moments when the most extensive empires were active, those centred on two cities in central Mexico which grew to importance at different moments in Mesoamerican history, Teotihuacan (with a peak in population ca. 200–600 AD), and Tenochtitlan (growing steadily from ca. 1325 CE until its development was truncated by the Spanish invasion). Conceived as a "world-system", Mesoamerica was a political economy in which a small urban elite extracted surplus raw materials from a periphery for use in manufacturing in the core, where labour increased the value of these unworked materials.

From my perspective, a weakness of this model is the failure to account for one of the most historically interesting things about the transactions recognized as "economic" among this network of societies: the unusual nature of the basic media of exchange and standards of value. The Mesoamerican economy is famously where, as Rene Millon (1955) put it, "money grew on trees", in the form of the seeds extracted from cacao pods, which could be converted into the raw material for chocolate, and were recorded as used for payments to political leaders. The Mesoamerican economy, especially in its most hierarchical tribute states and empires, also used a second organic material, cotton, as another standard of value, in the form of cotton cloth. Both of these perishable and renewable organics are unusual as media of exchange when compared to other ancient economies. That both cotton and cacao could be cultivated easily in the peripheries of the two highland cities that centred proposed Mesoamerican world systems challenges their control by authorities. With the added consideration of limitations on transport due to the lack of domesticated animals and consequent reliance on human porters, it is clear that these materials do not lend themselves to accumulation at the political centres.

What was completely feasible, and is clearly evident in sources from a variety of Mesoamerican societies, is the use of cloth and cacao as measures of value. Individual cacao seeds and packages of 400 seeds were basic units of counting tribute in the world system centred on Tenochtitlan (Berdan & Anawalt, 1992). Measured lengths of cloth served as the second standard of value for tribute, one that is attested both for Tenochtitlan and in public records of courtly life for the earlier Classic Maya (250–800 CE) city-states (Halperin, 2011).

I have argued that these two organic materials became standards of value due to their embeddedness in specific forms of social relations and have to be understood in terms of the social practices that gave them meaning for specific groups of people (Joyce, 2000). Cotton cloth played a particularly important role throughout its history as a concentrated index of work, sometimes but not always very skilled work, undertaken by groups of people who lived together and formed what archaeologists recognize as households. Cacao drinks, required for marriage alliances (Gillespie & Joyce, 1997), were used in transactions between groups of humans and supernatural beings, as a ritually powerful substance equated with the animating force of organic beings (Meskell & Joyce, 2003: 139–140). Even other media of value that don't immediately seem unusual, such as beads made from greenstone (jade), attained their value as a consequence of their pragmatic use in social relations. Jade beads were a store of wealth that was deployed in marriage alliance, probably in part due to their long history of use in accounting for harvest and for counting in divinatory practices (Freidel et al., 2017; Gillespie & Joyce, 1997). What cloth and cacao shared, beyond their status as perishable organic materials, was that in the societies where they constituted standards of value, their processing and conversion into valuable forms was undertaken by individuals who were gendered female, and their value was thus intertwined with the constitution of gender difference.

Cloth

The special role of cotton cloth as tribute payment has been recognized for as long as scholars have developed arguments about "the Mesoamerican economy". In sixteenth-century Mexico, Spanish administrators authorized the production of a register of tribute payments owed to the Mexica (or Aztec) empire centred in Tenochtitlan which they sought to continue to administer (Berdan & Anawalt, 1992). Entry after entry in this book detailed tribute paid in specific numbers of *mantas*, lengths of cloth woven on backstrap looms. Some towns were listed as providing more elaborate cloth, ornamented through additional techniques such as resist dyeing (Anawalt, 1981). While credited as payments from the town, all of this cloth—simple plain weave or complex—was the product of women's work, carried out within the houses and courtyards of residences.

Nor was the importance of cloth, and its implication of demands on women's labour, unique to the late conquest empire created by the Mexica. Images and texts from the city-states of Maya people, occupied five centuries or more earlier in Guatemala, also identified cloth as a major tribute good, in this case, rendered to the ruler of a city-state by lords of subordinate towns (Baron, 2018a; Halperin, 2008, 2011).

While the cloth produced generally does not survive in the tropical environment, archaeological analyses examine a database parallel to the historical information derived from texts about the Mexica and inscriptions recorded by the Maya. Tools for spinning and weaving cloth formed part of excavated assemblages in late Mexican sites (Overholtzer, 2015), those of many Classic Maya city-states (Ardren et al., 2010; Halperin, 2008; Hendon, 1997, 1999), and in other areas of Mesoamerica such as Oaxaca where the textual record has not yet been completely deciphered (King, 2011; McCafferty & McCafferty, 2000). Spindle whorls, battens, and weaving picks were and continue to be recorded when archaeologists in the region carry out excavations of the small-scale settings of everyday face-to-face life, house compounds.

Yet such items are not found everywhere, and not everywhere in the same abundance or with the same degree of elaboration. In the Maya area, secondary industries produced enhanced tools discarded preferentially around the houses of the apparent ruling and noble families (Hendon, 1997, 1999). In Oaxaca, weaving tools made of precious materials, effigies too delicate to be used, were placed in major family tombs (McCafferty & McCafferty, 1994). These carefully crafted tools do not simply place production in a "domestic sphere". They show that cloth production was particularly important to households of the wealthy and powerful. Through the identification of considerable investment in secondary industries to provide tools to these spinners and weavers, archaeological assemblages underline the social importance of cloth making.

Two ways of thinking about these material patterns have emerged in recent scholarship. On one side we see common sense claims that women's work was appropriated by men—men of their families, men of the state, men of the empire—without any credit remaining for the crafting women. In this view, strongly influenced by anthropological naturalization of sex-based hierarchies, women became a kind of captive force working against their will only to lose the alienable products of their labour. At first glance, this interpretation seemed consistent with early colonial data showing how demands for cloth increased, as village-level cloth tribute levels did not decline in parallel with the loss of population that followed the violence of Spanish campaigns of colonization. Key work by feminist archaeologist Elizabeth Brumfiel, however, identified changes in spinning technology that she argued accompanied decreasing concern about the quality of cloth after the Spanish took over administration (Brumfiel, 1996, 1997). The corollary is the realization that prior to the change to the European tribute system, even when the Mexica conquered and incorporated subject towns, the production of cloth remained a practice requiring skill and knowledge, what Kohler and his colleagues (Kohler et al., 2017) call embodied wealth.

Even for the Mexica of Tenochtitlan, who incorporated vast numbers of towns and villages in an extractive state, there are implications of tribute in cloth that go beyond its potential to be accumulated and trafficked in a marketplace. The tribute-owing unit was not an individual, but a community. While cloth extracted from these towns became anonymous in the markets of Tenochtitlan, where the Mexica nobility converted it to other goods, in the towns where the work of cloth production took place, weaving and spinning would have been visibly associated with known persons, potentially recognized for their skill and expertise—what anthropologist Julia Hendon (2006) describes as their craft knowledge, a form of embodied wealth that is inherently inalienable at the scale of face-to-face society.

In texts Spanish-trained clerics recorded using the European alphabet to transcribe the indigenous Nahuatl language, spinning and weaving are characterized as activities valued in part because they are how the subjective skill and personality of women are formed (McCafferty & McCafferty, 1996). The specific texts we have come from informants who were part of the ruling nobility and merchant group. They characterize the epitome of womanhood for these classes or segments of society, the "good woman", as skilled craft producers. This emphasis is echoed in the vocabulary for special tribute cloth types recorded in works produced for the new Spanish administration that incorporate terms for the specialized techniques that some, but not all, textile producers knew (Berdan & Anawalt, 1992). They receive material inflection through the production for some crafters of highly ornamented tools, through the skilled craftwork of others. The distribution of spinning and weaving tools around the houses of wealthy and politically powerful Classic Maya families has similar implications.

I suggest that we need to consider the likelihood that tribute in cloth was more than simply a way for ancient states in this region to accumulate goods that they would then exchange in the marketplace for capital. Cloth was substantively connected to groups of women who spun and wove, and through them to other people of the community who provided the cultivated cotton and produced the tools with which it was worked. Cloth assembled the people and things that constituted a specific place. The literal emplacement of the backstrap loom—attached normatively to a support beam of the house structure—performatively connected the cloth produced with the people who made a place, a world, in the towns that sent cloth to the cities.

Cacao

The centrality of social relations to the value of cloth in these societies, while sometimes minimized, has been more broadly recognized than the importance of social relations to the second standard of value to which I now want to turn, before assessing what this case study can tell us about the contemporary world and the way archaeological models of economy can serve us today. Where cloth is understood as a specialized currency that circulated as a sign of hierarchy in political relations, cacao has at times been characterized as a generalized currency (Millon, 1955; Baron, 2018b). Yet nothing about the selection of this organic material as a standard of value, or its persistence in use as a valuable material for thousands of years, suggests that it was understood as a simple medium of exchange.

Cacao seeds are derived from plants of the genus *Theobroma cacao* and the less-prized *Theobroma bicolor*. Both appear to be species introduced from further south, although of great antiquity in the region, with residues detected in pottery vessels discarded before 1000 BCE excavated in multiple areas (Powis et al., 2011; Joyce & Henderson, 2010). Residues of chemicals diagnostic of *Theobroma cacao* remained in vessels I excavated in Honduras dating to ca. 1150 BCE, whose distinctive forms suggest the beverage being stored was alcoholic (Joyce & Henderson, 2010). Archaeologists working on assemblages from slightly later (around 700 BCE) in Mexico's Gulf Coast also identified evidence of alcohol brewing combined with the chemical diagnostic of cacao, theobromine (Seinfeld, 2007). After this, vessels with traces of cacao residues assume shapes associated with the serving of non-alcoholic cacao, frothed just before presentation (Powis et al., 2002).

Based on the forms and contexts of the earliest vessels with traces of cacao, and the culinary chemistry that transforms raw cacao seeds into dried cacao beans through a necessary stage of fermentation, I have argued that cacao was probably originally exploited as part of a suite of plants converted into alcoholic beverages used in hospitality by groups at the scale of a household (Joyce & Henderson, 2007). The serving of these beverages employed well-crafted ceramic vessels, many mimicking gourd containers. In Mexico, scholars working at the site of Paso de la Amada, another area with early use of cacao, suggest the earliest fired clay containers there were inspired by the desire to socially mark serving in drinking events at a similar scale (Clark & Gosser, 1995).

The use of cacao as a measure of value, like the value of cloth, rests on its social significance in activities in which women were key participants. Manuscripts created by the Mixtec people of Oaxaca in the last few centuries before colonization portray marital alliances between noble families through images of the couple presenting jars of foaming cacao, often ornamented with signs of additions such as flowers (Jansen, 1992). The addition of ground cacao seeds to fermented cacao liquid ultimately resulted in the creation of non-alcoholic versions of cacao drinks. The preparation of a variety of cacao beverages, including the addition of other condiments (chile, vanilla, fruit pits, and flowers) is reflected in Classic Maya inscriptions and colonial texts as well as in Mixtec images (Gillespie & de MacVean, 2002; Beliaev et al., 2010). These complex procedures of preparation, and particularly the fresh preparation of seasoned cacao beverages at the point of serving, would have allowed the preparer to receive (some of) the social credit for the hospitality in which these beverages were offered, the moment recorded in Mixtec codices.

Today, cacao maintains associations of hospitable provisioning, including when it is offered to deities in contemporary ceremonies like the *compostura* or earth-offerings of the Lenca of Honduras. Contemporary and historic Lenca sources specifically associate the offering of cacao beverages as significant in restoring health to the land (Sheptak, 2013). An association between cacao as a kind of animating liquid of the organic world of plants, and blood as the animating liquid of the organic world of animals, including humans, binds these apparently disparate practices together (Meskell & Joyce, 2003: 139–140).

Ignoring these associations of cacao seeds in order to treat them as a neutral measure of value is motivated more by the belief of archaeologists that a great empire like that of the Mexica must have had something equivalent to coinage, than by serious consideration of indigenous sources. Texts from the sixteenth century written in Nahuatl, the language of the Mexica, note that cacao was restricted to consumption either in ceremony or, more generally, by the members of the most exclusive social group, who were treated in many ways as divine beings.

Discussion

To help us conceptualize the Mesoamerican materials, we might turn to a third contemporary synthetic deep history of the domain archaeologists designate as "the economy", in particular, to think about what these data tell us about how women's activities were recognized (or not) as economic: David Graeber's book *Debt: The First 5,000 Years*. Graeber offers a much more dynamic, and explicitly revisionist view of the same millennia as Scott, often dealing with the same places. In contrast to *Against the Grain*, the index for *Debt* includes a dense cluster of key terms relating to women, with a great deal of historical specificity. The discussion of patriarchal hierarchy (Graeber, 2014: 178–179) is particularly significant, as it occurs as part of a reading of changes in the Mesopotamian world from the time of the Sumerians—when, Graeber (2014: 178) writes, "women are everywhere", as "doctors, merchants, scribes, and public officials... generally free to take part in all aspects of public life". Graeber identifies the need to finance wars as a driving force behind the commodification of labouring bodies that, over the next 1000 years of his narrative, reduces women's prominence and scope of action. It is not just an effect of particular features of female bodies that leads to this development. As families needed funds for taxation, the bodies of family members became sources of security for loans, and ultimately, were transactable directly through sale into slavery (Graeber, 2014: 179–185). In this discussion, far from a unified category of women and a second unified category of men, we see cross-cutting dimensions of age-based authority, property ownership, and activity that distinguish among male and female persons.

What makes Graeber more successful at seeing women as complex actors is, among other things, his critical project, which questions the way a certain set of concepts about "the economy" have become taken for granted background terms. His discussion of the language of debt and credit draws directly from classic works of what were once described as "substantivist" anthropologies of the economy, such as the different circulation of goods among the Tiv. Graeber (2014: 146–148) emphasizes the views of the Tiv themselves of the potential for what he calls a "human economy" to slide into a market economy. This is the context that Graeber describes in which people of various categories—including women—see their bodily integrity commodified and the social value of their contributions erode. Graeber links the shift from a human economy to a market economy to precisely the reduction of persons to tokens that, in naturalized form, haunts the other deep histories I have discussed:

> In a human economy, each person is unique, and of incomparable value, because each is a unique nexus of relations with others. A woman may be a daughter, sister, lover, rival, companion, mother, age-mate, and mentor to many different people in different ways. Each relation is unique, even in a society in which they are sustained through the constant giving back and forth of generic objects... In one sense, those objects make one who one is– a fact illustrated by the way that objects used as social currencies are so often things otherwise used to clothe or decorate the human body, that help make one who one is in the eyes of others... to make a human being an object of exchange, one woman equivalent to another, for example, requires first of all ripping her from her context; that is, tearing her away from that web of relations that she is, and thus, into a generic value capable of being added and subtracted and used as a means to measure debt. (Graeber, 2014: 158–159)

This perspective becomes a ground from which to re-examine how women's participation in activities recognized or unrecognized as "economic" by archaeologists might contribute to contesting the naturalization of present-day reduction of people to the value of their labouring bodies.

Separate Spheres? Rethinking the Archaeological Economy

Graeber begins his work on debt from the grounding of his previous anthropological reconsideration of value (Graeber, 2001). For Marxist feminists in the 1970s and 1980s, the question of women's unwaged work was also a question of value—specifically, whether in capitalist economies, this work had any value, and if so, what kind. Most often, the first generation of these writers concluded that what they then called housework was properly excluded from consideration of labour value (Kaluzynska, 1980). Subsequent scholars harshly criticized this as naturalizing not just a specific sexualized position of work, but one that was inherently heterosexist in its imagination of transcultural family life. Feminists who responded critically to these initial formulations, including Nona Glazer-Malbin (1976), Dorothy Roberts (1997), and Dorothy E. Smith (1987), sought to rework Marxist formulations to broaden understandings of value so that work in unwaged, everyday settings was understood to be productive of value.

This research has had important impacts on broader economic practice and even economic theory. Commenting on the exclusion of much of the work women do from contemporary measures of "the economy" for the World Economic Forum, Diane Coyle (2016) pointed to pioneering feminist writing such as Marilyn Waring's *If Women Counted* (1988) that called attention to the effects of not seeing this work as valuable. Citing mainstream studies, Coyle (2016) writes:

> In a well known alternative to GDP proposed in 1972 by William Nordhaus and James Tobin, the "Measure of Economic Welfare" (MEW), their estimate for the amount and value of "non-market production" in the mid-1960s was equivalent to about 40% of conventionally measured economic output economy… In a 2011 study, the OECD concluded that home production would add between 20% and 50% to the GDP of its member countries. The US Bureau of Economic Analysis said it would have added 26% to US GDP in 2010.

As Rebecca Winter and Jasmina Brankovich (2016) summarized the issue, "by presenting reproductive labour as not being 'real work,' women's labour is devalued, which allows capitalists to easily exploit it, while also perpetuating patriarchal social relations which privilege paid work in the 'public' sphere when performed by men".

Yet others have seen a danger in trying to treat work that women largely do unpaid in domestic or residential settings in the same way that work in factories is described. These critics call attention to the naturalizing of a specific way of thinking about some practices as "the economy" that this perpetuates, an approach that is profoundly embedded in precisely the kind of exploitation from which it seeks to emancipate us. Feminist economists Geoff Schneider and Jean Shackelford, in a conference paper originally called "Ten Principles of Feminist Economics" proposed that "values enter into economic analysis at many different levels", singling out such things as the view that consumerism is a positive goal that underlies conventional economics as a problem (Schneider & Shackelford, 2001). Their third principle for feminist economics is that "the household is a locus of economic activity" of a kind *contrasted to* the individualism that conventional economics identifies in work done outside the household. This echoes Graeber's (2014) contrast between the market economy and a human economy.

In ancestral Mexico and Central America household compounds, the spaces controlled by co-residential groups, served as the sites of primary production for most goods, for the reproduction of skilled crafting, and for the transmission of goods through hospitality. One way to think about this is to see the household as part of the broader economic sphere, not a separate "domestic" space (Hendon, 1996). It is not just maintenance work, or reproduction, that was located in these spaces, but the primary productive activities on which states rested. To the extent that some kinds of work were associated with specific social positions, including gender, these kinds of work offered the potential for value to become identified with persons of those subject positions. Cloth, whose exchange marked hierarchies between rulers and those they ruled, began its economic life in gendered and highly visible productive relationships in household compounds through which women demonstrated craft skill, which we can view as a form of embodied wealth (Kohler et al., 2017). The abundant images that have survived associating cloth production with feminine identities among the Maya, the Mexica, and the Mixtec of Oaxaca, including supernatural or mythical persons shown as weavers, created and reinforced broader visibility for the association of feminine gender and textile value. The preparation of complex foods such as cacao, bringing together a crop that was exotic to most places it was consumed with other rare materials in spiced drinks whose performative preparation and serving by female-gendered persons is portrayed in images in the same areas, created another relationship between the production of economic value and gendered personhood.

I have tried in this paper to demonstrate that in ancestral Mexico and Central America, theorizing an "economy" disembedded from social relations would distort one of the most interesting things we know from historical texts and archaeological research: that two of the primary standards of value and media for at least some economic exchanges were perishable, organic materials transformed into media of social relations through women's work. The processes used to support the production of cloth spawned additional crafting of tools that socially foregrounded spinning and weaving and associated them with divine capacities of creation. Cloth production represented the cumulation of efforts by a wide range of social actors, drawing together residents of small agricultural settlements representing themselves as autonomous within wider social relations.

These gendered associations of cloth production have to be seen as emerging from social relations, not simply the appropriation of already alienable bodily labour that is either inherent to female sex or naturally associated with it. Here, the deep historical dimension available is helpful. Examining the associations of textile tools in hundreds of burials in Tlatilco in Central Mexico, a village occupied between 1000 and 700 BCE, I noted that despite significant evidence for matrilineal kinship joining members of long-lived houses, textile tools were not restricted to one sex (Joyce, 2001a). So for this early period, I would argue that this value, and its role in the human economy, had not yet emerged.

When textile production is represented as women's work, as it was among the later Classic and Postclassic Maya and Postclassic Mixtecs and Mexica, it clearly has more significance than simply being "what women do": it is one of the ways that some people assumed a gendered position, in social relations that involved more than simply two genders corresponding to two natural sexes (Joyce, 2001b). In the emergence of cacao seeds as a second tribute good and a measure of value, again, it is social relations and meanings, not scarcity or inherent value, that made cacao worthwhile. Cacao, served to visitors in small-scale encounters, presented to supernatural beings responsible for the health of the earth, and consumed by human leaders who claimed a divine-like standing, was the material for performances of social provisioning and hospitality that marked food preparation as something more than the natural role of (all) women.

These standards of value made it impossible for the people of these societies to ignore the work done within what modern economics would label the domestic sphere, work that anthropologists and economists alike tend to assign to women. As feminist scholars of the contemporary economy have long noted, large areas of economic activity by women are routinely excluded in modern analyses of market economies. The exclusion of household maintenance work rests on a tacit distinction between household labour (as intimate, domestic, and presumed to be ruled only by naturalized relations of sex and age) and extra-domestic labour, seen as creating value.

For the societies of ancient Central America, such a division simply did not exist. A large part of the organization of agricultural labour built on household relations. Specialist craft production in residential locales, by women and men, was critical to broader social, political, and hence economic relations. In the period of greatest socioeconomic stratification, in these societies, cloth produced by women working in domestic spaces became one of the enduring standards of value, specifically important in tribute payments that established and perpetuated political hierarchies. Cloth's use in this fashion cannot be disentangled from the social relations in which it was embedded. Nor can the social relations which gave value to other key media used in economic exchanges, for example, in the cultivation, preparation, and consumption of cacao, the second standard of value. Even when market relations were transacted in the marketplace of Tenochtitlan, using counts of cacao seeds as a means to establish equivalent value of other materials, they were embedded in a human economy of moral relations (Joyce, 2001b: 140–143). In that human economy, dimensions of difference, including gender, mattered. The matter of gender may actually account for the most distinctive feature of the ancient Mesomerican economy, the selection of perishable organic materials as standards of value. Beyond this unique aspect, this case study suggests that when we examine ancient economies we need to explore the social relations that gave value to materials in each historical situation with attention to how value was produced, through what relations, by what kinds of actors. This may make comparative measurement less feasible, but it will keep us from simply projecting modern economic rationalisms on pasts which they poorly fit.

References

Agarwal, S., Beauchesne, P., Glencross, B., Larsen, C. S., Meskell, L., Nakamura, C., Pearson, J., & Sadvari, J. W. (2015). Roles for the sexes: The (bio)archaeology of women and men at Çatalhöyük. In I. Hodder & A. Marciniak (Eds.), *Assembling Çatalhöyük* (pp. 87–95). Routledge.

Anawalt, P. (1981). *Indian clothing before Cortés: Mesoamerican costumes from the codices.* University of Oklahoma Press.

Ardren, T., Kam Manahan, T., Wesp, J., & Alonso, A. (2010). Cloth production and economic intensification in the area surrounding Chichen Itza. *Latin American Antiquity, 21,* 274–289.

Bahrani, Z. (2001). *Women of Babylon: Gender and representation in Mesopotamia.* Routledge.

Baron, J. (2018a). Ancient monetization: The case of Classic Maya textiles. *Journal of Anthropological Archaeology, 49,* 100–113.

Baron, J. (2018b). Making money in Mesoamerica: Currency production and procurement in the Classic Maya financial system. *Economic Anthropology, 5,* 210–223.

Beliaev, D., Davietshin, A., & Tokovinine, A. (2010). Sweet cacao and sour atole: Mixed drinks on Classic Maya ceramic vases. In J. E. Staller & M. Carrasco (Eds.), *Pre-Columbian foodways: Interdisciplinary approaches to food, culture, and markets in ancient Mesoamerica* (pp. 257–272). Springer.

Berdan, F., & Anawalt, P., eds. (1992). *The Codex Mendoza.* University of California Press.

Blanton, R., & Feinman, G. (1984). The Mesoamerican world system. *American Anthropologist, 86,* 673–682.

Bolger, D. (2010). The dynamics of gender in early agricultural societies of the Near East. *Signs, 35,* 503–531.

Brumfiel, E. (1996). The quality of tribute cloth: The place of evidence in archaeological argument. *American Antiquity, 61,* 453–462.

Brumfiel, E. (1997). Tribute cloth production and compliance in Aztec and Colonial Mexico. *Museum Anthropology, 21,* 55–71.

Clark, J. E., & Gosser, D. (1995). Reinventing Mesoamerica's first pottery. In W. Barnett & J. Hoopes (Eds.), *The emergence of pottery: Technology and innovation in ancient societies* (pp. 209–222). Smithsonian Institution Press.

Coyle, D. (2016). *The way we measure economies is inherently sexist.* World Economic Forum. http://www.weforum.org/agenda/2016/04/why-economic-policy-overlooks-women. Accessed 19 May 2019.

Freidel, D. A., Masson, M. A., & Rich, M. (2017). Imagining a complex Maya political economy: Counting tokens and currencies in image, text and the archaeological record. *Cambridge Archaeological Journal, 27,* 29–54.

Gillespie, S., & de MacVean, A. L. (2002). Las flores en el Popol Vuh. *Revista de la Universidad del Valle de Guatemala, 12,* 10–17.

Gillespie, S., & Joyce, R. A. (1997). Gendered goods: The symbolism of Maya hierarchical exchange relations. In C. Claassen & R. Joyce (Eds.), *Women in prehistory: North America and Mesoamerica* (pp. 189–207). University of Pennsylvania Press.

Glazer-Malbin, N. (1976). Housework. *Signs, 1,* 905–922.

Graeber, D. (2001). *Toward an anthropological theory of value.* Palgrave MacMillan.

Graeber, D. (2014). *Debt: The first 5,000 years* (2nd rev. ed.). Melville House Publishing.

Halperin, C. (2008). Classic Maya textile production: Insights from Motul de San Jose, Peten, Guatemala. *Ancient Mesoamerica, 19,* 111–125.

Halperin, C. (2011). Late Classic Maya textile economies: An object history approach. In W. E. Little & P. A. McAnany (Eds.), *Textile economies: Power and value from the local to the transnational* (pp. 125–146). Altamira.

Hendon, J. A. (1996). Archaeological approaches to the organization of domestic labor: Household practice and domestic relations. *Annual Review of Anthropology, 25,* 45–61.

Hendon, J. A. (1997). Women's work, women's space, and women's status among the Classic-Period Maya elite of the Copán Valley, Honduras. In C. Claassen & R. A. Joyce (Eds.), *Women in prehistory: North America and Mesoamerica* (pp. 33–46). University of Pennsylvania Press.
Hendon, J. A. (1999). Spinning and weaving in Pre-Hispanic Mesoamerica: The technology and social relations of textile production. In B. K. de Arathoon, N. L. Gonzalez, & J. M. Willemsen Devlin (Eds.), *Mayan clothing and weaving through the ages* (pp. 7–16). Museo Ixchel del Traje Indígena.
Hendon, J. A. (2006). Textile production as craft in Mesoamerica: Time, labor and knowledge. *Journal of Social Archaeology, 6,* 354–378.
Hoyman, M. (1987). Female participation in the informal economy: A neglected issue. *The Annals of the American Academy of Political and Social Science, 43,* 64–82.
Jansen, M. (1992). Mixtec pictography: Conventions and contents. In V. Bricker (Eds.), *Supplement to the handbook of Middle American Indians, volume 5: Epigraphy* (pp. 20–33). University of Texas Press.
Joyce, R. A. (2000). High culture, Mesoamerican civilization, and the Classic Maya tradition. In J. Richards & M. Van Buren (Eds.), *Order, legitimacy, and wealth in ancient states* (pp. 64–76). Cambridge University Press.
Joyce, R. A. (2001a). Burying the dead at Tlatilco: Social memory and social identities. In M. Chesson (Eds.), *New perspectives on mortuary analysis* (pp. 12–26). Archaeology Division of the American Anthropology Association.
Joyce, R. A. (2001b). *Gender and power in Prehispanic Mesoamerica.* University of Texas Press.
Joyce, R. A. (2004). Mesoamerica: A working model for archaeology. In J. A. Hendon & R. A. Joyce (Eds.), *Mesoamerican archaeology: Theory and practice* (pp. 1–42). Blackwell.
Joyce, R. A. (2008). *Ancient bodies, ancient lives.* Thames and Hudson.
Joyce, R. A., & Henderson, J. S. (2007). From feasting to cuisine: Implications of archaeological research in an early Honduran village. *American Anthropologist, 109,* 642–653.
Joyce, R. A., & Henderson, J. S. (2010). Forming Mesoamerican taste: Cacao consumption in Formative Period contexts. In J. E. Staller & M. Carrasco (Eds.), *Pre-Columbian foodways: Interdisciplinary approaches to food, culture, and markets in ancient Mesoamerica* (pp. 157–173). Springer.
Kaluzynska, E. (1980). Wiping the floor with theory: A survey of writings on housework. *Feminist Review, 6,* 27–54.
King, S. (2011). Thread production in Early Postclassic coastal Oaxaca, Mexico: Technology, intensity, and gender. *Ancient Mesoamerica, 22,* 323–343.
Kohler, T. A., Smith, M. E., Bogard, A., Feinman, G. M., Peterson, C. E., Betzenhauser, A., et al. (2017). Greater post-Neolithic wealth disparities in Eurasia than in North America and Mesoamerica. *Nature, 551,* 619–623.
Kohler, T. A., Smith, M. E., Bogard, A., Peterson, C. E., Betzenhauser, A., Feinman, G. M., Oka, R. C., Pailes, M., Prentiss, A. M., Stone, E. C., Dennehy, T. J., & Ellyson, L. J. (2018). Deep inequality. In T. A. Kohler & M. E. Smith (Eds.), *Ten thousand years of inequality* (pp. 289–317). University of Arizona Press.
Kohler, T. A., & Smith, M. E., eds. (2018). *Ten thousand years of inequality.* University of Arizona Press.
McCafferty, S. D., & McCafferty, G. G. (1994). Engendering Tomb 7 at Monte Albán. *Current Anthropology, 35,* 143–166.
McCafferty, S. D., & McCafferty, G. G. (1996). Spinning and weaving as female gender identity in Post-Classic Mexico. In M. B. Schevill & J. C. Berlo (Eds.), *Textile traditions of Mesoamerica and the Andes: An anthology* (pp. 19–44). University of Texas Press.
McCafferty, S. D., & McCafferty, G. G. (2000). Textile production in Postclassic Cholula, Mexico. *Ancient Mesoamerica, 11,* 39–54.
McCorriston, J. (1997). The fiber revolution: Textile extensification, alienation, and social stratification in ancient Mesopotamia. *Current Anthropology, 38,* 517–549.

Meillassoux, C. (1981). *Maidens, meal, and money: Capitalism and the domestic community.* Cambridge University Press.

Meskell, L., & Joyce, R. A. (2003). *Embodied lives: Figuring ancient Egypt and the Classic Maya.* Routledge.

Millon, R. F. (1955). *When money grew on trees: A study of cacao in ancient Mesoamerica.* Ph.D. Dissertation, Columbia University.

Overholtzer, L. (2015). Dwelling on the past: The materiality of everyday life at Xaltocan, Mexico. *Archaeological Papers of the American Anthropological Association, 26,* 87–104.

Peterson, C. E., & Drennan, R. D. (2018). Letting the Gini out of the bottle: Measuring inequality archaeologically. In T. A. Kohler & M. E. Smith (Eds.), *Ten thousand years of inequality* (pp. 39–66). University of Arizona Press.

Powis, T. G., Cyphers, A., Galkwad, N. W., Grivetti, L., & Kong, C. (2011). Cacao use and the San Lorenzo Olmec. *Proceedings of the National Academy of Sciences, 108,* 8595–8600.

Powis, T. G., Valdez, Jr, F., Hester, T. R., Hurst, W. J., & Tarka, Jr, S. M. (2002). Spouted vessels and cacao use among the Preclassic Maya. *Latin American Antiquity, 13,* 85–106.

Roberts, D. (1997). Spiritual and menial housework. *Yale Journal of Law and Feminism, 9,* 51–80.

Schneider, G., & Shackelford, J. (2001). Economics standards and lists: Proposed antidotes for feminist economists. *Feminist Economics, 7,* 77–89.

Scott, J. C. (2017). *Against the grain: A deep history of the earliest states.* Yale University Press.

Seinfeld, D. M. (2007). *Molecular archaeological investigations of Olmec feasting in ceramics from San Andrés, Tabasco, Mexico.* MA thesis, Florida State University.

Sheptak, R. N. (2013). *Colonial Masca in motion: Tactics of persistence of a Honduran indigenous community.* Faculty of Archaeology, Leiden University. http://hdl.handle.net/1887/20999.

Smith, D. E. (1987). *The everyday world as problematic: A feminist sociology.* University of Toronto Press.

Smith, M. E., & Berdan, F. (2000). The Postclassic Mesoamerican world system. *Current Anthropology, 41,* 283–286.

Smith, M. E., Kohler, T. A., & Feinman, G. M. (2018). Studying inequality's deep past. In T. A. Kohler & M. E. Smith (Eds.), *Ten thousand years of inequality* (pp. 3–38). University of Arizona Press.

Stone, E. C. (2018). The trajectory of social inequality in ancient Mesopotamia. In T. A. Kohler & M. E. Smith (Eds.), *Ten thousand years of inequality* (pp. 230–261). University of Arizona Press.

Waring, M. (1988). *If women counted: A new feminist economics.* HarperCollins.

Winter, R., & Brankovich, J. (2016). The wages for housework campaign and "women's work" under capitalism. *Collective Action.* http://www.collectiveaction.org.au/2016/09/26/the-wages-for-housework-campaign-and-womens-work-under-capitalism. Accessed 19 May 2019.

Wright, R. P. (1996). Technology, gender, and class: Worlds of difference in Ur III Mesopotamia. In R. P. Wright (Eds.), *Gender and archaeology* (pp. 79–110). University of Pennsylvania Press.

Chapter 4
"The Economy Has No Surplus": Harry W. Pearson's Contribution Revisited, 60 Years Later

Svend Hansen

Abstract In the influential volume *Trade and Market in the Early Empires. Economies in History and Theory* edited by Karl Polanyi, Conrad M. Arensberg und Harry W. Pearson (Chicago 1957) Pearson published his provocative article "The Economy has No Surplus". He rejected a mechanistic view of development in which surplus was considered as the precondition of "complex" societies with priests and a ruling class. He stressed the question of the preconditions of the surplus: "There are always and everywhere potential surpluses available. What counts is the institutional means for bringing them to life". It provoked a number of statements by Marvin Harris, Ernest Mandel, Maurice Godelier and others, which criticised Pearson's standpoint and insisted on the "evolutionary" view of surplus. In this contribution, I will sketch this debate and discuss its relevance to the beginnings of the Neolithic. The topicality of Harry W. Pearson's essay lies in the fact that he pointed out that the surplus product did not have a natural cause, but was organised and that it came from a society that was already no longer egalitarian.

Introduction

The study of so-called "primitive societies" was from its very beginning in the eighteenth century not only of academic character. Their description was also often used as an implicit or explicit critique of the present society. Joseph-François Lafitau is the most prominent early anthropologist to draw an alternative picture of primitive societies.

In the nineteenth century John Lubbock (1874 [1865]), Edward Burnett Tylor (1865), and Lewis Henry Morgan (1976 [1877]) were the most eminent anthropologists, who described the indigenous peoples of the "New World" in terms of evolutionary stages ranging from primitive to developed on four levels: social, intellectual, juridical and religious. Karl Marx and Friedrich Engels studied the works

S. Hansen (✉)
Deutsches Archäologisches Institut, Eurasien-Abteilung, Berlin, Germany
e-mail: svend.hansen@dainst.de

S. Gimatzidis and R. Jung (eds.), *The Critique of Archaeological Economy*, Frontiers in Economic History,
https://doi.org/10.1007/978-3-030-72539-6_4

of the evolutionist researchers like James G. Frazer, John Lubbock, Lewis Henry Morgan and others very intensively (Marx, 1976). Morgan's book *Ancient Society* (Morgan, 1976 [1877) was the basis for Engels's *Der Ursprung der Familie, des Privateigentums und des Staats* (Engels, 1962 [1884]). Along with evolutionism, the idea of societies, that had to go through various stages came up in Marxist theory. That is, the classless society was only possible on the basis of a fully developed capitalist society (Foucault, 1978: 48). Tied to this, however, was the assurance of progress and the "principle" (*Naturgesetz*) of a development, which would overcome capitalism (Salvadori, 2008). The other kind of progress was defined by the constant growth of surplus or the control over nature (*Naturbeherrschung*), which was seen as the basis for socialism (Honneth, 2015: 65–83). Morgan's Ancient Society had been translated into the German language by Karl Kautsky, a well-known Social Democrat, who later founded the USPD (Unabhängige Sozialdemokratische Partei Deutschlands), but returned to the SPD (Sozialdemokratische Partei Deutschlands) already in 1922 (Morgan, 1976 [1877]). The interest in early societies was not academic, yet it was considered necessary for an understanding of the driving forces of history.

After the breakdown of evolutionism in anthropology as a consequence of Bronislaw Malinowski's groundbreaking field research on the Trobriand Islands (Malinowski, 1922), evolutionist thinking became important again in the 1950s (Steward, 1955). The models of the evolution of political systems sketched by Morton Fried (1967) and Elman R. Service (1975) were widely accepted. Service was undoubtedly the most precise and most influential anthropologist at that time (Service, 1958, 1962; Sahlins & Service, 1960).

Since the 1970s the interest in the study of primitive societies has become very widespread in western societies. It was an enormous awareness to find even larger societies that were not structured in states (Sigrist, 1983). They served not as a model, but as a kind of historical source that society could be organised other than in states. Ethnology became a kind of *Leitwissenschaft* (leading field in science). People wanted to understand not only the economic and political structures, but also the wisdom, the spiritual potential of American and African tribes. Moreover, in the 1980s, the interest in the economy and the political evolution of primitive societies grew enormously as well. At that time Marshall Sahlins' concept of the original affluent societies became very influential. The idea of "the original affluent society" was first presented during the conference *Man the Hunter* in 1966, which had enormous consequences for the anthropological study of hunter-gatherers in European archaeology, too. Marshall Sahlins, invited as discussant, made his response to the contributions of the conference participants (Sahlins, 1968, 1974).

He argued against the common belief that hunters enjoined continuous work just to survive, "affording them neither respite nor surplus, hence not even the 'leisure' to 'build culture'. Even so, for all his efforts, the hunter pulls the lowest grades in thermodynamics-less energy/capita/year than any other mode of production. And in treatises on economic development he is condemned to play the role of bad example: the so-called 'subsistence economy'. The traditional wisdom is always refractory. One is forced to oppose it polemically, to phrase the necessary revisions dialectically:

in fact, this was, when you come to examine it, the original affluent society" (Sahlins, 1968).

The term "affluent society" was taken from Kenneth Galbraith, who had criticised western capitalist societies for their social inequalities. Sahlins wrote: "The familiar conception, the Galbraithean way, makes assumptions peculiarly appropriate to market economies: that man's wants are great, not to say infinite, whereas his means are limited, although improvable: thus, the gap between means and ends can be narrowed by industrial productivity, at least to the point that 'urgent goods' become plentiful. But there is also a Zen road to affluence, departing from premises somewhat different from our own: that human material wants are finite and few, and technical means unchanging but on the whole adequate. Adopting the Zen strategy, a people can enjoy an unparalleled material plenty-with a low standard of living. That, I think, describes the hunters" (Sahlins, 1968).

Sahlins really had in mind to argue against a very old misconception: "Probably it was one of the first distinctly neolithic prejudices, an ideological appreciation of the hunter's capacity to exploit the earth's resources most congenial to the historic task of depriving him of the same. We must have inherited it with the seed of Jacob, which 'spread abroad to the west, and to the east, and to the north', to the disadvantage of Esau who was the elder son and cunning hunter, but in a famous scene deprived of his birthright. Current low opinions of the hunting-gathering economy need not be laid to neolithic ethnocentrism, however. Bourgeois ethnocentrism will do as well. The existing business economy, at every turn an ideological trap from which anthropological economics must escape, will promote the same dim conclusions about the hunting life" (Sahlins, 1974: 3).

In the meanwhile Sahlins' remarks about the hunter-gatherer society belong to the basic knowledge of cultural discourses: "A good case can be made that hunters and gatherers work less than we do; and, rather than a continuous travail, the food quest is intermittent, leisure abundant, and there is a greater amount of sleep in the daytime per capita per year than in any other condition of society" (Sahlins, 1974: 14).

In his last book "The Western Illusion of Human Nature" again the lifestyle of small-scale societies is emphasised. It is a splendid essay about the ancient sources of the Hobbesian worldview of a presocial and antisocial human nature. According to Sahlins, western society has been built upon a perverse and mistaken idea of human nature. By contrast, the truly universal character of human sociality is expressed in symbolically constructed kinship relations. Kinsmen are members of one another: they live each other's lives and die each other's deaths (Sahlins, 2008).

Sahlins' point is a critique of modern society: "Above all, what about the world today? One-third to one-half of humanity are said to go to bed hungry every night. In the Old Stone Age the fraction must have been much smaller. This is the era of hunger unprecedented. Now, in the time of the greatest technical power, starvation is an institution. Reverse another venerable formula: the amount of hunger increases relatively and absolutely with the evolution of culture. This paradox is my whole point" (Sahlins, 1974: 23).

So, Sahlins pinpointed that "Ethnologists and archaeologists have become neolithic revolutionaries, and in their enthusiasm for the Revolution spared nothing denouncing the Old (Stone Age) Regime" (Sahlins, 1974: 5). In line with this notion, recent books describe the historical step from Palaeolithic hunter-gatherer to Neolithic economies with a certain lack of understanding of why people stepped from the Palaeolithic paradise of much leisure and less work into the Neolithic hell of hard work and unhealthy food (Hariri, 2014; Meller, 2015; Scott, 2017). Claude Lévi-Strauss also saw the negative consequences of Neolithic accomplishments (Lévi-Strauss, 2013: 51–69). Indeed, sedentism and basic innovations such as stock-raising and agriculture fundamentally changed the way of life of human beings, who had lived for thousands of years as gatherers and hunters. V. Gordon Childe, who first coined the term "Neolithic Revolution" (Childe, 1936), would have never criticised the peoples of the tenth and ninth millennia BC, for having tried to survive in what seemed the best way. Childe was unambiguous in his view that hunger and inequalities in the modern world should be abolished by modern societies.

Sahlins' idea of the real "affluent society" became a standard in cultural anthropology and also in archaeology. Critical contributions are rare (Bird-David, 1992; Rowley-Conwy, 2001). Nonetheless, the high infant mortality, which does not fit with an affluent society, has been emphasised. The observation of the high proportion of "leisure time" in Kung society in Namibia has been explained by the necessity to stay in the shade when temperatures are very high (Kaplan, 2000: 315). It seems that Sahlins' affluent society is so successful in anthropology because it is not considered that their affluence is bound to their "Zen strategy".

As recent publications indicate, there seems to be a reawakened interest in these themes (Morehart & De Lucia, 2015; Bogaard, 2017). David Graeber (2011) also combined ethnological reflections with a kind of political activism. Possibly responsible for this reawakened interest is the present-day feeling of insecurity, brought about by globalisation with its social and psychic upheavals and by digitalisation together with rapid changes in so many spheres of life and work (Jullien, 2017).

Economy as Instituted Process and Harry Pearson

Karl Polanyi had a different focus. His starting point was the Age of Enlightenment and the development of concepts of economy and market: Hobbes, Locke, Smith and Marx. His writings were ambitious, towards understanding the complete tradition of western philosophy and social theory, and challenging for the reader to follow his intellectual brilliance.

Polanyi was born in Vienna and already in his youth he was part of the leftish and intellectual life in Budapest, where he started to study law and philosophy (Dale, 2016). Also his family background can be described as extraordinary. It suffices only to mention his brother Michael Polanyi, who was an excellent chemist and later a well-known philosopher. Karl Polanyi had to leave Austria in 1935 for London. Later he was able to move to the United States where he became Professor at Columbia

University (1947–1953). His wife, however, a member of the Communist party, did not receive an entrance visa into the United States. For this reason, they moved to Canada. Throughout his whole adult life Polanyi was politically torn between his wife, an active communist, and his liberal brother Michael.

Now in the Anthropocene epoch (Renn & Scherer, 2015), what Polanyi wrote in 1947 sounds very familiar: "The present condition of man can be described in simple terms. The Industrial Revolution, some 150 years ago, introduced a civilization of a technological type. Mankind may not survive the departure; the machine may yet destroy man; no-one is able to gauge whether, in the long run, man and the machine are compatible. But since industrial civilization cannot and will not be willingly discarded, the task of adapting it to the requirements of human existence *must* be solved, if mankind shall continue on earth. Such, in common sense terms, is the bird's eye view of our troubles" (Polanyi, 1947).

After retiring from his teaching position at age 67, Karl Polanyi received a grant from the Ford Foundation to continue interdisciplinary research on "Economic Aspects of Institutional Growth". Together with Conrad Arensberg and with assistance from Harry Pearson as executive secretary of the project, Karl Polanyi directed the research of a group of younger scholars. The result was "Trade and Market in the Early Empires" (1957), which includes Polanyi's seminal paper on "The Economy as Instituted Process". In their introduction to the volume, they argue against the generality of a market system and the claim of formal economics to historically universal applicability. The substantivist analysis has to penetrate the maze of social relationships, in which economy was embedded. "This is the task of what we will here call institutional analysis".

One of the basic premises of economic anthropology from its very beginnings onwards was, that surplus production was the prerequisite for development in society, the formation of a priest caste and a ruling class. Melville J. Herskovits, one of the leading ethnologists at that time, noted: "Whatever the case, the almost universal inequities which seem to mark the distribution of surplus economic goods is striking. This surplus wealth, it is apparent, goes to two groups, those who govern, and those who command techniques for placating and manipulating the supernatural forces of the universe" (Herskovitz, 1952: 414). This apparent matter-of-fact was questioned in the article by Harry W. Pearson, "The Economy has no Surplus. Critique of a Theory of Development" (1957).

Harry Waldemar Pearson was a longtime collaborator of Karl Polanyi. I tried to find out some biographical details about him, but was not very successful. Even in the Polanyi archive, where I asked for more information, there is no biographical material. In the archive, one can only find a manuscript by Pearson entitled "The Transformation Economic Society", which is an attempt to find out about an intellectual crisis after the death of Polanyi and the edition of Karl Polanyi's *The Livelihood of Man. Studies in Social Discontinuity* in 1977.

H.W. Pearson died in 1998. In an obituary, which I received from the Polanyi Archive, Walter C. Neal described Pearson as "a dear friend to many of the older members, a guide and inspiration to us all, and the mainstay of the group of scholars who gathered around Polanyi in the 1950s". Some biographical details are in the following: "Harry earned his BA at Lawrence College in 1943, served in the U.S. Army in Egypt during the Second World War, and then became a union organizer in Arkansas. In 1947 he entered the graduate program in Economics at Columbia University and shortly became a great admirer of Karl Polanyi and his work. From 1953 through 1958 he served as secretary, one might better say secretary-general, of the post-graduate seminar and subsequent projects originated by Polanyi. In addition to the regular chores of the position he was advisor to us all on innumerable matters. He bore the major share of the editing of *Trade and Market in the Early Empires* .... During these years he taught at Adelphi College, becoming Chair of the Economics Faculty and, as Acting President during 1964–1965, saw the College through some difficult times. During the 1970s Harry edited Polanyi's previously unpublished notes and lectures from the 1940s and 1950s, publishing them as *The Livelihood of Man* (by Karl Polanyi, Harry W. Pearson, editor. New York, San Francisco, London: Academic Press, 1977). After his retirement in 1983, he moved to Virginia".

In his article of 1957, Pearson first drew attention to the posit, that surplus would be a key for evolutionary change: "When employed as the key to evolutionary change, the surplus theorem has two essential parts. There is first the very concept of such a surplus. It is taken to represent that quantity of material resources which exists over and above the subsistence requirements of the society in question. Such surpluses are supposed to appear with advancing technology and productivity, and serve to distinguish one level of social and economic organization from another. The second part of the surplus theorem is the expectation that the surplus has an enabling effect, which allows typical social and economic developments of prime importance to take place. Trade and markets, money, cities, differentiation into social classes, indeed civilization itself, are thus said to follow upon the emergence of a surplus" (Pearson, 1957: 321).

Pearson identified this position in the works of Melville J. Herskovits, V. Gordon Childe, Leslie White and others (Pearson, 1957: 321). Herskovitz, for example, argued in his very influential book *Economic Anthropology* for a connection between population size and surplus: "It is to be recalled that the societies having the simplest economies, crudest technologies, and surpluses either nonexistent or so slight as to be of little significance, also have the smallest populations. On the other hand, it is evident that among the most populous nonliterate peoples, the surplus is large enough to enable these groups to support considerable numbers of persons not engaged in the production of subsistence goods. This point is the more striking if the literate historic cultures are included, since these comprise both greater populations, greater economic surpluses, and larger leisure classes than are found elsewhere" (Herskovitz, 1952: 413; for a broader discussion, cf. Heath Pearson, 2010).

With so many effects of surplus, for Pearson, citing Herskowitz, the question remains: "Just why the surplus is produced remains obscure" (Pearson, 1957: 322). Pearson viewed the basic needs of humans not as biological, but rather as a social construct. Therefore, he maintained that there is no absolute surplus, that is, no "absolute measure". Instead, surplus would be definable only by the entirety of the needs of a society. Relative surplus would then be present, when food for a specific feast would be produced and stored. These relative surpluses are initiated by the society in question.

Pearson identified Friedrich Engels as having introduced the surplus concept into anthropology: Engels: "In the middle stage of barbarism we already find among the pastoral peoples a possession in the form of cattle which, once the herd has attained a certain size, regularly produces a surplus over and above the tribe's own requirements, leading to a division of labor between pastoral peoples and backward tribes without herds, and hence to the existence of two different levels of production side by side with one another and the conditions necessary for regular exchange. The upper stage of barbarism brings us the further division of labor between agriculture and handicrafts, hence the production of a continually increasing portion of the products of labor directly for exchange, so that exchange between individual producers assumes the importance of a vital social function" (Engels, 1962 [1884]).

Pearson furthermore discussed the origin of the concept "surplus" as it was typical for Polanyi's school in historical depth and identified it in the works of the French Physiocrats in the Age of Enlightenment. Pearson found the idea of an absolute (that is, natural) surplus inadequate, and saw in that idea a typical figure of thought of economic liberalism, which he ascribed to John Locke. But this line of thought will not be pursued here in detail.

Surplus is, as the plausible theory goes, not natural, and thus must be viewed as a relative surplus within the frame of "definitive institutional requirements for the creation of relative surpluses". For example, it needs a redistributive system, in which fees for the redistribution of goods can be charged. "One of the most common of all means of surplus accumulation has been the power of arms to plunder and secure booty" (Pearson, 1957: 336). The elite exchange of prestigious goods would be a motor for mobilising surpluses. In short, "There are always and everywhere potential surpluses available. What counts is the institutional means for bringing them to life" (Pearson, 1957: 339).

Pearson's contributions have consequences for three fields: first, a theory of development/evolution as part of Marxian theory; second, the re-evaluation of the Neolithic; and third, possible consequences for consideration of the technical world.

Marx and Surplus

Marx argued that surplus value arises through the non-paid working time of workers; the surplus value is included in the surplus product. Pearson remarked: "Marx was perhaps the first to emphasize the institutional origin of relative surpluses in a market economy by focusing on the contractual relationship between worker and capitalist" (Pearson, 1957: 340, note 33). However, it is advisable to reserve the terms "surplus" (*Mehrprodukt*) for the *Stone Age Economics* (Sahlins, 1974), or other precapitalistic formations and—oppositely—the terms "surplus value" for commodity production which requires labour (Marx, 1962 [1867]: 189–191). So it would be better to speak of the appropriation of surplus which would name the precapitalist form of exploitation, and surplus value which is based on labour and exchange.

Nonetheless, Marx never challenged the production of surplus produce. Why? Because only the enormous wealth of the capitalist world would make people free "to hunt in the morning, fish in the afternoon, rear cattle in the evening, criticize after dinner" (Marx & Engels, 1958 [1845–1846]: 33). Marx is the complete opposite of the Zen road mentioned by Sahlins.

In reply to Pearson's article, Marvin Harris emphasised oppositely the importance of the existence of the surplus, which he attached to the measurable calorie requirement of humans (Harris, 1959). Everything that exceeded this was surplus. With this statement, Harris defended a manner of natural mechanism in social differentiation and development, which excluded the question of the motor of surplus production. George Dalton replied that surplus "is used as a *deus **ex** machina* which allegedly explains complex social structure or some unobserved socio-economic development" (Dalton, 1960: 485).

Ernest Mandel argued in the same direction; he viewed the concept of social excess products as essential for the Marxian analysis of economics (Mandel, 1968: 45–49, 2002). Mandel especially turned against the assumption of a constant supply of food. Only with the Neolithic Revolution did people become able to control their daily nourishment. Mandel explicitly refers to a "permanent surplus" as a result of the Neolithic Revolution (Mandel, 1968: 30). He wrote: "Every increase in the productivity of labour beyond this low point makes a small surplus possible; and once there is a surplus of products, once man's two hands can produce more than is needed for his own subsistence, then the conditions have been set for a struggle over how this surplus will be shared". One gets the impression that surplus production is comparable to learning to walk: Every day one step more.

Although he welcomed Pearson's differentiations, Maurice Godelier, too, remained firm about the relevance of the concept of surplus, by referring to it as a necessary condition for the future in capitalistic times (Godelier, 1972: 317–319). Neither Mandel nor Godelier succeeded in freeing their form of Marxian economic theory from the evolutionist trap.

Surplus in the Neolithic

Nowadays, Neolithic society has become a synonym for the simple beginnings of farm life. It is thought of as a time in which people lived together with their animals, still in harmony with nature. The Neolithic is also regarded by many as the time of matriarchy and the worship of a mother goddess (Gimbutas, 1995). Also, in the neo-evolutionist scheme for the development of society, early farmers formed egalitarian societies that did not have a marked hierarchical structure. The elder men had the say; they were eventually replaced by younger men who were in charge. The division of labour in Neolithic settlements was not noticeably distinct: "The economic basis of Neolithic society was farming and stock-raising. The division of labour was relatively low, whereby age and even more so gender were determinant for the scope and kind of activities to be carried out. The basic economic unit comprised autonomous farmsteads, likely organised on a kinship basis" (Veit, 1996: 201). And correspondingly, Neolithic households are described as autonomous units, which produced more or less everything on their own; very little exchange took place, above all, for desired articles from afar or prestigious goods.

But strong asymmetries in power and wealth did obviously occur, already in the fifth millennium BC, as is clearly demonstrated by the cemetery in Varna on the Bulgarian coast of the Black Sea. Many graves in Varna held only a few grave gifts or none at all, whereas some burials, by contrast, were lavishly furnished with goods, there among objects made of copper and gold. A total of 1.5 kg of gold was placed with the deceased in graves 4 and 43 each. According to available radiocarbon dates, the graves in Varna cover a time span of at least 100 years (4550–4450 calBC), or basing on more recent datings—up to 250 years (4650–4390 calBC) (Higham et al., 2007: 174; Krauß et al., 2014: 385, fig. 12; Windler et al., 2013).

Jean-Paul Demoule (2007: 78–89) commented that the graves in Varna would historically mark the beginning of social inequality. Colin Renfrew was the first who explicitly emphasised that with the cemetery in Varna the limits of domestic production had obviously been exceeded (Renfrew, 1986: 141–143). The duration of the settlement in Pietrele in South Romania was likely about 300 years (4600–4300 calBC), and there the economic base of such lavish grave goods can be described as a tributary system based on the division of labour (Hansen, 2018).

The more primitive picture of the Neolithic has been disrupted in the past three decades. New excavations in settlements of the preceramic Neolithic in Eastern Turkey and Northern Syria have revealed a hitherto unknown world of monumental architecture and figural sculpture (Hauptmann & Schmidt, 2007). There the beginnings of a producing economy could be pushed back into the tenth millennium BC through the "radiocarbon revolution". Likewise, in the Southern Levant the primary process of Neolithisation can be described for the first time through radiocarbon dating.

Cultic houses built of stone in Nevalı Çori, larger than life-sized statues and stone circles in Göbekli Tepe with pillars up to 5 m in height show that these were not at all tentative beginnings. Instead the contexts strongly suggest that represented here are organised processes, which demanded a considerable amount of labour. The stone circles and the sculptures are visible surplus products which were only possible because their producers were fed by people who produced more than was necessary for biological survival. There is no doubt that Nevalı Çori and Göbekli Tepe are not the only sites where large special buildings were erected and stone sculptures produced. Further research will uncover similar sites, which are already identified. These monumental buildings originated during a transitional time period, in which the old lifestyle as hunter and gatherer declined and a new more sedentary life with plant cultivation and later animal domestication arose. It was a deep-going crisis, in which the hunted game disappeared and with that peoples' basis of their traditional life. It is hardly possible to understand Neolithisation in the paradigm of Marshal Sahlins "affluent society".

It has become clear that the process of Neolithisation lasted much longer than hitherto thought in research. Nevalı Çori and Göbekli Tepe were not local developments, but instead represent a regional phenomenon with interactions in communication and exchange. It is quite unclear how labour was organised and how many people were involved, but there are some good arguments that work was under the control and direction of persons, who had the special protection of imagined supernatural powers, powers which were perhaps as rendered in the large-size statue found in Urfa (Hauptmann, 2003). All of this hardly offers a basis for considering the beginnings of the Neolithic period as an egalitarian organised process. The world of special buildings and sculpture disappeared in the eighth millennium BC. A more egalitarian model seems to have been the basis for the colonisation processes since the seventh millennium BC, when the Neolithic way of life entered new geographical areas, until it became established in central Europe in the first half of the sixth millennium BC.

Consequences for the Technical World

More than 20 years ago Jaret Diamond in his book *Guns, Germs and Steel* posed the question as to where the historical origins of present-day inequalities between the continents should actually be sought (Diamond, 1999). His answer was: in the Neolithic. Only in Eurasia were enough animals available to domesticate for husbandry. This answer is not as clear as it might seem. On the one hand, it is true that in Eurasia several species of mammals existed that could be domesticated, in Australia by contrast—none. But we should not make the nature and the number of domesticates responsible for the inequality in the modern world. It was a strict rule of the founder of sociology, Émile Durkheim, to explain that which is social solely with social facts and not with nature or religion.

Since then interest in the early history of techniques and knowledge has increased noticeably (Hariri, 2014; Kaube, 2017; Renn & Hyman, 2012). But already V. Gordon Childe (1958) and later Jack Goody (2010) viewed technological development as a key to understanding global disparities. Childe spoke of a technological differentia. Yet only later could this aspect in history be pursued, basing upon a solid chronology and on a global scale. This became possible as a result of the *radiocarbon revolution*, which provided a secure chronology. The end of the bloc division in 1989 made it easier for research worldwide. In addition, numerous new methods in scientific analyses throw light on the history of techniques (Smith et al., 2012). For example, the identification of natural resources enables the reconstruction of trade and exchange routes, which in turn throws light on ways of the transfer of knowledge. Thus, today an early history of mankind can be written, in which technical developments can be reconsidered adequately as preconditions and possibilities for economic, social and political processes, even though large gaps still exist that must be filled.

The examination of technical and social innovations can supply new impulses to the surplus-discussion of the Polanyi-School, and at the same time it gains important insights. Concerned here is the question: what was the framework within which the invention of technical devices and the development of techniques became possible. Or to use the famous Polanyi phrase, how were innovations "embedded" in society. The much-debated yet still unanswered question is whether innovative techniques arose during times of crises, in which creative solutions were urgently needed, or whether innovations were specially fostered by conditions of peace and intellectual freedom. Are technical innovations the preconditions for or the result of the emergence of a ruling class?

During the fourth millennium BC the world changed through a number of basic innovations: the fully developed metallurgy for practical purposes, the development of weapons which were in use for millennia in time, the wheel and the wagon, the domestication of the horse and the woolly sheep (Hansen, 2016). Here we see the foundations of a technological society which enabled class differentiation, states, slavery and permanent war.

Claude Lévi-Strauss and his famous distinction of "cold" and "hot" societies can help to converge to this observation. In his inaugural lecture at the College de France he stated: "The so-called primitive societies, of course, exist in history; their past is as old as ours, since it goes back to the origin of the species. Over thousands of years they have undergone all sorts of transformations; they have known wars, migrations, adventure. But they have specialized in ways that differ from those which we have chosen. Perhaps they have, in certain respects, remained closer to very ancient conditions of life, but this does not preclude the possibility that in other respects they are farther from those conditions than we are. Although they exist in history, these societies seem to have elaborated or retained a particular wisdom, which incites them to resist desperately any structural modification, that would afford history a point of entry into their lives. Those which have best protected their distinctive character appear to be societies predominantly concerned with preserving their existence. The way in which they exploit the environment guarantees both a standard mode of living and the conservation of natural resources (…) In short, these societies, which we might define as 'cold' in that their internal environment neighbours at the zero of historical temperature, are, through their limited total manpower and their mechanical mode of functioning, distinguished from those defined as 'hot' societies, which appeared in different parts of the world following the Neolithic revolution. In these 'hot' societies, differentiations between castes and classes are urged unceasingly in order to extract social change and energy from them" (Lévi-Strauss, 1966: 121).

With this we are able to understand much better the crucial distinctions between the technological, intellectual and mental developments in Eurasia and partly Africa, on the one hand, and North America and Australia, on the other hand. The Euro-Afroasian model of the Neolithic and its rapid dynamic development up to the emergence of cities and states is unparalleled in the world. States and civilisations emerged in South and Central America much later. In Eurasia the connection between technical innovations and social hierarchisation was much closer and flowed into cities and states. The result of these developments was undoubtedly the permanent increase in surplus production, interrupted only by diseases such as the plague or by major wars.

It enabled people to live today a much easier and healthy life than even 100 years before (Serres, 2019). The minority of people in the world enjoy a carefree life and the majority wants to have it. This represents a certain dilemma, because we all understand that this way of life is responsible for ecological and social catastrophes. Lévi-Strauss had only the social relations in mind, but not the ecological costs and climate change, when he wrote in 1986: "Perhaps that revolution [he is referring to the digital revolution, SH] allows us to glimpse the possibility of one day moving from a civilization that inaugurated historical change, but only by reducing human beings to the condition of machines, to a wiser civilization which would succeed—as we have begun to do with robots—in transforming machines into humans. Then, when culture had fully accepted the obligation to produce progress, society would be liberated from a millennial curse that constrained it to subjugate human beings for progress' sake. Henceforth, history would come to pass on its own, and society, placed outside and above history, could again enjoy the transparency and internal equilibrium by which the least damaged of the so-called primitive societies attest that such things are not incompatible with the human condition" (Lévi-Strauss, 2013: 74–76).

Conclusion

As is so often the case with influential theories and concepts, the slogan of the affluent society, with which Marshal Sahlins described the hunter-gatherers communities, was adopted only selectively. The other part, however, the Zen strategy of needlessness, was faded out. Thus the Neolithic Revolution became a power that destroyed forever the seemingly paradisiacal, in reality very precarious life of hunter-gatherers. The Neolithic period later became synonymous with the creation of the first surplus product. The surplus product or, in capitalist society, surplus value production has since been regarded as the prerequisite for a human future. Today, under the conditions of global warming, not only the fair distribution of the surplus product but also its sustainable production is on the agenda.

The topicality of Harry W. Pearson's essay lies in the fact that he pointed out that the surplus product did not have a natural cause, but was organised and that it came from a society that was already no longer egalitarian. Pearson challenged the common sense of surplus. The importance of his deliberations goes beyond simple terminology for emphasising the mechanism of how surplus products came into being in the first place. Pearson's contribution stresses the point of the decision-making for any surplus too far away to be something given by nature. His consideration touches upon certain fields of the future. This is how surplus production could be embedded in general public interest and welfare, on the one hand, and in the ecological necessity to stop climate warming, pollution and species extinction, on the other hand.

In the controversy with Marvin Harris, Polanyi's student George Dalton restated the problem in the form of a question: "When the tantalizing question is raised – 'How did they get to be priests and rulers?' – it is sometimes answered by saying that a food surplus must have arisen; because if no food surplus arose in a pre-stratified society, the potential priests and rulers would have had to produce food for themselves and hence could not have become priests and rulers" (Dalton, 1963: 389).

The question was why should a surplus have been produced in the first place and how could this have happened "so simply"? The answer was, that this **did not simply happen**; instead the surplus production was organised, and the origins for the organisation should be sought where they hitherto have not been imagined, namely in the egalitarian society.

Pearson and Dalton transferred a natural explanation into an institutional justification for surplus, in that they attached it with political control over the economy, for example, in a redistributive system. Dalton expressly noted that the assumption that a surplus emerged naturally and would not derive from class division would be an illusion: "It is not entirely apparent whether or not the anthropologist is aware that ***his*** Robinson Crusoe-hypothetical societies, in which all were food producers, perhaps, never existed" (Dalton, 1963: 394).

Acknowledgements I would like to thank Reinhard Jung and Stefanos Gimatzidis for their kind invitation to this inspiring symposium. I would also like to thank Professor Marguerite Mendell, Director of the Karl Polanyi Institute of Political Economy Montreal and Ana Gomez in the Karl Polanyi archive for their support. Emily Schalk translated an earlier version of this contribution.

References

Bird-David, N. (1992). Beyond "The Original Affluent Society": A culturalist reformulation. *Current Anthropology, 33*, 25–47.

Bogaard, A. (2017). The archaeology of food surplus. *World Archaeology, 49*, 1–7.

Childe, V. G. (1936). *Man Makes Himself.* Watts & Co.

Childe, V. G. (1958). *The prehistory of European society*. Cassell.

Dale, G. (2016). *Karl Polanyi: A life on the left*. Columbia University Press.

Dalton, G. (1960). A note of clarification on economic surplus. *American Anthropologist, 62*, 483–490.

Dalton, G. (1963). Economic surplus, once again. *American Anthropologist, 65*, 389–394.

Demoule, J.-P. (2007). L'origine des inégalités. In J.-P. Demoule (Eds.), *La révolution néolithique en France* (pp. 78–89). La Découverte.

Diamond, J. (1999). *Guns, germs, and steel. The fates of human societies*. Norton.

Engels, F. (1962 [1884]). *Der Ursprung der Familie, des Privateigentums und des Staats. Im Anschluss an Lewis H. Morgans Forschungen*, 25–173, Marx Engels Werke 21. Berlin: Dietz Verlag. [English translation taken from https://www.marxists.org/archive/marx/works/1884/origin-family].

Foucault, M. (1978). *Dispositive der Macht. Über Sexualität, Wissen und Wahrheit*. Merve.

Fried, M. H. (1967). *The evolution of political society*. Random House.

Gimbutas, M. (1995). *Die Sprache der Göttin. Das verschüttete Symbolsystem der westlichen Zivilisation*. Zweitausendeins.

Godelier, M. (1972). *Rationalität und Irrationalität in der Ökonomie*. Europäische Verlagsanstalt.

Goody, J. (2010). *The Eurasian miracle*. Polity.

Graeber, D. (2011). *Debt: The first 5,000 years*. Melville House.

Hansen, S. (2016). Prähistorische Innovationsforschung. *Das Altertum, 61*, 81–132.

Hansen, S. (2018). Arbeitsteilung, soziale Ungleichheit und Surplus in der Kupferzeit an der Unteren Donau 4600–4300 v. Chr. In H. Meller, D. Gronenborn, & R. Risch (Eds.), *Überschuss ohne Staat – Politische Formen in der Vorgeschichte. 10. Mitteldeutscher Archäologentag vom 19. bis 21. Oktober 2017 in Halle (Saale) / Surplus without the State – Political Forms in Prehistory. 10th Archaeological Conference of Central Germany, October 19–21, 2017 in Halle (Saale)*, Tagungen des Landesmuseums für Vorgeschichte Halle 18, 221–246. Halle (Saale): Landesamt für Denkmalpflege und Archäologie Sachsen-Anhalt.

Hariri, Y. N. (2014). *Sapiens: A brief history of humankind*. Vintage.

Harris, M. (1959). The economy has no surplus? *American Anthropologist, 61,* 185–199.

Hauptmann, H. (2003). Eine frühneolithische Kultfigur aus Urfa. In M. Özdoğan, H. Hauptmann, & N. Başgelen (Eds.), *Köyden Kente. From Village to Cities. Studies Presented to Ufuk Esin* (pp. 623–636). Arkeoloji ve Sanat Yayınları.

Hauptmann, H., & Schmidt, K. (2007). Anatolien vor 12000 Jahren. Die Skulpturen des Frühneolithikums. In *Vor 12000 Jahren in Anatolien. Die ältesten Monumente der Menschheit.* Ausstellungkatalog Badisches Landesmuseum Karlsruhe (pp. 67–82). Wissenschaftliche Buchgesellschaft.

Herskovitz. M. J. (1952). *Economic anthropology. A study in comparative economics.* Knopf.

Higham, T., Chapman, J., Slavchev, V., Gaydarska, B., Honch, N., Yordanov, Y., et al. (2007). New perspectives on the Varna cemetery (Bulgaria)—AMS dates and social implications. *Antiquity, 81,* 640–654.

Honneth, A. (2015). *Die Idee des Sozialismus. Versuch einer Aktualisierung.* Suhrkamp.

Jullien, F. (2017). *Es gibt keine kulturelle Identität.* Suhrkamp.

Kaplan, D. (2000). The darker side of the original affluent society. *Journal of Anthropological Research, 56,* 301–324.

Kaube, J. (2017). *Die Anfänge von Allem.* Rowohlt.

Krauß, R., Zäuner, S., & Pernicka, E. (2014). Statistical and anthropological analysis of the Varna necropolis. In H. Meller, R. Risch, & E. Pernicka (Eds.), *Metalle der Macht – Frühes Gold und Silber / Metals of Power – Early Gold and Silver.* 6. *Mitteldeutscher Archäologentag vom 17. bis 19. Oktober 2013 in Halle (Saale) /10th Archaeological Conference of Central Germany, October 17–19, 2013 in Halle (Saale),* Tagungen des Landesmuseums für Vorgeschichte Halle 11, 371–387. Halle (Saale): Landesamt für Denkmalpflege und Archäologie Sachsen-Anhalt.

Lévi-Strauss, C. (1966). The scope of anthropology. *Current Anthropology, 7,* 112–123.

Lévi-Strauss, C. (2013). *Anthropology confronts the problems of the modern world.* Belknap Press of Harvard University Press.

Lubbock, J. (1874 [1865)]). *Die vorgeschichtliche Zeit, erläutert durch die Überreste des Alterthums und die Sitten und Gebräuche der jetzigen Wilden (mit einem Vorwort von Rudolf Virchow) Bd. I–II.* (German translation of "Prehistoric Times: as illustrated by ancient remains and the manners and customs of modern savages": Jena Costenoble). Williams and Norgate.

Malinowski, B. (1922). *Argonauts of the western pacific: An account of native enterprise and adventure in the archipelagoes of Melanesian New Guinea.* E.P. Dutton & Co.

Mandel, E. (1968). *Marxistische Wirtschaftstheorie.* Suhrkamp.

Mandel, E. (2002). *An introduction to marxist economic theory.* Resistance.

Marx, K. (1962 [1867]). *Das Kapital. Kritik der politischen Ökonomie. Erster Band: Der Produktionsprozeß des Kapitals,* Marx Engels Werke 23. Dietz Verlag.

Marx, K. (1976). *Die ethnologischen Exzerpthefte.* Herausgegeben von Lawrence Krader. Suhrkamp.

Marx, K., & Engels, F. (1958 [1845–1846]). *Die deutsche Ideologie. Kritik der neuesten deutschen Philosophie in ihren Repräsentanten Feuerbach, B. Bauer und Stirner, und des deutschen Sozialismus in seinen verschiedenen Propheten.* Marx Engels Werke 3, 9–530. Berlin: Dietz Verlag [English translation taken from https://www.marxists.org/archive/marx/works/1845/german-ide oloy].

Meller, H. (2015). Vom Jäger zum Bauern – Der Sieg des Neolithikums. Der unumkehrbare Auszug des Menschen aus dem Paradies. In T. Otten, J. Kunow, M. M. Ring, & M. C. Trier (Eds.), *Revolution Jungsteinzeit*, Schriften zur Bodendenkmalpflege in Nordrhein-Westfalen 11,1 (pp. 20–28). Darmstadt: Theiss.

Morehart, C. T., & De Lucia, K. (Eds.). (2015). *Surplus. The politics of production and the strategies of everyday life.* University of Colorado Press.

Morgan, L. H. (1976 [1877]). *Die Urgesellschaft* (German translation of "Ancient Society"). Stuttgart 1908; Nachdruck Lollar/Lahn: Achenbach.

Pearson, H. (2010). Ground between two stones: Melville Herskovits and the fate of economic anthropology. *History of Political Economy, 42,* 165–195.

Pearson, H. W. (1957). The economy has no surplus. Critique of a theory of development. In K. Polanyi, C. Arensberg, & H. W. Pearson (Eds.), *Trade and market in the early empires: Economies in history and theory* (pp. 320–339). Gateway.

Polanyi, K. (1947). On belief in economic determinism. *Sociological Revue, 37,* 96–112.

Polanyi, K. (1957). Economy as instituted process. In K. Polanyi, C. Arensberg, & H. W. Pearson (Eds.), *Trade and market in the early empires: Economies in history and theory* (pp. 243–270). Gateway.

Polanyi, K. (1977). *The livelihood of man,* Studies in Social Discontinuity (edited by Harry W. Pearson). Academic Press.

Renfrew, C. (1986). Varna and the emergence of wealth in prehistoric Europe. In A. Appadurai (Ed.), *The social life of things: Commodities in cultural perspective* (pp. 141–168). Cambridge University Press.

Renn, J., & Hyman, M. D. (2012). The globalization of knowledge in history: An introduction. In J. Renn, & M. Planck (Eds.), *The globalization of knowledge in history.* Research Library for the History and Development Knowledge Studies 1 (pp. 15–44). Edition Open Access http://edition-open-access.de/studies/1. Accessed 23 May 2018.

Renn, J., & Scherer, B. (2015). *Das Anthropozän. Zum Stand der Dinge.* Matthes & Seitz.

Rowley-Conwy, P. (2001). Time, change and the archaeology of hunter-gatherers: How original is the 'Original affluent society'?' In C. Panter-Brick, R. H. Layton, & P. Rowley-Conwy (Eds.), *Hunter-gatherers: an interdisciplinary perspective* (pp. 39–72). Cambridge University Press.

Sahlins, M. (1968). Notes on the original affluent society. In R. B. Lee & I. DeVore (Eds.), *Man the hunter* (pp. 85–89). Aldine.

Sahlins, M. (1974). *Stone age economics.* Routledge.

Sahlins, M. (2008). *The Western illusion of human nature: With reflections on the long history of hierarchy, equality and the sublimation of anarchy in the West, and comparative notes on other conceptions of the human condition.* Prickly Paradigm Press.

Sahlins, M., & E. R. Service. (1960). *Evolution and culture.* University of Michigan Press.

Salvadori, M. L. (2008). *Fortschritt – Die Zukunft einer Idee.* Wagenbach.

Scott, J. C. (2017). *Against the grain. A deep history of the earliest states.* Yale University Press.

Serres, M. (2019). *Was genau war früher besser?* Suhrkamp.

Service, E. R. (1958). *A profile of primitive culture.* Harper & Row.

Service, E. R. (1962). *Primitive social organization: An evolutionary perspective.* Random House.

Service, E. R. (1975). *Origins of the State and Civilization: The Process of Cultural Evolution.* Norton.

Sigrist, C. (1983). Gesellschaften ohne Staat und die Entdeckung der social anthropology. In F. Kramer & C. Sigrist (Eds.), *Gesellschaften ohne Staat. Gleichheit und Gegenseitigkeit* (pp. 28–44). Syndikat.

Smith, M. E., Feinman, Gary M., Drennan, Robert D., Earle, T., & Morris, I. (2012). Archaeology as a social science. *Proceedings of the National Academy of Sciences of the United States of America, 109,* 7617–7621.

Steward, J. H. (1955). *Theory of culture change: The methodology of multilinear evolution.* University of Illinois Press.

Tylor, E. B. (1865). *Researches into the early history of mankind.* J. Murray.

Veit, U. (1996). *Studien zum Problem der Siedlungsbestattung im europäischen Neolithikum.* Waxmann.

Windler, A., Thiele, R., & Müller, J. (2013). Increasing inequality in Chalcolithic Southeast Europe: the case of Durankulak. *Journal of Archaeological Science, 40,* 204–210.

Chapter 5
Crafting Values in Chalcolithic Cyprus and Anatolia

Bleda S. Düring

Abstract In the Chalcolithic of Cyprus and Anatolia, we can document the emergence of exchange networks that were centred on highly standardized craft products. These exchange systems, organized around figurative items crafted from stone, set the stage for the later development of long-distance exchange networks of 'prestige goods' made from metals and gemstones of often distant provenance. This earliest exchange of figurative stone objects, which occurred in egalitarian societies, remains poorly investigated. Why were such objects considered desirable in the first place? How can we understand the rise of the shared *regimes of value* that they objectify? In this paper, I will present some first ideas to understand this problem in relation to anthropological studies on value, and I will argue that the initial creation of value was rooted in shared cultural repertoires of craftsmanship.

Introduction

When it comes to the study of economic systems of the past, archaeology faces an important challenge. Along with history and anthropology, it constitutes one of the few disciplines, that can provide data on societies whose economic systems were based on radically different parameters. Yet, recent scholarship abounds with studies suggesting that today's economic principles were equally pertinent to the deep past. Scholars such as Graeber (2011), Scott (2017) and Scheidel (2017) have recently reconstructed Bronze Age Mesopotamian economies as being not dissimilar to contemporary economic systems: having class societies, private property and exploitation and enslavement of workers by elites and state institutions. Further, they pushed the emergence of private property and competition over scarce resources back into the Neolithic, a view that is also held by some colleagues in archaeology (Mattison et al., 2016). In doing so, they not only legitimize modern economic and social practices by suggesting that they are part and parcel of human history from

B. S. Düring (✉)
Leiden University, Faculty of Archaeology, Leiden, The Netherlands
e-mail: b.s.during@arch.leidenuniv.nl

S. Gimatzidis and R. Jung (eds.), *The Critique of Archaeological Economy*, Frontiers in Economic History,
https://doi.org/10.1007/978-3-030-72539-6_5

the very beginning, but they also ignore the work of scholars who have studied these ancient societies up close and argue that ancient states were extremely weak and incapable of modern forms of exploitation (Richardson, 2012), and that there is no evidence for persistent (intergenerational) social inequalities in many Neolithic and Chalcolithic (that is pre-urban) societies (Price & Bar-Yosef, 2010; Hodder, 2014; Kohler et al., 2018).

Thus, a reconsideration of the nature of ancient economies is a desideratum, and the topic of the symposium at the origins of this volume was well chosen. However, if one studies the archaeological discourse of ancient economies, there is remarkably little to work with. Up to the 1980s the polemical debates between *formalists* and *substantivists*, initiated by Karl Polanyi and Moses Finley, on the degree to which exchange in the ancient world was or was not socially embedded, continued to determine the discourse of eastern Mediterranean archaeology (Polanyi et al., 1957; Finley, 1999; Warburton, 2011). The subsequent, and related, approach of distinguishing between *inaliable objects* and *commodities*, deriving from the seminal work of Appadurai and Kopytoff (Appadurai, 1986; Kopytoff, 1986; Appadurai, 2013), has been used mainly by Aegean archaeologists and has limited impact beyond (Voutsaki, 1997; van Wijngaarden, 1999). In recent years, however, with the exclusion of network analysis (Knappett et al., 2008; Ibáñez et al., 2016), relatively little work on ancient exchanges and economies has taken place.

Remarkably, discussions on ancient economies have focused almost exclusively on the nature of exchange systems, and more particularly, on how exchange was organized in relation to society. The *things* that were exchanged and *why* these things were exchanged has not been the focus of much research, and neither has their production and consumption received much attention, although this situation has started to change in recent years (Wilkinson, 2014; Massa & Palmisano, 2018). Thus, we have arrived in the paradoxical situation that the very objects that were central to exchange have often been regarded as epiphenomenal, and the study of ancient economies has been largely bypassed by the new materialism that has transformed so much of archaeology (Boivin, 2008). Here instead, I want to focus on what was being exchanged, what type of material and technology went into its production, and why these objects might have been considered worth pursuing. In other words: why were these objects considered valuable?

Setting the Scene

In the middle of the third millennium BCE a remarkable development occurred in the eastern Mediterranean, which could in effect be labelled the first globalization episode in this region of the world (following earlier globalization episodes in Mesopotamia and the Persian Gulf) (Frank & Thompson, 2005). Between about 2600 and 2200 BCE, the eastern Mediterranean witnessed the emergence of remarkably far-flung exchange networks, in which relatively modest places such as Troy were obtaining exotic substances such as *lapis lazuli* or amber from distant regions such as Afghanistan and the Baltic. Exquisitely crafted objects made from valuable materials were used by elites to distinguish themselves from commoners. Whether or not these elites were successful in their attempt to establish a class society at this time is a matter of debate. Although much work remains to be done to understand how economies worked in particular Early Bronze Age societies, *the prestige goods model* (Frankenstein & Rowlands, 1978; Kristiansen, 1987; but see Kienlin, 2017)—in which valuable objects, often made of exotic materials, were used by elites to underline their aspirations—has been more or less universally accepted (Bachhuber, 2009, 2015a).

Around the same time as the floruit of the EBA trade networks, ca. 2400 BCE, we can date the so-called 'Philia' horizon in Cyprus—which is often interpreted as an Anatolian colonization of groups bringing a distinctly Anatolian set of practices to the island, including ploughing, textile industries and rectangular buildings. Many scholars argue that these groups came to exploit Cypriote copper ores (Webb & Frankel, 2007, 2011; Bachhuber, 2015b). If we accept this hypothesis, this development further underlines the importance of trade, especially that in metals, in the mid-third millennium BCE.

The question how this interconnected, perhaps even globalized, world came into being has not been addressed much, as if the co-development of elites, crafted objects made from valuable materials and long-distance trade networks is self-evident and does not require further scrutiny. Some scholars have argued for a World Systems approach, in which these developments were triggered by a more developed Mesopotamian core (e.g. Bachhuber, 2015a: 150–151). This argument is problematic, however, as there is no substantial evidence that can be marshalled to demonstrate that a site like Troy was a Mesopotamian satellite of sorts. By contrast, there is much evidence that the emergence of trade networks, metallurgy and elites, are to be understood primarily as indigenous developments (see Stein, 2005 for a similar critique of Upper Mesopotamia as a World Systems dependency in the Uruk period). Of course, these local developments were connected to broader networks, and Anatolian societies did appropriate existing technologies and ideas from Mesopotamia (Rahmstorf, 2006), but this should not be construed as representing a relation of dominance.

Exchange networks have a long and dynamic history in the ancient Eastern Mediterranean. Well known, for example, are Neolithic exchange networks through which obsidian ended up as far as 2000 km away from its source of origin. The reconstruction of these obsidian exchange networks and modelling the mechanisms of exchange, has been one of the great success stories of archaeology (Düring, 2014; Ibáñez et al., 2016). Remarkably, these obsidian exchange networks can be documented alongside entrenched cultural differences between exchanging groups, for example, between central Anatolia and upper Mesopotamia. At the obsidian processing site of Kaletepe we even find Levantine knapping technologies (naviform cores), which are completely absent otherwise in Asia Minor, suggesting a production specifically for export (Binder & Balkan-Atlı, 2001). Subsequently, in the Later Neolithic and Chalcolithic (sixth and fifth millennia BCE) we see much less evidence for exchange networks in the Eastern Mediterranean, as well as an increasing fragmentation of cultural traditions in Asia Minor and Cyprus (but a very different trajectory occurs in Mesopotamia, with the rise of the Halaf and the Ubaid) (Düring, 2013).

It is only in the Chalcolithic that we see the re-emergence of exchange networks in the Eastern Mediterranean. Interestingly, we have evidence for what I think are the earliest traded craft objects: stone figurative objects that circulated in Chalcolithic Anatolia and Cyprus. In Anatolia, the earliest objects of this type are the so-called Kilia figurines, dated to the mid-fifth millennium BCE. On Cyprus, they take form of cruciform figurines, and date to the second half of the fourth millennium BCE. What these object types have in common is that they do not appear to be 'useful', and one wonders why these objects were exchanged by prehistoric people. Why and how were they of value to people?

The Kilia Case

I will focus first on the site of Kulaksizlar located in western Turkey, where a marble working workshop has been investigated by Turan Takaoğlu (2002, 2005, 2016, 2017; also Dinç, 1996) (Fig. 5.1).

Two types of marble objects were produced at this workshop: Kilia figurines and pointed beakers with perforated handles. Kilia figurines depict a stylized humanoid, most likely female, with a long neck, round sloping shoulders, arms folded upwards in front of the chest and a lozenge-shaped lower body and legs, with incisions to

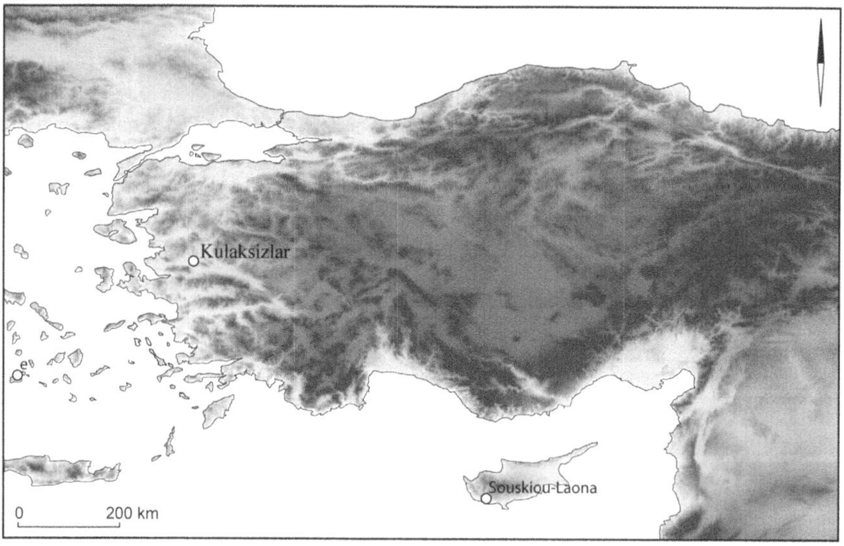

Fig. 5.1 Map of the northern part of the eastern Mediterranean showing the two main sites discussed in this paper. Produced by the author

indicate the legs and the pubic triangle (Seeher, 1992). Whereas the bodies are flat, the necks are cylindrical and the heads are much broader than the body and have raised facial features. The beakers are conical in shape and have two vertical lugs with piercings near the rim (Fig. 5.2).

Both the pointed marble beakers and the Kilia figurines have been found over large areas. While there may have been other production centres besides Kulaksızlar, the distribution of such artefacts does tell us something about prehistoric exchange patterns and cultural preferences. Similar pointed marble beakers have been found on

Fig. 5.2 Kilia figurine currently at the Getty Museum (object 88.AA.122). Reproduced with permission under CC-BY arrangement

the Aegean islands of Samos, Keos and Naxos; in the Troad, at Kumtepe and Beşik-Sivritepe; at Demircihöyük in the Eşkişehir Region, at Çukuriçi Höyük in Aegean Turkey and at Varna in western Bulgaria (Takaoğlu, 2002: 78–79; 2004: 3; Schwall, 2018: 243).

By contrast, Kilia figurines were found across western Anatolia, but seemingly not in the Aegean: at sites in the Troad such as Beşik-Yassıtepe, Hanaytepe and Troy; and in western Turkey, at Yortan, Alaağaç, Selendi, Gavurtepe and Aphrodisias. Kilia figurines are mainly found at sites dating to the Middle Chalcolithic. The EBA Kilia figurines, for example at Troy, are probably heirlooms (Seeher, 1992: 163; Takaoğlu, 2002: 80).

A large number of blanks, waste by-products, manufacture rejects and stone working tools were found at Kulaksızlar. These constitute about 90% of the surface assemblage at the site, with the remainder consisting of more ordinary domestic artefacts (Takaoğlu, 2002: 72). The marble raw material for these stone vessels and other rocks used in the manufacturing process such as gabbro, basalt and sandstone were located within walking distance of Kulaksızlar. The stone vessels and figurines were produced with a combination of hammering, drilling and grinding techniques. Notably, the raw material used for the production of the pointed beakers and Kilia figurines is present in many localities within the exchange networks.

I want to draw attention to two key aspects of these objects. First, they are objects of skilled craft. The Kulaksızlar workshop was clearly pushing the limits of what is possible in marble. The remarkable thing about both the pointed beakers and the Kilia figurines is that they have features that are very difficult to produce in stone: the beakers have perforated vertical lugs, and the figurines have round protruding heads set on a narrow and fragile neck. It is likely, that the consumers of these objects appreciated this aspect of craftsmanship. This is plausible given a pre-existing tradition of stone artefacts in Asia Minor.

The production of stone bracelets has been documented at Late Neolithic and Chalcolithic sites, such as Orman Fidanlığı and Kanlıtaş (Baysal et al., 2015), where numerous blanks and broken fragments were found. Stone bracelets are found at many late prehistoric sites in Asia Minor, such as Köşk Höyük, İkiztepe and Mersin-Yumuktepe. The ubiquity of these artefacts meant that people were familiar with producing stone artefacts and knew that they could easily break during production and use. Undoubtedly, this knowledge fed into the appreciation of the pointed beakers and the Kilia figurines. On another level, there is a rich tradition of figurine production and consumption in Anatolian Prehistory, although none of the types can be regarded as immediate predecessors of the Kilia figurines.

The second remarkable thing about the Kilia figurines is how standardized they are. There are a few small details that differ from one object to the other, such as the shape of the backward protrusion of the head, but overall they can be classified as variations of a type (Lesure, 2017 talks of *logos*). This is a point I will return to later in the discussion.

The Cruciform Case

In Cyprus, there is a tradition of cruciform stone figures that is completely unrelated in its development (no Kilia figurines were found on Cyprus and no cruciforms were found in Anatolia) (A Campo, 1994; Peltenburg & Webb, 2013; Lesure, 2017; Crooks, 2018). They are predominantly made of *picrolite*, a type of stone of green colour that is relatively soft and unique to Cyprus, occurring in seams in the Troodos Mountains. Picrolite blocks and pebbles range in size from a few centimetres to about 30 cm (maximum outlier). The smaller cruciforms are often pierced and show evidence of having been strung on a necklace or armlet, while the larger objects may have been stationary. Variations in ceramics and stone of cruciform figurines have also been found (Fig. 5.3).

Like the Philia figurines, the cruciforms are characterized by a high degree of stylistic standardization. All have outstretched arms, bent knees and parallel legs,

Fig. 5.3 Small pricolite figurine form the site of Chlorakas-*Palloures* (667_M1). Palloures excavation archives, photo by Ian J. Cohn

and tilted/protruding heads on elongated necks. Additional elements, such as facial features, occasional breasts or arms, which also form a figure, are optional extras adding a unique twist to a standard icon. It appears that, as for the Philia figurines, the intercomparability of these objects was of great importance.

As was the case for the Philia, there is a workshop site at Souskiou-*Laona* (Bolger, 2016; Peltenburg, 2019), but it is unlikely that the standardization of this type was the result of the centralization of production, and it is more likely that these objects were produced by multiple craftspeople at a variety of locations.

The cruciform figurines developed out of older types of figurines, made of other materials, such as stone and ceramics that existed in the Late Ceramic Neolithic on Cyprus (Peltenburg, 1982a). In the Early Chalcolithic, we see the earliest picrolite figurines that resemble cruciform. The type becomes common in the Middle Chalcolithic (3500–2900 BCE); hundreds are known from across the island. In the Late Chalcolithic they are still found, but it is not clear whether the production of this type continued. It would appear therefore that cruciforms developed out of a pre-existing figurative tradition in prehistoric Cyprus.

If we focus specifically on the use of picrolite as a raw material, we can trace its use back to the Late Aceramic Neolithic. There are various little ornaments and hooks dating to this period that were produced from this material (Peltenburg, 1991). The same types were made in the Ceramic Neolithic. It is plausible, that they were made of pebbles found in the stream beds of the Kouris and Karyotis rivers. Indeed, Picrolite pebbles have been found at a number of Neolithic sites. These pebbles are relatively small, and this is reflected in the limited size of these artefacts.

In the Chalcolithic, however, larger objects started to be produced from picrolite, and it is likely that picrolite was in part mined from its sources, where it occurs in veins, or plates in the rock. Peltenburg (1982b, 1991) has even suggested that this might have led to the first exploitation of copper. Interestingly, the cortex of the veins of picrolite is frequently visible in the cruciform figurines, as for example on the famous figurine from Yiali, where the cortex is visible on the knees. Indeed, the very shape of the cruciform, with its bent knees, outstretched arms and tilted head, is inherently problematic in a material that occurs in small sizes and plate-like veins. I think this was the point. Like in the Philia figurines, the Chalcolithic figurine makers were deliberately pushing the edge of what was possible in this particular material, and the products would have been appreciated as such because people knew what sizes and forms picrolite occurred in.

A Matter of Value

How then did these Chalcolithic trade networks start, and when and how did objects acquired through trade start to function as a means for social distinction? In my opinion, this leads to the question why these objects were considered valuable, which is worth pursuing.

What is value? In scholarship it is often defined as consumer value (what one is willing to exchange or pay for a product) or production value (how much labour went into the production of an object). While these two types of value can help to establish a relative exchange value, neither does actually do much to explain the *why* question. Why is an object desirable? Or, to use the terminology of Appadurai how does it fit into a culturally specific *regime of value*? The concept of *regimes of value* foregrounds how objects circulate in specific cultural horizons (Appadurai, 1986: 4; 2013: 60).[1] Many scholars have found the *regimes of value* concept useful to discuss how goods are meaningful in specific cultural settings (Myers, 2001; Flad, 2012; Papadopoulos & Urton, 2012: 17). Archaeologically, the *regimes of value* concept has not been explored much, but I believe it has much potential.

I would like to illustrate why I find the concept of *regimes of value* useful by considering an example from fieldwork in Turkey I executed about a decade ago, at the site of Barcın Höyük. At this excavation, we employed a group of Kurdish migrant workers hailing from southeastern Turkey, working as day labourers in agriculture and construction. They were magnificent workers, the best I ever encountered. They had curious collective habits I could not understand at the time. All the senior workers had packages of Marlboro cigarettes, instead of the much cheaper Turkish alternatives. Why, did these men, who earned very modest incomes, insist on smoking expensive cigarettes? (actually they seldom smoked them, but they did produce them at key moments). Then, a year later, these men had completely abandoned smoking. Instead, they all brandished fancy mobile phones (not smartphones, as these did not yet exist). Again, they rarely used these phones but they displayed them as often as they could.

Obviously, for these workmen the mobile phones substituted the purpose previously taken by the Marlboro cigarettes. Both clearly were important as markers of social identity: a serious man marks his achievement by an act of conspicuous consumption of an expensive product. The Marlboro cigarettes and phones were of key importance in the articulation of being a man, and it was particularly important to communicate ownership of these goods to peers.[2]

I will argue that this type of 'social value' has two characteristics. First, it builds on people's previous knowledge and experience. Second, standardization of objects facilitates the communication of values (this is why the workmen insisted specifically on Marlboro).

If we now compare this example to the Kilia and cruciform cases, we can note these two aspects. In the Philia and Cruciform exchange networks, we see that craftsmanship is important in that the limits of what was possible in stone production were deliberately pushed. In both cases, these objects reference older craft traditions and

[1]Graeber is very critical of this concept, arguing that the *regimes of value* as used by Appadurai is concerned mainly with power, or how elites manipulate the flow of goods to serve their own interests, and that there is little cultural content in the concept (Graeber, 2001: 32–33; also van Binsbergen & Geschiere, 2005: 19), although Graeber does not provide any such cultural content himself in his *Toward an Anthropological Theory of Value* (2011).

[2]These are not what economist call 'positional goods' (e.g. Brighouse & Swift, 2006), as the point was to signal membership of a collective rather than to communicate and individual status.

iconographic repertoires through which consumers could connect to these objects and appreciate their craftsmanship. Thus, these objects clearly linked to culturally specific knowledge of materials and craft technologies and, to a more limited degree, iconographic repertoires.

Further, in both the Philia and Cruciform exchange networks stylistic standardization was apparently of key significance. Thus, it was important not simply to have a well-crafted stone object that referenced previous cultural repertoires, but that object had to be a variation of a type, an iconic object. Thus, these objects most likely served to signal membership of a collective rather than individual status.

Thus, I argue that Chalcolithic regimes of value revolved around: first, referencing older categories of material culture; second, referencing widespread craft traditions; and third, required a substantial degree of standardization. Of course, we will never know the meaning that Philia and cruciform figurines had in Chalcolithic Asia Minor and Cyprus, even if it is highly likely that, like the Marlboro cigarettes and mobile phones of my dig workers, they would be important in the constitution and negotiation of social identities.

What is clear is that these are among the earliest craft objects exchanged in Asia Minor and Cyprus. Once the idea of exchanging craft products had caught on, and probably the use of these craft products for creating social distinctions, a new world opened up. In the wake of the Philia and cruciform exchange networks we see a marked increase in connectivity, reflected in the increased evidence for contact in ceramics, trade in craft products (such as imported faience beads and spurred annular pendants in Cyprus) (Peltenburg, 2018), and the emergence of metallurgy and the trade-in metals and metal artefacts, as exemplified in a copper axe recently found on Cyprus to be dated around 2600 BCE (Düring et al., 2018). Arguably, this process led towards the first globalization episode of the eastern Mediterranean which I have already introduced and which, as I am convinced, was rooted in the earlier development of exchange networks of crafted objects in the Chalcolithic.

Acknowledgements I would like to thank Reinhard Jung and Stefanos Gimatzidis for inviting me to Vienna to their wonderful symposium and for their patience with me while producing this paper.

References

A Campo, A. L. (1994). *Anthropomorphic representations in prehistoric cyprus: A formal and symbolic analysis of figurines, c. 3500–1800 B.C.* Paul Aströms Förlag.

Appadurai, A. (1986). Introduction: Commodities and the politics of value. In A. Appadurai (Eds.), *The social life of things: Commodoties in cultural perspective* (pp. 3–63). Cambridge University Press.

Appadurai, A. (2013). *The future as cultural fact.* Verso.

Bachhuber, C. (2009). The treasure deposit of Troy: Rethinking crisis and agency on the Early Bronze Age citadel. *Anatolian Studies, 59,* 1–18.

Bachhuber, C. (2015a). *Citadel and Cemetery in Early Bronze Age Anatolia.* Equinox.

Bachhuber, C. (2015b). The Anatolian context of Philia material culture in Cyprus. In A. B. Knapp & P. van Dommelen (Eds.), *The Cambridge prehistory of the Bronze and Iron Age Mediterranean* (pp. 139–156). Cambridge University Press.

Baysal, E., Baysal, A., Türkcan, A. U., & Nazarof, A. (2015). Early specialized production? A Chalcolithic stone bracelet workshop at Kanlitaş, Turkey. *Oxford Journal of Archaeology, 34,* 235–257.

Binder, D., & Balkan-Atlı, N. (2001). Obsidian exploitation and blade technology at Kömürcü-Kaletepe, Cappadocia, Turkey. In I. Caneva, C. Lemorini, D. Zampetti, & P. Biagi (Eds.), *Beyond tools: Redefining the PPN lithic assemblages of the Levant* (pp. 1–16). Ex Oriente.

Boivin, N. (2008). *Material cultures, material minds: The impact of things on human thought, society, and evolution.* Cambridge University Press.

Bolger, D. (2016). Re-making the self: Bodies, identities and materialities in Chalcolithic Cyprus. In M. Mina, S. Triantaphyllou, & Y. Papadatos (Eds.), *An Archaeology of prehistoric bodies and embodied identities in the Eastern Mediterranean* (pp. 47–54). Oxbow.

Brighouse, H., & Swift, A. (2006). Equality, priority, and positional goods. *Ethics, 116*(3), 471–497.

Crooks, S. (2018). The construction of value in Chalcolithic Cyprus: The picrolite cruciform figurines and pendants. In B. Horejs, C. Schwall, V. Müller, M. Luciani, M. Ritter, M. Giudetti, R. B. Salisbury, F. Höflmayer, & T. Bürge (Eds.), *Proceedings of the 10th International Congress on the Archaeology of the Ancient Near East, 25–29 April 2016, Vienna, Vol. 1* (pp. 397–410). Harrassowitz Verlag.

Dinç, R. (1996). 1994 yılı Akhisar-Kulaksızlar mermer atölyesi yüzey araştırması. *Araştırma Şonuçları Toplantısı, 13*(1), 11–41.

Düring, B. S. (2013). Apples and oranges? Comparing Neolithic horizons of upper Mesopotamia and Asia Minor. In R. Bernbeck, O. Nieuwenhuyse, P. M. M. G. Akkermans, & J. Rogasch (Eds.), *Interpreting the Late Neolithic of Upper Mesopotamia* (pp. 367–376). Brepols.

Düring, B. S. (2014). Material and craft networks in the prehistory of Asia Minor: Transformations in values and societies. In K. Rebay-Salisbury, A. Brysbaert, & L. Foxhall (Eds.), *Knowledge networks and craft traditions in the ancient world: Material crossovers* (pp. 7–22). Routledge.

Düring, B. S., Klinkenberg, V., Paraskeva, C., Kassianidou, V., Souter, E., Croft, P., et al. (2018). Metal artefacts in Chalcolithic Cyprus: New data from western Cyprus. *Mediterranean Archaeology and Archaeometry, 18*(1), 11–25.

Finley, M. I. (1999). *The ancient economy* [updated with a new foreword by Ian Morris]. University of California Press.

Flad, R. (2012). Bronze, jade, gold and ivory: Valuable objects in ancient Sichuan. In J. K. Papadopoulos & G. Urton (Eds.), *The construction of value in the ancient world* (pp. 306–335). Cotsen Institute of Archaeology.

Frank, A. G., & Thompson, W. (2005). Afro-Eurasian Bronze Age economic expansion and contraction revisited. *Journal of World History, 16,* 115–172.

Frankenstein, S., & Rowlands, M. (1978). The internal structure and regional context of early iron age society in south-western Germany. *Bulletin of the Institute of Archaeology, 15,* 73–112.

Graeber, D. (2001). *Toward an anthropological theory of value: The false coin of our own dreams.* Palgrave.

Graeber, D. (2011). *Debt: The first 5,000 years.* Melville House.

Hodder, I. (2014). Çatalhöyük: The leopard changes its spots: A summary of recent work. *Anatolian Studies, 64,* 1–22.

Ibáñez, J. J., Ortega, D., Campos, D., Khalidi, L., Mendez, V., & Teira, L. (2016). Developing a complex model of obsidian exchange in the Neolithic Near East: Linear regressions, ethnographic models and archaeological data. *Paléorient, 42*(2), 9–32.

Kienlin, T. L. (2017). World systems and the structuring potential of foreign-derived (prestige) goods: On modelling Bronze Age economy and society. In A. K. Scholz, M. Bartelheim, R. Hardenberg, & J. Staecker (Eds.), *Resource cultures sociocultural dynamics and the use of resources—Theories, methods, perspectives* (pp. 143–157). Universität Tübingen.

Knappett, C., Evans, T., & Rivers, R. (2008). Modelling maritime interaction in the Aegean Bronze Age. *Antiquity, 82,* 1009–1024.
Kohler, T., Smith, M. E., Bogaard, A., Peterson, C. E., Betzenhauser, A., Feinman, G. M., Oka, R. C., Pailes, M., Prentiss, A. M., Stone, E. C., Dennehy, T. J., & Ellyson, L. J. (2018). Deep inequality: Summary and conclusions. In T. A. Kohler & M. E. Smith (Eds.), *Ten thousand years of inequality* (pp. 289–318). University of Arizona Press.
Kopytoff, I. (1986). The cultural biography of things, commoditization as process. In A. Appadurai (Eds.), *The social life of things, commodoties in cultural perspective* (pp. 64–91). Cambridge University Press.
Kristiansen, K. (1987). Center and periphery in Bronze Age Scandinavia. In M. Rowlands, M. T. Larsen, & K. Kristiansen (Eds.), *Centre and periphery in the ancient world* (pp. 74–85). Cambridge University Press.
Lesure, R. G. (2017). Representation as visual exegesis: The stone figurines of Chalcolithic Cyprus. *Journal of Mediterranean Archaeology, 30,* 33–58.
Massa, M., & Palmisano, A. (2018). Change and continuity in the long-distance exchange networks between western/central Anatolia, northern Levant and northern Mesopotamia, c.3200–1600 BCE. *Journal of Anthropological Archaeology, 49,* 65–87.
Mattison, S. M., Smith, E. A., Shenk, M. K., & Cochrane, E. E. (2016). The evolution of inequality. *Evolutionary Anthropology: Issues, News, and Reviews, 25*(4), 184–199.
Myers, F. R. (2001). Introduction: The empire of things. In F. R. Myers (Eds.), *The empire of things, regimes of value and material culture* (pp. 3–61). School of American Research Press.
Papadopoulos, J. K., & Urton, G. (2012). Introduction: The construction of value in the ancient world. In J. K. Papadopoulos & G. Urton (Eds.), *The construction of value in the ancient world* (pp. 1–47). Cotsen Institute of Archaeology.
Peltenburg, E. (1982a). The evolution of the Cypriot cruciform figurine. *Reports of the Department of Antiquities*, 12–14.
Peltenburg, E. (1982b). Early copperwork in Cyprus and the exploitation of picrolite: Evidence from the Lemba Archaeological Project. In J. Muhly, R. Maddin, & V. Karageorghis (Eds.), *Early metallurgy in Cyprus, 4000–500 B.C.* (pp. 41–62). Pierides Foundation, Department of Antiquities Republic of Cyprus.
Peltenburg, E. (1991). Local exchange in prehistoric Cyprus: An initial assessment of picrolite. *Bulletin of the American Schools of Oriental Research, 282–283,* 107–126.
Peltenburg, E. (2018). The entry of Cyprus into the circum-Aegean world and the growth of regionalism on the Island. In S. Dietz, Ž. Tankosić, F. Mavridis, & T. Takaoğlu (Eds.), *Communities in transition: The Circum-Aegean Later Neolithic Stages (5000/4800–3200/3000 BC)* (pp. 435–467). Danish Institute at Athens.
Peltenburg, E. (2019). Picrolite procurement, manfucture and use. In E. Peltenburg, D. Bolger & L. Crewe L. (Eds.), *Figurine Makers of Prehistoric Cyprus: Settlement and Cemeteries at Souskiou.* (pp. 233–248). Oxford: Oxbow Books.
Peltenburg, E., & Webb, J. M. (2013). Figurines and other objects. In E. Peltenburg (Eds.), *Associated Regional Chronologies for the Ancient Near East and the Eastern Mediterranean* (pp. 251–297). Brepols.
Polanyi, K., Arensberg, C. M., & Pearson, H. W., eds. (1957). *Trade and market in the early empires: Economies in history and theory.* The Free Press.
Price, T. D., & Bar-Yosef, O. (2010). Traces of inequality at the origins of agriculture in the ancient Near East. In T. D. Price & G. M. Feinman (Eds.), *Pathways to power: New perspectives on the emergence of social inequality* (pp. 147–168). Springer.
Rahmstorf, L. (2006). Zur Ausbreitung vorderasiatischer Innovationen in die frühbronzezeitliche Ägäis. *Praehistorische Zeitschrift, 81,* 49–96.
Richardson, S. (2012). Early Mesopotamia: The presumptive state. *Past and Present, 21,* 3–49.
Scheidel, W. (2017). *The Great Leveler: Violence and the history of inequality from the stone age to the twenty-first century.* Princeton University Press.

Schwall, C. (2018). *Çukuriçi Höyük 2. Das 5. und 4. Jahrtausend v. Chr. in Westanatolien und der Ostägäis*, OREA 7. Verlag der Österreichischen Akademie der Wissenschaften.
Scott, J. C. (2017). *Against the grain: A deep history of the earliest states*. Yale University Press.
Seeher, J. (1992). Die kleinasiatischen Marmorstatuetten vom Typ Kiliya. *Archäologischer Anzeiger*, 153–170.
Stein, G. J. (2005). The political economy of Mesopotamian colonial encounters. In G. J. Stein (Ed.), *The Archaeology of colonial encounters: Comparative perspectives* (pp. 143–172). School of American Research.
Takaoğlu, T. (2002). Chalcolithic marble working at Kulaksizlar in Western Anatolia. *TÜBA-AR, 5,* 71–93.
Takaoğlu, T. (2004). Interactions in the fifth millennium BC Eastern Aegean: New evidence. *Anatolia Antiqua, 12,* 1–6.
Takaoğlu, T. (2005). *A Chalcolithic marble workshop at Kulaksizlar in Western Anatolia, an analysis of production and craft specialization*. Archaeopress.
Takaoğlu, T. (2016). On the modes of exchange in Prehistoric Lycia. In E. Dündar, Ş. Aktaş, M. Koçak, & S. Erkoç (Eds.), *Lykiarhissa: Festschrift für Havva İşkan* (pp. 649–657). Ege Yayınları.
Takaoğlu, T. (2017). Middle Chalcolithic finds from Dağdere in the Akhisar/Manissa region. *Anadolu (Ankara Üniversitesi Dil ve Tarih-Co[g]rafya Fakültesi Arkeoloji Bölümü Dergisi), 43,* 1–14.
van Binsbergen, W., & Geschiere, P. (2005). *Commodification: Things, agency, and identities (The social life of things revisited)*. Lit.
van Wijngaarden, G. J. (1999). An archaeological approach to the concept of value. *Archaeological Dialogues, 1,* 2–46.
Voutsaki, S. (1997). The creation of value and prestige in the Aegean Bronze Age. *Journal of European Archaeology, 5*(2), 34–52.
Warburton, D. A. (2011). Taking a stab at archaeological thought on ancient Near Eastern economics. In B. S. Düring, A. Wossink, & P. M. M. G. Akkermans (Eds.), *Correlates of complexity: Essays in Archaeology and Assyriology dedicated to Diederik J. W. Meijer in Honour of his 65th Birthday* (pp. 233–259). Nederlands Instituut voor het Nabije Oosten.
Webb, J. M., & Frankel, D. (2007). Identifying population movements by everyday practice: The case of 3rd millennium Cyprus. In S. Antoniadou & A. Pace (Eds.), *Mediterraenan crossroads* (pp. 189–216). Pireides Foundation.
Webb, J. M., & Frankel, D. (2011). Hearth and home as identifiers of community in mid-third millennium Cyprus. In V. Karageorghis & O. Kouka (Eds.), *On cooking pots, drinking cups, loom weights and ethnicity in Bronze Age Cyprus and neighbouring regions* (pp. 29–42). The A.G. Leventis Foundation.
Wilkinson, T. C. (2014). *Tying the Threads of Eurasia: Trans-regional routes and material flows in Transcaucasia, Eastern Anatolia and Western Central Asia*. Sidestone Press.

Chapter 6
The Bornhöck Burial Mound and the Political Economy of an Únětice Ruler

Roberto Risch, Harald Meller, Selina Delgado-Raack, and Torsten Schunke

Abstract The Circum-Harz group of the Central German Únětice Culture (c. 2200–1550 BCE), which finally unified the Late Neolithic Corded Ware and Bell Beaker Cultures, exhibits a remarkably high level of social complexity. Based on the funerary record and the structured composition of the metal hoards, it has been suggested that this social entity was developed into a state organisation ruled by a dominant leader and supported by armed troops. However, the surplus economy necessary to supply this army and other state servants, which would not work in agricultural production, has not been confirmed so far. In this sense, the burial mound of Bornhöck in the communal district of Raßnitz, Saalekreis district, near Dieskau with its well-known weapon hoards, offers new insight into the economic organisation of an Únětice community, especially with regard to its rulers. In this socio-historical context, the study of grinding equipment coming from the stone core protecting the central burial chamber turns to be of crucial importance. Our study shows that an exceptional number of highly efficient grinding slabs, specifically designed to carry out intensive grinding processes, was concealed in this funerary context. Moreover, these tools were markedly different from the grinding slabs present in the typical Únětice long-houses. As a result, the Bornhöck provides direct evidence of the existence of three characteristic elements of a state organisation, i.e. the centralisation of an important part of agricultural production, probably through some type of taxation mechanism, the control of surplus value by the dominant class of Únětice, and the existence of a substantial population dependent on this surplus. As an army seems the most plausible consumer of large amounts of food supplies, indirectly, the macrolithic tools of the Bornhöck confirm the monopoly on the use of force hold by the ruler buried in it.

R. Risch (✉) · S. Delgado-Raack
Departament de Prehistòria, Universitat Autònoma de Barcelona, Barcelona, Spain
e-mail: Robert.Risch@uab.cat

H. Meller · T. Schunke
Landesmuseum für Vorgeschichte, Landesamt für Denkmalpflege und Archäologie Sachsen-Anhalt, Halle, Germany

S. Gimatzidis and R. Jung (eds.), *The Critique of Archaeological Economy*, Frontiers in Economic History,
https://doi.org/10.1007/978-3-030-72539-6_6

Introduction

The recovery of the Sky Disk of Nebra from the illegal antique market in 2002 set out an array of research programmes devoted to the understanding of the society in which the first clear recognisable calendar known in Europe could have become a meaningful artefact.[1] This research has gradually lead to a better understanding that the Early Bronze Age of Central Germany, more specifically known as the Circum-Harz group of the Únětice Culture, saw the rise of a social and political entity, which does not conform well to conventional categories proposed by twentieth-century functionalist anthropology, such as chiefdom (Service, 1962 [1971]). This has revived the discussion about whether state societies could have risen in Europe, particularly during the Early Bronze Age (c. 2200–1600 BCE), independently and in a different way than from their Near Eastern, Egyptian, and probably also Aegean neighbours (Lull & Risch, 1995; Nocete, 2001; Chapman, 2003; Contreras, 2009–2010; Lull et al., 2011; Meller, 2019a, 2019b, 2019d). This discussion can easily drift into a sterile academic debate between different research traditions about which categories we use to communicate, if the distinctive socio-economic relations and the means of exploitation of the state are not addressed.

Beyond the teleological meaning that the different state theories have attached to this historical category, most of them probably coincide in relating the appearance of the state to the existence of stratified or class societies, in which individuals and social groups can clearly be distinguished in terms of their asymmetric access to wealth and power.[2] These privileges are warranted and legitimised in space and time through different mechanisms and institutions. Legally, this requires the imposition of some form of permanent, usually hereditary, property rights and the establishment of territorial limits, within which these privileges are imposed. The dynastic rule is another institution by which economic and political privileges are often fixed in time. Effectively, the enforcement of law and domination demands the existence of specific mechanisms of coercion and the concentration of means of violence in the hands of a dominant class. Apart from the violent imposition of privileges and rights, states always develop their own mechanism of psychological coercion, for example through rituals and imagery of violence, in order to give rise to individual fear and obedience, which form the subjective fabric of domination and hegemony. In general, the ideological and ceremonial paraphernalia of the state are essential to its legitimation.[3]

Economically, all state organisations are dependent on the production of surplus profit, rather than wealth. While the first always implies an unequal individual appropriation of social production directly or indirectly derived from the exploitation of workforce, wealth is the pool of goods and services accessible to a society, which can be distributed according to many different criteria (Risch, 2016). Rent, tribute but

[1] For informations on the Nebra Sky Disc see e.g. Meller (2010, 2013a).

[2] For a discussion of the different state theories, see Lull and Micó (2011).

[3] For a discussion of the glorification of violence see Risch (2020). For legitimation strategies in the Únětice Culture see Meller (2019d).

also plain robbery are some of the mechanisms that elites have conventionally drawn on in order to benefit from collective work. However, in state societies, surplus is no longer just the economic profit or ill-gotten gains of the dominant class. Through an increasingly complex circulation process, material goods and services are transformed into surplus value, which can be managed, stored and transformed into new goods and services that ultimately benefit the dominant group. The development of specific crafts, such as those devoted to the production of weapons, or setting up an army and a priestly caste, form part of this realisation process of surplus. Consequently, the production, as well as circulation of surplus profit or added value, in modern economic terminology, is critical to the qualification of any social group or archaeological entity as a state society.

While sociological approaches to the Early Bronze Age societies of central Europe have mainly been based on funerary evidence, hoarding praxis, and, lately, also to settlement patterns, the recent discovery of the Bornhöck burial mound, near Dieskau, Saalekreis district, has provided unexpected insights into the organisation of an Únětice community and the economic power of its rulers (Meller & Schunke, 2016). A substantial number of macrolithic tools were recovered from the remains of what appears to have been one of the largest funerary monuments of Central Europe. Most of these artefacts were intentionally deposited in the stone core that protected the large wooden funerary chamber, indicating a direct relation between these tools and the ruler buried inside. This paper aims to analyse this key source of palaeoeconomic information and to explore if socio-economic strategies emerged in the Únětice society that made the economic exploitation and the accumulation of surplus possible.

The Únětice Society of Central Germany

Towards the last centuries of the 3rd millennium BCE, the end of the Neolithic, marked the onset of profound political and economic change in Central Europe. As a consequence, a new social entity, commonly referred to as the Únětice Culture, emerged at the start of the Bronze Age. In many aspects, it was different both from earlier Corded Ware and Bell Beaker Cultures as well as from subsequent Bronze Age societies. The Circum-Harz group of the Central German Únětice Culture is of particular relevance. Its characteristic grave, settlement and hoard finds date from 2200 to 1550 BCE and can be found in the area north, east and south of the Harz mountain range (see, inter alia, Zich, 1996; Evers, 2012; Evers & Witt, 2019).

The Circum-Harz region, the so-called Lössbörde, is among the most fertile areas of the world. Its deep chernozem soil lies in the precipitation shadow of the Harz mountain range and thus provides ideal conditions for agriculture (cf. Kainz, 1999: 21–22, 27–29). After 2200 BCE, a new settlement pattern was established on these soils and in proximity to watercourses, which gave access to water and the waterways that form the natural communication routes of the region (e.g. Schunke, 2019). The basic socio-economic unit was the typical Únětice longhouse, which could stand

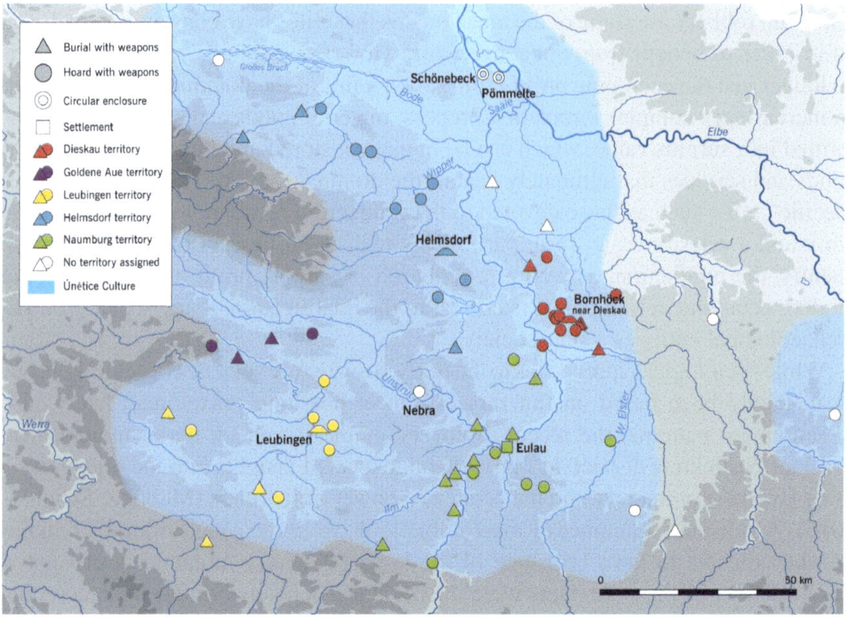

Fig. 6.1 Distribution map of the Circum-Harz Únětice group (c. 2200–1550 BCE) in central Germany and the sites mentioned in the text. The distribution of hoards and graves containing weapons, as well as natural boundaries, possibly indicates the existence of distinct territories. In the (putative) territories of Naumburg and the Goldene Aue princely graves have yet to be discovered. The hoard find of Nebra, which is located in between the different territories, has not yet been associated with any particular group (map by J.-H. Bunnefeld and B. Janzen, LDA Sachsen-Anhalt, based on data from von Brunn, 1959; Zich, 1996; Meller, 2014, with additions)

either isolated or forming loose hamlets of over 40 buildings, as has just been documented in the settlement of Pömmelte (Fig. 6.1). Their construction and ground plans are highly standardised and symmetrical, suggesting the existence of some notion of modular building (Meller & Zirm, 2019; Schunke & Stäuble, 2019). While the width of these two-aisled houses tends to be rather uniform (ca. 5.5–7 m), their length varies from less than 15 m to nearly 40 m (Schunke, 2019; Ganslmeier, 2019; Schunke & Stäuble, 2019). The rare and large three-aisled hall-like buildings can reach over 50 m in length and 11 m in width (Küßner & Wechler, 2019; Schunke & Stäuble, 2019). The high variability of the resulting living spaces (ca. 80–500 m^2) suggests the existence of notable differences in terms of the demographic and/or economic strength of longhouses. Although their original floor levels are missing due to erosion and ploughing, stall areas and storage facilities including large vessels containing animal fats have been identified in better-preserved buildings (e.g. Schüler et al., 2019; Walter et al., 2019). Besides the longhouses, settlements can also include auxiliary buildings of still undefined function, large workshop areas, wooden pathways, fenced areas and wells (Meller et al., 2019). All this reveals the existence of economic activities on a supra-domestic level.

Large-scale cooperation is attested in the construction, maintenance and use of circular enclosures since the late Bell Beaker period, such as Pömmelte or Schönebeck, both in the Salzlandkreis district (Spatzier, 2017, 2019). Both enclosures are located close to the river Elbe and at the northern fringes of the Circum-Harz Únětice territory and were in use up to the end of the 3rd millennium BCE.

The Pömmelte rondel was built around 2300 and intentionally destroyed by 2050 BCE presumably by pulling and burning the rondel's posts. The Schönebeck circular trench was built a little later and probably continued to function after Pömmelte was abandoned. Both structures were in use contemporarily during at least part of the twenty-two–twenty-first centuries BCE, but their function seems to be partially different. The Pömmelte rondel had a diameter of approximately 115 meters with 29 up to 1.3 meters deep shaft pits dug into the ditch. Pottery, animal bones, stone axes, but also different human bodies or body parts had been deposited in these shafts. Several skulls show trauma (Stecher & Alt, 2019), so that the possibility of human sacrifices can be considered. The deposits of individual grinding stones and coarse stone tools in these pits are particularly noteworthy. The neighbouring, somewhat younger Schönebeck rondel enclosure, however, was smaller with a diameter of approximately 90 m. The main difference, between them, however, is the lack of surrounding graves, and in particular shaft pits with sacrificial deposits in Schönebeck. The only deposit in the circular ditch of this site is a hoard made up of a cushion stone and a possible grinding stone (Bertemes, 2020). Both structures are likely to have had ritual significance due to their astronomical orientations (Meinike, 2019; Schlosser, 2019) and the sacrificial deposits. They clearly reflect the change from human sacrifice to more abstract religious ideas and actions (Meller, 2019a: 65–67).

A more detailed insight into the social structure of the Circum-Harz Únětice group is provided by the funerary structures. Its stratified character is mainly expressed by the barrow construction and burial furnishings—including weapons, tools and a fixed set of gold ornaments. These rich furnishings characterise the so-called princely graves of Leubingen, Sömmerda district (1942 ± 10 BCE), Helmsdorf, Mansfeld-Südharz district (1829/28 BCE), and the recently explored barrow Bornhöck, Saalekreis district (second half of the nineteenth century BCE/c. 1800 BCE) (Meller & Schunke, 2016; Meller, 2019a, 2019b, 2019d). The "overdisplay" of weaponry, represented by two axes, three daggers and a halberd, in the burial of Leubingen points towards the close ties between wealth and means of violence, on a symbolic as well as physical level. Palaeopathological evidence has confirmed that the prince of Helmsdorf was himself a victim of lethal violence inflicted by a dagger. He had been stabbed through his belly, into his shoulder blade and in his arm (Nicklisch et al., 2020). The social distance between the ordinary population and these political and military leaders is also illustrated by their diet, which was made up to an exceptional extent of animal products (Knipper et al., 2015).

Based on the distribution of grave and hoard finds as well as existing natural boundaries, the Circum-Harz group has been divided into five different political territories or "domains" (Zich, 2016). Taking into account landscape features and the distribution of Únětice finds, the borders of these territories have been subsequently slightly redefined (Meller, 2019a: 56–57; 2019c: 147–148) (Fig. 6.1). Moreover, after the discovery of the once monumental Bornhöck tumulus and its association to the Dieskau gold finds, discussed below, it seems highly plausible that, by 1850 BCE, the whole of the Circum-Harz Únětice group merged into a unified political unit.

The high-status group represented by the princely graves was accompanied by a second tier of individuals whose burials did not always contain weapons and were characterised by the presence of much less gold. The golden artefacts involved are hair-rings, a distinctive feature known since the Bell Beaker Culture (Meller, 2014: 616–628; 2019e; Schwarz, 2014: 719). The third tier included only a few burials containing axes and daggers, while the fourth tier consisted of graves characterised by bronze goods, often in the form of one or two pins. The two bottom tiers are made up of burials furnished only with pottery vessels, or completely unfurnished graves (Schwarz, 2014: 719–725).

The composition of the metal hoards has been recognised as a third source of information revealing the character of the Circum-Harz Únětice society and, more specifically, its forces of physical coercion (Meller, 2015, 2017, 2019a). The central German hoards known so far and which largely date from between 2000 and 1625 BCE, contain a total of 1178 axes, 26 halberds, 18 daggers and eight double axes, while jewellery (indeed, almost exclusively ring ornaments) is of secondary importance (Meller, 2019a, 2019c). In contrast, graves from the same period have only yielded 10 axes, 3 halberds and 27 daggers. The warriors' weapons were, therefore, preferentially placed in hoards, rather than graves.

To follow this trail, it needs to be noticed that many of the deposited axes, as well as halberds and daggers, display obvious traces of use (cf. Kienlin, 2008; Behrendt et al., 2015: 98). They were, therefore, not made specifically for deposition; rather, their handles were removed at the end of their use-life, before the weapons were permanently concealed in the earth. On the other side, metal analyses have shown that the axes from the individual hoards show a very similar composition (Rassmann, 2010: 813–815; Meller, 2017: Fig. 7). Therefore, it can be assumed that the axes from each hoard were the serial production of a single workshop. As no stone or fired clay molds are known from Central Germany so far, the materially and metrically highly standardised weapons probably were cast in forms of sand or unburned clay. The batch then stayed together during its whole use-life—as did their carriers—until they were deposited years later. But, which event lead these communities to collect, un-haft and conceal the metal blades?

The quantitative analysis of the hoards of Central Germany has revealed that the number of axes in hoards with more than ten axes is not coincidental. The smallest unit visible in the hoards comprised 10 or 15 axes. Larger hoards show a tendency to include ca. 30, 45, 60, 90, 120 or 300 axes. Moreover, the ratio between axes and halberds is 1:45, with daggers 1:65, and with double axes 1:150. Taking into account that these ratios involve weapons, these numerical sequences remind one of military hierarchies, as have been proven to exist throughout military history since antiquity (Meller, 2015; 2017; 2019a: 53–57). If this reading is correct, the smallest unit visible in the hoards comprised ca. 15 axes or "soldiers". The unit of 45 "soldiers" would then have been led by a halberd-bearer, and the unit of 65 "soldiers" would have been under the command of a dagger-bearer. The largest combat unit of 150 individuals would have been led by a double axe-bearer. In sum, the number of weapons in the hoarding seems to reflect the number of available warriors and corresponds to the meaning of the respective prince's grave (Fig. 6.1). It follows, that the princes of the Dieskau territory, who were buried in Bornhöck mound, could have warrior groups with a size of at least 300 warriors. Of course, the number of warrior groups cannot be established, as most hoards probably remain unknown.

The hierarchical structure of these troops might be expressed by the colours of the distinctive Únětice weapons, which were determined through the metal composition (Meller, 2019a: 57–62; 2019c; Wunderlich et al., 2019). Tin alloyed and, consequently, shiny gold-coloured weapons were preferentially placed in graves, but not deposited in hoards. The axe from the Dieskau I hoard even consists entirely of gold. These colour and material differences seem to mirror the clearly structured Únětice society.

The possibility that hoarded weapons legitimately represent actual "soldiers" and "military units" is strongly supported by the recent discovery of an Early Bronze Age hoard and an unusually large (44 × 11 m), three-aisled longhouse at Dermsdorf, Thuringia, located within sight of the Leubingen princely grave. The hoard consisted of 98 axes and two possible dagger or halberd blanks found in a pottery vessel near the ridge post of the longhouse. It dates to the transition of the phases Bz A2a and Bz A2b (c. 1850–1700 BCE), and is therefore later than the Leubingen princely burial (Behrendt et al., 2015; Küßner & Wechler, 2019). The length of the building compared to modern ethnographic examples suggests that it could easily have accommodated 98–100 people. The obvious conclusion is that the hoard may have been a deposition of axe blades that had belonged to "soldiers" garrisoned in what could be called a "men's house" (Meller, 2013b: 520–521; Schwarz, 2014: 727–728). This military garrison and the earlier prince of Leubingen who was buried nearby at the centre of the North Thuringian political territory show that there is some continuity of political power in this micro-region. The group of "soldiers" had possibly been issued the weapons by a prince and sacrificed them in front of their ritual building when he died. His successor expressed his power by supplying new axes to his army, thereby symbolically securing their loyalty. This military and ritual praxis explains the serial production and the closely connected use of sets of weapons, as opposed to a domestic production and use of particular objects. In the absence of texts, the coherence between location, size and composition of hoards and burials is probably the most reliable archaeological evidence that the Circum-Harz Únětice territory was ruled by a dominant class, which had armies at their disposal, and thus an enforcement or administrative staff.

However, the existence of coercive and administrative forces bound to a ruling class must have required a steady production of surplus value through tribute, *corvée*, slave labour, or a combination of these. Unfortunately, we know too little of the activities taking place in the longhouses of different sizes and the auxiliary structures identified in the settlements to trace the economic organisation of the communities. The discovery and excavation of the remains of the Bornhöck tumulus, constructed with materials and debris transported from settlements, has provided exceptional economic information.

The Bornhöck Funerary Monument

The largest Early Bronze Age burial mound in Central Europe, named Bornhöck once lay in the Raßnitz parish, of Saalekreis district, and very near to Dieskau, an area which is well-known for its weapon hoards. It was razed by workers from 1844 on, and in particular between 1850 and 1890 CE. Historical drawings and excavations carried out between 2014 and 2018 revealed that the original Bronze Age mound originally measured about 65 metres in diameter and 13 metres in height and had successively been enlarged until it reached more than 80 metres in diameter and an estimated 15 metres in height (Fig. 6.2). Like the princely barrows at Leubingen and Helmsdorf, the Bornhöck contained a tent-like wooden central construction protected by stone packing. The dismantling of this funerary monument between c. 1844 and 1890 CE only left parts of the lowest layer of the burial mount more or less unaltered. During the nineteenth century, fertile soil and stone were highly valued material, used

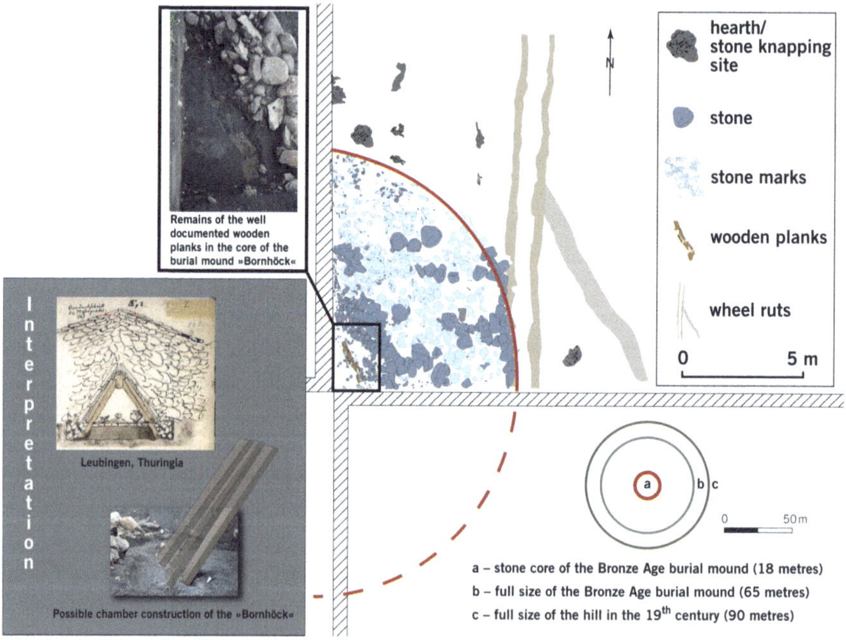

Fig. 6.2 Plan of the large burial mound Bornhöck near Dieskau. It shows the remains of the tent-like burial chamber, the stone packing and the wheel ruts made by the carts used to transport the construction materials (Graphic design by J. Filipp, Bad Bibra)

for agriculture, road construction and houses. By the time of its nineteenth-century destruction, the inner chamber had already been accessed through a shaft and robbed out around the year 1200 CE. Most of the oak beams and planks had decayed or were removed during the nineteenth century. However, well-preserved imprints of the structure's foundations make it possible to establish that the chamber's outer measurements were 5.8 m × 3.5 m which is considerably larger than the chambers of the Leubingen and Helmsdorf graves. As the imprints also allowed us to measure the angle of the diagonal "roof" planks, the height of the tent-like construction must have reached ca. 3 m (Mellerl, 2019a: Fig. 6). A 14C data series taken from preserved wood and charcoal dates the funerary monument to the second half of the nineteenth century or about 1800 BCE (Meller & Schunke, 2016).

According to written sources, the extraordinary gold hoard of Dieskau I was allegedly recovered only three kilometres away from the Bornhöck, in a place called the "Saures Loch" ("Sour or Acrid Hole") in 1874. It appears to have consisted of 13 gold artefacts. While eight of them seem to have been melted down by a Leipzig jeweller, the remaining five gold artefacts (a flanged axe, two ribbed bracelets, one open bracelet and a small lugged ring [*Ösenring*]) were sent to the former Royal Museum in Berlin, from where they were subsequently taken to the Pushkin State Museum in Moscow, Russia, after World War II (Filipp & Freudenreich, 2014). Different observations suggest that the dismantling of the Bornhöck and the discovery of the Dieskau gold are connected. It is most likely that the gold find originated from a secondary chamber of the Bornhöck and was moved to the nearby find-spot "Saures Loch" in an attempt to cover up the workers' illegal extraction of the artefacts from the barrow, which was the property of the local landowner (Meller, 2019a). Typological criteria date the find to the Únětice phase Bz A2b, between ca. 1775 and 1625 BCE, i.e. one to six generations later than the original burial in the Bornhöck.

The Dieskau gold finds represent a key assemblage, which is suitable for assessing both the nature of Circum-Harz Únětice society as well as the Early Bronze Age in Central Europe in general. Golden grave goods and particularly weapons cast in gold distinguish the most exceptional hoards and graves, including political rulers, from the late fourth millennium BCE onwards in Egypt, the Near East and south-eastern Europe (Primas, 1988; Hansen, 2001; Meller & Bunnefeld, 2020). Moreover, the micro-region around Dieskau has yielded the largest quantity of Early Bronze Age metal finds anywhere in Europe, comprising more than 150 kg of bronze and approximately 650 g of gold (cf. Filipp & Freudenreich, 2014)—and potentially more than 1 kg of gold, if the lost Dieskau artefacts are included. Both the Bornhöck mound and the hoards imply that this location was a centre of power over a period of several centuries, starting with the construction of the burial mound around the nineteenth century BCE, and lasting until the period between 1600 and 1550 BCE. Such a power structure has no comparisons in central European prehistory in terms of its longevity (Meller, 2013b: 520–523). With the emergence of a dynastic ruling class, technologies of time measurement, as provided by the Nebra sky, also become critical instruments of legitimation and coercion.

The number of weapons included in the hoards around the Bornhöck implies that the rulers of Dieskau, compared with the previous "princes", commanded the largest army and probably expanded their dominion over much larger territories, possibly comprising the entire Circum-Harz region. The resources and means used and concealed in the construction of their spectacular funerary monument confirm the exceptional economic power of this dominant class.

The Palaeoeconomic Analysis of the Macrolithic Tools of the Bornhöck Monument

The potential of macrolithic tools as key evidence for palaeoeconomic studies stems from the enormous variety of productive functions they performed in prehistoric societies (food processing, mining and metalworking, bone-, leather- and woodwork, tool maintenance and repairing, construction, etc.) and their durability and abundance in the archaeological record. They include abraders, smoothers, polishers, sharpeners, grinding tools, mortars, pestles, axes, moulds, anvils and so forth. Many of them were involved in working processes, which are otherwise hard to detect in the archaeological record. These tools provide crucial data on the social division of work, as well as on the scale of economic activities at the household, settlement and regional levels. Moreover, unlike most archaeological remains, they enable us to approach production quantitatively by assessing the amount of resources used or the number of people supplied, for example, with flour, which was the most common staple food of the European Bronze Age.

A considerable number of macrolithic tools were found in the stone core of the Bornhöck burial mound, which protected its central, tent-like funerary chamber. According to the structural evidence documented during the exploration of the remaining burial mound, the inner cairn had an original diameter of 18.5 m and a height of c. 4 m. The total volume of stones covering the funerary chamber has been estimated around 482 m^3, largely formed by complete or broken glacial boulders and stones broken from the bedrock (Schunke, 2018). Several thousand foundlings and other rocks, some of them measuring up to 0.9 m in length, must have been transported to the site from some distance, mostly 5–15 km and up to 25 km (Schiele, 2020). Many boulders were incorporated into the cairn without any further modification, while others were broken down into smaller stones. Concentrations of rock fragments and grit, identified on the original surface under the barrow, suggest that part of the boulders were crushed on the site (Schunke, 2018: 101). Taking into consideration the geology of the rocks, it can be estimated that the 482 m^3 were equivalent to a weight of 964,000 kg.

The Forces of Production

The productive and demographic implications of the exceptional economic resources placed in the Bornhöck cairn emerge if we consider in the first place the variety of macrolithic artefacts recovered in the remains of the Bornhöck. So far, 71 clearly definable and two unspecific tools have been recovered in the preserved lowest level of the cairn. Further insight is gained if this assemblage is compared with the macrolithic tools of contemporary settlements, such as Eulau, located c. 32 km southwest of the Bornhöck. Here, an excavation of 87,900 m^2, carried out between 2003 and 2005, allowed the discovery of a minimum of 19 typical Únětice longhouses. Although the original house floors were not preserved, 37 macrolithic tools were recovered, mostly from storage and/or garbage pits. While they do not represent the totality of the tools used in the settlements, pits are expected to provide a reliable picture of the everyday garbage and materials disposed of by the community during the occupation of the settlement, which is estimated to have spanned over 200 years, during the classic Únětice phase (Ganslmeier, 2019).

The lithic assemblage from the basal layer of the Bornhöck is not only larger when compared to the artefacts recovered during the extensive excavations of Eulau, but tool types also differ in variety and frequency between the two sites (Fig. 6.3). While grinding slabs and hammerstones are markedly overrepresented at the funerary site, clearly identifiable grinders as well as mortars are missing. As is observed in

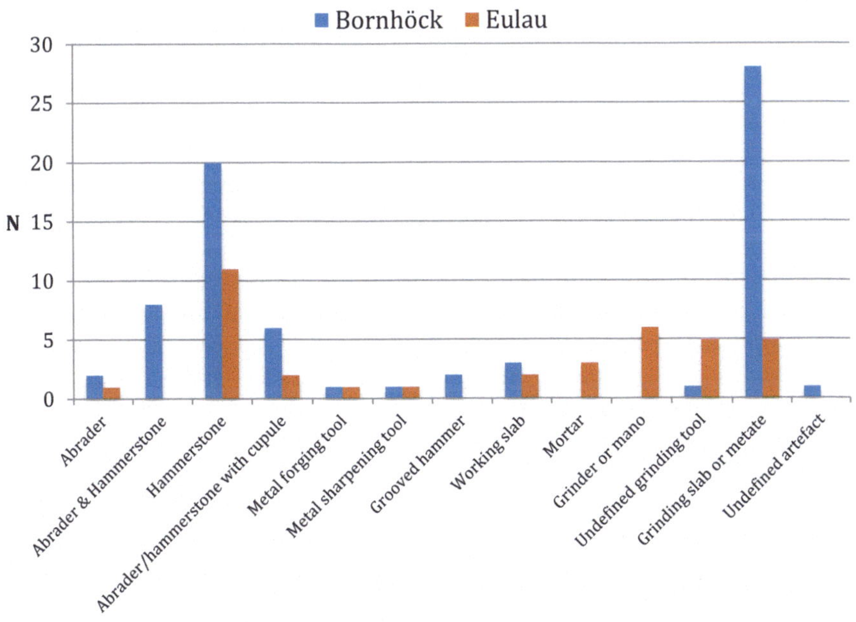

Fig. 6.3 Artefact categories identified in the Bornhöck cairn ($N = 73$) in comparison to the settlement of Eulau ($N = 37$)

Eulau, grinders should be more abundant in the archaeological record than grinding slabs, given their superior material wear (Delgado-Raack & Risch, 2016). Most of the hammerstones found in the Bornhöck show use-wear traces derived from the regular, usually weekly, maintenance of the grinding surfaces. It follows that two out of the three tool categories taking part in cereal processing were specifically selected to form part of the burial mound. The exclusion of the grinders, which are indispensable to carry out the cereal grinding process, is particularly surprising and reveals the specific decisions taken during the building of the barrow.

As grinding slabs and grinders form a tribologically linked equipment and wear concomitantly, it is questionable that the second could have continued in use, after the corresponding grinding slabs had been placed into the burial mound. Considerable abrasive processes would have been required to adjust the grinders to new surfaces, which would only have been possible if the grinders were not very worn down or, in other words, were sufficiently thick to allow the high material loss demanded by the adjustment process. This suggests that grinders might have been (ritually) deposited at a different place, either in a different part of the funerary monument, or, as we suspect, inside or close to the workspaces where they were used, as also seems to have been the case with metal axes (cf. Dermsdorf longhouse).

It cannot be ruled out that some of the artefacts found in the inner part of the Bornhöck might have been related to the construction of the funerary monument. Given the focused accumulation of grinding slabs and hammerstones as construction material, rare artefact types, such as the heavy hammerstones, could be related to the construction of the Bornhöck. This is probably also the case of two heavy grooved hammers. A complete example weighs over 4 kg, while the fragment of a second hammer suggests that this artefact was more than double the size and weight. Such hammers have been found in many El Argar settlements and are not to be mistaken for mining hammers (Delgado-Raack & Risch, 2017). Given the observed use-wear traces, their function seems to be related to construction activities, especially the placing of wooden beams in houses or maybe, during the construction of the funerary chamber of the Bornhöck. The working of the wooden planks and beams on the site was documented during excavations (Meller & Schunke, 2016: 449–452) and would also have required the use of metal axes and adzes, which need to be sharpened and repaired regularly. A sharpening tool and a hammer with traces derived from metal forging and repairing correspond to these activities. The same might also be the case with some of the multifunctional hammerstones/abraders (Fig. 6.3), particularly those showing patterns of pressure marks carried out with a pointed object, such as a bronze chisel or awl. These traces seem to be related to the severance or piercing of materials such as leather, reed or basketry, which were probably used as bags or baskets to carry smaller rocks, grit and earth from the charts, which transported this material to the large burial being constructed. Reed has also been confirmed during excavations and seems to have been used to line and cover the funerary chamber (Schunke, 2018: 101).

In order to identify the economic value of the productive forces placed in the Bornhöck, it is necessary to recognise that recent excavations could recover 12 m^3, or 24,000 kg, of the estimated 482 m^3, or 964,000 kg, of stones used to construct the cairn surrounding the funerary chamber in an unaltered state. In some places, this basal layer reached a maximal thickness of 0.6 m (Meller & Schunke, 2016: 441). Where the original filling had remained in situ, it was formed eminently of stone material, including macrolithic artefacts, while the proportion of soil and sand in the inner cairn was not more than c. 5% (Fig. 6.2). Contrary, few stones and lithic artefacts were observed in the exterior part of the mound with nearly 20,000 m^3 soil (Schunke, 2018: 109), indicating that a clear distinction between the stone and the earthern part of the burial mound was made by its Únětice builders.

The preserved 12 m^3 of the stone core contained the remains of 31 macrolithic artefacts, weighing 1,615.78 kg. Of these, 22 tools are more or less preserved grinding slabs, weighing 1,550.91 kg. This implies that c. 6.7% of the materials used to construct the excavated lowest 0.6 m of the stone cairn of the Bornhöck mound consisted of stone tools, mainly grinding slabs, some of which must have weighed over 175 kg. However, written reports from the nineteenth and twentieth centuries, describing the destruction of the funerary mound and some of its archaeological finds, suggest that large grinding slabs were also present in the upper layers of the stone core. If we take the material of the well-documented 12 m^3 as a reference, it is possible to establish that c. 64,900 kg of the cairn would be macrolithic artefacts, of which 62,295 kg correspond to grinding slabs. As the mean weight of the grinding slabs recovered from the Bornhöck can be estimated to have been 105 kg, *the total number of slabs is estimated to have been 593.*

A different method to estimate the total amount of tools placed in the cairn can be applied, using the minimum number of grinding slabs. Taking into account the degree of fragmentation of the 22 slabs recovered from the preserved 12 m^3 of the cairn, their minimum number corresponds to 13.6 tools. As nothing suggests that the proportion and distribution of macrolithic tools were uneven in the 482 m^3 of the stone core, the projection of this minimum number on the whole cairn implies that *546 grinding slabs were built into the burial mound.*

Such a volume of grinding tools clearly corresponds to a large population. How many artefacts were available at each moment in the longhouses is difficult to estimate, but our own ethno-archaeological studies in the compounds of extended families in northern Ghana and central Mali suggest that large households usually owned 2–3 grinding slabs and grinders, several small abraders and hammerstones, as well as some sharpening stones. Rarely, more than 6–10 stone tools are available at each time in a compound formed by 12–24 persons (see also Roux, 1986 for households in Mauritania; Gronenborn, 1994 for Northeast Nigeria; Hamon & Le Gall, 2013: Fig. 8 for Mali).

One factor, which appears particularly constant in cross-cultural comparisons, is the number of grinding tools available in the households. As cereal grinding in America, Africa and Asia is regularly assigned to women, the number of slabs and grinders tends to be equal to the number of adult women living in the houses (Horsfall, 1987; Hamon & Le Gall, 2013: 117–118; Robitaille, 2016: 429–456; Alonso, 2019). Some artefacts might be stored, in the foresight that production of flour needs to be increased or tools might break. Usually, women use the same tool kid until its material exhaustion or breakage, given the close kinetic relation between body weight and size, and the tools in this physically highly demanding activity. This work organisation only changes, if cereal grinding is carried out at a supra-domestic level, usually under the control of a state or a dominant class. These specialised workshops are well documented in the archaeological record and through iconographic evidence, as well as in texts (Grégoire, 1992). A large number of persons, both men and female, were working in these buildings and grinding cereal simultaneously on standardised tools. Slaves or captives are also reported to have been forced to carry out this strenuous work (Schirokauer & Brown, 2006: 89–90; Díaz del Castillo, 1992 [1577]). A particularly impressive example is provided by Hittite sources, which refer to blind prisoners who had to work in milling houses (Beal, 2016: 38–39; Trimm, 2017: 350–351). Before we continue to delve into the cereal economy illustrated by the Bornhöck macrolithic assemblage, it is necessary to analyse the technical features and intensity of the use of the grinding tools.

Artefact Wear Intensity

The preservation of tools is always a critical variable in order to understand the organisation of production and discard. The first difference noted between the macrolithic artefacts of the Bornhöck princely grave and the settlement of Eulau, is their different breakage pattern. Around 58% of tools recovered from the remnants of the funerary cairn are still complete, while small fragments only represent c. 30% of the sample (Fig. 6.4). Moreover, most of the fractures observed on the damaged artefacts show a recent sheen and not the patina resulting from meteorisation and oxidation, which usually appears on the original surfaces. It follows that most artefacts were broken

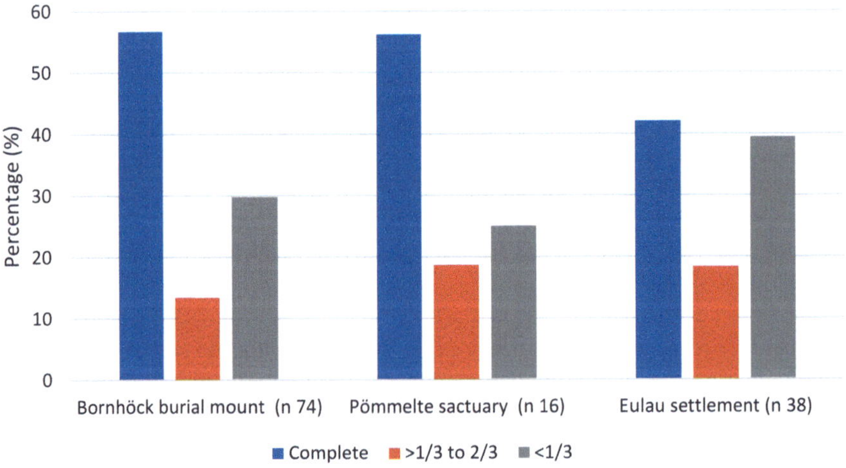

Fig. 6.4 Percentage values for the three categories of preservation of macrolithic artefacts

as a direct or indirect consequence of the dismantling of the burial in the nineteenth century AD. Two unpublished reports from 1915 to 1917 (Pritschöna, MQ, OA-ID 2039 and "Sammlung Berger") also mention the presence of complete and exceptionally large grinding slabs, which had been carried away—partly by horses—during the dismantling of the burial mound and were kept by private owners. As we found only seven fragments which refitted into three artefacts, all the missing parts must have been carried away from the site for constructive purposes. Contrary, in the case of Eulau, only 42% of the artefacts are complete, and 40% are fragments, presenting ancient fractures. The difference between both values (complete artefacts and fragments) corresponds to slightly damaged artefacts (for the methodological background, see Risch, 2002; Delgado-Raack, 2013). The material from the Bell Beaker and early Únětice ritual enclosure of Pömmelte, where several stone tool deposits have been defined (Spatzier, 2017), has a similar preservation stage as the Bornhöck after the nineteenth-century dismantling works (Fig. 6.4).

Another way to approach the wear intensity of tools is to measure the material loss that took place during their use-life in other words, their degree of mechanical exhaustion (Fig. 6.4). In the case of grinding tools, this loss is best expressed by the wear index of the querns (Risch, 2002: 54). The four more or less well-preserved querns from Eulau have a mean minimum thickness of 91.5 mm, with a standard deviation of 30.8 mm. In contrast, in the case of 15 grinding slabs of the Bornhöck where the original minimum thickness can still be measured, the mean value is 289 ± 92.4 mm. In conclusion, the Bornhöck grinding slabs are not only heavier but also less used than the Eulau examples (Fig. 6.5). Furthermore, the reports mention that the very large grinding slabs carried away in the nineteenth century AD were "noch wenig benutzt" (only slightly used) (Pritschöna, MQ, OA-ID 2039, page 9).

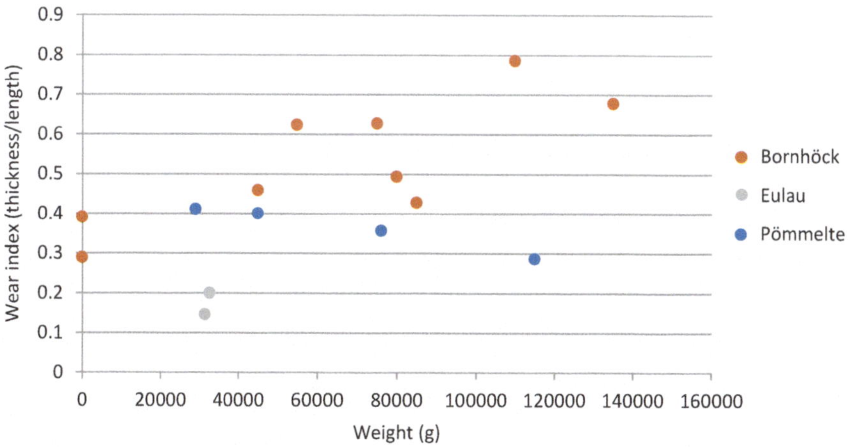

Fig. 6.5 Use intensity of complete grinding slabs in three different Únětice sites, expressed by the relation between absolute weight and relative wear index, in which high or low values represent a short or a long tool use, respectively

It follows that these grinding slabs were perfectly operative, when they were placed in the Bornhöck cairn. Experimental tests suggest that grinding slabs made out of sandstone and used daily in household contexts, wear down c. 10 mm in thickness, per year (Wright, 1993). This would imply that, on average, the Bornhöck querns could have been used for another 20 years before breaking, if they were used in a domestic context, which, as is still to be discussed, does not seem likely. Yet, it must also be taken into account that the Únětice grinding slabs were made of significantly harder rocks, such as granite, gneiss and porphyry, than the sandstone used by Wright. In any case, the Bornhöck querns were perfectly operative and could still have been used for the next decades, rather than years if they had remained in their original workspaces.

Similar calculations can be carried out with the smaller-sized artefacts used in percussion, pounding and abrading processes. In this case, however, their presence in the cairn could be due to different causes. Hammerstones are required for the regular roughening or sharpening of the grinding tools, while other tools could have served directly on-site performing building tasks when constructing the barrow (Fig. 6.6). Concentrations of rock fragments and grit, identified under the funerary mound, confirm that porphyry and sandstone blocks were crushed on the site (Schunke, 2018: 101). Taking into account the different technological and mechanical requirements of both types of activities, a bimodal use is reflected by differences in artefact weight and thickness (Fig. 6.7). Most of the hammerstones mirror the pattern known from settlements, such as Eulau, confirming that they were brought to the Bornhöck together with the grinding slabs, once they had fulfilled a certain amount of sharpening in relation to grinding equipment. A second thicker and heavier type of hammer, so far unknown in domestic contexts, seems to have been used during the preparation of the chamber for inserting beams or doing other kinds of "brickwork". In both cases, the macrolithic materials of the Bornhöck cairn were perfectly functional artefacts, and many of them were still at an initial stage of their use-life.

The Cereal Grinding Technology of Únětice

The technical characteristics of the purposefully buried grinding slabs provide the final clue to the meaning of the stone artefacts of the Bornhöck. The first outstanding aspect is their weight and dimensions. The size and shape of the working surfaces are directly linked to the amount of flour produced and to the workforce required by this production. The shapes of the surfaces are described in terms of their longitudinal and transversal profiles (Hürlimann, 1965; Zimmermann, 1988; Adams, 1993; Risch, 1995). Three mechanical premises play the determining role in the productivity of grinding equipment, which is understood as the amount of flour gained per unit of time: (a) the more accurate/precise the correspondence/matching between the active surfaces of grinding slab and grinder, the higher their efficiency, (b) the larger the contacting areas, the higher their efficiency and (c) the larger the contacting areas,

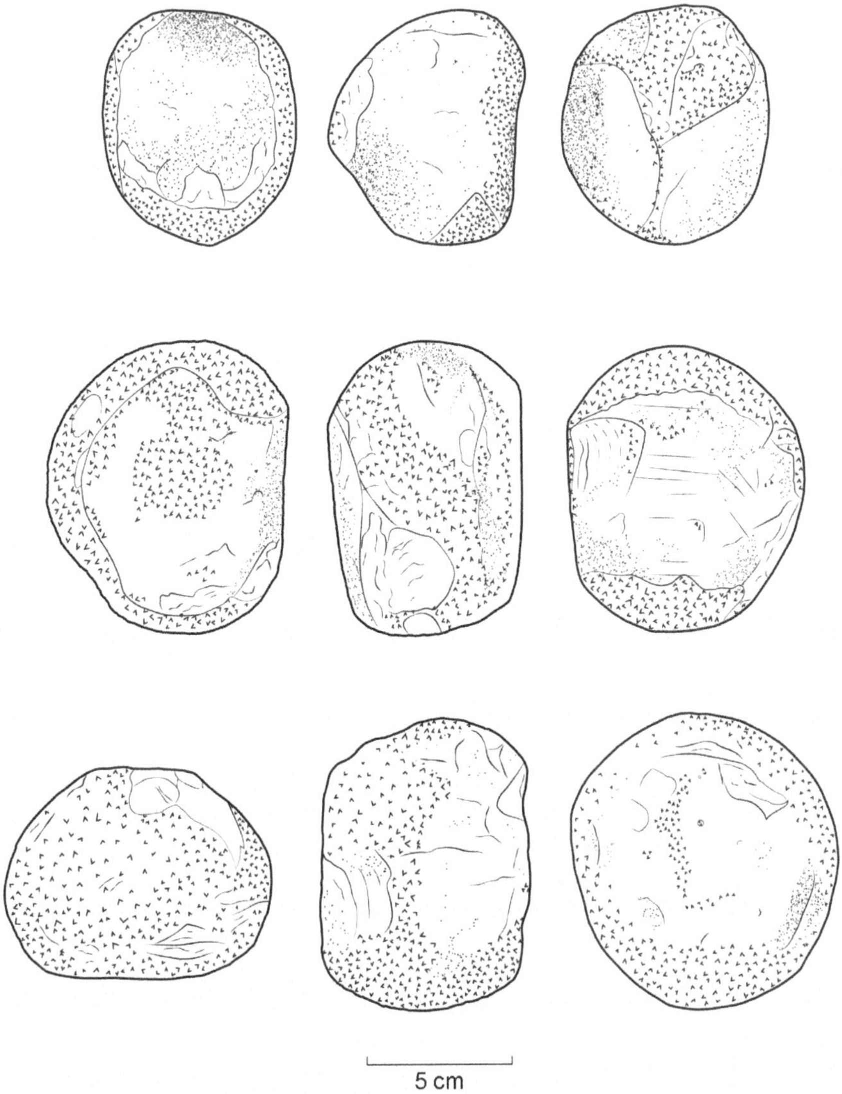

Fig. 6.6 Three hammerstones and pressure platforms shown from different sides, found in the Bornhöck barrow with use wear traces caused by roughening grinding slabs, crushing stone, and other heavy-duty tasks (drawing by M. Eguíluz)

the heavier the grinders and, consequently, the more physical strength that will be required to perform the grinding process.

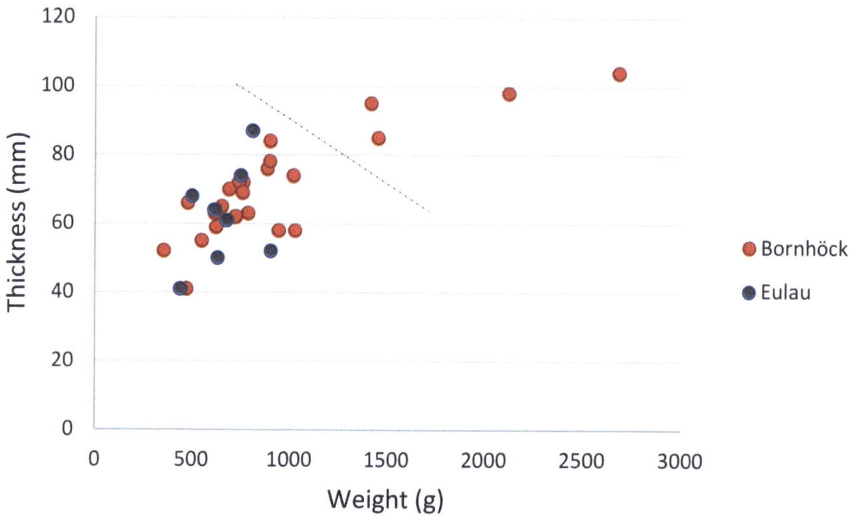

Fig. 6.7 Metric features of hammerstones/abraders used for different tasks

Four basic types of grinding equipment are found in the ethnological and archaeological records of cereal-based economies, using stone against stone technology.[4] In general terms, they can be divided into mechanisms using one-handed and two-handed grinders, which is often related to the surface area in their reciprocal contact. Two-handed grinders will exert much higher pressure on the grain than the one-handed grinders, allowing for faster processing of flour. Experiments have also confirmed that grinding in trough and flat grinding slabs was twice as productive as in wider, basin-shaped slabs (Adams, 1993). Additionally, grinders can be moved freely on the grinding surface or have fixed course, as in the case of overlapping, usually concave grinders, or of trough grinding slabs. In the latter case, a more standardised forth and back trajectory of the grinder along the longitudinal axis of the quern allows a fully mechanical movement, hindering lateral deviation of the grinder, which would cause unnecessary oblique movements. As a result, the use of basin-shaped as well as flat grinding slabs implies longer work processes in comparison with fixed grinding equipment. However, as Adams has already stated, the fixed grinding slabs do not allow the operator to vary his or her stroke in order to relieve muscle stress (Adams, 1993: 336–340).

In the specific case of the Bornhöck, these technological differences get even clearer. Compared with the Central European Neolithic as well as other Early Bronze Age assemblages, the Bornhöck grinding slabs are by far the heaviest and largest specimens discovered so far (Fig. 6.8). If we reconstruct the original size of some fragmented artefacts weighing 125 and 175 kg, some grinding slabs would have been

[4]Other material combinations are also possible, as is the case in south-east Iberia, where the use of wooden grinders and stone grinding slabs was experimentally and traceologically demontrated for the Early Bronze Age (Risch, 2002).

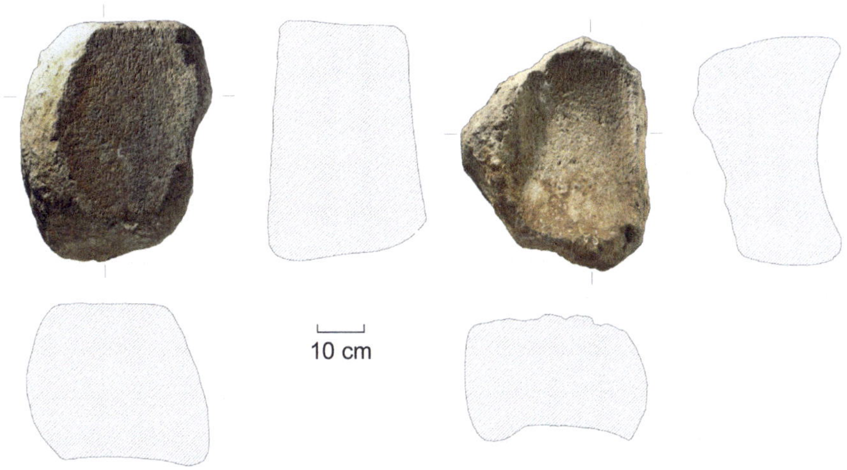

Fig. 6.8 Two complete grinding slabs from the Bornhöck cairn. The left slab shows a very early stage of use; the right one starts developing the typical trough (drawing by M. Eguíluz)

larger than 740 mm in length, 625 mm in width and 400 mm in thickness. Hence, the expected contact area between grinding slab and grinder was higher in the case of the grinding equipment of the Bornhöck than for any other known archaeological context in Prehistoric Europe. This suggests that an increased productive capacity was intended (in terms of flour yielded per unit of time), due to the wide area of grinding surfaces in reciprocal contact.

Regarding the morphological features of the grinding equipment, the Bornhöck shows another particularity (Table 6.1). During the preceding Neolithic period, overlapping, concave grinders were predominantly used on grinding slabs for cereal grinding (type A, Table 6.1), while flat grinding surfaces were only occasionally in use (type B, Table 6.1). At the end of this period, however, the number of flat tools clearly increased and their use lasted throughout the Bronze Age (Graefe, 2009: 76; Gundelach, 2012). In the Bornhöck a totally new kind of grinding technology appears, namely the trough-shaped grinding slab operated with a fixed grinder (type C2; Table 6.1). Many of the type B and C1 slabs found in the cairn would have also developed a clear trough had their use-life and wear been prolonged. Similar artefacts have been observed in the sanctuary of Pömmelte, where this technology is attested for the first time in the Early Bronze Age Saxony-Anhalt (c. 2300–2050 BCE). Here, both the grinding slabs and their grinders were deposited in the shaft-like deposition pits cut into the circular ditch (Fig. 6.9). In contrast, this technology is absent in the Eulau settlement (Table 6.1). Simple basin (type C1) and saddle-shaped slabs (type A) seem to have been the predominant equipment, and the size of their grinding surface is significantly smaller than at the Bornhöck, as should be expected in domestic contexts.

The presence of trough-shaped grinding equipment in ritual sites such as Pömmelte and Bornhöck does not seem to be a mere coincidence and highlights

Table 6.1 Absolute frequencies of morphologically described grinding elements (grinding slab and grinder) for Neolithic and Bronze Age settlements and ritual sites of Central Europe. *Following Zimmermann's typological proposal, Kegler-Graiewski (2007) and Graefe (2009) subdivided type C into two subtypes, which have been defined by Adams as basin and trough *metates*, well known among the Pueblo Indians (Adams, 1993: Fig. 2)

Types according to Zimmermann (1988)	A	B	C*		References
Morphology of grinding equipment	Concave-convex quern/overlapping grinder	Flat quern/flat grinder	(C1) Basin quern/Small, convex grinder	(C2) Trough quern/Large, fixed grinder	
Langweiler 8 (Early Neolithic)	All grinding stones belong to this type of equipment	–	–	–	Zimmermann (1988)
Breitenbach (Early Neolithic)	9/62	5/1	2/0	–	Zamzow (2020)
Goseck (Early Neolithic)	5/4	0/1	–	–	Zamzow (in preparation)
North Hesse (Recent and Late Neolithic)	64/121	9/1	4/0	–	Kegler-Graiewski (2007)
Central Europe (Neolithic)	Predominantly	Occasionally	–	–	Graefe (2009)
Pömmelte (Early Bronze Age)	–	0/1	6/0	2/3	Unpublished
Eulau (Early Bronze Age)	1/1	0/1	3/2	–	Unpublished
Bornhöck (Early Bronze Age)	–	9/0	10/0	5/0	Unpublished

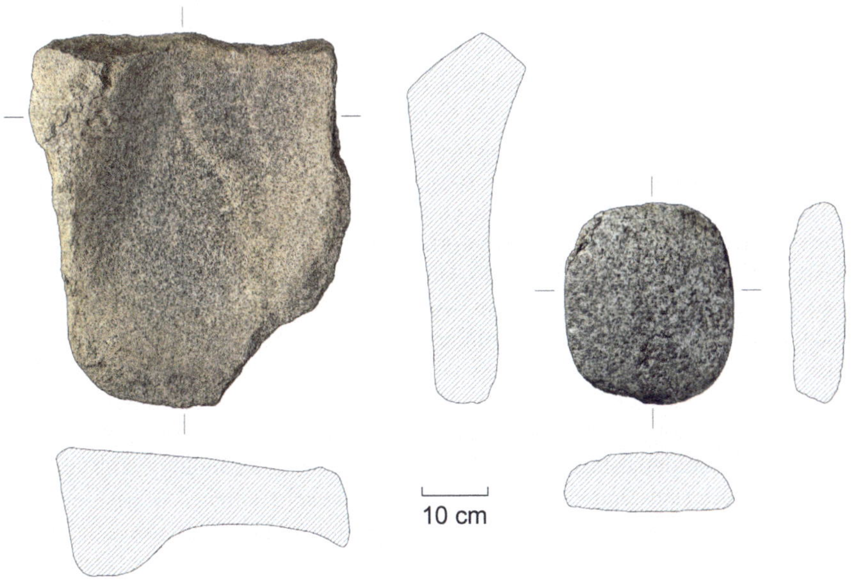

Fig. 6.9 Trough-shaped grinding slab (left) with corresponding grinder (right) from Pömmelte. The slab weighs 45 kg. The grinder weighs 11.5 kg (drawing by M. Eguíluz)

the link between a new, more intensive technology with monumental places of high ideological and political relevance. In comparison with the Neolithic grinding tradition, the trough type is an inverted version of type A grinding technology (Table 6.1), which implies a replacement of the overlapping grinders by much heavier grinders dragged through a trough, whose depth increases along with the use-life of the slab. On the other hand, unlike in the case of type A, the trough-shaped slabs would have favoured that grinding stock could stay longer on the active side before being totally ground. Pömmelte and Bornhöck were political and ritual sites with a much more intense flour production, and separated from the domestic sphere.

This grinding technology is exceptional in its European context. Although, a profound change has also been observed at the beginning of the El Argar Early Bronze Age in south-eastern Spain, around 2200 BCE, which saw the introduction of narrow concave/convex grinding tools operated with wooden grinders, no trough-shaped grinding slabs are known from El Argar sites (Delgado-Raack & Risch, 2015). They are also not known in the whole Aegean Neolithic and Bronze Age (Runnels, 1981). The development of grinding technologies is also different in the north of the Italian Peninsula (Dal Ri, 1994). Trough *metates* are well studied in the Southwest of the US, where they were introduced sometime after 200 AD (Adams, 1999). Their appearance has been linked to the introduction of a new variety of corn (*maíz del ocho*), though other socio-economic factors still need to be considered. A similar change occurred in central Germany at the transition from the Bell Beaker to the Únětice period. In comparison with all other archaeological and contemporary contexts, where information on the shape and weight of grinders is available, the Únětice C2 type tools are clearly exceptional (Table 6.2). In mean terms, they are nearly twice as heavy as the domestic grinders documented in present-day north-eastern Ghana and at least three times heavier than any Neolithic artefact recorded in Central Europe. As heavier grinders slow the path of the grinding stroke, large trough querns possibly represent the most efficient grinding technology before the introduction of the rotary mill. However, this efficiency, resulting from their larger abrasive surfaces, depends on greater work efforts and, consequently leads to greater physical exhaustion (Hard et al., 1996; Hamon & Le Gall, 2013: 116).

As grinding is always a strenuous work and no significant changes have been observed so far in the cereal record of the Early Bronze Age (Kretschmer & Harbig, 2019; M. Hellmund, LDA Saxony-Anhalt, personal communication), the introduction of a trough technology implies a change in the mode of production as well as of consumption. The more intense workload suggests that part of the cereal grinding activities left the domestic sphere, where the traditional technology with type A, concave/convex slabs and comparatively light grinders continued to be used. The exceptional size of the trough slabs and corresponding grinders even raises the possibility that the latter were operated by two persons, each placed on opposed ends of the slab.[5] The grinding slabs buried in the Bornhöck seem to point to a relation between the political organisation of Únětice and cereal production with this more specialised and work-intensive technology. The control of specific grinding technology, which was probably restricted to specific workshops, appears to be a critical factor in the maintenance as well as ideology of the Únětice ruling class, which needed to be massively underscored in its emblematic funerary monument.

Conclusion

The macrolithic material recovered from the remains of the Bornhöck burial mound offers the first evidence concerning the economic power of the ruling class in Únětice Bronze Age society. Considering the original dimension of the funerary monument which was dismantled during the nineteenth century CE, it has been possible to estimate that between 540 and 600 grinding slabs were transported and built into the stone cairn covering its central funerary chamber. In agricultural economies such as Únětice (Knipper et al., 2015), the number of grinding tools is directly related to the size of the community which needs to be sustained. According to ethnographic observations from domestic contexts of Africa, America and Asia, a cereal grinding stone tends to be used daily to obtain flour required to nourish 4–5 individuals (Risch, 2002: 232–236). In such a scenario, between 2400 and 2700 persons could be supplied with the means concealed in the Bornhöck barrow. However, it has been shown that the Bornhöck grinding technology is excessive in a domestic context. The size,

[5]First experimental tests support this operative option where one person is placed at each side of the grinding slab.

Table 6.2 Type and weight of grinders in different archaeological and contemporary contexts. *This weight belongs to a unique artefact, and is not representative. **The 9250 g grinder documented in Bende (Ghana) was considered by all other women, except the owner, an excessive tool and which they would not use

Context & Nr	Chronology	Shape	Weight-X	Weight- Std.dev.	Weight-Min.	Weight-Max	References
Langweiler 8 (*N* = 6)	LBK	Concave/convex	3873 g	1786 g	1805 g	6650 g	Zimmermann (1988: Fig. 645)
Paris Basin (*N* = c. 46)	Early Neolithic	Convex/convex	1378 g	–	c. 300 g	c. 2500 g	Hamon (2006: 45)
Dietfurt (*N* = 5)	Chamer K. (c. 3000–2700 BCE)	Variable	2970 g	1149 g	1490 g	4550 g	Böhner (1997) (grinders identified by authors)
Vinça, Central Balcans	c. 5400–4600 BCE	Variable	c. 1500 g	c. 1300 g	311 g	4329 g	Vučković (2019: Tables 6.1–6.4)
Alimizaraque (*N* = 15)	Copper Age 2850–2200 BCE	Highly variable	927 g	337 g	500 g	1900 g	Risch (2008: P0/5tab2)
Cerro de la Virgen, SE Iberia (*N* = 20)	Bell Beaker 2500–2200 BCE	Mainly straight/straight; convex/convex	484 g	216 g	278 g	1250 g	Delgado-Raack (2013)
La Bastida, SE Iberia	El Argar 2200–1550 BCE	Mainly concave/convex	2540 g	1233 g	554 g	11,600 g*	Ache (2019: 169ff.)
Marki Alonia, Cyprus (*N* = 32)	EC II-MCII 2400–1700 BCE	Convex/convex	5764 g	2040 g	2800 g	12,000 g	Frankel and Webb (2006: 224, Table 6.8)
NE Ghana (*N* = 5)	Twenty-first century CE	Concave/convex	5900 g	2091 g	4000 g	9250 g*	Unpublished
Pömmelte (*N* = 3) Kleinpaschleben (*N* = 1)	Bell Beaker-Únětice 2300–2050 BCE	C2 type (trough)	11,100 g	1606 g	9700 g	11,500 g	Unpublished

weight and shape of the grinding tools indicate a specialised cereal production, which demanded a large workforce, probably working more intensively than in a domestic sphere. Written documents report that in centrally controlled Mesopotamian mills, an average of 7 litres and up to 9.25 litres of flour could be produced per person/grinding slab per day (Grégoire, 1992: 331; 1999: 229). Larger and heavier grinding tools, together with longer grain processing sessions could easily have allowed a 50% increase of production, covering the daily needs in carbohydrates of 3600–4050 individuals.

The situation observed in Únětice settlements, such as Eulau, further implies that this production was not linked to the common longhouses, where the simpler technology, derived from Neolithic traditions, continued in use. It follows, that the large trough grinding slabs, with extensive working surfaces, supplied food to a different group of persons and/or at different occasions, unrelated to the domestic sphere. The fact that large trough querns have been found at a certain distance from longhouse settlements in Central Germany provides further support to the socio-economic difference between both subsistence technologies. It is also questionable whether these heavy grinding tools could have been operated by the dwellers of the usual longhouses, who continued to use the Neolithic technology for the everyday needs of the domestic sphere. The simultaneous use of the over 500 grinding tools placed in the Bornhöck mound, whose operation demands exceptional physical force, starts to highlight the existence of an exploited class, directly bound to the Dieskau rulers. In sum, slaves or servants and a clientele class are the suspected protagonists at each end of the production and consumption cycle. While the flour they produced could have supplied specialised craftsmen/women and above all the ruling class itself, the dimension of production implied by the artefacts placed in the Bornhöck mainly points towards a standing military force as the main recipient of this subsistence good.[6] It is difficult to oversee a ritual and political connection between the deposition of weapons in hoards and the concealment of the grinding equipment, which was indispensable to feed substantial forces or clientele, in the funerary monument of a dominant ruler. In both cases, the replacement of hundreds of weapons and food processing tools requires a supra-domestic level of economic organisation, such as that of a state, capable of mobilising substantial resources and extensive exchange networks.

The Bornhöck does not seem to have been the only Early Bronze Age funerary monument, which demonstrates this relation between grinding technology and political domination. The barrow of Szczepankowice Ia, dated around 1940–1885 cal BCE, contained 34 querns (Sarnowska, 1969; Pokutta, 2014: 139), of significant size and weight (Furmanek et al., 2015: 94). They also seem to have been present in

[6]Their variable wear and their position in the core of the mound exclude the possibility that these tools were manufactured and used specifically to supply the workforce in charge of the construction of the Bornhöck.

the well-known princely grave of Łęki Małe (Pokutta, 2014: 139); although this is not confirmed by Furmanek et al. (2015: 94).[7]

Our study suggests that the Únětice "princes" did not only derive their wealth from salt exploitation or central German copper, as has often been assumed (e.g. Montelius, 1900: 77–78; Jahn, 1950: 86), but also on the control of part of the cereal production and turned it into surplus profit. This economic power would have allowed to maintain a standing army and probably other types of clientele such organisation of specialised forces of production and of violence form the economic and military foundations of state societies.

Acknowledgements We acknowledge the support of Marina Eguíluz and José Antonio Soldevilla in the study and documentation of the macrolithic tools of Saxony-Anhalt. The authors are also grateful to Konstanze Geppert and Jan-Heinrich Bunnefeld for their feedback on a previous version of the paper and to Louis Nebelsick for editing the final text.

This research is supported by the State Office for Heritage Management and Archaeology of Saxony-Anhalt and by grants from the Spanish Ministry of Economy and Competitiveness (HAR2017-85962-P), the AGAUR of the Generalitat de Catalunya (2017SGR1044) and the ICREA Academia programme.

Bibliography

Ache, M. (2019). *Los artefactos macrolíticos de los asentamientos argáricos de La Bastida y Tira del Lienzo (Totana, Murcia): Una aproximación a la dinámica económica y social del sudeste de la Península Ibérica (2200–1550 cal ANE).* Tesis Doctoral Universitat Autònoma de Barcelona.

Adams, J. L. (1993). Towards understanding the technological development of manos and matates. *Kiva, 58,* 331–344.

Adams, J. L. (1999). Refocusing the role of food-grinding tools as correlates for subsistence strategies in the U.S., Southwest. *American Antiquity, 64,* 475–498.

Alonso, N. (2019). A first approach to women, tools and operational sequences in traditional manual cereal grinding. *Archaeological and Anthropological Sciences, 11,* 4307–4324.

Beal, R. H. (2016). Disabilities from head to foot in Hittite civilization. In C. Laes (Ed.), *Disability in antiquity* (pp. 37–46). Routledge.

Behrendt, S., Küßner, M., & Mecking, O. (2015). Der Hortfund von Dermsdorf, Lkr. Sömmerda – Erste archäometrische Ergebnisse. In T. Gluhak, S. Greiff, K. Kraus, & M. Prange (Eds.), *Archäometrie und Denkmalpflege 2015, Jahrestagung an der Johannes-Gutenberg-Universität Mainz 25.–28. März 2015.* Metalla Sonderhefte 7 (pp. 98–100). Deutsches Bergbaumuseum.

Bertemes, F. (2020). Ein fürstliches Opfer. In H. Meller & M. Schefzik (Eds.), *Die Welt der Himmelsscheibe von Nebra – Neue Horizonte. Begleitband zur Sonderausstellung im Landesmuseum für Vorgeschichte Halle (Saale), 4. Juni 2021 bis zum 9. Januar 2022* (pp. 136–139). Landesamt für Denkmalpflege und Archäologie Sachsen-Anhalt.

Böhner, U. (1997). *Die Felssteingeräte der endneolithischen Siedlung von Dietfurt a. d. Altmühl, Lkr. Neumarkt i. d. Opf.* Archäologie am Main-Donau Kanal 10. Verlag Marie Leidorf.

Chapman, R. W. (2003). *Archaeologies of complexity.* Routledge.

[7] "This is the only known case of worked stone being used as building materials in the princely graves of the Early Bronze Age Europe" (Furmanek et al., 2015: 94).

Contreras, F. (2009–2010). Los grupos agáricos de la alta Andalucía: patrones de asentamiento y urbanismo. El poblado de Peñalosa (Baños de la Encina, Jaén). *Anales de Prehistoria y Arqueología* 25–26: 49–76.

Dal Ri, L. (1994). La macine come problema archeologico. Alcune considerazioni. In *Il grano e le macine. La macinazione di cereali in Alto Adige dall'Antichità al Medioevo* (pp. 51–72). Museo Provinciale di Castel Tirolo.

Delgado-Raack, S. (2013). *Tecnotipología y distribución especial del material macrolítico del Cerro de la Virgen de Orce (Granada).* BAR International Series 2518. Archaeopress.

Delgado-Raack, S., & Risch, R. (2015). Social change and subsistence production on the Iberian Peninsula during the 3rd and 2nd millennia BCE. In J. Kneisel, M. Dal Corso, W. Kirleis, H. Scholz, N. Taylor, & V. Tiedtke (Eds.), *The third food revolution? Setting the Bronze Age table: Common trends in economic and subsistence strategies in Bronze Age Europe. Proceedings of the International Workshop "Socio-Environmental Dynamics over the Last 12,000 Years: The Creation of Landscapes III" (15th – 18th April 2013) in Kiel,* Universitätsforschungen zur prähistorischen Archäologie 283 (pp. 22–47). Habelt.

Delgado-Raack, S., & Risch, R. (2016). Bronze Age cereal processing in southern Iberia: A material approach to the production and use of grinding equipment. *Journal of Lithic Studies, 3*(3), 125–145.

Delgado-Raack, S., & Risch, R. (2017). La producción de las "mazas de minero" en el contexto clásico de los poblados argáricos del sudeste peninsular. In L. J. García-Pulido, L. Arboledas, E. Alarcón, & F. Contreras (Eds.), *Presente y Futuro de los Paisajes Mineros del pasado. Estudios sobre minería, metalurgia y poblamiento* (pp. 19–30). Universidad de Granada y la Sociedad Española para la Defensa del Patrimonio Geológico y Minero (SEDPGYM).

Díaz del Castillo, B. (1992 [1577]). *Historia verdadera de la conquista de la Nueva España.* Espasa Calpe.

Evers, M. (2012). *Die frühbronzezeitliche Besiedlung der Makroregion um Nebra.* Halle (Saale), unpublished Ph.D thesis, Martin-Luther-Universität Halle-Wittenberg.

Evers, M., & Witt, M. (2019). Die frühbronzezeitliche Besiedlung der Makroregion um Nebra – Siedlungsstrukturelle Untersuchungen und GIS basierte Geofaktorenanalysen. In H. Meller & F. Bertemes (Eds.), *Der Aufbruch zu Neuen Horizonten. Neue Sichtweisen zur europäischen Frühbronzezeit, Abschlusstagung der Forschergruppe FOR 550 vom 26.–29. November 2010 in Halle (Saale).* Tagungen des Landesmuseums für Vorgeschichte Halle 19 (pp. 293–323). Landesamt für Denkmalpflege und Archäologie Sachsen-Anhalt.

Filipp, J., & Freudenreich, M. (2014). Dieskau Revisited I. Nachforschungen zur „Lebensgeschichte" des Goldhortes von Dieskau und zu einem weiteren Grabhügel mit Goldbeigabe bei Osmünde im heutigen Saalekreis, Sachsen-Anhalt. In H. Meller, R. Risch, & E. Pernicka (Eds.), *Metalle der Macht – Frühes Gold und Silber, 6. Mitteldeutscher Archäologentag vom 17. bis 19. Oktober 2013 in Halle (Saale).* Tagungen des Landesmuseums für Vorgeschichte Halle 11 (pp. 743–752). Landesamt für Denkmalpflege und Archäologie Sachsen-Anhalt.

Frankel, D., & Webb, J. M. (2006). *Marki Alonia—An early and middle Bronze Age settlement in Cyprus: Excavations 1995–2000.* Paul Åströms.

Furmanek, M., Gralak, T., Mackiewicz, M., & Pokutta, D. A. (2015). Archaeological potential of the Early Bronze Age barrow burial ground in Szczepankowice: A geophysical survey and field evaluation. *Śląskie Sprawozdania Archeologiczne, 57,* 93–106.

Ganslmeier, R. (2019). Siedlungen des Spätneolithikums und der Frühbronzezeit auf der Lützen-Hohenmölsener Platte zwischen Saale und Weißer Elster (Eulau und Bösau, beide Burgenlandkreis). In H. Meller, S. Friederich, M. Küßner, H. Stäuble, & R. Risch (Eds.), *Siedlungsarchäologie des Endneolithikums und der frühen Bronzezeit - Late Neolithic and Early Bronze Age Settlement Archaeology, 11. Mitteldeutscher Archäologentag vom 18. bis 20. Oktober 2018 in Halle (Saale),* Tagungen des Landesmuseums für Vorgeschichte Halle 20 (pp. 325–340). Landesamt für Denkmalpflege und Archäologie Sachsen-Anhalt.

Graefe, J. (2009). Mahlsteine: Funktion, Fertigung und Verbreitung. *Archäologische Informationen, 32*(1–2), 75–81.

Grégoire, J.-P. (1992). Les grandes unités de transformation des céréales: l'exemple des minoteries de la Mésopotamie du sud à la fin du IIIe millénaire avant notre ère. In P. C. Anderson (Ed.), *Préhistoire de l'agriculture: nouvelles approches expérimentales et ethnographiques*. Monographie du CRA 6 (pp. 321–339). Editions du CNRS.

Grégoire, J.-P. (1999). Major units for the transformation of grain: The grain-grinding households of southern Mesopotamia at the end of the third millennium BCE. In P. C. Anderson (Ed.), *Prehistory of agriculture—New experimental and ethnographic approaches*. Institute of Archaeology Monograph 40 (pp. 223–238). UCLA.

Gronenborn, D. (1994). Ethnoarchäologische Untersuchungen zur rezenten Herstellung und Nutzung von Mahlsteinen in Nordost-Nigeria. In M. Fansa (Ed.), *Experimentelle Archäologie in Deutschland 8* (pp. 45–55). Oldenburg.

Gundelach, M. J. (2012). *Die Mahlsteine aus der spätneolithischen Siedlung Okolište (Bosnien-Herzegowina): von der Klassifikation zur sozialarchäologischen Aussage*. Kiel: unpublished MA thesis, Philosophische Fakultät der Christian-Albrechts-Universität.

Hamon, C. (2006). *Broyage et abrasion au Néolithique ancien. Caractérisation technique et fonctionnelle de l'outillage en grès du Bassin parisien*. BAR International Series 1551. Archaeopress.

Hamon, C., & Le Gall, V. (2013). Millet and sauce: The uses and functions of querns among the Minyanka (Mali). *Journal of Anthropological Archaeology, 32*(1), 109–121.

Hansen, S. (2001). Waffen aus Gold und Silber während des 3. und frühen 2. Jahrtausends v. Chr. in Europa und Vorderasien. In H. Born & S. Hansen (Eds.), *Helme und Waffen Alteuropas*, Sammlung Axel Guttmann 9 (pp. 11–59). Philipp von Zabern.

Hard, R. J., Mauldin, R. P., & Raymond, G. R. (1996). Mano size, stable carbon isotope ratios, and macrobotanical remains as multiple lines of evidence of maize dependence in the American Southwest. *Journal of Archaeological Method and Theory, 3*, 253–318.

Horsfall, G. (1987). Design theory and grinding stones. In B. Hayden (Ed.), *Lithic studies among the contemporary Highland Maya* (pp. 332–377). The University of Arizona Press.

Hürlimann, F. (1965). Neolithische Reibmühlen von einer Ufersiedlung am Greifensee. *Jahrbuch der Schweizerischen Gesellschaft für Ur- und Frühgeschichte, 52*, 72–86.

Jahn, M. (1950). Ein kultureller Mittelpunkt bei Halle/Saale während der frühen Bronzezeit. *Jahresschrift für Mitteldeutsche Vorgeschichte, 34*, 81–89.

Kainz, W. (1999). *Bodenatlas Sachsen-Anhalt. Teil 1: Beschreibung der Bodenlandschaften und Böden*. Geologisches Landesamt.

Kegler-Graiewski, N. (2007). *Beile – Äxte – Mahlsteine. Zur Rohmaterialversorgung im Jung- und Spätneolithikum Nordhessens*. Dissertation im Fach Ur- und Frühgeschichte der Philosophischen Fakultät der Universität zu Köln.

Kienlin, T. L. (2008). *Frühes Metall im nordalpinen Raum. Eine Untersuchung zu technologischen und kognitiven Aspekten früher Metallurgie anhand der Gefüge frühbronzezeitlicher Beile*. Universitätsforschungen zur prähistorischen Archäologie 162. Habelt Verlag.

Knipper, C., Held, P., Fecher, M., Nicklisch, N., Meyer, C., Schreiber, H., Zich, B., Metzner-Nebelsick, C., Hubensack, V., Hansen, L., Nieveler, E., & Alt, K. W. (2015). Superior in life—Superior in death: Dietary distinction of Central European prehistoric and medieval elites. *Current Anthropology, 56*(4), 579–589.

Kretschmer, S., & Herbig, C. (2019). Hausbau und Siedlungsmuster des Endneolithikums und der Frühbronzezeit in der Mikroregion Droßdorf-Kieritzsch, Lkr. Leipzig. In H. Meller, S. Friederich, M. Küßner, H. Stäuble, & R. Risch (Eds.), *Siedlungsarchäologie des Endneolithikums und der frühen Bronzezeit – Late Neolithic and Early Bronze Age Settlement Archaeology, 11. Mitteldeutscher Archäologentag vom 18. bis 20. Oktober 2018 in Halle (Saale)*. Tagungen des Landesmuseums für Vorgeschichte Halle 20 (pp. 341–376). Landesamt für Denkmalpflege und Archäologie Sachsen-Anhalt.

Küßner, M., & Wechler, K.-P. (2019). Der Großbau der Aunjetitzer Kultur und das zugehörige Depot von Dermsdorf, Lkr. Sömmerda – ein Vorbericht. In H. Meller, S. Friederich, M. Küßner, H. Stäuble, & R. Risch (Eds.), *Siedlungsarchäologie des Endneolithikums und der frühen*

Bronzezeit – Late Neolithic and Early Bronze Age Settlement Archaeology, 11. Mitteldeutscher Archäologentag vom 18. bis 20. Oktober 2018 in Halle (Saale). Tagungen des Landesmuseums für Vorgeschichte Halle 20 (pp. 433–466). Landesamt für Denkmalpflege und Archäologie Sachsen-Anhalt.

Lull, V., & Micó, R. (2011). *Archaeology of the origin of the state: The theories*. Oxford University Press.

Lull, V., Micó, R., Rihuete, C., & Risch, R. (2011). El Argar and the beginning of class society in the Western Mediterranean. In S. Hansen & J. Müller (Eds.), *Sozialarchäologische Perspektiven: Gesellschaftlicher Wandel 5000–1500 v. Chr. zwischen Atlantik und Kaukasus. Internationale Tagung 15.-18. Oktober 2007 in Kiel*. Archäologie in Eurasien 24 (pp. 381–414). Philipp von Zabern.

Lull, V., & Risch, R. (1995). El Estado Argárico. *Verdolay, 7*, 97–109.

Meinike, M. (2019). Zur Astronomie der Rondellanlage Pömmelte-Zackmünde. In H. Meller & F. Bertemes (Eds.), *Mensch und Umwelt im Ringheiligtum von Pömmelte-Zackmünde, Salzlandkreis*. Forschungsberichte des Landesmuseums für Vorgeschichte Halle 10/III (pp. 191–194). Landesamt für Denkmalpflege und Archäologie Sachsen-Anhalt.

Meller, H. (2010). Nebra: Vom Logos zum Mythos – Biographie eines Himmelsbildes. In H. Meller & F. Bertemes (Eds.), *Der Griff nach den Sternen. Wie Europas Eliten zu Macht und Reichtum kamen. Internationales Symposium in Halle (Saale) 16.–21. Februar 2005*. Tagungen des Landesmuseums für Vorgeschichte Halle 5 (pp. 23–73). Landesamt für Denkmalpflege und Archäologie Sachsen-Anhalt.

Meller, H. (2013a). The sky disc of Nebra. In H. Fokkens & A. Harding (Eds.), *The Oxford handbook of the European Bronze Age* (pp. 266–269). Oxford University Press.

Meller, H. (2013b). Der Hortfund von Nebra im Spiegel frühbronzezeitlicher Deponierungssitten. In H. Meller, F. Bertemes, H.-R. Bork, & R. Risch (Eds.), *1600 – Kultureller Umbruch im Schatten des Thera-Ausbruchs? – 1600 – Cultural change in the shadow of the Thera eruption? 4. Mitteldeutscher Archäologentag vom 14. bis 16. Oktober 2011 in Halle (Saale)*. Tagungen des Landesmuseums für Vorgeschichte Halle 9 (pp. 493–526). Landesamt für Denkmalpflege und Archäologie Sachsen-Anhalt.

Meller, H. (2014). Die neolithischen und bronzezeitlichen Goldfunde Mitteldeutschlands – Eine Übersicht. In H. Meller, R. Risch, & E. Pernicka (Eds.), *Metalle der Macht – Frühes Gold und Silber. Metals of Power – Early Gold and Silver, 6. Mitteldeutscher Archäologentag vom 17. bis 19. Oktober 2013 in Halle (Saale)*. Tagungen des Landesmuseums für Vorgeschichte Halle 11 (pp. 611–716). Landesamt für Denkmalpflege und Archäologie Sachsen-Anhalt.

Meller, H. (2015). Armeen in der Frühbronzezeit? In H. Meller & M. Schefzik (Eds.), *Krieg – eine archäologische Spurensuche. Begleitband zur Sonderausstellung im Landesmuseum für Vorgeschichte Halle (Saale) 6. November 2015 bis 22. Mai 2016* (pp. 243–252). Landesamt für Denkmalpflege und Archäologie Sachsen-Anhalt.

Meller, H. (2017). Armies in the Early Bronze Age? An alternative interpretation of Únětice Culture axe hoards. *Antiquity, 91*, 1529–1545.

Meller, H. (2019a). Princes, armies, sanctuaries. The emergence of complex authority in the Central German Únětice Culture. *Acta Archaeologica, 90*, 39–79.

Meller, H. (2019b). Fürsten, Goldwaffen und Armeen. Überlegungen zum Goldfund von Dieskau und dessen möglicher Herkunft aus dem frühbronzezeitlichen Großgrabhügel Bornhöck bei Dieskau, Saalekreis. In H. Meller & F. Bertemes (Eds.), *Der Aufbruch zu Neuen Horizonten. Neue Sichtweisen zur europäischen Frühbronzezeit, Abschlusstagung der Forschergruppe FOR 550 vom 26.–29. November 2010 in Halle (Saale)*. Tagungen des Landesmuseums für Vorgeschichte Halle 19 (pp. 101–111). Landesamt für Denkmalpflege und Archäologie Sachsen-Anhalt.

Meller, H. (2019c). Zur unterschiedlichen Farbigkeit der Waffen der mitteldeutschen Aunjetitzer Kultur und ihrer Interpretation als militärisches Ordnungssystem. In H. Meller & F. Bertemes (Eds.), *Der Aufbruch zu Neuen Horizonten. Neue Sichtweisen zur europäischen Frühbronzezeit, Abschlusstagung der Forschergruppe FOR 550 vom 26.–29. November 2010 in Halle (Saale)*.

Tagungen des Landesmuseums für Vorgeschichte Halle 19 (pp. 154–158). Landesamt für Denkmalpflege und Archäologie Sachsen-Anhalt.

Meller, H. (2019d). Das Fürstengrab von Leubingen neu betrachtet – Zur Konstruktion von herrschaftlicher Legitimität durch Bezugnahme auf die Vorgängerkulturen. In H. Meller & F. Bertemes (Eds.), *Der Aufbruch zu Neuen Horizonten. Neue Sichtweisen zur europäischen Frühbronzezeit, Abschlusstagung der Forschergruppe FOR 550 vom 26.–29. November 2010 in Halle (Saale).* Tagungen des Landesmuseums für Vorgeschichte Halle 19 (pp. 245–259). Landesamt für Denkmalpflege und Archäologie Sachsen-Anhalt.

Meller, H. (2019e). Vom Herrschaftszeichen zum Herrschaftsornat. Zur Entstehung des goldenen Ringschmucks in Mitteleuropa. In H. Meller, A. Reichenberger, & S. Kimmig-Völkner (Eds.), *Ringe der Macht – Rings of Power. Internationale Tagung vom 09. bis 10. November 2018 in Halle (Saale).* Tagungen des Landesmuseums für Vorgeschichte Halle 21 (pp. 283–300). Landesamt für Denkmalpflege und Archäologie Sachsen-Anhalt.

Meller, H., & Bunnefeld, J.-H. (2020). Glänzend wie Sonne und Mond – Goldene und silberne Waffen im 4.–2. Jt. v. Chr. In H. Meller & M. Schefzik (Eds.), *Die Welt der Himmelsscheibe von Nebra – Neue Horizonte. Begleitband zur Sonderausstellung im Landesmuseum für Vorgeschichte Halle (Saale), 4. Juni 2021 bis zum 9. Januar 2022* (pp. 118–123). Landesamt für Denkmalpflege und Archäologie Sachsen-Anhalt.

Meller, H., Friederich, S., Küßner, M., Stäuble, H., & Risch, R. (Eds.). (2019). *Siedlungsarchäologie des Endneolithikums und der frühen Bronzezeit - Late Neolithic and Early Bronze Age Settlement Archaeology, 11. Mitteldeutscher Archäologentag vom 18. bis 20. Oktober 2018 in Halle (Saale).* Tagungen des Landesmuseums für Vorgeschichte Halle 20. Landesamt für Denkmalpflege und Archäologie Sachsen-Anhalt.

Meller, H., & Schunke, T. (2016). Die Wiederentdeckung des Bornhöck – Ein neuer frühbronzezeitlicher „Fürstengrabhügel" bei Raßnitz, Saalekreis. Erster Vorbericht. In H. Meller, H. P. Hahn, R. Jung, & R. Risch (Eds.), *Arm und Reich – Zur Ressourcenverteilung in prähistorischen Gesellschaften. Rich and Poor. Competing for Resources in Prehistoric Societies, 8. Mitteldeutscher Archäologentag vom 22. bis 24. Oktober 2015 in Halle (Saale).* Tagungen des Landesmuseums für Vorgeschichte Halle 14 (pp. 427–466). Landesamt für Denkmalpflege und Archäologie Sachsen-Anhalt.

Meller, H., & Zirm, M. (2019). Neueste Ergebnisse am Ringheiligtum von Pömmelte, Salzlandkreis (Grabungskampagne 2019). In H. Meller, S Friederich, M. Küßner, H. Stäuble, & R. Risch (Eds.), *Siedlungsarchäologie des Endneolithikums und der frühen Bronzezeit – Late Neolithic and Early Bronze Age Settlement Archaeology, 11. Mitteldeutscher Archäologentag vom 18. bis 20. Oktober 2018 in Halle (Saale).* Tagungen des Landesmuseums für Vorgeschichte Halle 20 (pp. 319–324). Landesamt für Denkmalpflege und Archäologie Sachsen-Anhalt.

Montelius, O. (1900). *Die Chronologie der ältesten Bronzezeit in Norddeutschland und Skandinavien.* F. Vieweg und Sohn.

Nicklisch, N., Ramsthaler, F., & Reichenberger, A. (2020). Der Fürstenmord von Helmsdorf. In H. Meller & M. Schefzik (Eds.), *Die Welt der Himmelsscheibe von Nebra – Neue Horizonte. Begleitband zur Sonderausstellung im Landesmuseum für Vorgeschichte Halle (Saale), 4. Juni 2021 bis zum 9. Januar 2022* (pp. 94–99). Landesamt für Denkmalpflege und Archäologie Sachsen-Anhalt.

Nocete, F. (2001). *Tercer milenio antes de nuestra era. Relaciones y contradicciones centro/periferia en el valle del Guadalquivir.* Bellaterra.

Pokutta, D. A. (2014). Food and cooking in the Únětice Culture. In N. Boroffka, G. T. Rustoiu, & R. Ota (Eds.), *CARPATHIAN HEARTLANDS—Studies on the prehistory and history of Transsylvania in European contexts, dedicated to Horia Ciugudean on his 60th birthday.* Apulum 51 (pp. 135–159). Muzeul Naţional Al Unirii.

Primas, M. (1988). Waffen aus Edelmetall. *Jahrbuch des Römisch-Germanischen Zentralmuseums, 35,* 161–185.

Rassmann, K. (2010). Die frühbronzezeitlichen Stabdolche Ostmitteleuropas. Anmerkungen zu Chronologie, Typologie, Technik und Archäometallurgie. In H. Meller & F. Bertemes (Eds.),

Der Griff nach den Sternen. Wie Europas Eliten zu Macht und Reichtum kamen. Internationales Symposium in Halle (Saale) 16.–21. Februar 2005. Tagungen des Landesmuseums für Vorgeschichte Halle 5 (pp. 807–821). Landesamt für Denkmalpflege und Archäologie Sachsen-Anhalt.

Risch, R. (1995). *Recursos naturales y sistemas de producción en el sudeste de la península Ibérica entre 3000 y 1000 ane*. Bellaterra, Ph.D. thesis, Departament d'Història de les Societats Precapitalistes i d'Antropologia Social, Universitat Autónoma de Barcelona. https://www.tdx.cat/handle/10803/5524. Accessed 28 Dec 2020.

Risch, R. (2002). *Recursos naturales, medios de producción y explotación social. Un análisis económico de la industria lítica de Fuente Álamo (Almería), 2250–1400 antes de nuestra era*. Philipp von Zabern.

Risch, R. (2008). Grain processing technologies and economic organisation: A case study from the south-east of the Iberian Peninsula during the Copper Age. *The Arkeotek Journal, 2*(2), 1–20.

Risch, R. (2016). How did wealth turn into surplus profit? From affluence to »scarcity« in prehistoric economies. In H. Meller, H. P. Hahn, R. Jung, & R. Risch (Eds.), *Arm und Reich – Zur Ressourcenverteilung in prähistorischen Gesellschaften. Rich and Poor. Competing for Resources in Prehistoric Societies, 8. Mitteldeutscher Archäologentag vom 22. bis 24. Oktober 2015 in Halle (Saale)*. Tagungen des Landesmuseums für Vorgeschichte Halle 14 (pp. 34–48). Landesamt für Denkmalpflege und Archäologie Sachsen-Anhalt.

Risch, R. (2020). Glorification of violence at the dawn of class exploitation. In H. Meller, R. Risch, K. W. Alt, F. Bertemes, & R. Micó (Eds.), *Rituelle Gewalt – Rituale der Gewalt. Ritual Violence – Rituals of Violence, 12. Mitteldeutscher Archäologentag vom 10. bis 12. Oktober 2019 in Halle (Saale)*. Tagungen des Landesmuseums für Vorgeschichte Halle 22 (pp. 149–163). Landesamt für Denkmalpflege und Archäologie Sachsen-Anhalt.

Risch, R., Delgado-Raack, S., & Eguíluz, M. (2020). Ein Einblick in die wirtschaftliche Macht der Aunjetitzer Fürsten – Die Mahlsteine des Grabhügels Bornhöck. In H. Meller & M. Schefzik (Eds.), *Die Welt der Himmelsscheibe von Nebra – Neue Horizonte. Begleitband zur Sonderausstellung im Landesmuseum für Vorgeschichte Halle (Saale), 4. Juni 2021 bis zum 9. Januar 2022* (pp. 108–111). Landesamt für Denkmalpflege und Archäologie Sachsen-Anhalt.

Robitaille, J. (2016). The ground stone industry of the Mursi of Maki, Ethiopia: Ethnoarchaeological research on milling and crushing equipment (technique and function). *Journal of Lithic Studies, 3*(3), 429–456.

Roux, V. (1986). *Le matériel de broyage. Etude ethnoarchéologique à Tichitt (R.I. Mauritanie)*. Edition Recherches sur les civilisations, mémoire 58.

Runnels, C. (1981). *A diachronic study and economic analysis of millstones from the Argolid, Greece*. Thesis University of Indiana. University Microfilms (Ph.D thesis).

Sarnowska, W. (1969). *Kultura unietycka w Polsce 1*. Zakład Narodowy im. Ossolińskich.

Schiele, S. (2020). *Die Steinpackung des frühbronzezeitlichen Großgrabhügels Bornhöck – Charakterisierung und Herkunftsanalyse der verbauten Lithotypen*. Halle (Saale): unpublished MA thesis Martin Luther University Halle-Wittenberg.

Schirokauer, C., & Brown, M. (2006). *Breve historia de la civilización china*. Bellaterra.

Schlosser, W. (2019). Geometrisch-astronomische Bewertung der Rondellanlage von Pömmelte-Zackmünde. In H. Meller & F. Bertemes (Eds.), *Mensch und Umwelt im Ringheiligtum von Pömmelte-Zackmünde, Salzlandkreis*. Forschungsberichte des Landesmuseums für Vorgeschichte Halle 10/III (pp. 187–189). Landesamt für Denkmalpflege und Archäologie Sachsen-Anhalt.

Schüler, J., Eichentopf, J., Molina, E., Planert, M., & Friederich, S. (2019). Frühbronzezeitliche Häuser ohne Hausgrundriss-Strukturen? Merseburg-Beuna und Esperstedt-Obhausen, Saalekreis. In H. Meller, S. Friederich, M. Küßner, H. Stäuble, & R. Risch (Eds.), *Siedlungsarchäologie des Endneolithikums und der frühen Bronzezeit – Late Neolithic and Early Bronze Age Settlement Archaeology, 11. Mitteldeutscher Archäologentag vom 18. bis 20. Oktober 2018 in Halle (Saale)*. Tagungen des Landesmuseums für Vorgeschichte Halle 20 (pp. 475–490). Landesamt für Denkmalpflege und Archäologie Sachsen-Anhalt.

Schunke, T. (2018). Fahren oder Tragen? Methoden des Antransports von Baumaterial für bronzezeitliche Grabhügel. In B. Nessel, D. Neumann, & M. Bartelheim (Eds.), *Bronzezeitlicher Transport – Akteure, Mittel und Wege*. RessourcenKulturen 8 (pp. 85–115). Tübingen University Press.

Schunke, T. (2019). Siedlungen und Landschaft der Aunjetitzer Kultur in Sachsen-Anhalt – die Siedlungselemente, ihre Strukturierung und Lage. In H. Meller, S. Friederich, M. Küßner, H. Stäuble, & R. Risch (Eds.), *Siedlungsarchäologie des Endneolithikums und der frühen Bronzezeit - Late Neolithic and Early Bronze Age Settlement Archaeology, 11. Mitteldeutscher Archäologentag vom 18. bis 20. Oktober 2018 in Halle (Saale)*. Tagungen des Landesmuseums für Vorgeschichte Halle 20 (pp. 127–207). Landesamt für Denkmalpflege und Archäologie Sachsen-Anhalt.

Schunke, T., & Stäuble, H. (2019). Zum Verständnis der Aunjetitzer Langhäuser und der Versuch einer Typologie. In H. Meller, S. Friederich, M. Küßner, H. Stäuble, & R. Risch (Eds.), *Siedlungsarchäologie des Endneolithikums und der frühen Bronzezeit - Late Neolithic and Early Bronze Age Settlement Archaeology, 11. Mitteldeutscher Archäologentag vom 18. bis 20. Oktober 2018 in Halle (Saale)*. Tagungen des Landesmuseums für Vorgeschichte Halle 20 (pp. 393–418). Landesamt für Denkmalpflege und Archäologie Sachsen-Anhalt.

Schwarz, R. (2014). Goldene Schläfen- und Lockenringe – Herrschaftsinsignien in bronzezeitlichen Ranggesellschaften Mitteldeutschlands. Überlegungen zur Gesellschaft der Aunjetitzer Kultur. In H. Meller, R. Risch, & E. Pernicka (Eds.), *Metalle der Macht – Frühes Gold und Silber. Metals of Power – Early Gold and Silver, 6. Mitteldeutscher Archäologentag vom 17. bis 19. Oktober 2013 in Halle (Saale)*. Tagungen des Landesmuseums für Vorgeschichte Halle 11 (pp. 717–742). Landesamt für Denkmalpflege und Archäologie Sachsen-Anhalt.

Service, E. R. (1962 [1971]). *Primitive social organization: An evolutionary perspective* (2nd ed.). Random House.

Spatzier, A. (2017). *Das endneolithisch-frühbronzezeitliche Rondell von Pömmelte-Zackmünde, Salzlandkreis, und das Rondell-Phänomen des 4.–1. Jt. v. Chr. in Mitteleuropa*. Forschungsberichte des Landesmuseums für Vorgeschichte Halle 10/I-II. Landesamt für Denkmalpflege und Archäologie Sachsen-Anhalt.

Spatzier, A. (2019). The enclosure complex Pömmelte–Schönebeck: The dialectic of two circular monuments of the late 3rd to early 2nd millennium BC in Central Germany. In H. Meller & F. Bertemes (Eds.), *Der Aufbruch zu Neuen Horizonten. Neue Sichtweisen zur europäischen Frühbronzezeit, Abschlusstagung der Forschergruppe FOR 550 vom 26.–29. November 2010 in Halle (Saale)*. Tagungen des Landesmuseums für Vorgeschichte Halle 19 (pp. 421–443). Landesamt für Denkmalpflege und Archäologie Sachsen-Anhalt.

Stecher, M., & Kurt, W. A. (2019). Anthropologische Untersuchungen an den menschlichen Überresten aus dem Rondell Pömmelte-Zackmünde. In H. Meller & F. Bertemes (Eds.), *Mensch und Umwelt im Ringheiligtum von Pömmelte-Zackmünde, Salzlandkreis*. Forschungsberichte des Landesmuseums für Vorgeschichte Halle 10/III (pp. 9–116). Landesamt für Denkmalpflege und Archäologie Sachsen-Anhalt.

Trimm, C. (2017). *Fighting for the king and the gods: A survey of warfare in the ancient Near East*, Resources for Biblical Study 88. SBL Press.

von Brunn, W. A. (1959). *Die Hortfunde der frühen Bronzezeit aus Sachsen-Anhalt, Sachsen und Thüringen*. Deutsche Akademie der Wissenschaften.

Vučković, V. (2019). *Neolithic economy and macro-lithic tools of the Central Balkans*. Ph.D. thesis, Universitat Autònoma de Barcelona, Bellaterra. https://www.tdx.cat/handle/10803/669666. Accessed 28 Dec 2020.

Walter, D., Endrigkeit, A., Bartel, K., Schneider, S., Mecking, O., & Ettel, P. (2019). Häuser der frühen Bronzezeit in Thüringen. In H. Meller, S. Friederich, M. Küßner, H. Stäuble, & R. Risch (Eds.), *Siedlungsarchäologie des Endneolithikums und der frühen Bronzezeit – Late Neolithic and Early Bronze Age Settlement Archaeology, 11. Mitteldeutscher Archäologentag vom 18. bis 20. Oktober 2018 in Halle (Saale)*. Tagungen des Landesmuseums für Vorgeschichte Halle 20 (pp. 419–432). Landesamt für Denkmalpflege und Archäologie Sachsen-Anhalt.

Wright, M. K. (1993). Simulated use of experimental maize grinding tools from Southwestern Colorado. *Kiva, 58,* 345–355.

Wunderlich, C.-H., Bunnefeld, J.-H., & Meller, H. (2019). Buntmetall. Farbigkeit und ästhetische Eigenschaften von Legierungen der Aunjetitzer Kultur. In H. Meller & F. Bertemes (Eds.), *Der Aufbruch zu Neuen Horizonten. Neue Sichtweisen zur europäischen Frühbronzezeit, Abschlusstagung der Forschergruppe FOR 550 vom 26.–29. November 2010 in Halle (Saale).* Tagungen des Landesmuseums für Vorgeschichte Halle 19 (pp. 159–181). Landesamt für Denkmalpflege und Archäologie Sachsen-Anhalt.

Zamzow, E. (2020). *Gestein + Getreide = Gehöft. Die bandkeramischen Mahlsteine der Fundstelle Breitenbach Schneidemühle.* Masterthesis der Universität Halle.

Zamzow, E. (in preparation). Bandkeramische Mahlsteine und Gräber in der Umgebung der Kreisgrabenanlage Goseck. *Archäologie in Sachsen-Anhalt.*

Zich, B. (1996). *Studien zur regionalen und chronologischen Gliederung der nördlichen Aunjetitzer Kultur.* Vorgeschichtliche Forschungen 20. de Gruyter.

Zich, B. (2016). Aunjetitzer Herrschaften in Mitteldeutschland – »Fürsten« der Frühbronzezeit und ihre Territorien (»Domänen«). In H. Meller, H. P. Hahn, R. Jung, & R. Risch (Eds.), *Arm und Reich – Zur Ressourcenverteilung in prähistorischen Gesellschaften. Rich and Poor. Competing for Resources in Prehistoric Societies, 8. Mitteldeutscher Archäologentag vom 22. bis 24. Oktober 2015 in Halle (Saale).* Tagungen des Landesmuseums für Vorgeschichte Halle 14 (pp. 371–406). Landesamt für Denkmalpflege und Archäologie Sachsen-Anhalt.

Zimmermann, A. (1988). Steine. In U. Boelicke, D. von Brandt, J. Lüning, P. Stehli, & A. Zimmermann (Eds.), *Der bandkeramische Siedlungsplatz Langweiler 8, Gemeinde Aldenhoven, Kr. Düren.* Rheinische Ausgrabungen 28 (pp. 569–787). Rheinland-Verlag.

Chapter 7
Property and Markets: The Uses of Land in Pharaonic Egypt Beyond Redistributive and Neoliberal Approaches

Juan Carlos Moreno García

Abstract Ancient Egypt has been considered the quintessential example of a redistributive centralized economy. Neo-institutionalism, on the contrary, emphasizes that markets, law, institutions and private property reduced transaction costs, promoted economic rationalism and led to increased economic specialization. Pharaonic Egypt provides some evidence about private possession of land in which markets and a business-oriented mentality operated in a social and economic environment rational but alien to modern capitalist values. Kinship ties limited the emergence of individualist interests, but kings promoted such behaviour in an attempt to curve down the power of noble families. Yet individualist strategies remained limited because institutions (particularly temples and the crown) were crucial in the formation of private land portfolios and narrowed the possibilities for the emergence of a significant market of land.

Introduction

If there is a domain in which the contributions of pharaonic Egypt (that is to say, the period of Egyptian history preceding the Macedonian conquest in 332 BCE) to comparative history have been negligible, economic history comes immediately to mind. The reasons are diverse (Moreno García, 2014a). On the one hand, the priorities of research have focused traditionally on art history and religion, as it was prestigious monuments (mostly tombs and temples) that provided easily the kind of beautiful objects and spectacular discoveries avidly searched for by Egyptologists to satisfy the insatiable appetite of museums, collectors and national governments. On the other hand, the combined weight of the biblical story of Joseph, of the stereotype of a despotic hyper-centralized and all-encompassing "oriental" interventionist state, and the relative abundance of papyri (interpreted as the surviving evidence of a massive documentation produced by a meticulous bureaucracy at the service of

J. C. M. García (✉)
CNRS (UMR 8167), Sorbonne University, Paris, France

S. Gimatzidis and R. Jung (eds.), *The Critique of Archaeological Economy*, Frontiers in Economic History,
https://doi.org/10.1007/978-3-030-72539-6_7

kings), persuaded historians that markets, private economy and property had played a very minor role in the land of the pharaohs. Finally, concepts such as "redistribution" provided a respectable intellectual background (a Polanyian and social-sciences based one) that helped justify this traditional view about the ancient Egyptian economy (Bleiberg, 1996; Grandet, 1994; Janssen, 1975). However, a slight change in the perspective adopted shows that such a view is largely unjustifiable. Excavating temples, tombs and monuments built and used by the elite (a very tiny part of pharaonic society) forcibly provided abundant information about state institutions and their activities, much less about other actors whose economic importance was in all probability as significant (if not more) than those of institutions. Two examples may illustrate this point. The Wilbour papyrus, a detailed record of more than 3000 plots of land, their holders and the taxes they paid in a section of Middle Egypt, written around 1200 BCE, may convey an image of thorough administrative control. Yet this document only concerns about 5–10% of all the cultivable land in this area of the Nile Valley (Gardiner, 1948). As for a slightly early document, papyrus Harris I, it records massive donations of land, people, cattle and huge amounts of diverse kinds of goods to the temples of Egypt, to the point that it has been estimated that about one-third of the land of the country was actually in their hands (Grandet, 1994). But what about the other 66%, not to speak of the 90–95% of land not referred to in the Wilbour papyrus? In a similar vein, the archaeology of cities and of their economic activities (trading areas, workshops, etc.) is still in its infancy (Moeller, 2005). This means that crucial economic actors such as traders, craftsmen and other specialists are poorly documented in the archaeological and textual record, except when they worked at the service of kings, temples and the elite. It is in these cases that they happen to be mentioned in letters and administrative sources that help them emerge from the shadows in which they usually lie. As for the rural world, it still remains one of the greatest unknowns in Egyptian history, a paradox when one thinks that Egypt is very often characterized as one of the major breadbaskets of the ancient world. Little is known, for example, about the role played by wealthy peasants and their economic choices and land portfolios, about market-oriented crops, about peasant productive strategies and the organization of their domestic workforce, about the weight of different modalities of work prevailing in the countryside (sharecroppers, compulsory workers, leasers, etc.) and their seasonal mobilization depending on the needs of institutions and landholders, about the forms and uses of the landscape resulting from these strategies, not to mention the impact of state taxes on all these aspects and potential choices. The fact that wealthy peasants paid their taxes occasionally in gold directly to the royal treasury, or that huge amounts of precious metals were "laundered" by robbers through the acquisition of fields and orchards, reveals that some kind of proto-monetization was operative in the countryside and that a land market, even if modest, enabled modest and wealthy tenants to acquire agricultural plots (Moreno García, 2013c; Katary, 2000, 2001; McDowell, 1992).

Despite these severe limitations in our knowledge of pharaonic economy, scattered textual references, small archives and isolated documents, as well as occasional archaeological evidence, allow nevertheless to address topics relevant in on-going discussions on ancient economic history. Among them, one can think on potential economic growth in ancient societies, the role played by markets and profit-seeking economic activities, the emergence of "rational" economic behaviour, the importance of law and the use of contracts in the reduction of transaction costs, etc. (Kehoe et al., 2015). Many of these discussions have been inspired partly by an increasing popularity of neo-institutional models in the study of ancient near eastern societies (Jursa et al., 2010; van der Spek et al., 2015; Kleber & Pirngruber, 2016; Pirngruber, 2017; van Leeuwen & van der Spek, 2018), while the Polanyian paradigm (particularly its emphasis on redistribution) seems to have lost most of its former appeal and given way to alternative economic models based on a variable combination of redistribution, markets, private interests and selective interventions by the state. Another source of inspiration derives from a revival of neo-Marxist models. Their primary goal is to understand the circumstances that led to the emergence of capitalism and a market economy in the West and, in so doing, to discern if this particular historical and economic path was unique, an exception in history or if, rather, its roots are to be found in other parts of the world, including antiquity (Anievas & Nişancıoğlu, 2015; Banaji, 2018; Tedesco, 2018). In any case, the validity of the neo-institutional model for the analysis of pre-modern societies is currently subject to increasing criticism, particularly its claim that Western practices and institutional arrangements (as well as their cognitive and behavioural foundations, such as "rationality") are universally valid and not rooted, instead, on very distinctive historical conditions and balances of power among diverse actors that led, not only to the emergence of the modern state in Europe, but also to the gradual extension of capitalism in this part of the world (Sánchez León & Izquierdo Martín, 2002; Narotzky & Manzano, 2014).

To conclude this brief introduction, it should be noticed that the recent regain of interest in the study of markets, enterprise, "entrepreneurship", monetization and economic structure in the ancient Near East has hardly influenced or inspired discussions in Egyptology about the economic foundations of pharaonic Egypt and their changes over time. Only some attempts have tried to test and/or import the neo-institutional (Muhs, 2016) and neo-Keynesian paradigms (Warburton, 2016), but their impact seems quite limited on (if not utterly ignored by) an otherwise traditional narrative still solidly framed by the concepts of centralization, intense state interventionism and dominant redistributive networks, even if their actual pertinence has been rarely discussed seriously. With these ideas in mind, I will try to explore in the following pages the problem of the economic logic underlying the possession and transfer of land in an attempt to challenge these assumptions and to explore some venues of research that, I hope, may promote comparative research with other societies of the ancient world.

Private Ownership of Land and the Strategies Involving Its Possession and Management

One of the most enduring myths about the agricultural economy of ancient Egypt states that pharaohs owned all land in Egypt. A fact that, when coupled with the alleged interventionist and centralized nature of royal power, meant that private ownership of land was insignificant and that, as a consequence, a market of land in which private tenants bought and sold plots was simply absent. Furthermore, the all-encompassing redistributive economic organization supposedly implemented by the pharaohs also meant that pharaohs cared for the welfare of their subjects, covered their needs and that, under these conditions, private economic transactions (including those related to the use and transfer of land) were reduced to very modest exchanges in the domestic sphere between individuals and households. So, private transactions on land could only involve the transfer of rights over these fields as the king (and, secondarily, the institutions he controlled) always remained the eminent/effective owner of the fields exchanged. In this perspective, most of the Egyptian population would have consisted of a mass of poor peasants hardly able at all to purchase land (Baer, 1962).

Against such idealized depictions (see also Manning, 2003: 193–197) I would like to argue that the term peasantry covered in fact quite diverse conditions, from poor agricultural workers who cultivated the fields of other people and institutions to wealthy or, at least, affluent tenants capable to manage a substantial portfolio of landed assets including their own land, fields leased from other tenants as well as plots belonging to institutions such as temples or the crown (Moreno García, 2014b). As the private archive of Heqanakhte—a wealthy landowner who lived at the beginning of the second millennium BCE—shows, the letters he addressed to his subordinates contain very precise instructions about the management of his land and the allocation of resources to the members of his household. What emerges from them is that his agricultural choices were guided by purely private interests, as he sought to obtain the best possible returns. He controlled a substantial amount of land (at least 110–150 arouras of land or 27–37 ha), well above that usually ascribed to an average Egyptian peasant (about 1.25 ha), as well as a sizeable cattle herd, he employed several assistants and was also a creditor for about 25 neighbours who owed him grain. In his search for profit, he did not doubt to lease additional land from wealthy neighbours, a strategy that in all probability also intended to create a network of social relations in which he reinforced his status as local patron, accepted by his peers as member of a local (sub-)elite (Allen, 2002).

Having this example in mind, it is perhaps significant that the earliest extensive administrative inscription records precisely, among other dispositions, selling and buying land. Metjen was an official who lived around 2600 BCE, and he described in the texts of his tomb how he accumulated and managed the landed assets under his control: "He has acquired 200 arouras (=55 ha) of land from many royal colonists. He has given 50 arouras of land to (his) mother Nebesneit when she set up her will for the children, and their share was set down in a royal document for every office"

(Strudwick, 2005: 192). Another passage mentions again that "he has acquired 200 arouras of land from many royal colonists", and refers as well to the acquisition of two orchards and the inheritance of some property from his father: "a walled estate 200 cubits long and 200 broad, set out with fine trees, and a large pool made in it; it was planted with fig trees and vines. It is written down in a royal document, and their names are (recorded likewise) on (this) royal document. The trees and the vines were planted in great numbers, and the wine therefrom was produced in great quantity (or 'of great quality'). A garden was made for him on land of 1 kha and 2 ta within the enclosure, which was planted with trees. (They were called) Iymeres, a 'foundation of Metjen,' and Iatsobek, a 'foundation of Metjen.' The property of his father the judge and scribe Inpuemankh was given to him, without wheat and barley and the property of the house, but with dependents and herds of donkeys and pigs (?)" (Strudwick, 2005: 193). Finally, Metjen obtained other fields as remuneration for specific administrative duties he accomplished for the crown. Whereas the precise "legal" circumstances involved in these transactions are not indicated, the texts are exceptional in which they refer in detail to the diverse categories of land in possession of a high official: rewards for administrative duties, private acquisitions and, finally, property inherited from his father. That he made use freely of this property also transpires from the land he transferred to his mother (50 arouras) in order she provided for other sons (Strudwick, 2005: 192). In this case, the references to "shares" of the field did not normally describe physical division into separate plots of land, but rights to land for cultivation—which often meant rights to lease land—and claims to income from a proportional share of the crop (Eyre, 2013: 171). The inscription of Metjen appears thus as one of the rare examples in which an official describes in detail the formation, composition and disposal of his patrimony. Similar conditions are discernible in the will of prince Nykaure (late twenty-sixth century BCE), who enumerates fourteen agricultural domains spread in several provinces in Middle Egypt and the Delta and bequeathed to several members of his family (Strudwick, 2005: 200).

Despite the very scarce textual evidence about private transfers of real estate that has survived from the third millennium BCE, there are also examples in which individuals acquired houses (Strudwick, 2005: 185–186, 205–206) and tombs (Strudwick, 2005: 204), and that these transactions involved the use of sealed documents to validate the sales. Some statements in the tombs of dignitaries and officials also refer to transactions and acquisitions of wealth outside the circuit of royal rewards, particularly to payments to the artists and craftsmen who built and decorated the tombs (Strudwick, 2005: 251–260). These inscriptions stress in fact that it was the owner of the tomb who paid the artisans with his own property, without any intervention of the king. One of the most detailed is that of Remenuka at Giza, dating from the 6th dynasty (2345–2181 BCE): "this tomb was made for me in exchange of bread and beer which I gave to the workmen who made this tomb. For indeed I have given to them a large payment of all sorts of linen which they requested and they thanked god for it" (Strudwick, 2005: 257). Another example comes from the tomb of Akhetmehu at Giza, also dated from the 6th dynasty: "with regard to this my tomb of eternity, it was made for bread and beer; every workman who worked on it thanked all the gods for me. I gave them clothing, oil, copper and grain in great quantity" (Strudwick, 2005: 252). It seems then that metals (especially copper), cloth and, obviously, grain were not only part of the wealth owned by individuals, but also commodities freely used as "currency" for payments. An inscription from Giza confirms this use as it mentions a house that was sold in exchange for a prize evaluated in ten *shat*-units but actually paid with several pieces of furniture and cloth: "one piece of four-measure cloth: 3 shat; one wooden bed: 4 shat; one piece of two-measure cloth: 3 shat" (Strudwick, 2005: 205–206).

It is apparent then that real estate was bought and sold in the course of purely private transactions since an early date, that they involved what can be called very loosely "contracts" (or sealed documents), and that a world of private affairs—still poorly known—coexisted alongside the redistributive circuits controlled by the royal palace. One can evoke, for instance, a famous market scene represented in a tomb of Saqqara (late twenty-fifth century BCE). There, a man appears measuring out cloth by the cubit from a bale held by a second man, with the caption "(a?) cubit of cloth for 6,5 shat (=7.36 gr, perhaps of copper)" (Eyre, 1998: 179). In this sphere of exchanges, use of abstract units of measure and private affairs, it was not uncommon that land be evoked in some inscription as a commodity subject to similar operations of sale and purchase. The sudden recurrence in many private inscriptions following the end of the monarchy (*ca.* 2160 BCE) of themes such as indebtedness, loss of property (including members of the vendor's household, reduced to serfdom), acquisition of fields and praise of economic autonomy, points to the importance of the acquisition of land in the strategies of some members of the local sub-elites. Until 2160 BCE it was exceptional that officials mentioned at all the accumulation of wealth outside the circuits of rewards and remunerations awarded by the king. But with the end of the monarchy and the crisis of the palatial culture that followed, the dominant cultural codes (which restricted any mention to private sources of income) lost their former predominance. It was then that private inscriptions began to express new, alternative social values. Personal initiative, economic autonomy and accumulation of wealth became some of the most praised. The counterpart is that the sources of this period of the political division of Egypt (2160–2050 BCE) also evoke the dangers that hanged over private patrimonies. Indebtedness, conflicts around inheritances and the transmission of family assets, economic hardship and abuses from powerful potentates appear as the main challenges that put at risk the transmission of patrimonies, so the continuity of "the house of the father" became a major concern in the inscriptions of this period (Moreno García, 2000, 2015, 2016a). A fascinating set of texts called "letters to the dead" contain, precisely, pleas addressed to dead people by their living relatives in order to request their help face difficulties. A good example is the letter addressed by Shepsi to his deceased father Iyenkhenmut, dealing with the loss of Shepsi's fields because of the debts run up by his brother and never repaid (Willems, 1991; Strudwick, 2005: 183). In other cases, conflicts erupted because of divorces (and the subsequent disputes between former wives over the inheritance of the goods of their deceased husband), about succession to authority over a family between the tutor appointed by a deceased official and the son of the latter, in challenge to a written claim (Strudwick, 2005: 186–187; Eyre, 2013: 103–104), etc.

However, harsh conditions for some also created opportunities for personal enrichment and, consequently, others profited from distress to acquire land, people and property and to enhance their social status. That is why so many private inscriptions from the period between 2160 and 2050 BCE, when no central monarchy ruled over Egypt, refer to these circumstances. On the one hand, individuals proudly evoke that they had obtained their wealth thanks only to their own effort and, what is more, that they had also succeeded in preserving the "house of the father" intact; then they passed it on to the next generation, sometimes even enlarged and enriched (Moreno García, 1997: 32–45). On the other hand, they also boasted about acquiring prestigious possessions like fields, serfs, boats and cattle (Moreno García, 2000). Finally, there are many cases in which they rhetorically claimed that they had never enslaved a girl or deprived a man of his property in periods of distress and famine. In these cases, it was not rare that the monuments of such individuals were inscribed with meticulous enumerations of the property acquired by their own initiative, as in the case of the army commander Nuy: "I acquired 40 people, 54 bulls, 36 asses, 260 goats, 3 imu-ships and 6 depet-ships. (Furthermore,) I have bought (by contract?) 20 kha of fields [=about 50 ha] as well as (several) houses. (Finally,) I have dug a pool and planted 40 sycamores, and I did all that in excess of the goods of my father" (Musacchio, 2010). The stela of another official, Heqaib, who lived in the area of Thebes, epitomizes the new ideals so valued in the private inscriptions of this period: "I was an excellent 'modest one', speaking with his mouth and acting with his arm, who makes his town keep at a distance from him. I was a noble one in Thebes, a great pillar in the southern district. I surpassed every peer of mine in this city in respect of riches of every kind. So people said, when I was acting by my (own) arm: '[he is] one that is free from robbing another.' I provided this whole city with Upper Egyptian barley for many(?) years, not to speak of the […]. I gave bread to the hungry and clothes to the naked. I did not calumniate the great ones and I gave ease to the 'modest ones'. I gave a loan of corn (?) to Upper Egypt and Upper Egyptian barley to this northern district. I also gave oil to the province of Elkab after my town had been satisfied. I made a ship of forty (cubits) and a bark, for transporting cattle and for ferrying him who had no boat in the season of inundation. I appointed a herdsman to (my) cattle and (further) herdsmen to (my) goats and to (my) donkeys. My people were more numerous and my precious goods were greater in number than those of any peer of mine. I was a (real) master of my heart in times of turmoil, while everybody else was shutting his door. When the ruler counted my cattle, he found that my possessions had increased. As for everyone that had to deal with me, I caused him to bend his arm" (Morenz, 2006; Polotsky, 1930). Acting by oneself, according with his own initiatives, needs and expectations, without following the instructions of others (including the king), accumulating substantial wealth thanks to his own deeds, not to be matched by his peers, and sharing his prosperity and good counsils with neighbours and fellow citizens, especially in periods of turmoil and famine, convey the new ideal of the prosperous self-made man (Moreno García, 1997: 1–87).

Unfortunately, precise data about the amount of land bought (not to speak of prices paid) are very rare, but it seems that it could be quite substantial. A Nubian soldier proclaimed that he had obtained a field of 23 arouras (about 6.3 ha); a resident at the locality of Dendera bought a field of five *kha* (that is to say, 50 arouras, about 13.7 ha); Nuy, a chief of the army from this same locality, got 20 *kha* (that is to say 200 arouras, about 55 ha), while in several other instances an individual simply asserts that he had bought "a big field"; Bawi of El-Hawawish acquired many people as well as many fields and another contemporary, Beb, proudly declared that he had acquired four fields. In some of these cases, the inscriptions precise that the acquisition took the form of a (sealed) contract (Moreno García, 2000). Of course, these texts may simply refer to a practice that had been usual for centuries but never evoked in previous periods because of considerations of decorum and etiquette, when only royal endowments were considered worth recording in private inscriptions. Nevertheless, these considerable purchases of land (a field of 1.25 ha could support a standard Egyptian family), and the fact that they were inscribed on prestigious expensive monuments, reveal that the purchasers were not simple peasants but members of a local sub-elite with (easy?) access to land. The "letter to the dead" of Shepsi, mentioned previously, seems to correspond to a different social background. According to this document, an unreimbursed debt evaluated in 144 litters of barley (approximately two *khar* "sacks", an Egyptian measure of volume), led to the seizure of Shepsi's fields. This quantity of grain corresponds to the standard yield expected from a field of only 0.2–0.4 arouras (0.05–0.11 ha), so Shepsi apparently belonged to a social sector more modest than that of the purchasers mentioned before. Finally, the papyrus Brooklyn 16.205 (around 770 BCE), deals with the acquisition of several plots of land made by a certain Ikeni in a year of hard times. The plots were quite small (in three cases hardly more than half an aroura) and in several cases, they are described as located next to "the well of Ikeni" (Parker, 1962: 49–52). It seems as if Ikeni had followed a calculated strategy of purchase, seeking to acquire plots around a well that bore his own name or that of a member of his kin, even an ancestor. Given the small surface of the tenures, it is possible that they were devoted to horticultural production instead of the cultivation of cereals. Once again, bad times for some meant that they were forced to sell land and that others profited from their misfortunes to build a portfolio of landed assets.

A final intriguing point concerns the use of gold in private acquisitions of land. A common assumption about the Egyptian economy (and its alleged redistributive basis) was that any (pre-)monetary use of precious metals was unnecessary and that, accordingly, the role of market-oriented and profit-seeking production was irrelevant. These assertions are nevertheless problematic (Moreno García, 2016b). Fishermen, for instance, paid their taxes in silver according to several documents from the late second and early first millennium BCE, and the sums they delivered were in some cases quite substantial, so they probably sold their captures in markets where precious metals circulated and were exchanged for other goods. Even the army (or at least a fortress commander) shelled out huge amounts of silver to obtain supplies such as fish and wool in the late second millennium BCE (Wente, 1990: 120–121). In fact, gold and copper were already part of the wealth accumulated and stocked by officials of modest status around 2100 BCE: "[I surpassed everyone who was and] who will exist therein in people, Lower Egyptian grain and emmer, gold, copper, clothing, oil, [honey], … [cattle], goats, cargo ships and everything" (Fischer, 1968: 160). And one of the potential uses of the precious metals thus accumulated was to acquire land. A soldier from Edfu, Ha-ankhef (*ca.* 1550 BCE), returned from Nubia after having obtained 26 pieces of gold and a servant girl as payment for his military services for six years. He invested then this wealth in the purchase of three plots of land, one for himself, another for his wife and the last one for his children (Redford, 1997: 12). Penone, a sandal maker who lived in the Ramesside period, acquired 17 *nbyw* (?) of land in exchange for gold (Hassan & Ouda, 2018: 100). As for the famous robberies of the late New Kingdom, when huge amounts of silver and gold were stolen from temples and royal tombs, the documents of the trials reveal that the robbers used the booty for the acquisition, among other goods, of fields, slaves, grain and cattle, usually through the mediation of merchants (Peet, 1930: 118, 144, 149, 152, 157). Thus the overseer of the field of the temple of Amun, Akhenmenu, received 1 *deben* of silver (=91 gr) and 5 *kite* of gold (=45.5 gr) "in exchange for land", while the scribe Amenhotep "called Seret", of the temple of Amun, received 2 *deben* (=182 gr of silver) "in exchange for land", for 40 *deben* of copper and for 10 sacks of barley (Peet, 1930: 144; the ratio silver-copper at this time was 1:60). That enormous quantities of precious metals could be laundered in this way and, what is more, easily exchanged for modest amounts of common goods, means that their circulation, as well as the activities of traders, were far less rare than previously assumed in the local sphere and even among people of modest condition (Moreno García, 2014a, 2014b, 2016b). This may also explain why three tenants who cultivated some royal land assigned to a temple during this period are said to have paid their taxes in gold directly into the Pharaoh's treasury (Wente, 1990: 130–131).

Temple Land and Private Strategies

In other instances, transactions on land appear rather more ambiguous as they refer not necessarily to private property but to fields that belonged to temples and the crown. The tenants could buy, sell and transfer by inheritance their rights over their land and this possibility enabled people of some status to build and manage substantial land portfolios for their own profit, including members of the royal family (Moreno García, 2016c). Since the middle of the third millennium BCE, and particularly since 1550 BCE, temples became crucial institutions as providers of substantial income to the elites of the kingdom, both central and provincial. Their symbolic and economic importance put into the hands of kings a powerful tool to rally local chiefs and potentates to their authority, to reward dignitaries and agents of the crown (including the military) and to interfere in local affairs through donations of land that benefited selected members of the local elite. As for the families and potentates with access to this source of wealth, prestige and useful contacts with the royal palace, the income they obtained from temples (as priests, managers of temple property, beneficiaries of rewards, etc.) provided them with institutional and economic security on the long term. This land escaped indeed from the uncertainties brought by divisions of property (inheritances, divorces and family disputes) and from utter interference by other members of their kin and opened the possibility to develop individual strategies for them and for their direct descendants (Moreno García, 2013a).

Such conflicts are well documented from documents of all periods. Perhaps the best known is the dispute over a land grant to the naval officer Neshi in the reign of Ahmose (1550–1525 BCE). It had been run as an undivided family holding for centuries, but then been the subject of repeated dispute since the reign of Akhenaten (1352–1336 BCE). Later on, during the reign of Ramesses II (1279–1213 BCE), the dispute opposed a certain Khay on one side, to a lady Werel, her son Huy, his wife Nubnefer and their son Mose on the other. Mose's father had managed the estate, but control had then fallen into the hands of Khay. A court was constituted to study their claims and judge between them, and each party presented documents to support their positions (Eyre, 2013: 155–162). As Eyre has pointed out, "the core of the dispute was a breakdown of relations within an extended family over shares in agricultural land: originally a royal donation to reward the high-ranking military officer Neshi. Although it is not made explicit here, such endowments were characteristically inalienable and indivisible grants, to be inherited in a single line: 'son to son, heir to heir, for ever'. The testimony is partial and incomplete, but the best guess is that by the reign of Horemheb [1323–1295 BCE] a direct male line of succession had broken down, and that those members of the family who retained an interest were split in their opinions: whether it should remain as a unit or a clean division be made; if undivided, who should act as 'representative' for the 'brothers' (a term that includes siblings and cousins of both sexes); and who actually qualified as a brother, and was therefore entitled to share in the income from the land" (Eyre, 2013: 157). In other cases, "preventive" dispositions forbade that the goods affected to the mortuary cult of an official (and the income derived from it) were unduly appropriated by his kin, as the "legitimate" beneficiaries were the ritualists supposed to perform the ceremonies and/or his direct descendants (Strudwick, 2005: 185–207; Moreno García, 2013a).

Temple land, in principle, was (ideally) put under the protection of a god as it was part of his house(hold), it was (ideally) inviolable, and it increased thanks to donations, mostly royal. A kind of virtuous procedure made it possible for kings to transfer royal land to temples, both in the provinces as well as around the main cities of Egypt (Moreno García, 2013b). Then, this land was partly cultivated by tenants according to diverse modalities (compulsory work, leases, domains trusted to agricultural "entrepreneurs", etc.), partly granted to people of a certain status connected to sanctuaries in different ways, from priests to people that performed occasional rituals in exchange for revenue, from military personnel and administrators to potentates and dignitaries who received substantial fields as rewards from the king (Eyre, 1997; Katary, 2012; Moreno García, 2016c). The status of the fields thus granted varied significantly and inspired complex strategies of accumulation and use of temple land that cannot be reduced to the mere usufruct of the fields. For these reasons, temples appear as true "elite-building tools" in the hands of kings, an aspect often emphasized in both royal and private inscriptions: the high steward Amenhotep declared that the king had built a new temple close to Memphis, endowed it with fields and appointed priests and prophets from the children of the notables of Memphis (Moreno García, 2013b). In other cases, personal initiatives pursued the same goal: the priest Merenptah stated before the great court of Heliopolis that he had placed a statue of Ramesses III in the temple of Ptah at Memphis, equipped with ritual personnel and offerings; the court approved his measure as well as his appointments (which included Merenptah himself as main authority of the cult "from son to son, heir to heir", a sister and two other persons) and assigned offerings brought from the treasury of Ptah and the royal treasury. Royal statues placed in temples, endowed with fields (usually belonging to the category of "donation-fields"), offerings, cattle and other sources of income, were central in these strategies, and rent was paid to the possessor, as papyrus Wilbour and papyrus Golenischeff 1116A show (Moreno García, 2013a, 2013b). In this vein, Sataimau of Edfu claimed that king Ahmose (1550–1525 BCE) had appointed him second lector-priest in the temple of Horus and had granted him the income from a royal statue in the sanctuary endowed with about 36 arouras as well as many offerings (Davies, 2009: 34–36). Inversely, mere scribes and craftsmen (Fischer-Elfert, 2012; Hovestreydt, 1997) and high dignitaries alike made donations to royal statues and, in return, they were allowed to share in the god's offerings presented to the royal image or obtained rewards from the king and thus became associated to his retinue. Hence several fragments of an inscription found in the tomb of Wenennefer, a high priest of Osiris in Abydos, record many royal statues erected (?) in the years 21, 33, 30 + x, 38, 39 and 40 of Ramesses II and endowed with offerings of wine and milk as well as with substantial amounts of land (30 arouras in one case: Moreno García, 2013d: 1038). This policy recalls similar claims from other members of the Ramesside elite, like Penniut of Aniba (Frood, 2007: 213–218). In these cases, private donations of land were often followed, in return, either by offerings from the king's monuments or by authorization to control and derive an income from the endowment (a privilege which continued under the heirs of the donor). In both cases, the donor ensured that the goods donated remained in some way under his control by specifying that the goods transferred to a temple or to a royal statue were protected from outside interference.

In other examples, some tenants enjoyed considerable rights over the temple fields they possessed. A decree from the temple of Medamud, for instance, refers to the reorganization of its patrimony by a Theban king in the early sixteenth century BCE. The text mentions, on the one hand, the donation of fields for an amount of 39 arouras (10.7 ha) to the local temple of god Montu and, on the other hand, the reorganization of its entire landed patrimony (about 460 ha), with a particular clause: "as for anything therein which is in the possession of holders of endowments, make compensation for that [which is to be compen]sated for [on these] fields, plot for plot, threshing-floor [for threshing-floor, with respect to] this endowment of (god) Montu in Medamud. Those who are among the numerous holders of endowments […]" (Redford, 1997: 8). This very particular category of field is mentioned again in an administrative text known as the *Duties of the Vizier* (earliest versions from the middle-late fifteenth century BCE). According to this composition, one of the tasks of the vizier was described in these terms: "it is he who makes the endowment with every plot of land. As for any petitioner who says: 'our boundaries are moved', then one shall inspect that (i. e. whether) they (the boundaries) are under the seal of officials. If so, then he will take away the plots of the particular council which moved them (the boundaries)" (Van den Boorn, 1988: 185). From these texts, it appears that some people benefited from a particular category of endowment and that kings and local authorities (either temple overseers or local dignitaries) could not simply take away this land from their possessors, as they were at least to receive some compensation.

These measures made it possible for kings to get the support of local authorities and to build a provincial social basis formed by people loyal to their authority, sometimes of relative modest condition. In both cases grants of temple land were crucial. From the numerous donations of land recorded in the royal annals of the Early and Middle Bronze Age to the massive grants of fields, gardens, cattle and workers celebrated in the inscriptions and papyri monuments of the Late Bronze Age, temples provided kings with a powerful tool that helped guarantee that the interests of the highest elite of the kingdom and of a provincial "middle class" coincided with those of the sovereign. The Wilbour papyrus gives a detailed clue about what such social base of the pharaohs in the provinces may look like (Antoine, 2014; Katary, 1999, 2010). This document records more than three thousand plots, scattered over a stretch of 140 km in the Nile Valley around the Fayum and the adjacent southern area. Most of these plots (around 2800) are accompanied by the name of their possessors and their social position (titles, functions, etc.). It thus emerges a world of small tenants made of priests, women of a certain status, modest landowners, soldiers and military personnel, scribes, etc. The size of the allotments varied substantially, but the basic plot consisted of 3 or 5 arouras, and multiples of this amount were granted according to the rank, function and activities of their beneficiaries. Only in a very reduced number of cases (thirty-seven) does this document record "donation fields", but they were correlated with the funerary cults of Ramesses III and Ramesses V and with royal institutions, they were mainly located around the locality of Sharope (where many military personnel lived), and they seem related to royal statues endowed with fields. In general, the private possessors of the holdings recorded in the papyrus paid a "tax" or management fee to the administering institution on a variable, but usually minuscule, portion of their fields at a fixed rate per aroura. These smallholdings entailed rights of access to the land provided that their possessors honoured the institution's harvest claim. A study of the roster of smallholders indicates that there are more than 160 instances of split holding (a smallholder possessing more than one plot), comprising approximately 400 plots. Split holdings occur most often with high-ranking individuals, but most of the smallholders with more than one plot, however, were ordinary people identified as prophets, priests, soldiers and scribes. Thus, split holding was a significant element of land tenure on institutionally administered domains even though the percentage of the total plots is modest (Katary, 2000, 2001). When considering that the southern area covered by the papyrus lacks any significant historical and administrative source for the previous centuries, it seems that the pharaohs promoted an active policy of agricultural colonization of this region accompanied by the incorporation of the local elites. Temples were crucial as managerial and economic institutions in this process.

The opportunities for local promotion for those with access to temple holdings were considerable. In fact, wealthy peasants played quite often the role of private "entrepreneurs" at the service of the temples, as they cultivated substantial tracts of land (referred to as "domains"), up to 200 arouras (or 55 ha) according to the papyrus Wilbours. Then they delivered part of the harvest to the institution owner of the land, between one-fourth and one-third. The best-known category of such "entrepreneurs" was called *ihuty* (Moreno García, 2016c: 228–232). The *ihuty* were depicted in many literary texts as leading a miserable existence, prone to abuses by superiors and afflicted by bad harvests, pests, excessive taxes, etc. But in real life, their condition was quite diverse, from serfs forced to cultivate standard plots of 20 arouras (5.5 ha) and deliver 200 sacks of grain (one sack being equivalent to 76.8 L) to *ihuty* capable to deliver more than a thousand sacks. One of them, for instance, handed over 1421 sacks in several villages, and this gives an approximate insight into the geographical extent of his interests and his capacity to mobilize manpower in order to cultivate the land required (Gardiner, 1941: 56–58). This case was far from unique. As the interests of such wealthy *ihuty* extended over entire districts, they can be defined as local potentates. In such a role appears another *ihuty*, called Patjauemdiamun, involved in an obscure affair of stolen tunics and found guilty by an image of god Amun at a village near Thebes. He challenged this divine decision and took his case to other oracles in nearby villages hoping to have finally a favourable decision before "the people of the villages." The fact that such decisions were taken at several localities and involved many witnesses as well as his companions and members of his personnel, suggests that he enjoyed a high status in the local sphere (Kitchen, 2014: 236–237). A final example of the importance of temple land in the social and economic strategies developed by rich peasants is described in a late demotic literary composition. There a potentate (lit. a "great man") was also a priest in the local temple. This was a profitable source of income for him, as he obtained part of the agricultural income of the sanctuary because of his condition as a priest and, in addition, he also exploited some fields of the temple as a cultivator in exchange for a part of the harvest; the considerable wealth thus amassed allowed him to pay wages to the personnel of the temple, who were thus considered his clients (the text states that he had "acquired" them) and he could even marry his sons and daughters to priests and potentates (lit. "great men") of another town (Tait, 2008–2009: 115–124).

These examples reveal that temple land was a crucial asset in the composition of the patrimonies not only of the elite but also of moderately wealthy people, including the upper strata of the peasantry as well as scribes. The late second millennium BCE scribe Thutmose is a good example in which holding land, whether institutional or private, was a familial affair involving him and his son (Antoine, 2015). He owned two categories of land, one which explicitly belonged to him and his son ("our own land"), the administrative status thereof being difficult to identify (were these privately held fields on temple land, or simply private property?), and the other which quite probably consisted of estates pertaining to temples or secular institutions. Holding those two types of the fields was a sign of social prestige that confirmed Thutmose's high rank but, as in the case of another well-off tenant, Heqanakhte, who lived in the early second millennium BCE, the administrative or juridical nature of these fields was a secondary concern: his main goal was managing the land so as to obtain the best agricultural yield (Allen, 2002). Both Heqanakhte and Thutmose behaved like managerial landlords, closely watching over all the details of agricultural operations, and they were certainly not absentee landlords, who delegated the management of their fields to subordinates preoccupied only with the revenue generated. Their interests extended over a district and, in the case of Thutmose, his letters refer to grain stored in magazines in several villages, thus suggesting that other cultivators living nearby worked the estate alongside household members. In fact, the men labouring in the fields were perceived as having the same level of importance as his son and his family, as if they were part of his household. Links with temples also emerge in one of his letters, in which Thutmose mentions chariot-pulling donkeys that, apparently, belonged to a temple (Antoine, 2015). A papyrus scroll recently discovered records his financial accounts relating to the acquisition of copper tools and weapons, but also private affairs like an inventory of his amulets and jewellery and a report about the robbery of his personal belongings (Hölzl et al., 2018). Other examples of people of relative modest condition but involved in different business, including leasing land from temples and getting income from it, are the middle first-millennium *choachytes* (ritualists who took care of mummies in exchange for a remuneration) Djekhy (and his son) and Tsenhor (Donker van Heel, 2012, 2014). They accumulated priestly and/or administrative functions, alongside their agricultural affairs, and reveal a sector of the Egyptian society of this period in which the lines between peasantry and officialdom had become blurred.

A final word concerns some categories of tenants usually labelled "free tenants". They possessed temple land but (usually) not as holders of administrative or priestly positions and, apparently, not as beneficiaries of royal awards. The problem becomes even more controversial because it was common that officials and priests held in fact plots defined as "fields of free tenants". So, the central question seems more related to the categorization of a very specific type of land tenure than to the actual social position of its holders. The term *nemeh* is an excellent example of these problems (Moreno García, 2016c: 232–239). It designated originally the orphan, but its semantic field became gradually enlarged to encompassed further meanings, principally people who led an autonomous existence, based in the possession and management of their own land and whose means of subsistence, consequently, were independent of any service to other landholders, to institutions such as temples and royal departments and to the crown but subject, nevertheless, to state taxes (from the beginning of the New Kingdom). By the end of the New Kingdom, a new expression appeared, "field of *nemeh*", both in administrative texts and in documents dealing with the management of fields belonging to temples, the royal family and the members of the elite. The expression "field of *nemeh*" appeared for the first time around 1280 BCE, not in Egypt but in Nubia, then under Egyptian control, and it was not until two centuries later that it began to be attested in inscriptions and administrative papyri from Upper Egypt. The earliest attestations reveal that the "fields of *nemeh*" bordered fields of the king, of members of the royal family or of dignitaries. It appears then that "fields of *nemeh*" were probably held by local potentates, bearing no rank or function title, but enjoying a certain wealth and status. This may explain why "fields of *nemeh*" are so scarce in Ramesside and in later land registers, as if they were a special kind of tenure used by kings as a selective tool to honour and co-opt certain individuals. Seen in this light, similar conditions prevailed when *nemeh* involved in agricultural activities and "fields of *nemeh*" appeared for the first time in Egypt properly.

In a letter from Elephantine, dated from the eleventh century BCE (Wente, 1990: 130–131), the mayor of Elephantine informed his superiors about a field of the crown regularly tilled by some *nemeh*/free tenants who paid rent or tax in gold directly to the treasury of the Pharaoh while he, on the contrary, paid in grain (100 sacks) to the scribe of a temple for some temple land he cultivated near Kom Ombo, close to Elephantine. The fact that these *nemeh*/free tenants owned gold and paid with it their taxes or rent points to their well-off condition. Other documents, also dated from the eleventh century BCE, introduce for the first time the expression "fields of *nemeh*" (Gasse, 1988: 13, 37–38, 97, 105, 213–214). But even in these administrative land registers references to "fields of *nemeh*" are very rare when compared with other categories of plots. For example, in papyrus Louvre AF 6345 only three plots are so defined and, moreover, they only represented a small fraction of the extensive agricultural domains where each of them was located: 1 + x arouras out of 800 in the first case, 40.5 arouras out of 667 in the second and, finally, 10 arouras out of 1800 in the third, respectively.

From the beginning of the first millennium BCE references to "fields of *nemeh*" become more frequent, especially in the transactions passed on between members of the royal family and private people (Moreno García, 2016c: 232–239). This is the case, for instance, of the funerary endowment established by Sheshonq I (945–924 BCE) for the statue of his father in the temple of Osiris at Abydos, which included 100 arouras of "fields of *nemeh*" (Ritner, 2009: 166–172). Henuttawy, sister and wife of Smendes II, great priest of Amun, declared that she had bought some land, including "fields of *nemeh*" (Ritner, 2009: 138–143), while princess Maatkare obtained, when she was just a child, some property that she had bought as well as "anything of any sort that the people of the land sold to her" and which was recorded as goods of *nemeh*/free tenants (Ritner, 2009: 163–165). The most detailed example is that of Iuwelot, great priest of Amun and son of king Osorkon I (924–889 BCE) and the impressive inscription (the so-called *Apanage stela*). He acquired a domain measuring 556 arouras from eighteen tenants that he bequeathed to his son; the land, located in the domain of god Amun, was considered collectively as "fields of *nemeh*", and the stela records the surface of each plot, the different categories of land it encompassed as well as the presence of wells and trees in it. Finally, the document indicates the price paid for each field (Ritner, 2009: 271–278). Another high priest of Amun, Menkheperre, bought a field from about two dozen individuals designated as "the *nemeh*/free tenants of the town" (Ritner, 2009: 130–135). In other cases, "fields of *nmḥ*" were involved in transactions between ordinary people, as when an inscription from 655 BCE, found near Karnak, refers to the sale or donation of a "high field of *nemeh*" of 10 arouras, located in the domain of god Amun, between a scribe and a priestess. As for papyrus Louvre E 10,935, it makes it possible to follow the ups and downs of a "high field of *nemeh*" of about 5.5 ha over an extensive period of time (628–556 BCE). Located in the domain of god Amun in the region of Coptos, it was successively passed on to different members of the clergy and the royal household, until it was finally transferred to the pious endowment established for the mother of the ultimate buyer. A comparable situation transpires from papyrus British Museum 10,117, dated from 542 BCE, which deals with the sale of a "high field of *nemeh*" of about 8 ha located in the domain of god Amun and which had remained in the hands of the same family for four generations, including its sale to a third party and its later purchase by this same family again. An important aspect to consider is that both inscriptions and papyri reveal that transactions involving "fields of *nemeh*" are only attested in Upper Egypt, and this suggests that these land tenures are closely related to very particular regional agricultural conditions (Moreno García, 2016c: 232–239).

From all these references it is possible to draw three main conclusions. First, "fields of *nemeh*" were part of the landed assets of temples but they were exploited by people entitled to make free use of their rights over this category of land, such as selling or leasing it to a third party or bequeathing it to their heirs. Secondly, members of the royal family and of the highest elite of the country did not hesitate to buy this kind of fields from ordinary tenants in order to create private agricultural domains within a cult institution (as it happened with earlier categories of temple land discussed *supra*, as the decree from Medamud). Finally, their (usually) relatively modest size coupled with the scarce references to "fields of *nemeh*" in the inscriptions (about 150) that recorded donations of land to temples in the late second and early first millennium BCE (Meeks, 1979), suggest that their role was very limited in Egypt. However, their size was in many cases larger than the average tenure needed to feed a peasant family (about 5 arouras or 1.37 ha). Finally, "fields of *nemeh*" are also very rare (only one example) in the corpus of land leases dated between 700 and 400 BCE (Donker van Heel, 1995; Moreno García, 2016c: 239–246). Other documents relative to the exploitation of temple land and privately owned fields also lack any mention of this type of tenure. It may then be concluded that transactions concerning "fields of *nemeh*" only involved, on the one hand, members of the rural elite as well as small but relatively well-off landholders and, on the other hand, temples and members of the royalty and the high priesthood of Amun. Unfortunately, a crucial question remains unsolved: which was the origin of the "fields of *nemeh*" held by temples (purchase? Cession by individuals? Royal dispositions?). A possible explanation, based on the evidence discussed, is that individuals sold, transferred or donated private land tenures to temples, thus formally transformed into temple land but subject nevertheless to some restrictions. Thanks to these transactions the original owner of the field put himself under the protection of a sanctuary, established useful connections with a powerful institution (and its influential rulers), obtained institutional security for his interests in the long term and assured the transmission of the land in the hands of his direct descendants, ideally "from son to son, and from heir to heir", while avoiding any intrusion or claim from collateral branches of his own extended family, as stated in the famous Apanage stela discussed *supra* (Ritner, 2009: 271–278). As for the temple, it also profited from the transaction. It expanded its wealth and social influence and the land remained firmly in its hands, even if the rights over it could be sold, transferred or revoked. To sum up, transactions involving "fields of *nemeh*" point more to strategies aiming to preserve the patrimony of wealthy individuals and to enhance their social promotion than a particular modality of cultivation of institutional land. This may explain why "fields of *nemeh*" flourished in Upper Egypt, at a time of the political division of the country, of loss of the Egyptian empire (and the sources of income with went with it), and when the domain of god Amun became the most powerful and stable institution in Upper Egypt, the only region where "fields of *nemeh*" are attested (Moreno García, 2016c: 232–239).

As for Lower Egypt, it followed, apparently, a different strategy. Here "fields of *nemeh*" are absent but inscriptions recording donations of land to temples are ubiquitous from the very end of the second millennium BCE. Temples, too, were centres of institutional stability, of agricultural wealth and of reorganization of the local elites in northern Egypt. But instead of a single source of authority (like the domain of god Amun in Upper Egypt), Lower Egypt, by contrast, witnessed the emergence of a multitude of principalities. Donations of land to temples, celebrated in numerous stelae in Lower Egypt, may thus express the desire to visualize the prosperity of a local elite supported by temples in a dynamic and fluid society, well integrated in the vibrant exchange networks of the Mediterranean. However, as Donker van Heel has pointed out recently, it is quite possible that in some instances the differences between Upper and Lower Egypt are more apparent than real. From the study of donations of land to *choachytes*, he also discerns a strategy by which people in Lower Egypt may have donated land to the temples and then the sanctuaries transferred them to the *choachytes* in usufruct, just to finance the rituals they usually performed. In this case, it is significant that temples acted as mediators in operations between individuals (the donor and the *choachyte*), doubtless to provide security to the donor (Donker van Heel, 2017–2018).

Conclusion

From the evidence analysed, it is apparent that private land tenures are well attested in Egypt from the earliest times. The land was exchanged between individuals and made it possible to accumulate patrimonies, but it seems nevertheless that these transactions were limited, that their protagonists were usually wealthy or moderately wealthy people, and that a true market of land did not exist in Egypt. Other institutions, such as temples and domains of the crown, opened more possibilities for the creation of landed portfolios. However, leaving aside the abundant cases of people who obtained temple land as awards and remunerations from the king, in exchange for their services for the crown, there is also very limited evidence about the creation and transmission over long periods of time of (almost) private tenures located on temple land. They represented only a small fraction of the landed assets of temples and they could be expropriated (but their possessors should then be compensated). It is even possible that most of these (almost) private tenures consisted in fact in fields previously donated by individuals to the sanctuaries in exchange for specific services but, more generally, as a strategy seeking to secure at least part of their patrimony. In all, the scope of all these individualist strategies seems quite limited and reduced mostly to transactions carried out by wealthy individuals within the sphere of institutions (temples, crown land, royal grants of fields), with little impact outside them. What is more, the importance of these institutions (particularly temples) in the formation of private land portfolios meant in the end that they also limited the possibilities for the emergence of a significant market of land and that, accordingly, the formation of extensive private landholdings was only possible through regular access to temple and crown land, not to land markets.

References

Allen, J. P. (2002). *The Heqanakht Papyri*. Metropolitan Museum of Art.

Anievas, A., & Nişancıoğlu, K. (2015). *How the west came to rule: The geopolitical origins of capitalism*. Pluto Press.

Antoine, J.-C. (2014). Social position and the organisation of landholding in Ramesside Egypt: An analysis of the Wilbour Papyrus. *Studien zur Altägyptischen Kultur, 43,* 17–46.

Antoine, J.-C. (2015). Landholding and agriculture in Late Ramesside Theban documents. *Zeitschrift für Ägyptische Sprache und Altertumskunde, 142,* 104–119.

Baer, K. (1962). The low price of land in ancient Egypt. *Journal of the American Research Center in Egypt, 1,* 25–45.

Banaji, J. (2018). Globalising the history of capital: Ways forward. *Historical Materialism, 26,* 143–166.

Bleiberg, E. (1996). *The official gift in ancient Egypt*. Oklahoma University Press.

Davies, W. V. (2009). La tombe de Sataimaou à Hagar Edfou. *Égypte, Afrique Et Orient, 53,* 25–40.

Donker van Heel, K. (1995). *Abnormal hieratic and early demotic texts collected by the Theban Choachytes in the reign of Amasis. Papyri from the Louvre Eisenlohr Lot*. Autoprint.

Donker van Heel, K. (2012). *Djekhy & Son: Doing business in ancient Egypt*. American University Cairo.

Donker van Heel, K. (2014). *Mrs. Tsenhor: A female entrepreneur in ancient Egypt*. American University Cairo.

Donker van Heel, K. (2017–2018). Delta donations for doorkeepers, why? *Journal of the Society for the Study of Egyptian Antiquities, 44,* 205–218.

Eyre, C. (1997). Peasants and "modern" leasing strategies in ancient Egypt. *Journal of the Economic and Social History of the Orient, 40,* 367–390.

Eyre, C. (1998). The market women of Pharaonic Egypt. In N. Grimal & B. Menu (Eds.), *Le commerce en Égypte ancienne* (pp. 173–191). Institut Français d'Archéologie Orientale.

Eyre, C. (2013). *The use of documents in Pharaonic Egypt*. Oxford University Press.

Fischer, H. G. (1968). *Dendera in the third millennium BC, down to the Theban domination of Upper Egypt*. J.J. Augustin.

Fischer-Elfert, H.-W. (2012). A strike in the reign of Merenptah? *plus* the endowment of three cult statue(tte)s on behalf of the same king at Deir el-Medina (Pap. Berlin P. 23300 and P. 23301). In V. M. Lepper (Ed.), *Forschung in der Papyrussammlung: Eine Festgabe für das Neue Museum* (pp. 47–73). Akademie Verlag.

Frood, E. (2007). *Biographical texts from Ramessid Egypt*. Society of Biblical Literature.

Gardiner, A. H. (1941). Ramesside texts relating to the taxation and transport of corn. *The Journal of Egyptian Archaeology, 27,* 19–73.

Gardiner, A. H. (1948). *The Wilbour Papyrus. Vol. II: Commentary*. Oxford University Press.

Gasse, A. (1988). *Données nouvelles administratives et sacerdotales sur l'organisation du domaine d'Amon XXe-XXIe dynasties à la lumière des papyrus Prachov, Reinhardt et Grundbuch*. Institut Français d'Archéologie Orientale.

Grandet, P. (1994). *Le Papyrus Harris I (BM 9999)*. Institut Français d'Archéologie Orientale.

Hassan, K., & Ouda, A. M. (2018). Ramesside hieratic stela of the sandal maker Penōne in the Egyptian Museum Cairo (TR. 27.6.24.3). *Journal of the American Research Center in Egypt, 54*, 93–106.

Hölzl, R., Neumann, M., & Demarée, R. J. (2018). *The notebook of Dhutmose: P. Vienna AES 10321*. Brill.

Hovestreydt, W. (1997). A letter to the king relating to the foundation of a statue (P. Turin 1879 vso.). *Lingua Aegyptia, 5*, 107–121.

Janssen, J. J. (1975). Prolegomena to the study of Egypt's economic history during the New Kingdom. *Studien zur Altägyptischen Kultur, 3*, 127–185.

Jursa, M., Hackl, J., Janković, B., Kleber, K., Payne, E. E., Waerzeggers, C., & Weszeli, M. (2010). *Aspects of the economic history of Babylonia in the first millennium BC: Economic geography, economic mentalities, agriculture, the use of money and the problem of economic growth*, Alter Orient und Altes Testament 377. Ugarit Verlag Münster.

Katary, S. L. D. (1999). Land-tenure in the New Kingdom: The role of women smallholders and the military. In A. K. Bowman & E. Rogan (Eds.), *Agriculture in Egypt: From pharaonic to modern times* (pp. 61–82). Oxford University Press.

Katary, S. L. D. (2000). O. Strasbourg H 106: Ramesside split holdings and a possible link to Deir el-Medina. In R. Demarée & A. Egberts (Eds.), *Deir el- Medina in the third millennium AD: A tribute to Jac. J. Janssen* (pp. 171–208). Nederlands Instituut voor het Nabije Oosten.

Katary, S. L. D. (2001). Labour on smallholdings in the New Kingdom: O. BM 5627 in light of P. Wilbour. *Journal of the Society for the Study of Egyptian Antiquities, 28*, 111–123.

Katary, S. L. D. (2010). Distinguishing subclasses in New Kingdom society on evidence of the Wilbour Papyrus. In J. C. M. García (Ed.), *Élites et pouvoir en Égypte ancienne* (pp. 263–320). Université Charles-de-Gaulle-Lille 3.

Katary, S. L. D. (2012). Land tenure (to the end of the Ptolemaic period). In J. C. M. García & W. Wendrich (Eds.), *UCLA encyclopedia of egyptology*. UCLA. https://digital2.library.ucla.edu/viewItem.do?ark=21198/zz002bfks5.

Kehoe, D. P., Ratzan, D. M., & Yiftach, U. (Eds.). (2015). *Law and transaction costs in the ancient economy*. University of Michigan Press.

Kitchen, K. A. (2014). *Ramesside inscriptions translated and annotated: Translations* (Vol. VII). Wiley-Blackwell.

Kleber, K., & Pirngruber, R. (Eds.). (2016). *Silver, money and credit: A tribute to Robartus J. van der Spek on the occasion of his 65th birthday*. Nederlands Instituut voor het Nabije Oosten.

Manning, J. G. (2003). *Land and power in Ptolemaic Egypt: The structure of land tenure*. Cambridge University Press.

McDowell, A. (1992). Agricultural activity by the workmen of Deir el-Medina. *The Journal of Egyptian Archaeology, 78*(195), 206.

Meeks, D. (1979). Les donations aux temples dans l'Égypte du Ier millénaire avant J.-C. In E. Lipiński (Ed.), *State and temple economy in the ancient near East: Proceedings of the International Conference organized by the Katholieke Universiteit Leuven from the 10th to the 14th of April 1978* (Vol. II, pp. 605–687). Departement Oriëntalistiek.

Moeller, N. (2005). *The archaeology of urbanism in ancient Egypt: From the predynastic period to the end of the Middle Kingdom*. Cambridge University Press.

Moreno García, J. C. (1997). *Études sur l'administration, le pouvoir et l'idéologie en Égypte, de l'Ancien au Moyen Empire*. Centre d'informatique de Philosophie et Lettres.

Moreno García, J. C. (2000). Acquisition de serfs durant la Première Période Intermédiaire: une étude d'histoire sociale dans l'Egypte du IIIe millénaire. *Revue D'égyptologie, 51*, 123–139.

Moreno García, J. C. (2013a). Conflicting interests over the possession and transfer of institutional land: Individual *versus* family strategies. In E. Frood & A. McDonald (Eds.), *Decorum and experience: Essays in ancient culture for John Baines* (pp. 258–263). Griffith Institute.
Moreno García, J. C. (2013b). Land donations. In E. Frood & W. Wendrich (Eds.), *UCLA encyclopedia of egyptology*. UCLA. https://digital2.library.ucla.edu/viewItem.do?ark=21198/zz002hgp07. Accessed 18 Dec 2020.
Moreno García, J. C. (2013c). The limits of pharaonic administration: Patronage, informal authorities, mobile populations and "invisible" social sectors. In M. Bárta & H. Küllmer (Eds.), *Diachronic trends in ancient Egyptian history: Studies dedicated to the memory of Eva Pardey* (pp. 88–101). Czech Institute of Egyptology.
Moreno García, J. C. (2013d). The "other" administration: Patronage system and informal networks of power in ancient Egypt. In J. C. Moreno García (Ed.), *Ancient Egyptian administration* (pp. 1029–1065). Brill.
Moreno García, J. C. (2014a). Penser l'économie pharaonique. *Annales. Histoire, Sciences sociales, 69*, 7–38.
Moreno García, J. C. (2014b). L'organisation sociale de l'agriculture pharaonique: quelques cas d'étude. *Annales. Histoire, Sciences sociales, 69*, 39–74.
Moreno García, J. C. (2015). Climatic change or sociopolitical transformation? Reassessing late 3rd millennium Egypt. In H. Meller, R. Risch, R. Jung, & H. W. Arz (Eds.), *2200 BC—A climatic breakdown as a cause for the collapse of the old world? Proceedings of the 7th archaeological congress of Central Germany*, Tagungen des Landesmuseums für Vorgeschichte Halle 1 (pp. 79–94). Landesmuseum für Vorgeschichte Halle (Saale).
Moreno García, J. C. (2016a). Social inequality, private accumulation of wealth and new ideological values in late 3rd millennium BCE Egypt. In H. Meller, H. P. Hahn, R. Jung, & R. Risch (Eds.), *Arm und Reich — Zur Ressourcenverteilung in prähistorischen Gesellschaften*, Tagungen des Landesmuseums für Vorgeschichte Halle 14 (pp. 491–512). Landesmuseum für Vorgeschichte Halle (Saale).
Moreno García, J. C. (2016b). Economies in transition: Trade, "money", labour and nomads at the turn of the 1st millennium BC. In J. C. M. García (Ed.), *Dynamics of production in the ancient Near East, 1300–500 BC* (pp. 1–39). Oxbow Books.
Moreno García, J. C. (2016c). Temples and agricultural labour in Egypt, from the Late New Kingdom to the Saite Period. In J. C. M. García (Ed.), *Dynamics of production in the ancient Near East, 1300–500 BC* (pp. 223–256). Oxbow Books.
Morenz, L. D. (2006). Zwischen Kontext, Intermedialität, Intertextualität und Individualität: die Selbst-Präsentation eines Nedjes-iker (BM 1671). *Lingua Aegyptia, 14*, 389–407.
Muhs, B. (2016). *The ancient Egyptian economy 3000–30 BCE*. Cambridge University Press.
Musacchio, T. (2010). An unpublished stela from Dendera dating to the eleventh dynasty. In Z. A. Hawass & J. H. Wegner (Eds.), *Millions of jubilees: Studies in honor of David P. Silverman* (Vol. II, pp. 1–12). Conseil Suprême des Antiquités de l'Égypte.
Narotzky, S., & Manzano, E. (2014). The Ḥisba, the Muḥtasib and the struggle over political power and a moral economy: An enquiry into institutions. In J. Hudson & A. Rodríguez (Eds.), *Diverging paths? The shapes of power and institutions in Medieval Christendom and Islam* (pp. 30–54). Brill.
Parker, R. A. (1962). *A saite oracle papyrus from Thebes in the Brooklyn Museum (Papyrus Brooklyn 47.218.3)*. Brown University Press.
Peet, T. E. (1930). *The great tomb robberies of the twentieth Egyptian dynasty, being a critical study, with translations and commentaries, of the papyri in which these are recorded*. Oxford University Press.
Pirngruber, R. (2017). *The economy of late Achaemenid and Seleucid Babylonia*. Cambridge University Press.
Polotsky, H. J. (1930). The stela of Ḥeḳa-yeb. *The Journal of Egyptian Archaeology, 16*, 194–199.

Redford, D. B. (1997). Textual sources for the Hyksos period. In E. D. Oren (Ed.), *The Hyksos: New historical and archaeological perspectives* (pp. 1–44). Museum of Archaeology and Anthropology.
Ritner, R. K. (2009). *The Libyan anarchy: Inscriptions from Egypt's third intermediate period.* Society of Biblical Literature.
Sánchez León, P., & Martín, J. I. (2002). L'autismo della microeconomia. Per un'interpretazione non utilitarista della storia agraria. *Meridiana, 45,* 179–197.
Strudwick, N. C. (2005). *Texts from the pyramid age.* Society of Biblical Literature.
Tait, J. (2008–2009). Pa-di-pep tells Pharaoh the story of the condemnation of Djed-her: Fragments of Demotic narrative in the British Museum. *Enchoria, 31,* 113–143.
Tedesco, P. (2018). Late antiquity, early Islam, and the emergence of a "precocious capitalism": A review essay. *The Journal of European Economic History, 3,* 115–151.
Van den Boorn, G. P. F. (1988). *The duties of the Vizier: Civil administration in the early New Kingdom.* Kegan Paul International.
Van der Spek, R. J., van Leeuwen, B., & van Zanden, J. L. (Eds.). (2015). *A history of market performance: From ancient Babylonia to the modern world.* Routledge.
Van Leeuwen, B., & Van der Spek, R. J. (Eds.). (2018). *Money, currency and crisis: In search of trust, 2000 bc to ad 2000.* Routledge.
Warburton, D. A. (2016). *The fundamentals of economics: Lessons from the Bronze Age Near East.* Recherches et Publications.
Wente, E. (1990). *Letters from ancient Egypt.* Scholars Press.
Willems, H. (1991). The end of Seankhenptah's household (Letter to the Dead Cairo JdE 25975). *Journal of Near Eastern Studies, 50,* 183–191.

Chapter 8
Uneven and Combined: Product Exchange in the Mediterranean (3rd to 2nd Millennium BCE)

Reinhard Jung

Abstract This contribution deals with goods exchange in the Mediterranean Bronze Age by applying Marx's commodity definition in order to better characterize the economic aspects of that goods exchange and to understand how those aspects affected the societies involved. In the process of commoditization, the exchange value of products becomes distinct from their use value, and as this development typically appears first in exchange relations between societies, the examples discussed here refer to products exported from Cyprus and Mycenaean Greece among others. The exchange relationships between different Mediterranean societies involved products exhibiting a commodity character to various degrees, while showing a rough east-west gradient in this respect. Under specific circumstances, these exchange relationships led to a rapid acceleration in the development of socio-economic relationships within societies.

Introduction

In recent years, we seem to have witnessed a growing use of economic terms borrowed from contemporary capitalism for the description of Bronze Age economies outside Mesopotamia, the Levant and Egypt—terms such as "trade," "commodity," "markets" (e.g. Blake, 2014: 18–19, 219–220, 227, 238; Blackwell, 2018: 513, 525; Pullen, 2013; for the written sources referring to markets in Mesopotamia and Egypt see Rahmstorf, 2016a: 292–294), "World System" (Sherratt, 2000),[1] or even "flow of capital" and "capital accumulation" (Iacono, 2013: 60–61, 67). More often than not those terms are not properly or not at all defined, which seems to imply that scholars

[1] On the discussions regarding the possibilities of applying or adapting Wallerstein's world systems approach to pre-capitalist societies and especially to 4th to 2nd millennium Mesopotamia and the Near East, see Patterson (2003: 140–146).

R. Jung (✉)
Austrian Academy of Sciences, Austrian Archaeological Institute, Vienna, Austria
e-mail: Reinhard.Jung@oeaw.ac.at

S. Gimatzidis and R. Jung (eds.), *The Critique of Archaeological Economy*, Frontiers in Economic History,
https://doi.org/10.1007/978-3-030-72539-6_8

use them with the meaning they have in our current societies, though referring to societies of the third and second millennia BCE. The task of this paper is therefore twofold: first, to discuss basic definitions of economic terminology by reference to the work of Karl Marx and second, to test these definitions against some examples in the archaeological record in order to elucidate the economic character of various aspects of product exchange during the Bronze Age in the Mediterranean.

Part A—Theoretical Consideration

Value

The first question to answer is what we should understand by the term "commodity," Does it aid a deeper understanding of pre- and protohistoric economies to use this term interchangeably with "exchanged product" or anything that can be exchanged between humans, as we read in many papers (cf. Kopytoff, 1986: 71–72)?

Karl Marx in his *Kapital*, vol. I, established that a dual nature is the defining characteristic of a commodity. A commodity has both a use value and an exchange value. First, it is a "thing that by its properties satisfies human wants of some sort or another" (Marx, 1962 [1867]: 49). "The utility of a thing makes it a use value" (Marx, 1962 [1867]: 50). Second, the exchange value of a commodity depends on labor, but not in the way it does in classical economic theory. The value of a commodity is determined by "abstract human labor" measured in time units. This time is that which has to be spent on average in a given society under normal conditions of production and by normal intensity of work and skillfulness of the workman, in order to produce an average specimen of a specific commodity (Marx, 1962 [1867]: 53–54). In conclusion, not every product is a commodity. A commodity is a useful thing produced in order to be exchanged against other commodities on the basis of their exchange values.

Marx carefully studied pre-capitalist societies by reading written sources from many different periods and regions of the world, and he came to the conclusion that commodities are not confined to contemporary capitalism, but existed even on "the basis of the primitive community, of slave production, of small peasant [production]" (Marx, 1964 [1894]: 337). However, "Before capitalist production, a large part of the products was not produced as commodities, not to serve as commodities; while, conversely, a large part of the products [...] did not enter the production process as commodities. The conversion of products into commodities only occurs at individual points, is limited only to the surplus of production, or only to individual spheres of production (the products of manufacture), etc." (Marx, 2009 [1863/1864]: 25).

The anthropologist David Graeber, by contrast, suggested limiting the application of the categories "use value" and "exchange value" to capitalist societies (Graeber, 2001: 264). In a more recent paper, the economist Riccardo Bellofiore refers to critics of Marx's labor theory of value, who argue that "Marx himself shows that the social equalization among labors is achieved only when commodities are *actually* sold in circulation: before that, in production, we meet only concrete labors, which are *heterogeneous* and *non-additive*." Bellofiore responds by explaining that such positions "ignore the fact that for Marx, commodity exchange is universal *only* when the capitalist mode of production is dominant — that is, only when workers are compelled to sell their labor power to money as capital, as self-valorizing value" (Bellofiore, 2018).

Considering these points of critique, we can point out that among the pre-capitalist modes of production, the bureaucratic monarchies of the so-called Asiatic Mode of Production (on that Marxian concept in reference to Near Eastern societies of the 3rd and 2nd millennia BCE see Zaccagnini, 1981; on the research history see Nippel, 2020), did assess the value of labor in very direct ways, i.e., without the commodity fetish of capitalist production. So, for instance, Piotr Steinkeller (2015), in his introduction to the volume "Labor in the Ancient World," has remarked on the fact that around 2400 BCE the Sumerians were already thinking about human labor in abstract terms. As he explained, "… the Sumerian word á, whose basic and original meanings are 'arm, strength, power, physical exertion,' signified 'labor' in exactly the same way we understand it today, namely, a quantifiable physical effort resulting in the creation of goods and services. The Sumerians measured labor in the units of time (days) needed by an average grown man to complete a particular task." Moreover, the administrators were hiring workers from other institutions and neighboring provinces. In these transactions, the value of the labor was expressed in units of grain or even silver. This did not happen on a free labor market as in capitalist societies, but remained under state control (Steinkeller, 2015: 1–2, 20–21 n. 44; 23–24). This practice of counting labor in work days or man-days, themselves converted into grain units, was developed for managing and planning purposes by the early state administration in Mesopotamia and brings us surprisingly close to the "socially necessary labor" of Marx's exchange value concept.

In the Late Bronze Age Mycenaean palace regimes, the basis of calculation for the dependent work force of the palaces is not average time, but food rations were given out according to gender categories for adults and to age categories (independent of gender) for child workers, as classified by the administrators—a practice which was also used in Mesopotamia from the 3rd millennium BCE (Milani, 1977; Nosch, 2020). These rations are the foodstuffs needed to sustain labor power (i.e., to keep alive the work forces for an envisaged working period), which those administrators used to plan work projects. In other words, the most important aspect determining the value of the labor of those workers (cf. Marx, 1962 [1867]: 184–187) is directly registered in this way (housing and clothes not being registered).

Thus, either registering the average personal labor, which is equivalent to the production time for the goods necessary to reproduce the workforce, or, alternatively, listing those subsistence goods themselves would have enabled the bureaucrats of those palace- and temple-based economies to calculate the *surplus labor* of the workers—i.e., that part of their daily labor time during which they would have produced new goods to the exclusive benefit of the rulers (Marx, 1962 [1867]: 249–250; on surplus labor in precapitalist economies). We can therefore expect the administrators to have been well informed about the labor expenditure needed in the production of goods that either went into consumption, distribution, or exchange.

Returning to the subject of exchange value, Marx found that the more regular an exchange relationship becomes, the more products tend to be produced in order to be exchanged. Therefore, a separation starts to occur between the utility of the product for consumption and its utility for exchange purposes—i.e., its use value becomes distinguished from its exchange value. Furthermore, the quantitative proportions, in which commodities are exchanged against each other, become directly dependent on their production. "Custom stamps them as values with definite magnitudes" (Marx, 1962 [1867]: 103).

Much research in social anthropology, archaeology, and history clarified a wide variety of ways in which human societies ascribe value to the things their members appropriate from nature (Graeber, 2001). In a Marxist reading, all the culturally and ideologically determined categories of value—such as those of the famous *kula* exchange system for example—appear as specific expressions of use value. Once products obtained by exchange between societies enter distribution and consumption processes in one society, its members imbue them with value according to the social rules and traditions of their own society and then exchange them further or remove them from circulation, etc. (Kopytoff, 1986). They are thus re-interpreted and re-evaluated, sometimes simply because knowledge about them is not fully transferred along with them (Appadurai, 1986: 56), but often also in light of the fact that they come from foreign, distant areas, which may add to their value (Helms, 1988: 111–130). This may happen separately from the fact that the transport itself was labor-intensive or else in such a way that this labor input becomes ideologically concealed, i.e., fetishized. The resulting new value ascription can, of course, differ markedly from that of the society which manufactured those products.

It follows then that society-specific systems of use value cannot be generalized for explaining product exchange systems functioning *between* two different societies with *diverging value systems*. By contrast, the exchange value based on the "socially necessary labor time" offers a measure independent from society-specific use values that are not convertible between two different societies. In Marx's own words, "… when we bring the products of our labour into relation with each other as values, it is not because we see in these articles the material receptacles of homogeneous human labour. Quite the contrary: whenever, by an exchange, we equate as values our different products, by that very act, we also equate, as human labour, the different kinds of labour expended upon them. We are not aware of this, nevertheless we do it" (Marx, 1962 [1867]: 88).

So, Marx gives us some criteria for determining if products did assume the character of commodities—criteria for which we can also find archaeological correlates. We may ask (1) if certain artifacts were produced with the purpose of being exchanged; (2) which quantities were actually exchanged; and (3) if the exchange processes in which those products changed hands were of a regular, recurring nature and thus had the potential to influence the economic and social relations of the participating exchange partners.

In a developed stage of commodity exchange, social and economic mechanisms lead to the fixation of one specific commodity as a **general, socially accepted value equivalent**—i.e., a value equivalent, in which all other commodities express their value. Money is invented (Marx, 1962 [1867], 82–83; for a concrete historical case study centering on the start of coinage see e.g. Furtwängler, 2016).

In other words, in pre-capitalist societies, the commodity character of products may have taken shape gradually, "revealing" (so to speak) their exchange value by expressing it in more and more other commodities and ultimately in a general value equivalent—though this did not necessarily happen in a continuous and progressive way and in all interacting societies contemporaneously. That commodity character of products is best captured by referring to the Marxian "exchange value"—as opposed to Appadurai's a-historical concept of "the commodity situation in the life of any 'thing'" coupled with his rejection of the production perspective (Appadurai, 1986: 13), which obscures precisely the important point, when the use value and the exchange value of a product become separated.

Functions of money according to Marx

1. Measure of value. It expresses the value of commodities and functions as a general social equivalent (*allgemeines gesellschaftlich gültiges Wertäquivalent*), because it is itself a product of labor (Marx, 1962 [1867]: 83–85, 101, 109, 113).[2]
2. Standard of price. (Imagined) weighable metal units with their subdivisions become standards of price (Marx, 1962 [1867]: 112).
3. Means of circulation, expressed by the formula commodity—money—commodity (Marx, 1962 [1867]: 118–143).

Ad 1 and 2. "As *measure of value*, and as *standard of price*, money has two entirely distinct functions to perform. It is the measure of value inasmuch as it is the socially recognised incarnation of human labour; it is the standard of price inasmuch as it is a fixed weight of metal" (Marx, 1962 [1867]: 113).

[2]"It is because all commodities, as values, are realised human labour, and therefore commensurable, that their values can be measured by one and the same special commodity, and the latter be converted into the common measure of their values, *i.e.*, into money. Money as a measure of value, is the phenomenal form that must of necessity be assumed by that measure of value which is immanent in commodities, labour-time" (Marx, 1962 [1867]: 109).

Capital

Capital is defined by Marx as being a *value*, which *valorizes* itself (Marx, 1962 [1867]: 169).[3] For its appearance, certain historical preconditions have to be met. The first is the existence of *free* laborers owning their labor power as a commodity. The second precondition is a labor market, on which the laborer is selling the only commodity he/she possesses, his/her "labor power," to an owner of some means of production, to a capitalist, on a temporary basis (Marx, 1962 [1867]: 182–183). By paying him/her a wage, the capitalist buys the labor power, the commodity of the laborer, according to its exchange value. As is the case with any other commodity, the exchange value of the labor power is determined by the socially necessary time needed for its production, i.e., for the production of the goods the laborer needs to survive (including the goods for dependent family members). Having bought the labor power, the capitalist puts it to work and he/she seeks to extend the work time of the laborer, in order to extract surplus value. Surplus value is created by unpaid labor, i.e. by the extra time span, the laborer works for the capitalist after the subtraction of the wage (Marx, 1962 [1867]: 184–189, 230–232, 244).

The described factors hold good for industrial capital, and we may agree that in the economic systems of the Bronze Age, no significant labor market existed in the countries surrounding the Mediterranean (on the mobilization of labor in the Mycenaean palatial system see Palaima, 2015; for the mobilization of labor at Ugarit see Heltzer, 1999). However, there is also merchant capital, which according to Marx, historically precedes the formation of industrial capital.

Merchant's Capital: Buying in Order to Sell Dearer (Marx, 1962 [1867]: 170)

Merchant's capital "merely promotes the exchange of commodities; yet this exchange is not to be conceived at the outset as a bare exchange of commodities between direct producers. [...] The merchant buys and sells for many. [...] But whatever the social organisation of the spheres of production whose commodity exchange the merchant promotes, his wealth exists always in the form of money, and his money always serves as capital. [...] Money, the independent form of exchange-value, is the point of departure, and increasing the exchange-value an end in itself" (Marx, 1964 [1894]: 338). The characteristic circulation of merchant's capital is money—commodity—money (M—C—M'), which is at the same time the general formula of capital (Marx, 1962 [1867]: 170).

[3]"Denn die Bewegung, worin er [der Wert] Mehrwert zusetzt, ist seine eigne Bewegung, seine Verwertung als Selbstverwertung". In the English translation this becomes: "For the movement, in the course of which it [the value] adds surplus-value, is its own movement, its expansion, therefore, is automatic expansion," quoted after https://www.marxists.org/archive/marx/works/1867-c1/ch04.htm.

Marx goes on to explain that "So long as merchant's capital promotes the exchange of products between undeveloped societies, commercial profit not only appears as out-bargaining and cheating, but also largely originates from them. Aside from the fact that it exploits the difference between the prices of production of various countries (and in this respect it tends to level and fix the values of commodities), those modes of production bring it about that merchant's capital appropriates an overwhelming portion of the surplus-product" (Marx, 1964 [1894]: 343).

A good example for such a mechanism from the Bronze Age is provided by the city of Assur on the Tigris River during the nineteenth and eighteenth centuries BCE, for the economy of Assur largely depended on trade, by export of woolen textiles, tin and lapis lazuli to and import of gold and silver from central Asia Minor. Almost all the commodities traded by family firms of that city-state, which at that time did not feature a palace and did not rule an empire, were produced in faraway regions (textiles being a partial exception, because they were also locally produced). However, the detailed clay tablet archives from the *kārum* outpost (trading quarter) at the city of Kanesh convey that Assyrian traders were able to appropriate a large surplus product, as is indicated by huge price differences for silver when bought at Kanesh in Asia Minor and then exchanged for southern imports at Assur in Mesopotamia (Veenhof, 2010). In fact, when those archives for the first time in human history preserve the expression "to make money"—literally "to make silver"—and also state the goal "to covert merchandise [again] into silver" (Veenhof, 1997: 363) they reveal the very essence of merchant's capital. However, Assyriologists classify this kind of silver-focused exchange as "a much more 'monetarian' economy than anywhere else in the ancient Near East" (Veenhof, 1997: 340).

Part B—The Mediterranean Bronze Age Evidence

The Beginnings in the 3rd Millennium and the Early 2nd Millennium

In the early 3rd millennium BCE we witness the introduction of a Near Eastern weight system—perhaps first on the western coast of Asia Minor and then spreading to the Aegean islands and the Greek mainland (Rahmstorf, 2016b). Sphendonoid to rectangular weight shapes were first employed in Mesopotamia around 3000 BCE (Rahmstorf, 2016b: 254; Rahmstorf, 2016c: 29–31, Fig. 2.3). In the early 3rd millennium, the Aegean communities created a specifically regional spool-shaped type—often made of colorful stone and reproducing different Mesopotamian and Syrian weight units (Horejs, 2016; Rahmstorf, 2016b: 238–256). We are dealing mainly with small weights. The heaviest mainly range between 91.8 and 190 g (Rahmstorf, 2006: 80, Fig. 17). However, a late EH II context at Ayía Iríni on the Cycladic island of Keos yielded a large weight of 3790 g (almost exactly 400 times a weight of 9.4 g, or else 8 minas or 4 double minas), together with two further spools and a large piece of litharge (Rahmstorf, 2006: 76–78, Fig. 13–14). Already some of the earliest Aegean weights were part of assemblages related to metal production and therefore possibly also to the exchange of metals (Rahmstorf, 2015: 164–166, Fig. 12; Rahmstorf, 2016b: 250–251, 253–255). So, the first step to express abstract human labor objectified in products (almost certainly including metals) that were exchanged had been taken. It was the introduction of Mesopotamian weight systems for exchange processes that allowed the precise measurement of that objectified labor; as the work required to produce a product could now be related directly to its mass. However, in the absence of texts, we do not know if any general, socially accepted value equivalent did exist in Greece or Asia Minor in the 3rd millennium BCE. We also do not know if the Mesopotamian system of daily rations for alienated labor existed in the Aegean at that time.

The Later 2nd Millennium

Proceeding to the second half of the 2nd millennium BCE, we are now much better informed about Mediterranean exchange processes. Letters in the royal and non-royal archives—e.g., at Tell el-Amarna in Upper Egypt and Ugarit in coastal northern Syria—document large-scale goods exchange taking place between kings as well as recording goods exchanges between rulers and their subordinates. Both on the level of formalized gift exchange and in openly commercial interactions, value equivalents could be registered by giving prices in silver quantities, i.e., the general value equivalent, which was socially accepted among the kingdoms around the eastern Mediterranean. In formalized gift exchange, such references to silver quantities would often only be implicit. However, even in such cases, the kings expressed concern about the equivalent values of the gifts they received (Zaccagnini, 1973: 79–80). Finished objects of refined craftsmanship functioning as status symbols of the ruling classes such as chariots, weapons, and vessels, often specifically named as products of this or that country or made in a specific country's style, became even more appreciated when a gift received from a foreign king was re-used, as it was given to a third king (Liverani, 2001: 157–158). This would be a clear example of the concept of an ideologically determined use value.

From Ugarit, we know quite a number of prices for different products (and even plots of land), expressed in shekels of silver, but these products were not necessarily commodities exchanged between two owners (Courtois, 1990). It is furthermore interesting to note that the palace used the value equivalent of silver to register debt obligations, which then were paid by the debtor in the form of labor conducted for the palace (McGeough, 2015: 88–89). Weighed quantities of silver as a general value equivalent of course have a long history in Bronze Age Mesopotamia (see also above). This metal was even used in tax collection as the final means of payment to the palace, i.e., by middlemen, who collected the payment in kind from peasants and herders and then converted it into silver in the early second millennium Babylonia (Van De Mieroop, 2014).

In stark contrast to Ugarit, in Mycenaean Greece the Linear B texts from the different palaces do not provide us with any indications for the use of a **general, socially accepted value equivalent** for the internal economic affairs of the palatial administration. Occasionally products were offset against quantities of other products, i.e., a textile (of unspecified quantity!) against a quantity of cereals (Montecchi, 2007). It seems that any kind of product could become a means of payment to the palace (Montecchi, 2007: 489; Luján, 2011: 25). As for transactions, the palace of Knossós, for instance, recorded in two cases that a certain person bought a slave from another person—though without mentioning the price, for the palatial administrators were seemingly only interested in monitoring the fact that these transactions took place (Olivier, 1987 [with the hypothesis that these texts were only extracts of unpreserved purchase contracts]; Montecchi, 2007: 488; Zurbach, 2017: 665–666).

Finally, Julien Zurbach has recently put forward good arguments for the existence of debt slavery, citing the "slaves of the divinity" and connecting them to loans of so-called "holy" or "temple gold" by Mycenaean temples. However, the relevant Linear B texts he refers to do not provide detailed evidence as to how that mechanism of lending gold (*Hackgold* in Zurbach's interpretation) may have worked (Zurbach, 2017). At the end of his argument, Zurbach suggests that the very objective of granting loans in gold might even have been the enslavement of indebted people as a mechanism used by the temples for acquiring additional workforce (Zurbach, 2017: 669). This would mean the temples managed to turn their gold into capital, but so far, this is a hypothesis (on debt slavery in general see Zeuske, 2013: 102, 106–107). However, according to Eugenio Luján, the Linear B texts do not provide any other evidence for gold and silver functioning as a means of exchange or as a means of payment (Luján, 2011: 30).

Now, in the exchange processes with other societies—unfortunately not documented in the Linear B record—things may have been quite different, for here the Mycenaean palaces had to take part in established exchange practices operating on the basis of value equivalents expressed in weighed quantities of precious metals (Montecchi, 2007: 490). The existence of Near Eastern weight types at Mycenaean settlement sites offers some concrete indication in that respect (Rahmstorf, 2008: 159–163). Moreover, at the thirteenth-century Mycenaean palace of Thebes, a weight assemblage came to light which includes both disc-shaped weights of Aegean type and sphendonoid weights of Near Eastern type. One of the five sphendonoid weights is marked with a circle—apparently denoting one unit. Its weight seems to fit with a well-known Mycenaean unit of about 20 g (also identified in the Linear B record), while at the same time, all five weights apparently correspond to different quantities of the "Ugaritic shekel," which itself would be half the quantity of the Mycenaean unit. Therefore, the Mycenaean palace administration at Thebes seems to have taken measures to ensure the convertibility of value expressions for external exchange relations—involving luxury goods, precious metals, or bulk metals such as copper and tin, which all had to be imported to Greece from various other Mediterranean regions (Aravantinos & Alberti, 2006). At this point, one must not forget that exploitation of the Attic silver ores already formed part of the Mycenaean economy (for Mycenaean mining see Spitaels, 1984; Mountjoy, 1995) and that silver figured among the Mycenaean products exported to the east—be it in the shape of ingots or in the form of finished luxury objects such as vessels (Wardle & Wardle, 1997: 99; Jung, 2015: 253–255).

It is possible that *Hackgold* was used in these exchange relations too, for the aforementioned small weights were suited for such quantities of gold. This is also indicated by the finds from the Uluburun ship from the fourteenth century BCE, which had apparently been bound for the Aegean and had two Mycenaean palace officials on board (Pulak, 2005; cf. Kilian, 1993; Jung, 2005). It carried an assemblage of gold and silver in the form of scrap as well as ring ingots (Yalçın et al., 2005: 611–614), found in an area where weights and the personal belongings of crew members, including Mycenaean and Egyptian seals, were present as well—all pointing to a voyage undertaken in connection with royal goods exchange (Kilian, 1993; Pulak, 2008; for the use of ingots as well as gold and silver scrap as payment in the eastern Mediterranean see Gestoso Singer, 2015).

Copper Ingots

Regarding the possible commodity character of the products exchanged across the eastern Mediterranean, a well-known class of product that travelled long distances and in huge quantities was copper ingots. The well-known Uluburun cargo of the late fourteenth century comprised c. 10 t of copper (in the shape of oxhide as well as plano-convex ingots) and 1 t of tin (Pulak, 2000a), which would result in 11 t of bronze with a 9% tin content, an optimal alloy attested frequently in that period. However, one must allow for a loss of material, as both the copper of the oxhide ingots and that of the plano-convex ingots contained considerable amounts of slag from the smelting process—apparently in contrast to the tin of the tin ingots (cf. Pulak, 2000a: 152). It is blister copper in need of further refinement (Hauptmann et al., 2002). Now, even assuming that only 10 t of bronze could have been produced with that cargo and taking into consideration some 20% of metal loss during casting, grinding, and polishing, that amount of metal would, for example, have been enough to produce 33,684 Mycenaean swords of Sandars' type D (with an average mass of 237.5 g),[4] common at the time and attested on the shipwreck itself.

It is beyond doubt that mass production of copper was practiced in Cyprus at least since around 1350 BCE. First, we have the Uluburun shipwreck. Second, we have the contemporary palace archive from Akhetaton (Amarna) with letters recording amounts such as 100 talents, 200 pieces (ingots), 500 (ingots), 120 (ingots)—all

[4]The calculation is based on measurements at the National Archaeological Museum in Athens. EAM 3196, sword from chamber tomb 91 at Mycenae (Tsountas' excavations, Xenaki-Sakellariou, 1985: 260, pls. 127, VIII): 249 g.—EAM 3197, sword from chamber tomb 91 at Mycenae (Tsountas' excavations, Xenaki-Sakellariou, 1985: 260, pls. 127, VIII): 231.5 g.—EAM 6634, sword from chamber tomb 25 at Prósimna (Blegen, 1937: 330, Fig. 198 [top]): 232 g.—Metal loss during casting, grinding and polishing estimated by Mathias Mehofer (VIAS, University of Vienna).

originating in Alašiya, i.e., Cyprus (Knapp, 2011: 250–251). Metal analyses of oxhide ingots found all around the Mediterranean prove their Cypriot provenance for the fourteenth, thirteenth, and twelfth centuries BCE (Begemann et al., 2001; Gale & Stos-Gale, 2012). In addition, recent results from the ongoing excavations at Hala Sultan Tekke prove that during the thirteenth and twelfth centuries primary copper smelting processes could take place in a major coastal city, i.e., close to the harbor rather than to the ore deposits in the interior of the island (Mehofer, 2014; Fischer, 2018). Finally, in some of the Amarna letters, the king of Alašiya refers to payments for the delivered copper (Gestoso Singer, 2015: 93–94). One may conclude that this large-scale copper production for wide-ranging exchange purposes meets several conditions for a commodity exchange regime.

However, we must not forget the often-noted variable sizes of both oxhide and plano-convex ingots. The oxhide ingots from the Uluburun wreck seem to target a mass of around 23.5 kg (Pulak, 2000a: 143, Fig. 7), while the mass of excavated oxhide ingots from all over the Mediterranean oscillates between 21 and 39 kg (Knapp, 2011: 250). Thus, any calculation of copper amounts that was based on simple ingot counts at the harbor would have been a quite imprecise procedure. Weighing during each exchange transaction may have taken place in the harbors (Pulak, 1997: 238), and heavy weights of several kilos did exist at e.g., Ugarit (including a single weight of 28.9 kg for the unit of one talent, see Bordreuil, 2004; Bordreuil, 2006), in Mycenaean administrative buildings (Aravantinos & Alberti, 2006: 302–304; cf. also Verdelis, 1964: 166, pl. 120α) and on the Uluburun ship as well (though these are exceptions among the many small weights, see Pulak, 2000b: 253 tab. 17.1 [nos. W 129 and W 130], 263–264). Yet, in view of the fact that blister copper was shipped, only medium to long-term experience on the part of the importer could establish a numeric relation to the desired end product.

In conclusion, there was neither a precise relationship between the socially necessary labor time and one ingot on the side of the producer nor a precise relationship between the imported raw material and the pure copper needed for bronze production on the side of the importer—a Mycenaean palace, for instance. The latter is remarkable in light of the fact that the Mycenaean palatial administration kept records of (a) quite small amounts of copper or bronze (e.g. 1.5 kg, 3 kg, 5 kg, 6 kg) as assignments to smiths for producing bronze objects (Smith, 1992–1993) and (b) used and damaged bronze objects in store (Ventris & Chadwick, 1973: 336–337). However, when drawing conclusions from these practices, one needs to note that the mentioned records all come from the palace of Pylos. We do not have records from the other palaces that refer to copper/bronze production in similar detail. In addition—and perhaps more important—all the Linear B tablets were fired in conflagrations destroying the palaces. There are good reasons to believe that these destructions were man-made and followed economic and political crisis situations (Jung, in press).

Unfortunately, we do not know how the Mycenaean palaces organized the import of copper and tin, but given the vital importance of these two metals in the production of tools, weapons, and armor, one has to suppose some kind of record keeping. One can only speculate, on which scribal media and at which places this might have happened, as the Linear B documents from the palace archives are almost totally silent on import and export matters (for indirect hints in some texts see Killen, 2008: 181–189).

In conclusion, it seems first that the Cypriot copper traded between the different eastern Mediterranean state societies did have a commodity character, though defining its precise exchange value in terms of objectified abstract human labor (whether expressed in silver or other value equivalents) must have been a difficult undertaking and certainly did not reach the precision known from modern metal trading. Second, as follows from what has been said before, it appears that bulk copper trading cannot be classified as market exchange, but was strongly determined by political factors. Finally, there are no indications—neither in the Linear B texts nor in the archaeological record—that the imported metals continued to circulate as commodities upon entering the Mycenaean economy.

Mycenaean Pottery

Regarding Mycenaean exports, it is worth exploring whether products stored in ceramic vessels or the pottery vessels themselves may have assumed a commodity character. Painted Mycenaean ceramics of the second half of the 14th and the first half of the thirteenth century BCE constitute a specific class of widely distributed products. Wherever chemical analyses have been conducted on Mycenaean vessels of that period—found by the hundreds at sites in Egypt, Palestine, Syria, or Cyprus—the results have shown that the vast majority of the analyzed pots came from the northern Argolid, i.e., the region of Mycenae (Jung, 2015; Mountjoy, 2015). Moreover, for export to the Levant and Cyprus specific types were chosen that resemble local, traditional Cypriot and Levantine pottery shapes (which in those regions were regularly produced without painted decoration). Examples are the amphoroid krater and the shallow strap-handled bowl. These are shapes only rarely used in Greece itself (Jung, 2015: 246–251).

Specific quality traits—in terms of very well levigated clay, good firing as well as shiny paint and surface—make Mycenaean painted pottery from the Argolid stand out in comparison with many Cypriot and Levantine pottery classes. For this quality to be reached, all production operations required very well-educated personnel and lengthy preparation procedures in the workshop facilities. Those workshops themselves have not been discovered yet (the potter's kiln at Berbati being earlier in date, Schallin, 2002), but their output quantities known today hint at quite large installations. The meagre Linear B evidence provides us with some additional information, though unfortunately not from the region of the specialized export manufacture. Texts from Pylos in Messenia show that some Mycenaean potters were directly part of the royal economic sector. In addition, they could hold estates and also fulfilled administrative duties as functionaries of the palace (for a thorough survey of all the Linear B evidence related to Mycenaean potters see Boulotis, 2014).

We can therefore safely assume the existence of a centrally administered Mycenaean pottery production in the region of Mycenae with a large output targeting consumers in Cyprus, the Levant, and Egypt. When that export manufacture stopped around 1250 BCE (i.e., some decades before the breakdown of the Mycenaean palace state) no other Greek region filled that gap. There were only some limited shipments of Mycenaean pottery produced in Cyprus and Asia Minor to the Levant (for the latter, see Mountjoy & Mommsen, 2015: 487–488, Fig. 14). All of this suggests that its production and its export from the Argolid were economic processes organized and supervised by the palatial administration itself.

Finally, Cypriot, Levantine, and Egyptian archaeological evidence indicate that the population of those regions began to ascribe rather high relative values to imported Mycenaean pots. The basis for comparison and for the tentative assessment of the relative value (which cannot be differentiated into use and exchange value) is the association of imported Mycenaean pots with other objects in closed contexts. The prominent presence of Mycenaean imports not only in rich tombs in Cyprus (especially the class with pictorial decoration, see Keswani, 2004: 142) but also in different Levantine and Egyptian palaces such as Ugarit and Qatna may suggest that the royal exchange mechanisms—assigned to high-ranking merchants—were at least partially responsible for the importation of that pottery and its contents (Jung, 2015: 261–263). At Akhenaten's residence city Akhetaten (Tell el-Amarna), the predominant use of Mycenaean pottery inside the palace and the rather marginal presence in the town (Hassler, 2008) argue in favor of that hypothesis.

The large quantities produced in the Argolid and shipped over several decades to the coasts of the eastern Mediterranean suggest that the Mycenaean palace economy would have aimed at an improvement of production organization for controlling the quantity and quality of product output. This, in turn, would have necessitated an improvement in time management and administration. In such processes, average production time (socially necessary labor) automatically becomes the factor determining the exchange process to a large extent. Time management would have determined how many amphoroid craters with chariot representations, how many shallow bowls with added white paint, and how many small stirrup jars filled with unguents could be sent e.g., to a king in Amurru on the Syrian coast and at what intervals certain amounts were available for different external exchange partners. Through the repeated exchange, the Mycenaean side would also have acquired a better idea of how fast what amounts of desired goods could be received in return. This would have pointed ultimately and effectively to value equivalents between Mycenaean and Amorite products.

In conclusion, Argive Mycenaean pottery vessels exported to Egypt, Cyprus, and the Levant did have some commodity qualities—but we cannot say against which specific products they were exchanged by the exporting palatial administration (and its agents). The specialized and at the same time centralized Argive production and the distribution pattern of Argive ceramic products in the different kingdoms of the eastern Mediterranean both suggest that we are again not dealing with market exchange, but with largely politically determined and regulated product exchange mechanisms.

Canaanite Jars

The ovoid to conical so-called Canaanite jars represent another pottery class, some of which seem to have been especially manufactured in large quantities to be exported to other regions and therefore merit a brief mention here. In contrast to the Mycenaean pots, the only function of the (mostly) unpainted Canaanite jars was to serve as containers for the goods that were meant to be exchanged, i.e., a wide variety of agricultural products (mainly wine, oils, resin), and they appear in different size classes (Pedrazzi, 2007, 2016). Petrographic and chemical analyses in combination with typological studies and distribution maps show that basically all societies along the Levantine coasts exported products packaged in such jars (most recently Day et al., 2020 with bibliography). However, specific jar types seem to have been characteristic for bulk exchange between different palace states (Pedrazzi, 2016: type 5-4). Yet, even those specialized types exhibit not only size clusters but show considerable variability of capacity even within each size class, so that the jars themselves did not convey specific units of the products they carried (Cateloy, 2016; Monroe, 2016). This is a phenomenon similar to the oxhide ingots that could not simply be counted to assess the amount of copper they contained (see above), but Monroe stresses the rather low exchange value (expressed in silver) of the wine and resin transported in Canaanite jars on the Uluburun ship, if compared to the metal cargo of the same ship (Monroe, 2016: 91–92). In the case of Canaanite jars, inscriptions could be applied to them, when precise product quantities were of interest. This may have happened when an Egyptian temple estate administration was directly involved in agricultural production in the Levant (Bavay, 2015). However, in the latter case, we may not be dealing with commodities to be exchanged, but rather with products of an Egyptian institution that were produced outside Egypt (i.e., in the Levant), though under the direct control of that institution.

Markets and Merchant's Capital

Even though the commoditization of products occurred to various degrees in eastern Mediterranean societies, one has to note that it has so far not been possible to identify structures functioning as marketplaces or *suqs*—neither on Cyprus nor in Greece (though their existence has been purported, see Pullen, 2013). Even at Ugarit with its large-scale excavations of the thirteenth-century-BCE town, no such urban structure could be identified with certainty (McGeough, 2007: 308). Recently, Adelheid Otto tentatively interpreted the *Grand Place* in the southern part of town as a marketplace and based her argument on certain spaces opening to the square (possible shops) and on finds of a few weights and seals (Otto, 2019: 206–209), though balance weights were common in many Ugaritan houses (McGeough, 2007: 307–308). Though one has to admit the difficulties in identifying the function of open spaces (be it in settlements or at harbor sites), the lack of architecturally defined marketplaces/*suqs* seems to be a significant indicator for the non-dominant role of commodity exchange in those economies, while one has to keep in mind that not all kinds of commodity exchange would require the existence of marketplaces and market mechanisms in the first place (cf. the trade between kings/palaces, see above).

Regarding the issue of whether the possible commodity exchange between eastern Mediterranean societies could have included the formation of merchant's capital, the key problem is proving that a merchant has owned his merchandise. Of the two categories of Ugaritic merchants known from the texts, those of the first group had to pay taxes to the king (supposedly on their profits) and were called "royal dependents," while those of the second group were personal traders of the king ("of his feet") and were granted exemptions from taxes (Heltzer, 1988: 8). In either case, it is difficult to decide whether during his trading activity a merchant was only the prolonged arm of the king and the ruling class of palatial bureaucrats or if he was at least temporarily the immediate owner of the merchandise and therefore could realize the merchant's capital.

In the late thirteenth century, a man called Yabninu resided in a spacious building immediately to the south of the king's palace at Ugarit. He himself was not a part of the royal family, so it seems. Yet, he played quite an important role in the kingdom's diplomatic affairs. On one journey to Amurru—further south along the Syrian coast—he took with him 100 shekels of gold and textiles and poured oil on the head of the Amurru princess. Another text, a kind of "account" of Yabninu, lists oil products, wood products, etc., the value of which is given as 600 shekels of silver (McGeough, 2015). Apparently, his linked economic and diplomatic activities made him a rich man. Persons like him may foreshadow independent traders of the Iron Age, and conflicts between such individuals and the ruling classes of kings and bureaucrats might have contributed to the breakdown or overthrow of the palace economies (cf. Liverani, 1987: 69–73). The result would have been that holders of means of production and commodities, who had been acting on behalf of the palace, would have become owners of these means and thus were ultimately able to realize merchant's capital in the true sense of the word.

Contacts to Pre-state Societies in the Later 2nd Millennium

A quick look at pre-state economies in the central Mediterranean and their contacts to the east may serve as a last step in this investigation. In Italy, the use of specialized stone weights of two different basic shapes started in the Italian Middle Bronze Age 2 or 3—so most probably around 1400 BCE (Cardarelli et al., 1997; Ialongo, 2019; Ialongo & Rahmstorf, 2019). It seems that the Italian weight system(s) followed an Aegean prototype or was created to correspond in some points with the Aegean system (Ialongo, 2019: 216, Fig. 10; 218). Thus the introduction of those weights may have been motivated by constant Italo-Aegean contacts, which in the south of the Apennine peninsula evidently go back to the seventeenth century BCE, as Mycenaean pottery imports prove (Jones et al., 2014). However, the two basic weight shapes, lentoid with a groove and globular to piriform with a pierced lug, are local inventions. The masses of those weights, ranging from 295 g to 848 g (Cardarelli et al., 1997:

633–634, Figs. 361–362), would be suited to weighing small and medium to large quantities of metal—e.g., of copper and tin, the basic metals for making means of labor and weapons.

In the last few years, chemical and lead isotope analyses have successfully unraveled the central Mediterranean copper and bronze circulation from the fourteenth to the eleventh century BCE. The basic results are as follows:

- Italian bronze workers from the Po plain in the north to Apulia and Calabria in the south mainly relied on copper imports from the Trentino region in the Southern Alps (Jung et al., 2011; Villa & Giardino, 2019; Jung 2020; Jung et al., 2021; Jung et al., in press).
- By contrast, there are no indications for copper export to Mycenaean Greece in the form of ingots. Only certain classes of finished bronze weapons and implements were shipped east (Jung & Mehofer, 2013: 178).
- A limited overlap of raw copper circulation between Italy and Greece did occur, but was confined to the very south (as imported Cypriot copper ingot fragments from Apulia indicate, see Jung et al., in press).

The mentioned innovative stimulus for producing specialized weights may well be due to Italo-Aegean exchange relationships. However, the invention of specific Italian weight shapes and the absence of Aegean-type weights in Italy in combination with the distribution pattern of Trentino copper, which overlaps with the distribution pattern of the Italian weights (most recently Ialongo & Rahmstorf, 2019: 114–115, Figs. 9–10), suggests that this innovation basically served exchange relationships along the central Mediterranean coasts. Copper from the Southern Alps was apparently systematically produced for regular exchange purposes spanning the whole of the Apennine peninsula. Weighing of metal quantities seems to have played an important role in those exchange relationships.

Interestingly, after the fall of the Mycenaean palaces, a weight of Italian type was in use at Lefkandí on Euboea in the second half of the twelfth century BCE (Pare, 2013: 511, Fig. 29.2.5, 520). This is a period, for which we have good evidence suggesting that in Greece the palace economy (Asiatic Mode of Production) had given way to a new mode of production based on private ownership of the means of production, i.e., the mode of production usually perceived as an οἶκος economy continuing into the Early Iron Age (cf. Donlan, 1997). In southern continental Italy, the observation that large-scale storage appears dispersed both in larger settlements (with pithos magazines present in several houses) and in hamlets (pithos magazines scattered throughout the rural landscape) suggests a similar mode of production based on private rather than communal property. This may have come about with the intensified exchange relationships between those two Mediterranean regions, which is visible in the wide range of artifact classes in both Greece and Italy (D'Agata et al., 2012; Jung & Mehofer, 2013; Jones et al., 2014; Iacono, 2019). Interestingly, the adoption of Aegean storage techniques—i.e., the production and use of huge jars (pithoi)—from c. 1200 BCE onwards was followed by a considerable increase in stored surplus products during the following decades. In Apulia and Calabria, one can observe quantities of stored agricultural products (most probably wine and olive oil) that amounted to several thousands of liters per house and thus surpassed stored products in coeval Mycenaean houses (Jung & Pacciarelli, 2017). It seems that new production techniques, which elude us for now, are responsible for that economic success in the Italian south—a production increase that was not coupled with centralized storage as it was practiced in the Mycenaean palaces. At this point, it is important to note that the communities in the south of Italy never went through the stage of a palatial economy that characterized southern and central Greece in the fourteenth and thirteenth centuries. Instead, they seem to have established a mode of production based on private landed property (as indicated by the dispersed large-scale storage) in the twelfth century BCE, i.e., roughly at the same time as an analogous mode of production was introduced in Late Mycenaean Greece. However, those communities in southern Italy were departing from big men or small chiefdom societies with small-scale tributary economies. Marco Pacciarelli and I have tried to explain these phenomena with reference to Leon Trotsky's concept of uneven and combined development (Jung & Pacciarelli, 2017).

To be sure, for more than 20 years this specific theoretical approach has been in the focus of a methodological debate, mainly in the fields of international relations (in political science) and modern history. That debate centered on the question, whether (1) "uneven and combined development" is a transhistorical phenomenon and (2) whether this approach offers a method in its own right, able to solve the problem of "the international" (dimension of the social world). Critics gave a negative answer to the second question, and several of them proposed using the approach in conjunction with a thorough analysis of the modes of production of the societies involved in specific historical relations with one another (Callinicos in Callinicos & Rosenberg, 2008: 82, 101; Rioux, 2015: 507). The latter is precisely what the author who formulated the approach had done. Trotsky conceptualized his "laws" of uneven combined development as parts of historical materialism, in order to enlarge its scope to a global scale and to apply its methodology to economic, social, and political relations between different societies (Trotzki, 1973 [1930]: 13–23)—at the time motivated among other things by a reaction to the dead-end paradigm of Stageism, which insisted on a pre-described way of development for every human society (i.e., passing through a series of necessary stages). His was in fact one of many Marxist attempts to understand and explain the development of non-European societies, while preceding postcolonial and subalternist theories by many decades (Chibber, 2013: 291–293).

Uneven and combined developments may very well have led to economic and social "jumps" accelerating the progress from mode of production A toward a new mode of production C in one society without passing through mode of production B, which a second society did form after A and prior to arriving at C. However, the concrete historical conditions and driving forces enabling such a development need to be analyzed. Although some have claimed the opposite (Post, 2018), nothing excludes the possibility that this happened also in societies antedating the first formation of a capitalist mode of production by hundreds or thousands of years.

Conclusions

In conclusion, applying a classical Marxist approach allows us to detect specific economic characteristics of goods exchange, which in the cases examined here include:

- Various, often discontinuous stages of commodification processes in the 3rd and 2nd millennia BCE.
- Variable degrees of commodification for different product classes and different regions/societies during those two millennia (often not involving market exchange).
- The fixation of a general, socially accepted value equivalent only in the societies of Mesopotamia, Asia Minor, Egypt, and the Levant.
- Probable references by the Mycenaean palatial administration to the general, socially accepted value equivalents of exterior exchange partners (for those exchange purposes).
- Roughly an east-west gradient regarding commodification, contact-induced developments, under specific circumstances leading to a rapid acceleration in the development of socio-economic relationships inside societies (*uneven and combined development*).

Acknowledgements I wish to thank Kostas Passas for discussing with me various Marxian economic concepts. Of course, all errors remain mine.

References

Appadurai, A. (1986). Introduction: Commodities and the politics of value. In A. Appadurai (Eds.), *The social life of things: Commodities in cultural perspective* (pp. 3–63). Cambridge University Press.

Aravantinos, V., & Alberti, M. E. (2006). The balance weights from the Kadmeia, Thebes. In M. E. Alberti, E. Ascalone, & L. Peyronel (Eds.), *Weights in context: Bronze Age weighing systems of Eastern Mediterranean: Chronology, typology, material and archaeological contexts. Proceedings of the International Colloquium, Roma, 22–24 November 2004* (pp. 293–313). Istituto Italiano di Numismatica.

Bavay, L. (2015). Canaanite jars and jar sealings from Deir el-Medina: Scattered evidence of Egypt's economic relations with the Levant during the New Kingdom. In B. Eder & R. Pruzsinszky (Eds.), *Policies of exchange: Political systems and modes of interaction in the Aegean and the Near East in the 2nd millennium B.C.E. Proceedings of the International Symposium at the University of Freiburg, Institute for Archaeological Studies, 30 May–2 June 2012* (pp. 129–140). OREA 2. Austrian Academy of Sciences Press.

Begemann, F., Schmitt-Strecker, S., Pernicka, E., & Schiavo, F. L. (2001). Chemical composition and lead isotopy of copper and bronze from Nuragic Sardinia. *European Journal of Archaeology, 4*, 43–85.

Blackwell, N. G. (2018). Contextualizing Mycenaean hoards. *American Journal of Archaeology, 122*, 509–539.

Blake, E. (2014). *Social networks and regional identity in Bronze Age Italy*. Cambridge University Press.
Blegen, C. W. (1937). *Prosymna: The Helladic settlement preceding the Argive Heraeum*. Cambridge University Press.
Bellofiore, R. (2018). The multiple meanings of Marx's value theory. *Monthly Review, 69*(11). https://monthlyreview.org/2018/04/01/the-multiple-meanings-of-marxs-value-theory/. Accessed 5 Nov 2020.
Bordreuil, É. (2004). Les systems pondéraux. In G. Galliano & Y. Calvet (Eds.), *Le royaume d'Ougarit. Aux origines de l'alphabet* (pp. 135–139). Somogy éditions d'art, Musée des Beaux-Arts.
Bordreuil, É. (2006). Preliminary considerations for a typology of the weights of the Late Bronze Age at Ras Shamra-Ugarit. Archaeological and textual data. In M. E. Alberti, E. Ascalone, & L. Peyronel (Eds.), *Weights in context: Bronze Age weighing systems of Eastern Mediterranean: Chronology, typology, material and archaeological contexts. Proceedings of the International Colloquium, Roma, 22–24 November 2004* (pp. 203–232). Istituto Italiano di Numismatica.
Boulotis, C. (2014). Κεραμεύς (*ke-ra-me-u*) και (*ke-ra-me-ja*) στις μυκηναϊκές πινακίδες Γραμμικής B. In P. Valavanis & E. Manakidou (Eds.), *Essays on Greek pottery and iconography in honour of professor Michalis Tiverios* (pp. 19–34). University Studio Press.
Callinicos, A., & Rosenberg, J. (2008). Uneven and combined development: The social-relational substratum of "the international"? An exchange of letters. *Cambridge Review of International Affairs, 21*, 77–112.
Cardarelli, A., Pacciarelli, M., & Pallante, P. (1997). Pesi da bilancia dell'età del bronzo? In M. Bernabò Brea, A. Cardarelli, & M. Cremaschi (Eds.), *Le Terramare. La più antica civiltà padana* (pp. 629–642). Electa.
Cateloy, C. (2016). Trade and capacity studies in the eastern Mediterranean: The first Levantine trade amphorae. In S. Demesticha & A. Bernard Knapp (Eds.), *Maritime transport containers in the Bronze-Iron Age Aegean and Eastern Mediterranean* (pp. 39–55). Studies in Mediterranean Archaeology and Literature PB 183. Åströms förlag.
Chibber, V. (2013). *Postcolonial theory and the specter of capital*. Verso.
Courtois, J.-C. (1990). Poids, prix, taxes et salaires à Ougarit (Syrie) au IIe millénaire. *Res Orientales, 2*, 119–127.
Day, P. M., Hein, A., Kardamaki, E., Maran, J., Tenconi, M., & Waiman-Barak, P. (2020). Maritime commodity trade from the Near East to the Mycenaean heartland: Canaanite jars in final palatial Tiryns. *Jahrbuch des Deutschen Archäologischen Instituts, 135*, 1–99.
D'Agata, A. L., Boileau, M.-C., & De Angelis, S. (2012). Handmade burnished ware from the island of Crete: A view from the inside. *Rivista di Scienze Preistoriche, 62*, 295–330.
Donlan, W. 1997. The homeric economy. In I. Morris & B. Powell (Eds.), *A new companion to Homer* (pp. 649–667). Mnemosyne Supplement 163. Brill.
Fischer, P. (2018). Notes on metal production in CQ1 and CQ2. In P. Fischer & T. Bürge, *Two Late Cypriot city quarters at Hala Sultan Tekke: The Söderberg Expedition 2010–2017* (pp. 489–492). Studies in Mediterranean Archaeology CXLVII. Astrom Editions.
Furtwängler, A. E. (2016). Wertmesser, Finanzmanipulationen und die Geburt des Münzgeldes in der Antike. In H. Meller, H. Peter Hahn, R. Jung, & R. Risch (Eds.), *Arm und Reich – Zur Ressourcenverteilung in prähistorischen Gesellschaften. 8. Mitteldeutscher Archäologentag vom 22. bis 24. Oktober 2015 in Halle (Saale)/Rich and Poor—Competing for Resources in Prehistoric Societies. 8th Archaeological Conference of Central Germany, 22–24 October 2015 in Halle (Saale)* (pp. 599–610). Tagungen des Landesmuseums für Vorgeschichte Halle 14. Landesamt für Denkmalpflege und Archäologie Sachsen-Anhalt.
Gale, N. H., & Stos-Gale, Z. A. (2012). The role of the Apliki mine region in the post c. 1400 BC copper production and trade networks in Cyprus and in the wider Mediterranean. In V. Kassianidou & G. Papasavvas (Eds.), *Eastern Mediterranean metallurgy and metalwork in the second millennium BC: A Conference in honour of James D. Muhly, Nicosia ,10–11 October 2009* (pp. 70–82). Oxbow Books.

Gestoso Singer, G. (2015). Small ingots and scrap metal in the Eastern Mediterranean during the Late Bronze Age. In J. Mynářová, P. Onderka, & P. Pavúk (Eds.), *There and back again—The crossroads II. Proceedings of an International Conference held at Prague, 15–18 September 2014* (pp. 85–127). Charles University in Prague, Faculty of Arts.

Graeber, D. (2001). *Toward an anthropological theroy of value: The false coin of our own dreams.* Palgrave.

Hassler, A. (2008). Mykenisches in Amarna – Funde der Deutschen-Orient Gesellschaft im Ägyptischen Museum Berlin. *Ägypten & Levante, 18,* 129–143.

Hauptmann, A., Maddin, R., & Prange, M. (2002). On the texture and composition of copper and tin ingots excavated from the shipwreck of Uluburun. *Bulletin of the American School of Oriental Research, 328,* 1–30.

Helms, M. W. (1988). *Ulysses' Sail: An ethnographic Odyssey of power, knowledge, and geographic distance.* Princeton University Press.

Heltzer, M. (1988). Sinaranu, son of Siginu, and the trade relations between Ugarit and Crete. *Minos, 23,* 7–13.

Heltzer, M. (1999). The economy of Ugarit. In W. G. E. Watson & N. Wyatt (Eds.), *Handbook of Ugaritic studies* (pp. 423–454). Handbuch der Orientalistik, erste Abteilung, der Nahe und Mittlere Osten 39. Brill.

Horejs, B. (2016). Neue Gewichtssysteme und metallurgischer Aufschwung im frühen 3. Jahrtausend – ein Zufall? In M. Bartelheim, B. Horejs, & R. Krauß (Eds.), *Von Baden bis Troia. Ressourcennutzung, Metallurgie und Wissenstransfer. Eine Jubiläumsschrift für Ernst Pernicka* (pp. 251–272). OREA 3. Verlag Marie Leidorf.

Iacono, F. (2013). Westernizing Aegean of LH IIIC. In M. E. Alberti & S. Sabatini (Eds.), *Exchange networks and local transformations: Interaction and local change in Europe and the Mediterranean from the Bronze Age to the Iron Age* (pp. 60–79). Oxbow Books.

Iacono, F. (2019). *The archaeology of Late Bronze Age interaction and mobility at the gates of Europe: People, things and networks around the Southern Adriatic Sea.* Bloomsbury Academic.

Ialongo, N. (2019). The earliest balance weights in the west: Towards an independent metrology for Bronze Age Europe. *Cambridge Archaeological Journal, 29,* 103–124.

Ialongo, N., & Rahmstorf, L. (2019). The identification of balance weights in pre-literate Bronze Age Europe: Typology, chronology, distribution and metrology. In L. Rahmstorf & E. Stratford (Eds.), *Weights and marketplaces from the Bronze Age to the early Modern Period. Proceedings of Two workshops funded by the European Research Council (ERC)* (pp. 105–126). Weight & Value 1. Wachholtz Verlag Kiel/Hamburg—Murmann Publishers.

Jones, R., Levi, S. T., Bettelli, M., & Vagnetti, L. (2014). *Italo-Mycenaean pottery: The archaeological and archaeometric dimensions.* Incunabula Graeca CIII. CNR—Istituto di Studi sul Mediterraneo Antico.

Jung, R. (2005). Aspekte des mykenischen Handels und Produktenaustauschs. In B. Horejs, R. Jung, E. Kaiser, & B. Teržan (Eds.), *Interpretationsraum Bronzezeit. Bernhard Hänsel von seinen Schülern gewidmet* (pp. 45–70). Universitätsforschungen zur prähistorischen Archäologie 121. Dr. Rudolf Habelt GmbH.

Jung, R. (2015). Imported Mycenaean pottery in the east: Distribution, context and interpretation. In B. Eder & R. Pruzsinszky (Eds.), *Policies of exchange: Political systems and modes of interaction in the Aegean and the Near East in the 2nd millennium B.C.E. Proceedings of the International Symposium at the University of Freiburg, Institute for Archaeological Studies, 30 May–2 June 2012* (pp. 243–275). OREA 2. Austrian Academy of Sciences Press.

Jung, R. (2020). [with an appendix by M. Mehofer, R. Jung, and E. Pernicka]. Frattesina between Continental Europe and the Eastern Mediterranean. *Padusa*, 56, 173–202.

Jung, R. (in press). Sprenger der Ketten im Mittelmeerraum. In S. Hansen & R. Krause (Eds.), *The early history of war and conflict. Proceedings of the 4th International LOEWE Conference, 7–9 October 2019, Goethe-Universität Frankfurt a. M.*

Jung, R., & Mehofer, M. (2013). Mycenaean Greece and Bronze Age Italy: Cooperation, trade or war? *Archäologisches Korrespondenzblatt, 43,* 175–193.

Jung, R., Mehofer, M., & Pernicka, E. (2011). Metal exchange in Italy from the middle to the final Bronze Age (14th–11th cent. BCE). In P. P. Betancourt & S. C. Ferrence (Eds.), *Metallurgy: Understanding how, learning why. Studies in honor of James D. Muhly* (pp. 231–248). Prehistory Monographs 29. INSTAP Academic Press.

Jung, R., Mehofer, M., Pacciarelli, M., & Pernicka, E. (2021). The metal finds from Punta di Zambrone and other sites, and the Bronze Age metal supply in southern Calabria. In R. Jung (Ed.), *Punta di Zambrone I. 1200 BCE—A time of breakdown, a time of progress in Southern Italy and Greece* (pp. 345–395). OREA17. Austrian Academy of Sciences Press.

Jung, R., Mehofer, M., & Pernicka, E. (in press). Metal exchange in Bronze Age Italy: The final Bronze Age hoards from Roca Vecchia, Apulia. In R. Guglielmino & F. Iacono (Eds.), *Roca: A Bronze Age Port on the Adriatic Sea. Aegean type pottery and late Bronze Age sequence of area IX*.

Jung, R., & Pacciarelli, M. (2017). Greece and Southern Italy 1250–1050 BCE: Manifold patterns of interaction. In M. Fotiadis, R. Laffineur, Y. Lolos, & A. Vlachopoulos (Eds.), *Έσπερος/Hesperos—The Aegean seen from the west. Proceedings of the 16th International Aegaean Conference, University of Ioannina, Department of History and Archaeology, Unit of Archaeology and Art History, 18–21 May 2016* (pp. 185–204). Aegaeum 41. Peeters.

Keswani, P. (2004). *Mortuary ritual and society in Bronze Age Cyprus*. Monographs in Mediterranean Archaeology. Equinox Publishing.

Kilian, I. (1993). Überlegungen zum spätbronzezeitlichen Schiffswrack von Ulu Burun (Kaş). *Jahrbuch des Römisch-Germanischen Zentralmuseums Mainz, 40*, 333–352.

Killen, J. T. (2008). Mycenaean economy. In Y. Duhoux & A. Morpurgo Davies (Eds.), *A companion to Linear B. Mycenaean Greek texts and their world 1* (pp. 159–200). Bibliothèque des Cahiers de l'Institut de Linguistique de Louvain 120. Peeters.

Knapp, A. B. (2011). Cyprus, copper, and Alashiya. In P. P. Betancourt & S. C. Ferrence (Eds.), *Metallurgy: Understanding how, learning why: Studies in honor of James D. Muhly* (pp. 249–254). Prehistory Monographs 29. INSTAP Academic Press.

Kopytoff, I. (1986). The cultural biography of things: Commoditization as process. In A. Appadurai (Ed.), *The social life of things: Commodities in cultural perspective* (pp. 64–91). Cambridge University Press.

Liverani, M. (1987). The collapse of the Near Eastern regional system at the end of the Bronze Age: The case of Syria. In M. Rowlands, M. Larsen, & K. Kristiansen (Eds.), *Centre and periphery in the ancient world* (pp. 66–73). Cambridge University Press.

Liverani, M. (2001). *International relations in the ancient Near East, 1600–1100 BC*. Studies in Diplomacy. Palgrave.

Luján, E. R. (2011). Payment and trade terminology on Linear B tablets. In M. Paz Garcia-Bellido, L. Callegarin, & A. Jiménez Díaz (Eds.), *Barter, money and coinage in the Ancient Mediterranean (10th–1st centuries BC). Actas del IV Encuentro Peninsular de Numismática Antigua*. Consejo Superior de Investigaciones Científicas, Instituto de Historia.

Marx, K. (2009 [1863/1864]). *Das Kapital 1.1. Resultate des unmittelbaren Produktionsprozesses*. Dietz Verlag [English translation taken from https://www.marxists.org/archive/marx/works/1864/economic/].

Marx, K. (1962 [1867]). *Das Kapital. Kritik der politischen Ökonomie. Erster Band: Der Produktionsprozeß des Kapitals*. Marx Engels Werke 23. Dietz Verlag [English translation taken from https://www.marxists.org/archive/marx/works/1867-c1/].

Marx, K. (1964 [1894]). *Das Kapital. Kritik der politischen Ökonomie. Dritter Band: Der Gesamtprozeß der kapitalistischen Produktion* (F. Engels, Ed.). Marx-Engels Werke 25. Dietz Verlag [English translation taken from https://www.marxists.org/archive/marx/works/1894-c3/].

McGeough, K. M. (2007). *Exchange relationships at Ugarit*. Ancient Near Eastern Studies Supplement 26. Peeters.

McGeough, K. M. (2015). "What is not in my house you must give me": Agents of exchange according to the textual evidence from Ugarit. In B. Eder & R. Pruzsinszky (Eds.), *Policies of exchange: Political systems and modes of interaction in the Aegean and the Near East in the 2nd millennium B.C.E. Proceedings of the International Symposium at the University of Freiburg, Institute for Archaeological Studies, 30 May–2 June 2012* (pp. 85–96). OREA 2. Austrian Academy of Sciences Press.

Mehofer, M. (2014). A note on the copper-working remains from Area 6 W, Stratum 2. In P. Fischer & T. Bürge, The New Swedish Cyprus Expedition 2013. Excavations at Hala Sultan Tekke. Preliminary Results. *Opuscula, 7,* 75.

Milani, C. (1977). Lavoro e razioni nelle iscrizioni micenee delle serie Aa Ab Ad di Pilo. *Aevum, 51,* 89–111.

Monroe, C. M. (2016). Measure for "measure": Connecting text to material through Late Bronze Age shipping jars. In S. Demesticha & A. B. Knapp (Eds.), *Maritime transport containers in the Bronze-Iron Age Aegean and Eastern Mediterranean* (pp. 79–96). Studies in Mediterranean Archaeology and Literature PB 183. Åströms förlag.

Montecchi, B. (2007). Le misure del valore nell'economia micenea. *Rivista Italiana di Numismatica e Scienze Affini, 108,* 483–490.

Mountjoy, P. A. (1995). Thorikos mine no. 3: The Mycenaean pottery. *The Annual of the British School at Athens, 90,* 195–227.

Mountjoy, P. A. (2015). The North-East Peloponnese and the Near East: Ceramic evidence for contacts in LH III. In A.-L. Schallin & I. Tournavitou (Eds.), *Mycenaeans up to date: The archaeology of the North-Eastern Peloponnese: Current concepts and new directions* (pp. 533–554). Swedish Institute at Athens.

Mountjoy, P. A., & Mommsen, H. (2015). Neutron activation analysis of Aegean-style IIIC pottery from 11 Cypriot and various Near Eastern sites. *Ägypten & Levante, 25,* 421–508.

Nippel, W. (2020). Von Marx zum Marxismus. Das Formationsschema und die „Asiatische Produktionsweise". In C. Deglau & P. Reinard (Eds.), *Aus dem Tempel und dem ewigen Genuß des Geistes verstoßen? Karl Marx und sein Einfluss auf die Altertums- und Geschichtswissenschaften* (pp. 87–106). Philippika 126. Harrassowitz Verlag.

Nosch, M.-L. (2020). How to become a textile worker? Training and apprenticeship of child labourers in the Bronze Age. In L. Quillien & K. Sarri (Eds.), *Textile Workers: Skills, labour and status of textile craftspeople between the prehistoric Aegean and the ancient Near East. Proceedings of the workshop Held at 10th ICAANE in Vienna, April 2018* (pp. 91–108). Austrian Academy of Sciences Press.

Olivier, J.-P. (1987). Des extraits de contrats de vente d'esclaves dans les tablettes de Knossos. *Minos* 20–22 [*Studies in Mycenaean and Classical Greek Presented to John Chadwick*], 479–498.

Otto, A. (2019). Marketplaces in Syro-Mesopotamia in the second millennium BC in the light of new archaeological research. In L. Rahmstorf & E. Stratford (Eds.), *Weights and marketplaces from the Bronze Age to the early Modern Period. Proceedings of two workshops funded by the European Research Council (ERC)* (pp. 203–217). Weight & Value 1. Wachholtz Verlag Kiel/Hamburg—Murmann Publishers.

Palaima, T. (2015). The Mycenaean mobilization of labor in agriculture and building projects: Institutions, individuals, compensation and status in the Linear B tablets. In P. Steinkeller & M. Hudson (Eds.), *Labor in the ancient world: A colloquium held at Hirschbach (Saxony), April 2005* (pp. 617–648). International Scholars Conference on Ancient Near Eastern Economies 5. Islet.

Pare, C. (2013). Weighing, commodification, and money. In H. Fokkens & A. Harding (Eds.), *The Oxford handbook of the European Bronze Age* (pp. 508–527). Oxford University Press.

Patterson, T. C. (2003). *Marx's ghost: Conversations with archaeologists.* Berg.

Pedrazzi, T. (2007). *Le giare da conservazione e trasporto del Levante. Uno studio archeologico dell'economia fra Bronzo Tardo II e Ferro I (ca. 1400–900 a.C.).* Ricerche di archeologia del Vicino Oriente 2. Edizioni ETS.

Pedrazzi, T. (2016). Canaanite jars and the maritime trade network in the northern Levant during the transition from the late Bronze to the Early Iron Age. In S. Demesticha & A. B. Knapp (Eds.), *Maritime transport containers in the Bronze-Iron Age Aegean and Eastern Mediterranean* (pp. 57–77). Studies in Mediterranean Archaeology and Literature PB 183. Åströms förlag.

Post, C. (2018). The use and misuse of uneven ad combined development: A critique of Anievas and Nişancıoğlu. *Historical Materialism, 26*(3), 79–98.

Pulak, C. (1997). The Uluburun shipwreck. In S. Swiny, R. L. Hohlfelder, & H. W. Swiny (Eds.), *Res maritimae. Cyprus and the Eastern Mediterranean from prehistory to late antiquity. Proceedings of the Second International symposium "cities of the sea", Nicosia, Cyprus, 18–22 October 1994* (pp. 233–262). Cyprus American Archaeological Research Institute Monograph Series 1. American Schools of Oriental Research.

Pulak, C. (2000a). The copper and tin ingots from the Late Bronze Age shipwreck at Uluburun. In Ü. Yalçın (Ed.), *Anatolian Metal I* (pp. 137–157). Der Anschnitt Beiheft 13. Deutsches Bergbau-Museum Bochum.

Pulak, C. (2000b). The balance weights from the Late Bronze Age shipwreck at Uluburun. In C. F. E. Pare (Ed.), *Metals make the world go round: The supply and circulation of metals in Bronze Age Europe. Proceedings of a Conference held at the University of Birmingham in, June 1997* (pp. 247–266). Oxbow Books.

Pulak, C. (2005). Who were the Mycenaeans aboard the Uluburun ship? In R. Laffineur & E. Greco (Eds.), *Emporia: Aegeans in Central and Eastern Mediterranean. Proceedings of the 10th International Aegean Conference/10e Rencontre égéenne internationale, Athens, Italian School of Archaeology, 14–18 April 2004* (pp. 295–310). Aegaeum 25. Université de Liège, University of Texas at Austin.

Pulak, C. (2008). The Uluburun shipwreck and late Bronze Age trade. In J. Aruz, K. Benzel, and J. M. Evans (Eds.), *Beyond Babylon: Art, trade, and diplomacy in the second millennium B.C.* (pp. 288–305). Yale University Press.

Pullen, D. J. (2013). Crafts, specialists, and markets in Mycenaean Greece: Exchanging the Mycenaean economy. *American Journal of Archaeology, 117*, 437–445.

Rahmstorf, L. (2006). Zur Ausbreitung vorderasiatischer Innovationen in die frühbronzezeitliche Ägäis. *Praehistorische Zeitschrift, 81*, 49–96.

Rahmstorf, L. (2008). *Kleinfunde aus Tiryns. Terrakotta, Stein, Bein und Glas/Fayence vornehmlich aus der Spätbronzezeit.* Tiryns XVI. Reichert Verlag.

Rahmstorf, L. (2015). The Aegean before and after c. 2200 BC between Europe and Asia: Trade as a prime mover of cultural change. In H. Meller, H. Wolfgang Arz, R. Jung, & R. Risch (Eds.), *2200 BC—A Climatic breakdown as a cause for the collapse of the old world? 7th archaeological Conference of Central Germany, 23–26 October 2014 in Halle (Saale)* (pp. 149–180). Tagungen des Landesmuseums für Vorgeschichte Halle 12. Landesamt für Denkmalpflege und Archäologie Sachsen-Anhalt.

Rahmstorf, L. (2016a). Die Rahmenbedingungen des bronzezeitlichen Handels in Europa und im Alten Orient einschließlich Ägyptens. In U. Luise Dietz & A. Jockenhövel (Eds.), *50 Jahre „Prähistorische Bronzefunde" – Bilanz und Perspektiven. Beiträge zum internationalen Kolloquium vom 24. bis 26. September 2014 in Mainz* (pp. 291–310). Prähistorische Bronzefunde XX 14. Franz Steiner Verlag.

Rahmstorf, L. (2016b). Emerging economic complexity in the Aegean and Western Anatolia during earlier third millennium BC. In B. Molloy (Ed.), *Of Odysseys and oddities: Scales and modes of interaction between prehistoric Aegean societies and their neighbours* (pp. 225–276). Sheffield Studies in Aegean Archaeology 10. Oxbow Books.

Rahmstorf, L. (2016c). From 'value ascription' to coinage: A sketch of monetary developments in Western Eurasia from the Stone to the Iron Age. In C. Haselgrove & S. Krmnicek (Eds.), *The 'archaeology of money'*, University of Tübingen, October 2013 (pp. 19–42). Leicester Archaeology Monograph 24. School of Archaeology & Ancient History, University of Leicester.

Rioux, S. (2015). Mind the (theoretical) gap: On the poverty of international relations theorising of uneven and combined development. *Global Society, 29*, 481–509.

Schallin, A.-L. (2002). Pots for sale: The late Helladic IIIA and IIIB ceramic production at Berbati. In B. Wells (Ed.), *New research on old material from Asine and Berbati in celebration of the fiftieth anniversary of the Swedish Institute at Athens* (pp. 141–155). Acta Instituti Atheniensis Regni Sueciae 8°, XVII. Paul Åströms Förlag.

Sherratt, S. (2000). Circulation of metals and the end of the Bronze Age in the Eastern Mediterranean. In C. F. E. Pare (Ed.), *Metals make the world go round: The supply and circulation of metals in Bronze Age Europe. Proceedings of a Conference Held at the University of Birmingham in June 1997* (pp. 82–98). Oxbow Books.

Smith, J. (1992–1993). The Pylos Jn series. *Minos, 27–28,* 167–259.

Spitaels, P. (1984). The early Helladic period in mine no. 3 (theatre sector). In *Rapport préliminaire sur les 9ᵉ, 10ᵉ, 11ᵉ et 12ᵉ campagnes de fouilles*, by Herman F. Mussche, Jean Bingen, Jean Servais, and Paule Spitaels, Thorikos 8—1972/1976 (pp. 151–174). Comité des Fouilles Belges en Grèce.

Steinkeller, P. (2015). Introduction—Labor in the early states: An early Mesopotamian perspective. In P. Steinkeller & M. Hudson (Eds.), *Labor in the ancient world: A colloquium held at Hirschbach (Saxony), April 2005* (pp. 1–35). International Scholars Conference on Ancient Near Eastern Economies 5. Islet.

Trotzki, L. (1973 [1930]). *Geschichte der russischen Revolution. Erster Teil: Februarrevolution.* Fischer.

Van De Mieroop, M. (2014). Silver as a financial tool in ancient Egypt and Mesopotamia. In P. Bernholz & R. Vaubel (Eds.), *Explaining monetary and financial innovation* (pp. 17–29). Financial and Monetary Policy Studies 39. Springer International Publishing Switzerland.

Veenhof, K. R. (1997). "Modern" features in Old Assyrian trade. *Journal of the Economic and Social History of the Orient, 40,* 336–366.

Veenhof, K. R. (2010). Ancient Assur: The city, its traders, and its commercial network. *Journal of the Economic and Social History of the Orient, 53,* 39–82.

Ventris, M., & Chadwick, J. (1973). *Documents in Mycenaean Greek* (2nd ed.). Cambridge: Cambridge University Press.

Verdelis, N. M. (1964). Ανασκαφή Μυκηνών: εκατέρωθεν της Δυτικής Οικίας. *Πρακτικά της εν Αθήναις Αρχαιολογικής Εταιρείας, 1961,* 161–166.

Villa, I. M., & Giardino, C. (2019). Analisi isotopiche del piombo su reperti bronzei di Frattesina. In A. M. Bietti Sestieri, P. Bellintani, & C. Giardino (Eds.), *Frattesina: un centro internazionale di produzione e di scambio nella tarda età del bronzo del Veneto* (pp. 255–262). Atti della Accademia Nazionale dei Lincei, Classe di Scienze Morali, Storiche e Filologiche, Memorie serie IX, Vol. XXXIX. fascicolo 1. Bardi Edizioni.

Wardle, K. A., & Wardle, D. (1997). *Cities of legend: The Mycenaean world.* Bristol Classical Press.

Xenaki-Sakellariou, A. (1985). *Οι θαλαμωτοί τάφοι των Μυκηνών. Ανασκαφές Χρ. Τσούντα (1887–1898). Les tombes à chambre de Mycènes. Fouilles de Chr. Tsountas (1887–1898).* Diffusion de Boccard.

Yalçın, Ü., Pulak, C., & Slotta, R. (Eds.). (2005). *Das Schiff von Uluburun – Welthandel vor 3000 Jahren. Katalog der Ausstellung des Deutschen Bergbau-Museums Bochum vom 15. Juli 2005 bis 16. Juli 2006.* Deutsches Bergbau-Museum Bochum.

Zaccagnini, C. (1973). *Lo scambio dei doni nel Vicino Oriente durante i secoli XV–XIII.* Oriens Antiqui Collectio XI. Centro per le Antichità e la Storia dell'Arte del Vicino Oriente.

Zaccagnini, C. (1981). Modo di produzione asiatico e Vicino Oriente antico. *Dialoghi di Archeologia, 3,* 3–65.

Zeuske, M. (2013). *Handbuch Geschichte der Sklaverei. Eine Globalgeschichte von den Anfängen bis zur Gegenwart.* De Gruyter.

Zurbach, J. (2017). Esclaves, dette, monnaie en Grèce mycénienne. In M.-L. Nosch & H. L. Enegren (Eds.), *Aegean scripts: Proceedings of the 14th international colloquium on Mycenaean studies,* Vol. 1, Copenhagen, 2–5 September 2015 (pp. 659–672). Incunabula Graeca CV.1. Istituto di Studi sul Mediterraneo Antico.

Chapter 9
Tripod Dedication: Gift and Commodity Exchange in Ancient Greece

Stefanos Gimatzidis

Abstract Early Greek economic relations were previously examined through a gift exchange perspective inspired by epic literature and ethnography. A structured society and economy were presumed in subsequent interpretative narratives, suggesting that valuable goods were exchanged mainly among and for the benefit of elite members. This paper argues for an alternative understanding of the early Greek economy through a new approach to the ritual dedication of bronze tripods in Greek sanctuaries that has been traditionally perceived as an emblematic practice of gift exchange. In this paper, tripod dedication is understood instead as a pronounced manifestation of wealth exchange and accumulation in early Greece. This practice is further scrutinised as a paradigm of border fluidity between gifts and commodities depending on the social context of their circulation.

Introduction

An era of political fragmentation and decentralisation began in the Mediterranean shortly before the end of the second millennium BCE. This was a transformative period that followed the collapse of the palatial states in the eastern Mediterranean and preceded the rise of the city-state, the polis, which was the cell of the Greek culture in the Archaic and Classical period. During the Early Iron Age many small kingdoms emerged in the territories of earlier large empires in the Aegean, Asia Minor and the Syro-palestinian coast. The political organisation of the new states is less well known. Especially in the Aegean there is only indirect information deriving from epic literature and a rather fragmented archaeological record. In contrast to the Near East the archaeological landscape of the Early Iron Age Aegean is better known through mortuary than settlement evidence. Simplistic models of political hierarchies comprising kings and aristocrats, and economic relations based on gift exchange have been reconstructed for this period founded mainly on textual evidence.

S. Gimatzidis (✉)
Austrian Archaeological Institute, Austrian Academy of Sciences, Vienna, Austria
e-mail: stefanos.gimatzidis@oeaw.ac.at

S. Gimatzidis and R. Jung (eds.), *The Critique of Archaeological Economy*, Frontiers in Economic History,
https://doi.org/10.1007/978-3-030-72539-6_9

The political change that followed the collapse of the centralised palatial hierarchies of the Late Bronze Age gave rise to massive economic and social transformations. Economic transactions passed into the control of the newly emerged Greek, Cypriot, Phoenician, Neo-Hittite, Aramaean and other small states. A transition from a centrally controlled economy to economic relations driven by smaller institutions or individuals is usually assumed in this new political context. The paradigm of wandering Odysseus and his economic transactions overseas inspired archaeological and historical interpretive models and narratives. Despite the continuing scholarly debate that has been going on since the times of Marcel Mauss and Moses Finley, archaeology still lacks, nevertheless, empirical evidence and a theoretical framework for the reconstruction of this transformative period's economy.

This paper undertakes a new reading of economic relations in Early Iron Age Greece after reconsidering the available textual, archaeological and scientific evidence through a theoretical approach that diverges from the until now dominant consumption-oriented perspective. The starting point for the definition of early Greek economy as "good-faith" or "self-interest", which previously formed the main explanatory trajectories in economic history, is the exploration of exchange value. This is a requirement for the understanding of economic properties of goods that were exchanged either as gifts or commodities accordingly regulating social relations (see the introductory chapter in this book). Finally, it is the validity of these very same dichotomies—"good-faith" or "self-interest" and gift or commodity—that is put into question.

The Exchange Value of Copper in Ancient Texts

Early literature and other forms of texts present valuable information about exchange values during the Early Iron Age and the immediately preceding period in the economy of the Mediterranean. This is a privilege in the archaeology of early historic periods that not only supplements but also significantly determines the interpretation of the archaeological record. First and most significant are the cuneiform clay tablets from Ugarit in Syria, including hundreds of administrative and economic texts with information about economic transactions before the destruction of the city in the early twelfth century BCE. This large corpus, supplemented by other texts from Syria and Egypt, presents a rare opportunity for the reconstruction of exchange values on interregional terms in the eastern Mediterranean. The second source of textual evidence is Greek epic literature. This does not present direct information about the form of transactions and values as the Ugaritic tablets and Egyptian papyri do, but nevertheless still constitutes significant evidence for the reconstruction of economic relations.

A first conclusion that can be immediately drawn after consideration of the available Aegean and Levantine textual evidence is that copper was one of the most valuable products that was extensively exchanged in the Aegean and in eastern Mediterranean. Almost all sources about ancient values agree on this point. Although the Uluburun shipwreck has been repeatedly discussed in the past from a variety of approaches and perspectives, questions still remain about the exchange values and properties of the cargo and its entrepreneurial motives (Gates, 2011). The famous ship sank in the fourteenth century BCE off the south-western coast of Asia Minor carrying a cargo of ten tons of copper and one ton of tin ingots. The second largest cargo comprised 149 Canaanite jars containing resin or wine, or probably both. Other products were also on board such as glass ingots, Egyptian ebony logs, ivory blanks and finished products such as bronze tools, weapons, gold and silver scrap, ivory artefacts and of course ceramic vessels and foodstuffs.

A systematic study of the available textual evidence that achieved to convert the value of the Uluburun ship to silver shekels of Ugarit's standard reveals that its most valuable cargo was by far raw metal. The ten tons of copper and one ton of tin were thus estimated to have cost approximately 7000 shekels, while the assumed cargo of 1000 L of resin and wine would have cost 24.5 shekels. According to this estimation a single horse costing 35 silver shekels was more valuable than the whole cargo of the 149 jars of wine and resin in the Uluburun ship (Monroe, 2010, 2016).

An interesting aspect in overseas transactions during the Late Bronze Age that becomes immediately apparent was the disproportionally large value of cooper and tin compared to other commodities of probably similar bulk. In other words, the low value of wine and resin is in stark contrast to their large bulk. These properties of the Uluburun cargo have already been discussed to some extent and the symbolic value of wine and other bulky goods such as pottery, as lubricants of other economic transactions, has been previously suggested (Sherratt, 1999, 2015: 77).

The indisputable value of metals and particularly copper is further attested by Greek epics. Bronze and iron in the form of cauldrons or ingots are listed in the Iliad among the most common prizes awarded to the winners of the funeral games organised by Achilles for Patroclus (Homer, Iliad 23.263–858). The first prize for the chariot race was thus a large tripod of 22 measures and a female slave "skilled in goodly handiwork". A smaller, unused cauldron of four measures was the third prize in the same race. The final fifth prize was a simple bowl probably also made of bronze as were the tripods, while two talents of gold were given only as the fourth prize in the same race. A large tripod of value equal to twelve oxen was the first prize in wrestling. Iron was offered for the winners in throwing the discus and archery. A silver bowl of six measures and a silver-studded sword were the first prizes in the foot race and boxing contests, respectively. The tripod was also given as the first prize in the chariot race, which was the most popular game of all, at another instance in the Iliad. This was a chariot race in Elis, where Nestor's father wanted to participate with a four-horse chariot team (Homer, Iliad 11.698–702).

The award of tripods as first prizes in chariot races is indicative of these artefacts' value. Chariot races was not only the most popular but also the most prestigious game in the legendary Homeric world and in later historical periods. Participating in the games of ancient Greek festivals with a chariot was an expression of high social status. Owning and breeding horses was an expensive hobby enjoyed by aristocratic families, who displayed their status in chariot races (Fisher, 2009: 535; Kyle, 1992: 89). Some of the victors in chariot races who were most commemorated in lyric poetry were tyrants, who celebrated their victories by erecting precious dedications in Panhellenic sanctuaries. The most valuable prize, 140 amphoras filled with oil, awarded at the games organised during the Panathenaic festival in 370 BCE, was offered to the winner of the two-horse chariot race (Neils, 1992: 16).

In the Homeric economy tripods seem to have had a universal exchange value. This was defined—as in the case of other commodities—by comparison to oxen, which constituted some of the most common "universal equivalents" used to facilitate exchange. Oxen were thus first in the Homeric list of the exchangeable goods presenting simple and common value equivalents. The definition of Homeric values seems to have been up to a certain point rational: a large tripod cost twelve oxen and a female slave four (see above). A piece of golden armour cost one hundred oxen, whereas a piece of bronze armour cost only nine (Homer, Iliad 6.234–236).

Most puzzling in this respect was a particular transaction between Glaucus and Diomedes, who exchanged golden for bronze military gear. The Homeric poet ascribed this to Zeus' intervention, who took over Glaucus' mind and made him accept a gift of much lower value than that offered by him. This uneven transaction cannot be adequately explained as a display of higher status from the side of Glaucus in the context of competitive giving and generosity, and was understood as a public declaration of Diomedes' superiority. This is not the only unequal exchange in the Homeric world that implies variable perceptions and manipulation of values (Cook, 2016; Donlan, 1982, 1989).

Almost all commodities exchanged as gifts or prizes in the Homeric world shared at the same time social-symbolic and economic values. Tripods that usually appear in modern historical representations as primarily symbolic artefacts obviously had an acknowledged economic value that exceeded that of any other gift or commodity. Particularly illuminating in this respect is a passage in the Odyssey (13.10–23) that records the gifts given by the Phaeacians to Odysseus before his departure from their island. King Alcinous had already gathered cloths, gold and other gifts brought by Phaeacian aristocrats in a chest, but all these were apparently not enough for a fitting farewell to Odysseus. The king therefore exhorts his people "come now, let us give him a great tripod and a cauldron, each man of us, and we in turn will gather the cost from among the people ("demos"), and repay ourselves. It were hard for one man to give freely, without requital". In the next day they "brought the bronze, that gives strength to men" and the king himself supervised the stowing of the apparently numerous tripods and cauldrons in the ship so that the large cargo would not hamper the crew at their rowing. Tripods were apparently perceived as more valuable and more greatly appreciated than the other gifts. The king himself stresses the value of these objects by explaining that since the local aristocracy could not afford them, taxes would have to be collected from the "demos" to compensate them for the high expenses. The motive behind offering such valuable gifts without expecting material recompense was not only to present Alcinous as a generous host, but also to exhibit his authority among his people (cf. Hooker, 1989: 82–84; Papalexandrou [2005: 13–52] regards the tripods also as "material tokens of leadership" endowed by the Phaeacians to Odysseus, or as payment for information regarding navigation, or as territorial marks). His reward was the enhancement of his reputation since his generosity was commemorated three times in later episodes of the Odyssey by the main actor of the epos himself. In one of these instances Odysseus lists "stores of bronze and gold and raiment" by citing the most precious gift first in this order (Homer, Odyssey 23.341). The literary picture of a ship loaded with tripods sailing through the Aegean was probably not a Homeric invention but could have derived from real life. This is at least what the archaeological record in Greece implies about the use and exchange value of tripods as we shall see.

Tripod Dedication as Material Expression of Peer Competitive Attitudes

"Gift exchange" has usually been understood as the framework of the Homeric economy. Interestingly, direct exchanges of gifts between two parties were, however, extremely rare—amounting to only three in number—in Homeric texts, where gifts were mainly offered as prizes, rewards, tributes to chiefs, ransom, loans and within a marriage contract or guest friendship (Donlan, 1989: 3; Hooker, 1989). There may therefore have been further aspects in the "gift exchange" economy of the Early Iron Age than those implied in the Greek epics or reconstructed in modern archaeological literature.

Any attempt to recognise the material residue of "gift exchange" in past societies is a difficult exercise. Early Iron Age Greece presents extra challenges in this respect because settlements of this period are not well preserved or studied. The Early Iron Age is mainly known in Greece through its mortuary material culture. Burial gifts, however, represent different cultural relations that were defined by mortuary ideology and deserve separate treatment. Based on a non-systematic survey of the available settlement material from Greece it was previously assumed that metal objects were rarely used in domestic contexts, while they were more common in allegedly sacred spaces within settlements (Morris, 1986). Be that as it may, the more profound, large assemblages of metal artefacts were offered to Greek sanctuaries. Personal belongings such as fibulae, pins, amulets and other kinds of jewellery, weapons or even horse gear, as well as locally produced metal and clay figurines and pottery were dedicated in great numbers in Panhellenic and regional sanctuaries throughout Greece, already before the Archaic period that witnessed the erection of votive statues and other monuments. However, the oldest, most precious and also common votive offering in many Greek sanctuaries was the bronze tripod, which was originally a cooking vessel comprising a cauldron standing on three attached feet.

These artefacts were initially produced exclusively as cooking vessels in the service of a few elite members of certain communities. Over the course of time they acquired elaborate decoration with figurines attached to the ring-handles and cast legs with incised decoration, and gradually lost their functionality. Most of them were actually produced and used as objects of display. Their value was thus not only defined by the scarcity of the metal but also by the handicraft in their manufacture and mainly by their symbolism. Although such artefacts have attracted scholarly attention for a long time and have been intensively studied at sites such as Olympia (Maaß, 1978; Willemsen, 1957) and Delphi (Rolley, 1977), their socio-economic implications in Homeric society are still not fully explored.

Tripods with attached cauldrons were dedicated as offerings to at least 28 out of ca. 100 sanctuaries that have been archaeologically recorded all over continental and insular Greece (the mapping of Early Iron Age sanctuaries in Kiderlen, 2010 and Kiderlen et al., 2016 represents an earlier standpoint that does not include more recent finds). They were particularly common at the Panhellenic sanctuary of Olympia, where they were dedicated throughout the Early Iron Age, and Delphi, where they continued to be offered also in the following Archaic period. Not less than 1000 fragments belonging to several hundreds of tripods were found at Olympia. At the sanctuary of Apollo at Delphi 230 tripods have been catalogued so far. The archaeological record is echoed in the text of Theopompos (FGrH 1, 314) who relates that in the remote past bronze tripods rather than statues were erected at the Delphi sanctuary. It is also reflected in the popularity enjoyed by the scene showing the struggle for the Delphic tripod between Apollo and Heracles in Attic pottery after the mid-sixteenth century BCE. This figurative scene was probably not an allusion to the cultic tripod of Apollo but rather implied the robbery of the sanctuary's treasures or the competitive spirit of the games organised there (Sakowski, 1997: 113–163).

At the end of the Geometric period, under oriental influence cauldrons were equipped with attachments in the form of protomai of sirens, bulls, lions but most usually griffins, and continued to be offered in large numbers at Greek sanctuaries (for Olympia see Herrmann, 1979). The Archaic cauldrons with protomai were constructed separately from the rod tripod they used to stand on, which could also be elaborately decorated (Raubitschek, 1997: 77–96). With 14 hammered and 286 cast griffin protomes the sanctuary of Hera on Samos presents one of the most impressive contexts of Late Geometric and early Archaic cauldrons decorated with attached figures (Matthäus, 2008; Gehrig, 2004: 3). A fifth century BCE allusion to the concentration of such votive offerings on Samos is represented by the legend of Kolaios, who offered a monumental cauldron with griffins to the Heraion of Samos as a tribute after a profitable sea voyage to distant Tartessos in the Iberian peninsula (Herodotus 4.152).

In early Greek figurative art, the tripod was already shown as a prize, depicted between two horses or next to a single horse, which was already an aristocratic attribute. Next to these Late Geometric figurative scenes there were also vases of the same chronological phase showing tripods in rows. From the end of the Geometric period onwards tripods appeared between boxing men and later in association with other athletic games (wrestling, running) or chariot races, although in most cases they had long since ceased to be offered as prizes at such events (Sakowski, 1997). In fact their original use during earlier times, before the establishment of the athletic and chariot games at Olympia and Delphi, is also not undisputed (Morgan, 1990: 46–47).

Nevertheless, with a weight ranging between 6 and 30 kg and in some cases reaching 100 kg they constituted some of the most precious objects circulating in

Early Iron Age Greece, not only because of their material but also due to their value as finished artefacts, incorporating social symbolisms and representing elite attributes.

Already during the Late Bronze Age the use of tripods was associated with elites, and was thought to have represented power relations as their contextual analysis implied (Matthäus, 1980). Their common function as precious votive offerings in sanctuaries in later periods demonstrates their continuous perception as objects of particular value.

During recent decades there has been unanimity in classical scholarship regarding the interpretation of tripod offering; this is viewed as a practice of deliberate wealth disposal by competitive elite groups that wanted to enhance their reputation and further establish their authority (according to another view their concentration also suggests some kind of political centralisation; see Kiderlen, 2010 with literature; Morris, 1986). However, the assumed aristocratic competition that was thought to have been manifested by the offering of metal votives in the Greek sanctuaries is only one—and indeed a rather simplistic—aspect in the interpretation of this social practice.

Earlier archaeological approaches that focused on the undeniable symbolic value of tripods in the definition of social status blurred our understanding of certain economic implications in the practice of their offering. Tripods have been the subject of numerous studies so far, almost all of which have in common their understanding as prestige artefacts manipulated by peers for the purpose of social antagonisms via their offering and display in public places. These studies focused on aspects of use value, consumption and symbolisms of tripods, aligning with the zeitgeist of postprocessual critique in archaeology (McGuire, 2008: 84). Their material properties were thus downplayed and tripods were removed "both culturally and materially, from the social relations involved in their production, exchange, and distribution" (Patterson, 2005: 378). This paper will attempt to explore further social and economic aspects in the exchange of these conspicuous objects by overcoming biases of individual agency and treating other aspects of social behaviour.

New Empirical Data in the Exploration of Tripod Production and Exchange Modes

Recent scientific analyses have presented new empirical data that radically challenges the traditional perception of the use and exchange value of tripods. Chemical and lead isotope analyses showed that tripods at Olympia, and partly also at Delphi, were made from the Protogeometric to the beginning of the Late Geometric period with copper from the Faynan mines in modern Jordan (Kiderlen et al., 2016; for the provenance of copper during the Late Geometric, cf. Bode et al., 2020). The analytical evidence implies the operation of a stable exchange network that supplied the Aegean with large quantities of copper required for the production of bulky artefacts such as tripods, over a long period of time. The continuous supply of Faynan copper, that partly replaced the previous domination of Cypriot ores in Aegean metalworking, lasted at least three centuries and began after the end of Late Bronze Age (Jung & Mehofer, 2013). It is questionable if the numerous small states that emerged from the end of the Late Bronze Age could have developed similar institutionalised gift exchange mechanisms to those that operated in the previous period under the control of palatial hierarchies. In other words, the available archaeological record suggests that the circulation of copper over such extended and culturally variable political landscapes, during the Early Iron Age involved the participation of several different agents in distant places, complicating the development of personalised relations.

The exploration of some aspects, until now neglected and probably misunderstood, in the production and circulation of such conspicuous artefacts as the tripods requires the definition of their origin of production. Previously it was unthinkable that these precious artefacts were produced at the sanctuaries where they were dedicated. By means of typological and stylistic analyses scholars used to attribute them to one or the other assumed centre of Greek metalwork production such as Corinth and Argos (Coldstream, 2003: 105; Morgan, 1990: 36–37; cf. Maaß, 1981: 18, who suggests the production by wandering workshops). Neutron Activation Analysis of the clay core and residues of the casting moulds on the surface of tripods from Olympia have shown that they were indeed locally produced. Interestingly, only one of the five tripods analysed that were offered to the sanctuary of Kalapodi in Locris appeared to have been locally produced in Locris. All the other four tripods from Kalapodi were also made at Olympia (Kiderlen et al., 2017). The new empirical data allows a new reading of the tripods' value not only in terms of raw material but also as finished products. While personalised social relations could not have defined—at least over a long period—the international exchange mechanisms that supplied Greece with copper during the Early Iron Age, the circulation and offering of the finished products (tripods) followed different social trajectories.

Gifts to Gods and Gifts to Men: Disguised Economic Strategies in Greek Sanctuaries

The dedication of tripods to Greek sanctuaries cannot be understood in the same social and cultural context as that of other metal offerings that were personal belongings such as pins, fibulae or weapons. Tripods appear to have had a particular exchange and symbolic value that other artefacts in Homeric epics did not. Most interestingly, they incorporated an impressively consistent practice in votive offering that lasted centuries, from the Early Iron Age to the Classical period; furthermore, they marked the Greek cultural landscape through their massive production and dedication at certain sanctuaries, contrasting with their almost complete absence from domestic contexts.

The archaeological contexts where tripods were finally deposited at Olympia were abandoned wells and an extended black layer that further contained charcoal, animal bones, pottery and votive figurines representing sacrifice residue. Most usually parts of cast legs were preserved, which were intentionally fragmented. It is obvious that tripods were neither found at the original site of their deposition in the sanctuary, nor were they discarded after having fallen into disuse and becoming obsolete. It was instead assumed that preserved fragments from single tripods were secondarily deposited as *partes pro toto*, while all the other parts of these artefacts had been melted down. The purpose of recycling was associated by Helmut Kyrieleis (2006: 97–98), one of Olympia's excavators, with the economy of the sanctuary itself, since it was thought that dedicated artefacts could not be removed outside the sacred place.

The deposition of tripods in the Greek sanctuaries had scarcely anything in common with the practice of hoarding metal artefacts in continental Europe, a practice that also included accumulation and fragmentation of metal artefacts, often of the same type (Bradley, 1990: 7–9). Such hoards appeared for the first time in the Copper Age, while from 1700/1600 BCE they also included intentionally fragmented artefacts. The interpretation of the European hoards, which often comprised older objects covering a time span of three of four centuries, still puzzles scholarship. Earlier the practice of hoarding was interpreted as a response to economic crises in periods of social turbulence. Since a few decades, however, the deposition of precious artefacts in watery or land environments has been predominantly understood as a ritual practice; this conclusion nevertheless does not exclude other interpretation models for certain finds. The dedication of objects of great value as a gift to the gods cannot be explained in terms of rational economic thinking. Less structured, egalitarian communities may have offered precious votives to their gods in order to ease tensions that may have resulted after wealth accumulation by individual members. The latter not only avoided social exclusion in this way but also achieved enhancement of their social status (Hänsel, 1997: 14). Objects such as Richard Wagner's ring of the Nibelungen, inspired by German and Scandinavian traditions, could not become private wealth due to their supernatural powers; it was primarily for the protection of their potential owners that such objects had to be taken out of circulation (Bradley, 2017: 142–156). Nevertheless, many questions remain open, especially with regard to hoards of fragmented metal artefacts that are alternatively interpreted in economic, symbolic or other social terms (Hansen, 2013, 2016).

While the purpose of European hoarding was to permanently remove from circulation already formed groups of metal artefacts, possibly in a similar way to the Potlach ritual of the Native Americans in north-west America, the artefact assemblages dedicated to the Greek sanctuaries were gradually accumulated through a complex exchange mechanism in order to be displayed. Even if European hoards comprised artefact complexes that were displayed prior to their deposition, as Richard Bradley (2017: 80–105) has recently suggested, there is still a considerable difference from the practice of tripod dedication, since the latter were never permanently taken out of circulation.

By dedicating tripods to sanctuaries, their donors rather re-contextualised than put out of circulation these artefacts that were appreciated as top-ranking gifts in the Homeric world. At this point it is useful to observe that the earliest of these votive offerings were originally produced as functional cooking vessels. This is at least suggested by traces of use and repair on some of the earliest tripods from Olympia (Janietz, 2001: 28–29) that were probably used for common domestic purposes such as cooking or preparing water for a warm bath, as Homer implies. Such vessels were probably dedicated in sanctuaries after being used in local feasts of peers, who could afford the use of metal vases instead of common coarse ceramic jars, such as those frequently found in settlement contexts. Soon, tripods began to be produced exclusively as non-functional votive objects and were dedicated immediately after production.

Restricted accessibility to precious artefacts such as tripods emphasised the social implications of this votive offering and enhanced the donor's status in an alleged—as already stated—competitive exchange ceremony (cf. Gregory, 1980: 646). Sacrifices did not significantly differ from this practice as they also represented gifts to the gods through alienation of goods. On the one hand, the notion of alienation has been variously understood either through a Marxist perspective that regards labour as a matter of the self as well as value for the self or as a change of property rights from a Maussian point of view. On the other hand, Marcel Mauss (1966 [1925]: 43–47) defined as inalienable those gifts that even after exchange are still felt as originally owned by their giver, whose properties they continue to bear. This dichotomy complicates the understanding of past economic transactions since gift-debt and commodity-debt are usually thought to differ, in that they are created by the exchange of inalienable and alienable objects, respectively. Christopher Gregory (1980: 640; 1982: 7–8) and Marilyn Strathern (1988) suggested that an object becomes alienable through its exchange as commodity, and accordingly understood inalienability in the social context of gift exchange. Nevertheless, while gifts are generally inalienable things, they may still be alienated once they are dedicated to gods. This is the economic trajectory followed in the ritual exchange and accumulation of tripods in Greek sanctuaries: "alienation is a pre-condition for accumulation, and while alienation is impossible in a gifts-to-man system, it is the very basis of a gifts-to-god system which means that the potential for accumulation exists in such a system" (Gregory, 1980: 641).

The interpretation of the dedication of tripods to otherworldly powers as a ritual practice of aristocrats, aiming to convert valuables into prestige, is in contrast with the textual evidence. Tripods are namely offered and used in every possible context and manner in the Homeric epics, but never appear as dedications in sanctuaries. It is worth stressing that the sanctuary of Delphi, where large assemblages of tripods were deposited, is already mentioned once in the Odyssey (8.79–82). The fact that tripods are exchanged in the epics on several different occasions but never as votive offerings, which surprisingly is their predominant archaeological manifestation, may not imply biases in the formation of the archaeological record, or poetic conventions, but instead underlying perceptions in their use as dedications.

The practice of dedication did not necessarily alienate tripods' producers from their labour, since these objects were not directly appropriated or consumed by any elite group; they were instead exchanged in a gift-to-god system that allowed the accumulation of assets in public institutions. Sanctuaries thus represented not just fields of competitive gift exchange, as has been repeatedly assumed in the past, but rather institutions for the accumulation and potential redistribution of wealth. Sanctuaries accommodated the concentration of wealth, which was otherwise practiced by elites in structured societies and redistributed, for example through liturgies in ancient Athens (Graeber, 2001: 160; Mauss, 1966 [1925]: 66). The available evidence implies that, in addition to the ritual symbolism in the formation of power relations, there were also some significant economic aspects in the dedication of tripods that have been previously misunderstood.

Patterns of Ritual Wealth Accumulation in Ancient Greece

Tripod dedication in some aspects resembles votive deposition and display practices that took place in later periods in Greek sanctuaries. The large tripod concentrations at Olympia and Delphi in fact represent the archaeologically most visible accumulation of wealth in Early Iron Age and early Archaic Greece. From the second half of the seventh century BCE onwards, when the ritual practice of tripod dedication at these two sanctuaries declined, wealth accumulation was manifested in the form of treasuries. Treasure-houses were constructed as small temples in some of the most famous Greek sanctuaries, housing not only valuable dedications but also money offered by city-states and their rich citizens. The most prominent and numerous treasuries were erected in the two Panhellenic sanctuaries, at Olympia and Delphi, which previously had attracted tripod dedications. With few exceptions erected by tyrants, treasuries were dedications made by communities, not individuals. They were dedicated by city-states and were tightly linked with them. Cities even used to import building material from their territories for their construction in order to symbolically mark these links. Ancient literary evidence implies that some of the reasons for the erection of treasuries included the expression of devotion to the gods, the commemoration of victories and, of course, the display of wealth. The latter was a common denominator in the erection of both Archaic treasuries and earlier tripods. In both cases, the dedication was a political decision that expressed an elitist ideology (Neer, 2001). While, however, treasuries represented distinct political entities, where individual votive offerings were situated in the framework of single city-states and were ethnically identified, tripods were dedicated during the Early Iron Age as non-personalised objects, at a time when the major sanctuaries functioned as regional rather than Panhellenic institutions.

Tripods continued to incorporate symbolic values in the Archaic and Classical periods, when they were commonly erected to commemorate victorious events of any kind. The most renowned of all was certainly the Plataean tripod which was made of gold and which stood on the head of three intertwined bronze snakes. Greek cities erected this monument at Delphi to commemorate their victory against the Persians at the battle of Plataea in 479 BCE. From the Archaic period onwards, tripods were most usually offered as prizes in festivals such as the famous dramatic contests of the Dionysia in Athens. In turn, winners used to dedicate their prizes in sanctuaries in order—among other reasons—to commemorate their victory in public. This is precisely what Hesiod (Opera 654–657) did after having been awarded a tripod in a poetic contest in Chalkis, a prize which he eventually offered to the Sanctuary of the Muses at Helicon in his homeland.

The dedication of tripods that has been archaeologically attested at Olympia, Delphi and Samos during the Early Iron Age and early Archaic periods subsequently became a common practice at other Greek sanctuaries. Particularly indicative in this respect is a story recorded by Pausanias (4.12.8–10) about a territorial dispute between the Messenians and the Lacedaemonians. According to a Delphic oracle, those who would offer one hundred bronze tripods at the sanctuary of Zeus on Mount Ithome would gain the Messenian land. The Messenians did not have the money required and therefore produced one hundred wooden instead of bronze tripods. However, the Lacedaemonians, who had planned a similar trick, were the first to offer one hundred terracotta tripods to the sanctuary. This narrative contains an implicit indication about the economic value of tripods, namely, their perception as objects of particular exchange value.

The archaeological record of Boeotia demonstrates how the dedication of monumental tripods was manipulated by public institutions at Ptoon and Orchomenos (Papalexandrou, 2008). Twenty-five bases of tripods, inscribed with the names of victors in the musical contests in honour of Dionysos, have survived at Orchomenos where they were erected in a public place within or close to the agora. The interesting aspect in the dedication of these monuments is that they were awarded by the state as prizes to prominent citizens of Orchomenos; it was then intended that they would be returned to the city and displayed in a central public place, this time inscribed with the names of the victors. The display of the social status of certain individuals was only one objective fulfilled through this ritual practice. Another assemblage of tripod bases—this time of monumental size—preserved at the sanctuary of Ptoios at Kastraki allowed a reconstruction of their original setting, suggesting that they were erected as part of the sanctuary's scenery. The tripods formed two alignments—with nine and 19 tripod bases preserved, respectively—that used to frame and monumentalize the approach to the sanctuary as the Street of the Tripods did in Athens. Interestingly, this imposing syntax of tripods, with heights ranging between 1.50 and 2.50 m., was not only planned but fully implemented by the state, the city of Akraiphia itself. The significance of the tripod in Boeotian public life is further attested by the collective rite of *tripodephoria* (ceremonial transferences of tripods) on several occasions, yet also by its common appearance in the iconography of Geometric and early Archaic local pottery (Sakowski, 1997; on the perception of the tripod in Messene after its foundation by the Boeotians in 370/369 BCE, see Papalexandrou, 2014).

Epigraphic evidence in Boeotia attests that tripods were dedicated either by individuals who won in a musical contest at Orchomenos, or by the state itself at Ptoon. Two questions that immediately arise are, firstly, why the state undertook such an expense by erecting numerous tripods in its sanctuaries and, secondly, if the dedication of tripods gained by individuals was indeed a personal choice dependent on freewill. An answer to the latter question is provided by a story recorded by Herodotus about the games organised by the Doric league, which originally comprised six cities, in honour of Triopian Apollo close to Cnidus in south-western Asia Minor. When a man from Halicarnassus broke the law that obliged winners to dedicate their prizes to the temple of Apollo by taking his tripod back home, they expelled his home-city from the league. This is how the original Doric federation of six cities (Hexapolis) became Pentapolis (Herodotus 1.144). Greek literature implies that the deposit of tripods, which were previously awarded in contests or games, to sanctuaries was a common practice in Greece. Although tripod-prizes were not directly perceived as public property, they were still treated as objects that could not be alienated and privatised. Textual and archaeological evidence elucidates further the erection of tripod monuments as communal projects. Their use as markers in the planning of public space not only in Boeotia but also in Athens and elsewhere, as well as the costs involved, suggest that they cannot solely be explained in terms of cultural symbolism for the profit of individuals.

The tripods at Olympia had been made locally with imported copper ores and had been dedicated in large numbers by Elian aristocrats before the sanctuary became a Panhellenic institution. While the practice of tripod deposition gradually ceased at Olympia after the end of the Geometric period, it continued without any interruption in the early Archaic period at Delphi. This sanctuary, which has yielded the second largest assemblage of tripods in Greece, had a different political and social organisation (Osborne, 2009: 191). Namely, it was run by a religious league of neighbouring states known as the Amphictyony. The tripods at Delphi were the material manifestation of ceremonial dedications by more than one state.

Greek sanctuaries were not only arenas of social antagonisms but were primarily places where wealth was accumulated throughout their long history (Arafat, 2009). The Gauls who invaded Greece in the early Hellenistic period were aware that Greece's treasures were kept in its sanctuaries (Pausanias 10.19.9). The management of this wealth and its economic implications have been a rather misunderstood topic in Greek archaeology. There is, however, adequate textual evidence demonstrating that sacred funds, primarily in the form of valuable dedications, were not expropriated only for the purposes of the sanctuary itself or by looters, but were also at the disposal of the states in charge of these institutions. This is at least suggested by the Lacedaemonians choosing to entrust their gold and silver at a particular time to the sanctuary of Delphi, wealth which they in turn brought back to their city, Sparta, on a later occasion (Posidonius, FGrHist 87 F 48c). Thucydides' report (1.121.3 and 1.143.1) that the Peloponnesians could borrow money from the sanctuaries of Olympia and Delphi without committing any impiety contains the same implications about the relationship of certain states with the Panhellenic sanctuaries. It is relevant to consider in the same respect the textual—both literary and epigraphic—evidence from Classical Athens regarding the sacred resources of the temple of Athena Parthenos and other deities that were regularly used to fund military and building projects (Samons II, 1993). These resources included among others "the sacred vessels for the processions and games" and "the gold ornaments of Athena herself; for the statue contained forty talents of pure gold and it was all removable" (Thucydides 2.13.4–5).

The Commodification of Tripods

Tripods have been perceived in the past as votive offerings that were brought to Olympia from other regions in southern Greece and dedicated by individuals, whereas the sanctuary of Delphi was thought to have received them as public offerings (Morgan, 1990: 43–47, 140). The dominant interpretation of the motives for their dedication focused on social competition and accordingly defined the early history of Greek sanctuaries. This Maussian perspective, however, provided only a spotlight on the long social and cultural processes that began with the production of tripods and further involved their exchange, appropriation and consumption. The practice of tripod dedication cannot be approached through comparison to the institution of "the potlatch" that incorporates the best known ethnographic paradigm of competitive gift exchange (Mauss, 1966 [1925]). Closer consideration of the purposes and objectives of this economic transaction that took place in Greek sanctuaries has shown that this was not an expression of contempt for private possessions, as the potlatch was, but a means to accumulate wealth (Graeber, 2001: 160). A gift exchange institution such as the potlach requires unequal social relations and aims at constructing relations of dependency. The acceptance of a gift in the potlach is an act of recognition of the higher social status of the giver (Graeber, 2001: 225). In the case of tripod exchange the final recipient is always a public institution. By focusing on issues of exchange, previous scholarship downplayed modes of production and failed to elucidate certain disguised socio-economic aspects in tripods' consumption (Josephides, 1983). A major bias in previous archaeological and historical representations was the simplistic perception of private ownership that overlooked social complexity in pre-modern societies and alternative conceptualizations of value and access to the resources beyond individualism (Strathern, 1988: 142–143).

Social antagonisms and ceremonial votive practices are obviously not sufficient arguments to explain the accumulation of precious artefacts of the same form and type that made sanctuaries such as those at Olympia, Delphi and Samos look like treasuries filled with bronze ores imported from remote places in the Levant. Early Iron Age tripods did not have any individual personality, as other votive offerings did. Even when they were inscribed in later periods, they still rarely exerted individual agency. An exception is Athens during the late Classical period when the city experienced significant social transformations. Tripod dedication then looked more like an individual social performance, and tripod monuments were known by their donor's names such as Lysicrates, Thrasyllos and Nikias. Although tripod offering was an institutionalised practice aiming to display wealth and power, allegedly by individuals, the long-term objective was obviously not associated with personal strategies, at least in pre-Classical periods. A reciprocal gift from the gods was thus not expected after tripod dedication, since this votive practice incorporated economic benefits exclusively for the community (cf. Osborne, 2004: 2).

Tripod deposition was the oldest and longest practice of wealth accumulation that is archaeologically attested in ancient Greece. These artefacts were deposited at sacred places after having circulated within an exchange mechanism that was controlled by the states in charge of the sanctuaries. In earlier periods, the main actors in this gift exchange system were probably individual peers, competing with each other and probably representing different clans. The result was the concentration of wealth in the form of precious metal artefacts for the benefit of the community. The awarding of tripods as prizes was—at least in later periods—nothing more than the performative, ceremonial framework of a similar exchange mechanism that facilitated the concentration of tripods at sanctuaries. The symbolism of these artefacts was recycled through manipulation of their materiality: they were awarded as prizes by the community to its most distinctive members to enable them to negotiate their social status and enhance prestige, before they were finally returned to the community as votive dedications by the aristocrats. Tripods were "donated" as personalised and inalienable gifts by the state to elite individuals, and were subsequently alienated and re-appropriated by the state as gifts to the gods. The inscribed names on them did not record physical owners but, instead, holders of their symbolic value.

The alienation of tripods through their exchange between state and individuals, and their final dedication to the gods, neither immediately implies their commodification nor the function of sanctuaries as "market" places. The latter notion has often been abused in classical studies resulting in the construction of narratives biased by modern preconceptions. Small-scale votive offerings at Greek sanctuaries, other than personal belongings such as figurines and miniature vases that were produced in situ, were usually thought to have been "sold" to visitors (Morgan, 1990: 44). The question that consequently arises is with what money did such transactions take place, and to what extent were property rights defined; in other words, if any kind of market economy can be reconstructed, in contrast to Karl Polanyi's expectations. "Market" is a rather fluid notion that has been variously defined depending on the social contexts of transactions or the purchasability of goods (Hahn, 2018; Harris & Lewis, 2016). Moreover, from non-market to market societies there is a lot of space for alternative concepts that can be subsumed as "partial markets" (Andreau, 2002: 36–37; see more analytically North, 1977; there is therefore not much sense in the dispute over the dating of the introduction of the market in Greece, see e.g. Redfield, 1986; Morris, 1986). Equally fluid is the social process of commodification, exemplified by the transformation of personal into anonymous goods that can be sold and bought by anyone (commodities).

The notion of commodity emerged according to the original Marxist definition in the social context of capitalist economies, and was used to describe an object produced for exchange. However, Marx (1977 [1867], 97) left some space for the application of the notion of commodity also in the exploration of pre-capitalist economic relations, by suggesting that it appeared for the first time in a disguised manner much earlier in history. In recent decades anthropologists attempted to explore the multifaceted nature of this concept by highlighting its fluid borders to barter and gift (see Appadurai, 1986: 9–13; see also the introduction chapter in this book). The practice of tripod accumulation at Greek sanctuaries still cannot be fully understood through Appadurai's (1986: 13–16) perspective that seeks to break "with the production-dominated Marxian view of the commodity" and focuses instead on the history of individual objects, which at some time in their "career" may "meet the requirements of commodity candidacy". In this manner Appadurai, in his much cited paper, examined alternative ways to understand processes of commodification in pre-modern societies. By focusing on consumption and the self-centred spirit of commodities he failed, however, to present a holistic approach that would also consider their materiality and modes of production (Graeber, 2001: 30–33). Economics, including also studies of ancient economy, cannot be purged of ideologies. It therefore makes more sense to highlight political ideologies behind economic theorizing, as David Graeber does, and to assess their impact on interpretative models, than to question the politically unmasked approach to economics as "personal vision" and "social activism" (Papadopoulos & Urton, 2012: 20).

The exchange of tripods can also not be interpreted in terms of the mainstream division between gifts and commodities, that perceived the first as the qualitative outcome of personal relations and the second as goods of quantitative equivalence that were impersonally exchanged (Gregory, 1982). This theoretical perspective understands gifts as goods offered to enhance the social status of the giver through wealth distribution, and commodities as goods accumulated to create private wealth (Graeber, 2001: 36). Tripod exchange incorporated both properties.

A handicap in archaeology is its inability to directly observe and document social dynamics that defined modes of past transactions. This is a privilege of anthropology, which however can no longer be taken to represent a theoretical quiver of models and paradigms for the reconstruction of past social relations. Archaeological evidence at Greek sanctuaries suggests that tripods were initially exchanged in ceremonial feasts, where inalienable objects were commodified and subsequently accumulated. This transaction did not serve the individual purposes of a particular chief, as did, for example, the use of shell valuables in barter and gift exchange by the Roviana people on New Georgia, Solomon Islands (Aswani & Sheppard, 2003). Archaeological, historical and ethnographic data rejected any clear-cut dichotomy between gift and commodity in the exchanges of this Melanesian people. It was argued instead that a shift between such exchange modalities was not uncommon in pre-modern societies, depending on the transaction of objects among different social and cultural spheres. Roviana shell artefacts and Greek tripods underwent different processes of commodification and de-commodification. Some of the most valuable shell rings were initially exchanged as alienated commodities and then de-commodified through their dedication to sanctuaries or hoarding, to serve the purposes of the chief's authority by financing his ceremonial exchanges or wars. As inalienable objects, shell rings could return to circulation or be permanently removed from it. Tripods, on the other hand, were alternatively exchanged as gifts or commodities, but their alienation and accumulation was not intended to further enhance the social status of any individual, which was achieved by the performance of dedication. Similarly, their detachment from circulation was not a means to display elite control over the means of production or exchange through appropriation by elite groups of subordinates' labour. Following a different economic trajectory, tripod accumulation was a process of commodity alienation that in a ceremonial way placed wealth at the disposal of the community. Although tripods were initially provided with a certain biography, which in later periods was expressed through an inscription, they were institutionally alienated through their exchange and accumulation in sanctuaries, to be ultimately appropriated as commodities for communal use.

Conclusions

The understanding of the use and exchange value of tripods in this paper deviates from previous interpretations through its production-oriented approach to their materiality. It is in fact assumed that tripods were produced in large numbers and dedicated at the sanctuary of Olympia by elite members of regional communities who were in charge of the sanctuary without, however, alienating producers from their surplus in the Marxist sense. This perception of tripod exchange therefore renders the question of how donors paid for them appear futile (Kyrieleis, 2006: 101).

The grand narratives about the social and economic structure of Early Iron Age Greece used to depend more on textual rather than the available archaeological evidence (Finley, 1973; Murray, 1993; Stein-Hölkeskamp, 2015; cf. Whitley, 1991; and several papers in Morris & Powell, 1997; Sherratt & Bennet, 2017). The Hero of Lefkandi who was given an exceptional burial with his spouse in an elaborate building is, nevertheless, still without any parallel in Protogeometric and Geometric Greece. On the other hand, the spatial organisation of the settlement structure that came to light under the Archaic temple of Apollo Daphnephoros in Eretria, Euboea implies that industrial metalworking activities and "aristocratic feasts" could have taken place in the same settlement quarter (Verdan, 2013). The ritual practice of tripod dedication may be more eloquent about the socio-economic organisation of early Greece than the available mortuary record that forms the largest part of the archaeological dataset of this period but at the same time conveys socially and culturally biased evidence.

The transaction of tripods is here understood as a communal matter, whose outcome affected all community members equally. Similarly, tripod accumulation did not imply the creation of capital, but rather a concentration of wealth that was available for eventual redistribution or common use of another kind. This practice was common in Greek sanctuaries from the Early Iron Age onwards, with tripods symbolising peer antagonism in the first place, but also principally incorporating public strategies of wealth management. The scientifically attested circulation of tripods that were produced at Olympia at other sanctuaries such as Kalapodi can be understood in the context of interstate economic relations. The finds from Kalapodi are the archaeological manifestation of the Homeric picture of travelling ships loaded with valuable tripods. They represent common modes of exchange among peers from distant communities, and economic strategies that formed the background of the shaping of social relations in Early Iron Age and Archaic Greece. While ores from Faynan reached Greece as commodities exchanged between several different actors probably using the same non-personalised trajectories of economic transactions through the centuries, tripods may have circulated in Greece as personalised gifts to be finally deposited at Olympia, Kalapodi and elsewhere as alienated goods.

References

Andreau, J. (2002). Twenty years after Moses I. Finley's The ancient economy. In W. Scheidel & S. von Reden (Eds.), *The ancient economy* (pp. 33–49). Routledge.

Appadurai, A. (1986). Introduction: Commodities and the politics of value. In A. Appadurai (Ed.), *The social life of things: Commodities in cultural perspective* (pp. 3–63). Cambridge University Press.

Arafat, K. W. (2009). Treasure, treasuries and value in Pausanias. *The Classical Quarterly, 59*(2), 578–592.

Aswani, S., & Peter S. (2003). The archaeology and ethnohistory of exchange in precolonial and colonial Roviana: Gifts, commodities, and inalienable possessions. *Current Anthropology* 44, S5, Special Issue Multiple Methodologies in Anthropological Research, S51–S78.

Bode, M., Moritz K., Georgios P. M., Eleni F., & Yannis B. (2020). Das Kupfer der griechischen spätgeometrischen Dreifußkessel (ca. 750–700 v. Chr.): eine Diskussion der chemischen und bleiisotopischen Analysen. In H. Gönül Yalçın & O. Stegemeier (Eds.), *Metallurgica Anatolica: Festschrift für Ünsal Yalçın anlässlich seines 65. Geburtstags / Ünsal Yalçın 65 Yaşgünü Armağan Kitabı* (pp. 329–348). Ege Yayınları.

Bradley, R. (1990). *The passage of arms: An archaeological analysis of prehistoric hoards and votive deposits*. Cambridge University Press.

Bradley R. (2017). *A geography of offerings: Deposits of valuables in the landscapes of Europe*. Oxbow insights in archaeology. Oxbow Books.

Coldstream, J. N. (2003). *Geometric Greece, 900–700 BC* (2nd ed.). Routledge.

Cook, E. (2016). Homeric reciprocities. *Journal of Mediterranean Archaeology, 29*(1), 94–104. https://doi.org/10.1558/jmea.v29i1.31048.

Donlan, W. (1982). Reciprocities in Homer. *The Classical World, 75*(3), 137–175.

Donlan, W. (1989). The unequal exchange between Glaucus and Diomedes in light of the Homeric Gift-Economy. *Phoenix, 43*, 1–15.

Finley, M. I. (1973). *The ancient economy*. University of California Press.

Fisher, N. (2009). The culture of competition. In K. A. Raaflaub & H. van Wees (Eds.), *A companion to Archaic Greece* (pp. 524–541). Blackwell.

Gates, M.-H. (2011). Maritime business in the Bronze Age eastern Mediterranean: The view from its ports. In K. Duistermaat & I. Regulski (Eds.), *Intercultural contacts in the ancient Mediterranean. Proceedings of the International Conference at the Netherlands-Flemish Institute in Cairo, 25th to 29th October 2008* (pp. 381–394). Peeters.

Gehrig, U. (2004). *Die Greifenprotomen aus dem Heraion von Samos*. Samos 9. Habelt.

Graeber, D. (2001). *Toward an anthropological theory of value: The false coin of our own dreams*. Palgrave.

Gregory, C. A. (1980). Gifts to men and gifts to god: Gift exchange and capital accumulation in contemporary papua. *Man* (n.s.), 15(4), 626–652.

Gregory, C. A. (1982). *Gifts and commodities*. Academic Press.

Hahn, H. P. (2018). *Introduction*. Markets as places: Actors, structures and ideologies. In H. P. Hahn & G. Schmitz (Eds.), *Market as place and space of economic exchange: Perspectives from archaeology and anthropology* (pp. 1–18). Oxbow Books.

Hänsel, B. (1997). Gaben an die Götter—Schätze der Bronzezeit Europas—eine Einführung. In A. Hänsel & B. Hänsel (Eds.), *Gaben an die Götter. Schätze der Bronzezeit Europas. Ausstellung der Freien Universität Berlin in Verbindung mit dem Museum für Vor—und Frühgeschichte, Staatliche Museen zu Berlin—Preußischer Kulturbesitz* (pp. 11–27). Staatliche Museen zu Berlin—Preußischer Kulturbesitz and Freie Universität, Seminar für Ur- und Frühgeschichte.

Hansen, S. (2013). Bronze age hoards and their role in social structure: A case study from South-Western Zealand. In S. Bergerbrant & S. Sabatini (Eds.), *Counterpoint: Essays in archaeology and heritage studies in honour of Professor Kristian Kristiansen* (pp. 179–192). BAR Internat. Ser. 2508. Archaeopress.

Hansen, S. (2016). A short history of fragments in hoards of the bronze age. In H. Baitinger (Ed.), *Materielle Kultur und Identität im Spannungsfeld zwischen mediterraner Welt und Mitteleuropa / Material Culture and Identity between the Mediterranean World and Central Europe. Akten der Internationalen Tagung am Römisch-Germanischen Zentralmuseum Mainz, 22–24. Oktober 2014* (pp. 185–208). Verlag des Römisch-Germanischen Zentralmuseums.
Harris, E. M., & Lewis, D. M. (2016). Introduction: Markets in classical and Hellenistic Greece. In E. M. Harris, D. M. Lewis, & M. Woolmer (Eds.), *Markets, households and city-states in the Ancient Greek economy* (pp. 1–36). Cambridge University Press.
Herrmann, H. V. (1979). *Die Kessel der orientalisierenden Zeit. 2, Kesselprotomen und Stabdreifüsse.* Olympische Forschungen 11. W. de Gruyter.
Hooker, J. T. (1989). Gifts in Homer. *Bulletin of the Institute of Classical Studies, 36*, 79–90
Janietz, B. (2001). *Untersuchungen an geometrischen Bronzen.* Dissertation, University of Freiburg 1989. https://www.freidok.uni-freiburg.de/volltexte/199/. Accessed 28 October 2020.
Josephides, L. (1983). Equal but different? The ontology of gender among the Kewa. *Oceania, 53*, 291–307.
Jung, R., & Mehofer, M. (2013). Mycenaean Greece and Bronze Age Italy: Cooperation, trade or war? *Archäologisches Korrespondenzblatt, 43*, 175–193
Kiderlen, M. (2010). Zur Chronologie griechischer Bronzedreifüße des geometrischen Typus und den Möglichkeiten einer politisch-historischen Interpretation der Fundverteilung. *Archäologischer Anzeiger*, 91–105.
Kiderlen, M., Bode, M., Hauptmann, A., & Bassiakos, Y. (2016). Tripod cauldrons produced at Olympia give evidence for trade with copper from Faynan (Jordan) to South West Greece, c. 950–750 BCE. *Journal of Archaeological Science: Reports, 8*, 303–313.
Kiderlen, M., Anno, H., Hans M., & Noémi S. M. (2017). Production sites of Early Iron Age Greek bronze tripod cauldrons: First evidence from Neutron Activation Analysis of casting ceramics. *Geoarchaeology: An International Journal*, 32: 321–42.
Kyle, D. G. (1992). The Panathenaic games: Sacred and civic athletics. In J. Neils (Ed.), *Goddesse and Polis: The Panathenaic festival in ancient Athens* (pp. 77–101). Princeton University Press.
Kyrieleis, H. (2006). *Anfänge und Frühzeit des Heiligtums von Olympia. Die Ausgrabungen am Pelopion 1987–1996.* Olympische Forschungen 31. W. de Gruyter.
Maaß, M. (1978). *Die geometrischen Dreifüße von Olympia.* Olympische Forschungen 10. W. de Gruyter.
Maaß, M. (1981). Die geometrischen Dreifüsse von Olympia. *Antike Kunst, 24*, 6–20.
Marx, K. (1977 [1867]). *Das Kapital. Kritik der politischen Ökonomie.* Dietz Verlag.
Matthäus, H. (1980). *Die Bronzegefäße der kretisch-mykenischen Kultur.* Prähistorische Bronzefunde II, 1. Beck.
Matthäus, H. (2008). Review of 'Die Greifenprotomen aus Dem Heraion von Samos' by Ulrich Gehrig and Gerwulf Schneider. *American Journal of Archaeology, 112*(4), 771–773.
Mauss, M. (1966 [1925]). *The gift.* London: Cohen & West LTD (Essai sur le don. Forme et raison de l'échange dans les sociétés archaïques. *L'année sociologique* 1, 1923–24 [1925] 30–186).
McGuire, R. (2008). Marxism. In A. Bentley, H. Maschner, & C. Chippindale (Eds.), *Handbook of archaeological theories* (pp. 73–93). Altamira Press.
Monroe, C. M. (2010). Sunk Costs at Late Bronze Age Uluburun. *Bulletin of the American Schools of Oriental Research, 357*, 19–33.
Monroe, C. M. (2016). Measure for 'measure': Connecting text to material through late bronze age shipping jars. In S. Demesticha & A. Bernard Knapp (Eds.), *Maritime transport containers in the Bronze-Iron age Aegean and Eastern Mediterranean* (pp. 79–96). Studies in Mediterranean archaeology and literature, PB 183. Åströms förlag.
Morgan, C. (1990). *Athletes and Oracles: The transformation of Olympia and Delphi in the eight century BC.* Cambridge University Press.
Morris, I. (1986). Gift and commodity in Archaic Greece. *Man, New Series, 21*(1), 1–17.
Morris, I., & Barry B. P. (1997). *A new companion to Homer.* Brill.
Murray, O. (1993). *Early Greece* (2nd ed.). Harvard University Press.

Neer, R. T. (2001). Framing the gift: The politics of the Siphnian treasury at Delphi. *Classical Antiquity, 20*(2), 273–344.
Neils, J. (1992). The Panathenaia: An introduction. In J. Neils (Ed.), *Goddesse and Polis: The Panathenaic festival in Ancient Athens* (pp. 13–27). Princeton University Press.
North, D. C. (1977). Markets and other allocation systems in history: The challenge of Karl Polanyi. *Journal of European Economic History, 63*(3), 703–716.
Osborne, R. (2004). Hoards, votives, offerings: The archaeology of the dedicated object. *World Archaeology, 36*(1) The Object of Dedication, 1–10.
Osborne, R. (2009). *Greece in the making, 1200–479 BC* (2nd ed.). Routledge.
Papadopoulos, J. K., & Urton, G. (2012). Introduction: The construction of value in the ancient world. In J. K. Papadopoulos & G. Urton (Eds.), *The construction of value in the ancient world* (pp. 1–47). Cotsen advanced seminar series, 5. Cotsen Institute of Archaeology Press.
Papalexandrou, N. (2005). *The visual poetics of power: Warriors, youths, and tripods in early Greece.* Lexington Books.
Papalexandrou, N. (2008). Boiotian tripods: The tenacity of a Panhellenic symbol in a regional context. *Hesperia: The Journal of the American School of Classical Studies at Athens, 77*, 251–282.
Papalexandrou, N. (2014). Messenian tripods: A Boiotian contribution to the symbolic construction of the Messenian past? In B. Alroth & C. Scheffer (Eds.), *Attitudes towards the past in antiquity creating identities. Proceedings of an International Conference held at Stockholm University, 15–17 May 2009* (pp. 127–137). Acta Universitatis Stockholmiensis. Stockholm Studies in Classical Archaeology 14. Edita Bobergs AB.
Patterson, T. C. (2005). The turn to agency: Neoliberalism, individuality, and subjectivity in late-twentieth-century anglophone archaeology. *Rethinking Marxism, 17*(3), 373–384.
Raubitschek, I. K. (1997). *The metal objects (1952–1989).* Isthmia 7. American School of Classical Studies at Athens.
Redfield, J. M. (1986). The development of the market in Archaic Greece. In B. L. Anderson & A. J. H. Latham (Eds.), *The market in history* (pp. 29–58). Taylor & Francis.
Rolley, C. (1977). *Les trépieds à cuve clouée.* Fouilles de Delphes 5, 3. De Boccard.
Sakowski, A. (1997). *Darstellungen von Dreifußkesseln in der griechischen Kunst bis zum Beginn der Klassischen Zeit.* Europäische Hochschulschriften, Reihe XXXVIII, 67. Peter Lang.
Samons II, L. J. (1993). Athenian finance and the treasury of Athena. *Historia: Zeitschrift für Alte Geschichte, 42*(2), 129–138.
Sherratt, S. (1999). E pur si muove: pots, markets and values in the second millennium Mediterranean. In J. P. Crielaard, V. Stissi, & G. J. van Wijngaarden (Eds.), *The complex past of pottery: Production, circulation and consumption of Mycenaean and Greek pottery (Sixteenth to early fifth centuries BC). Proceedings of the ARCHON international conference, held in Amsterdam, 8–9 November 1996* (pp. 163–211). J. C. Gieben.
Sherratt, S. (2015). Cyprus and the Near East: Cultural contacts (1200–750 BC). In A. Babbi, F. Bubenheimer-Erhart, B. Marín-Aguilera, & S. Mühl (Eds.), *The Mediterranean mirror cultural contacts in the Mediterranean Sea between 1200 and 750 B.C. International Post-doc and Young Researcher Conference Heidelberg, 6th–8th October 2012* (pp. 71–83). Verlag des Römisch-Germanischen Zentralmuseums.
Sherratt, S., & J. Bennet. (2017). *Archaeology and Homeric epics.* Sheffield Studies in Aegean Archaeology. Oxbow Books.
Stein-Hölkeskamp, E. (2015). *Das archaische Griechenland. Die Stadt und das Meer.* C.H. Beck.
Strathern, M. (1988). *The gender of the gift: Problems with women and problems with society in Melanesia.* University of California Press.
Verdan, S. (2013). *Le sanctuaire d'Apollon Daphnéphoros à l'époque géométrique.* Eretria. Fouilles et recherches 22. Infolio.
Whitley, J. (1991). *Style and society in Dark Age Greece: The changing face of a pre-literate society 1100–700 BC.* Cambridge University Press.
Willemsen, F. (1957). *Dreifußkessel von Olympia.* Olympische Forschungen 3. W. de Gruyter.

Chapter 10
Happily Connected? The Interconnectivity Paradigm and the Debate About the Ancient Economy

Jan Paul Crielaard

Abstract This contribution deals with the recent paradigm shift in thinking about Mediterranean connectedness and how this affected prevalent ideas about the functioning of the ancient economy. It sketches the intellectual, cultural and academic contexts in which connectivity thinking has developed over the last 50 years and discusses some of its basic tenets, notably the notion of unlimited, Mediterranean-wide connectedness and individual economic agency. A blind spot in the current vision of a connected Mediterranean concerns the evidence of regional differentiality in connectivity and the ways and means that connectedness and networks were manipulated to create or reinforce power relations—a point which is illustrated with the help of a long-term study of seaborne and terrestrial connections in the southern part of the Greek island of Euboia.

Introduction

Over the last decades, Mediterranean archaeologists and historians have shifted from models emphasizing small, static units and rigid socioeconomic structures towards a new paradigm emphasizing connectedness and the fluidity of the movement of people, goods and ideas, both in a geographical and a social sense. Peregrine Horden and Nicholas Purcell's *The Corrupting Sea* has been a landmark in this development (Horden & Purcell, 2000). Other sources of inspiration for this interconnectivity paradigm are today's network society, the current internet culture and information society, and such related phenomena as globalization and increased economic interdependence.

The interconnectivity paradigm has led to all kinds of sweeping statements about mobility, ever-expanding networks, small worlds, mutability, cultural homogenization, loss of sense of place, breakdown of spatially bounded cultures, etc.—almost to the point that interconnectivity is taken as gospel truth and is becoming a new

J. P. Crielaard (✉)
Faculty of Humanities/CLUE+, VU University, Amsterdam, The Netherlands
e-mail: j.p.crielaard@vu.nl

S. Gimatzidis and R. Jung (eds.), *The Critique of Archaeological Economy*, Frontiers in Economic History,
https://doi.org/10.1007/978-3-030-72539-6_10

ideology. In this contribution, I offer some reflections on the interconnectivity model and its basic tenets. I do not offer a detailed critique of the various contributions to this debate, but rather sketch the intellectual, cultural and academic contexts in which connectivity thinking has developed over the last 40 or 50 years. After briefly discussing the dominant ways of thinking about Mediterranean connectivity in the decades preceding the publication of *The Corrupting Sea*, I evaluate the direction the debate has subsequently taken and identify some issues that still need to be addressed. One of the positive things about the current interest in Mediterranean connectivity is that its scope is much wider in comparison to the earlier focus on trade and economy. On the other hand, it goes without saying that ideas about a connected ancient world have a direct bearing on how the ancient economy is perceived and for this reason the debate about interconnectivity should be taken it into consideration if we wish to offer a critique on archaeological economy.[1]

Ideas About Mediterranean Connectedness

At the risk of oversimplifying, we can discern three important schools of thought or models that were current in the 1980s and 1990s and had a considerable influence on how Mediterranean connectivity was perceived before *The Corrupting Sea*. The first may be dubbed the "cellular self-sufficiency" model. One of its basic tenets is that the operation of ancient societies and economies was determined by powerful institutions and deeply rooted structures. Most ancient Mediterranean people were supposedly engaged in self-supporting agriculture, which created little surplus and small aggregate demand. Simple technology, a limited information flow and high transport costs prevented people from moving far and often, and divided the Mediterranean into small, static regions and geographically bounded cultures. Needless to say, this model of cellular self-sufficiency was heavily influenced by substantivism, owing much to the work of Moses Finley and, through him, Max Weber. Keywords are fragmentation, immobility and the disconnectedness of the ancient Mediterranean world. Trade and, more generally, connectivity were thought to be embedded in social institutions and to be especially the domain of elites. As Ian Morris remarks, for proponents of this model it was perfectly acceptable that "emperor Hadrian might tour from one end of the Mediterranean basin to the other and have similar philosophical conversations, drink similar wines, and eat off similar gold plates at every stop, while for 99 per cent of its people the 'Mediterranean world' was just a few hours' walk across" (Morris, 2003: 30–31, 37–38).

[1] I wish to express my thanks to Dr. Reinhard Jung and Dr. Stefanos Gimatzidis for the invitation to participate in the symposium and to contribute to this volume. I also wish to thank the symposium organizers and participants for their feedback on an earlier version of this paper. My contribution draws upon a synthesizing study as part of a research project titled "The sea and land routes of southern Euboea, ca. 4000–1 BCE. A case study in Mediterranean interconnectivity", funded by the Netherlands Organization for Scientific Research (NWO) as project no. PR-14-08 (abbreviated SESLR).

A second school of thought, in contrast, explicitly acknowledges Mediterranean connectivity, but perceives these connections in terms of centre–periphery relations, drawing on the world systems theory that Immanuel Wallerstein developed to explain the origins of Europe's early modern world economy (Wallerstein, 1974). Despite criticism that it is inappropriate to apply world systems theory to pre-capitalist societies, and Wallerstein's cautionary remarks about the matter, centre–periphery models have been fervently embraced particularly by prehistorians working not only in the Mediterranean and the Near East but also in north-western Europe, and have been widely used to explain connections between dissimilar parts of the world (e.g. Rowlands et al., 1987; Champion, 1989; Sherratt & Sherratt, 1991, 1993; Sherratt, 1993; Kristiansen, 1998; Harding, 2000. Critical: Stein, 1998. Centre–periphery models remain popular in addition to the connectedness model: see e.g. Kümmel, 2001; Sommer, 2004; Vianello, 2008). Centre–periphery models imply frequent and intensive economic interactions, often over long distances, between more developed centres and less complex societies in marginal areas. The periphery supplies raw materials and human resources, often in return for manufactured goods provided by the centre. The result is an asymmetrical socio-political and economic relationship; that is, there is a mutual dependency among the parties involved, but the centre dominates the relationships.

A third, influential school of thought that we can identify also acknowledges Mediterranean connectedness but very much in terms of people and ideas travelling from east to west. It is rooted in the cultural historical traditions of *ex oriente lux*. This was the dominant model among twentieth-century prehistorians, starting with Gordon Childe, who suggested that agriculture, together with a package of technological and cultural advancements, spread from the Near East through Anatolia and the Balkans to Europe (Childe, 1925). This more recent version of *ex oriente lux*-thinking focuses less on economic relationships than on cultural transmission. Such scholars as Walter Burkert, Martin Bernal, Sarah Morris and Martin West emphasize the impact of the ancient civilizations of Egypt and the Near East on the "younger" Mediterranean cultures, including classical Greece (Burkert, 1992 [1984], 2004; Bernal, 1987–2006; S. Morris, 1992; West, 1997; see also Kristiansen & Larsson, 2005). The idea that Greeks were "learning in the east and south" has been accepted by classicists—however, in a somewhat milder form and with the addition that the Greeks in their turn were "teaching in the west and north" by disseminating Greek civilization "to people in Italy and western Europe who were less advanced culturally and technologically" (Boardman, 1998: 8). In essence, this is a variation of the *ex oriente lux* idea, only with an intermediary role for the Greeks and the Greek genius. Much importance is attached to individuals acting as intermediaries, like Burkert's immigrant craftsmen and travelling healers and singers. What this view on east–west relations has in common with the more economically oriented centre–periphery models is that the flow of people, goods, practices, ideas, ideologies and technologies is thought to be basically unidirectional, implicitly assuming the existence of asymmetrical relationships and attributing a passive role to receptor communities.

The view of a fragmented Mediterranean underlying the cellular self-sufficiency model—or of a hierarchically divided Mediterranean, as adherents of centre–periphery models see it—was to a large extent a reflection of the fragmented state of the academic landscape: the study of the ancient Mediterranean itself was fragmented and divided, along often highly arbitrary disciplinary, chronological and geographical lines, created by long-established scholarly traditions or nationalist or otherwise ideologically tainted sentiments. These boundaries not only separated prehistory from classical archaeology or classics from medieval history, but also created an even greater divide between the study of Classical antiquity and that of the ancient cultures of the Near East or of "barbarian" Europe. Particularly within the field of archaeology, nation states formed the principal frame of reference for research on the past. This slowly started to change, however, when from the mid-twentieth century onwards, as part of a broader movement in the humanities and social sciences, historians increasingly recognized the importance of large-scale historical processes that transcended the boundaries of national states. In search of large-scale zones of interaction to bring these processes into focus, sea and ocean basins were identified as useful frameworks for the analysis of some historical processes, for instance regarding commercial, biological and cultural exchange that influenced the development of both individual societies and the larger region as a whole (Bentley, 1999; see further e.g. Bodle, 2007; Land, 2007). This was combined, especially from the 1990s onwards, with a new interest in connections and networks in the past. Sources of inspiration for models focusing on interconnectivity are the World Wide Web (e.g. Crielaard, 1998), the contemporary network society and information economy, and such related phenomena as globalization, mobility, increased economic interdependence and—once more—the demise of the sovereign nation state (Castells, 2004). The different way of perceiving the economy and trade in the past also seems to be influenced by the socioeconomic processes that we are currently experiencing in our world: nation-based industries are giving way to business networks that ignore national borders, which goes hand in hand with new sociopolitical and economic discourses, including the orientation towards entrepreneurial rather than state-building values, and towards identity formation rather than political or economic ideologies (Douw, 2017: 513).

Examples of connecting sea basins that shaped different phases in history were found in coastal Atlantic Europe (Cunliffe, 2001), the Atlantic Ocean basin (Bailyn, 2005; Egerton, 2007; Benjamin, 2009; Thornton, 2012), the Black Sea (King, 2004), the Baltic (Rönnby, 2003), the North Sea basin (Jordan, 2004; Van de Noort, 2011; Ayers, 2016) and, of course, the Mediterranean. The Mediterranean connectivity model gained ground very quickly, first of all because there was already a highly influential source of inspiration and point of orientation in the shape of Fernand Braudel's *La Méditerranée et le monde méditerranéen à l'époque de Philippe II* (Braudel, 1949), and secondly—and more importantly—thanks to the publication of Horden and Purcell's voluminous study *The Corrupting Sea* in 2000. This book became a watershed in Mediterranean studies. In an article published only three years after the appearance of *The Corrupting Sea*, Ian Morris felt confident to conclude that a paradigm shift, which he labelled the "new Mediterraneanism", was taking place, and that "the connectedness model is here to stay: it reveals new dimensions of antiquity and gives antiquity new significance for understanding the world around us" (I. Morris, 2003: 50–51).

The Corrupting Sea and The Ancient Economy

The starting point of Horden and Purcell's project is that the Mediterranean is "no barrier to communications, but the medium of all human intercourse from one region to another" (Horden & Purcell, 2000: 133). The subject of *The Corrupting Sea* is, to quote from the Introduction, "the human history of the Mediterranean Sea and its coastlands over some three millennia. Its immediate contention is that this history can profitably be treated as material for a unified and distinct discipline" (Horden & Purcell, 2000: 9). In the view of the authors, an interconnected Mediterranean means "history either of the whole Mediterranean or of an aspect of it to which the whole is an indispensable framework" (Horden & Purcell, 2000: 2). Their aim is to challenge simplistic notions of Mediterranean cultural unity and instead consider how divergent forms of variation, similarity and difference throughout the Mediterranean are interacted. Horden and Purcell take into account the heterogeneity of the Mediterranean region—being an assemblage of physically differentiated micro-regions—and stress the crucial and distinctive significance of local variability in Mediterranean history; however, they conceptualize this heterogeneity in holistic terms, pointing out that it is the variety and fragmentation that make the Mediterranean an entity, "the differences which resemble each other" (Horden & Purcell, 2000: 339). It is the relatively high degree of differentiation between micro-regions and the "natural" human response to risks caused by the marginality of the Mediterranean environments that forces these regions to continually interact, creating interdependent relationships and networks that foster cultural homogeneity across ecological divides.

The Corrupting Sea has directly or indirectly sparked a host of studies on the Mediterranean (Abulafia, 2011; Blake & Knapp, 2005; Harris, 2005; Broodbank, 2013; Horden & Purcell, 2019), Mediterranean interconnectivity and globalization (LaBianca & Scham, 2005; Harris, 2006; Hodos, 2006, 2017; Antoniadou & Pace, 2007; Maran, 2007; Tabak, 2008; Van Dommelen & Knapp, 2010; Demand, 2011; Jennings, 2011; Kistler, 2012; Pitts & Versluys, 2015), Mediterranean and Aegean networks (Crielaard, 1998; Malkin, 2011; Knapett et al., 2011; Knapett, 2013; van den Berg, 2018; Iacono, 2019), Aegean island and coastal archaeology (Broodbank, 2000; Rainbird, 2007; Berg, 2010; Bevan & Conolly, 2013; Tartaron, 2013) and interconnectivity between the Mediterranean and the Atlantic basin (Cunliffe, 2008, 2017). Many of these studies have in common that they adopt a long-term perspective and cut across the traditional disciplinary, chronological and geographical division lines. This "new Mediterraneanism" indeed proved to be a paradigm shift, most of all because it represents a clear break with many of the tenets current in the 1980s and 1990s. For example, in contrast to centre–periphery models, the Mediterranean connectivity paradigm does not work with dominant cultures, nor does it distinguish between central and peripheral areas. By their nature, interrelationships are believed to be rather symmetrical, in contrast to the unidirectional flows of raw materials and manufactured goods envisaged by centre–periphery models.

But the most radical and fundamental break has been with the traditional substantivist school of thought. Finley had stressed that production was more or less the same everywhere due to the sameness of the Mediterranean milieu, which discouraged large-scale trade and fostered autarkic home consumption. Horden and Purcell, in contrast, argue that the small differences in ecology forced micro-regions to continually interact and trade goods that in other regions were either entirely or temporarily unavailable or of a different quality. Whereas substantivists ("minimalists" in the terminology of Horden and Purcell) traditionally viewed the ancient economies as stagnant, agrarian and embedded in social and formal institutional systems (Horden & Purcell, 2000: 146–147 for critique on Finley's views on trade and economy in Antiquity), adherents of the Mediterranean connectedness models see fluidity, flexibility and dynamic relations, often taking place outside institutional frameworks.

Horden and Purcell stress that even if substantivists are right in their belief that ancient trade in some periods was about low-bulk, high-value goods, took the form of "directed trade", was connected to a command economy, or operated without a price setting market, it could still include very considerable movements of capital and people and be of socioeconomic significance and accompanied by considerable connectivity (Horden & Purcell, 2000: 149). In their view, cabotage played an important role in sustaining Mediterranean connectedness over the centuries. Hugging the shores or island hopping, caboteurs are thought to have been responsible for local, casual and short-distance contacts. They were highly flexible actors in the sense that they could easily adapt to seasonal changes and make year-to-year adjustments. Within the small-scale networks of coastal contacts, caboteurs knew what was available and what was wanted in each region. Horden and Purcell argue that, in aggregate, cabotage (sometimes in combination with petty piracy) was responsible for the bulk of the movement of people and goods around the sea. In this connection they make a distinction between "high commerce" and "low commerce". The former typically concerns long-distance exchanges of luxury and prestige goods, generated by the interests and purchasing power of aristocracy, state and army. It is the type of exchange that we encounter in literary texts and that plays a leading role in the dominant, historical narrative about ancient trade. This applies in particular to narratives constructed by substantivist/minimalist historians who, according to Horden and Purcell, give too much credit to normative thinking on the part of ancient elites trying to marginalize those who were engaged in commerce. The authors want to move away from this dualism, pointing out that high and low commerce were inextricable. High commerce was sophisticated and well organized, whereas low commerce was more casual, with caboteurs visiting informal harbours rather than the important ports. Together, however, they formed the fundamental ingredients in the social and economic history of the Mediterranean. At the same time, Horden and Purcell point out that thanks to the dense and mutable pattern of movement of cabotage and the existence of interconnected cabotage circuits, small traders were responsible for the redistribution of a tremendous quality, quantity and variety of goods, exceeding by far the volume of high commerce. Whereas high commerce fluctuated through history, low commerce formed the stable undercurrent of Mediterranean interconnectivity during both Antiquity and the Middle Ages, catering for the widespread and lasting interdependence of Mediterranean micro-regions (Horden & Purcell, 2000: 140–144, 150–151; for different forms of cabotage and differences between cabotage and tramping, see Arnaud, 2005, 2011: 61–63).

Some Critical Thoughts on Mediterranean Connectivity

For most of the latter half of the twentieth century, the substantivist–formalist debate kept many students of the ancient economy divided (Cartledge, 2002: 13–16). Towards the end of the second millennium, positions had become less polarized (see e.g. Bresson, 2016), but the "new Mediterraneanism" made this controversy seem superfluous, irrelevant and outdated. As said, it critiques especially substantivists' axioms, but what may be also noted is that the connectedness model projects some modern economic ideas or ideals into the past, and in that sense it provides a vehicle for the continuity of formalist thinking. For example, in the connectedness model there is little room for fixed exchanges or trade routes (Horden & Purcell, 2000: 137–140), and the emphasis is on decentralized movement and uncoordinated actions by individual travellers and traders. Great importance is attached to horizontal and flexible relationships, providing freedom of movement of goods, people and ideas. Mariners practicing cabotage epitomize this freedom of movement. Following Braudel, Horden and Purcell call caboteurs the "proletarians of the sea" (Horden & Purcell, 2000: 140, 144). This is a rather deceptive qualification: although caboteurs may have been involved in casual, informal trading and doing the "dirty work" of sailing up and down the coasts to distribute goods, purchasing and maintaining a seagoing vessel (even if it was small and used only for coastal shipping) required considerable investments, while selling, buying and exchanging goods en route or paying taxes in ports meant that a tramping captain had to possess certain financial means.[2] Horden and Purcell may be right that the role of the invisible caboteur has been systematically underestimated, but the fact that caboteurs are historically and archaeologically invisible also makes it hard to assess their share in seaborne interrelationships, and by implication makes it difficult to assess the intensity of Mediterranean interconnectivity itself. What is more, the qualifications that Horden and Purcell attribute to caboteurs are not those typical of proletarians: their supposed flexibility and ability to adapt to changing circumstances, and especially their role in bringing together supply and demand, make them look rather like modern brokers and traders. One cannot help but detect certain modernist, neoliberal overtones in the

[2] This point is illustrated by the examples of ships that, according to Horden and Purcell (2000: 142, 149), retained "close links with cabotage", namely the medieval Serçe Liman wreck which carried a valuable glass cargo, and the mid-fifth-century BCE Greek and Phoenician ships mentioned in the Elephantine palimpsest as paying substantial taxes in an Egyptian port.

way ancient and medieval caboteurs are supposed to have contributed to a connected Mediterranean world as autonomous agents. As champions of free enterprise and free economic exchange, these pre-modern entrepreneurs bridge the gap between Antiquity, the Middle Ages and our own modern world.

It is not my intention to try to revitalize the substantivist–formalist debate, but in my view current archaeological and historical approaches towards ancient interconnectivity could benefit from a bit of substantivism. I wish to make two closely related and partly overlapping points. First, most recent studies on the history of Mediterranean interconnectivity take a *longue durée* perspective—something they share with other historical studies of connecting sea basins or global connectedness. Also in this respect the points of orientation are Braudel and Horden and Purcell. One of the main aims of Horden and Purcell's study is to bring to the fore "certain continuities … across the extremes of time" (Horden & Purcell, 2000: 5). In this view, the Mediterranean is interconnected in terms not only of space but also of time. This has certain methodological consequences, as it allows a great deal of freedom to assemble from very different periods evidence that is normally used in a chronologically more restricted fashion. There is also the hazard of re-creating the stereotyped image of a timeless Mediterranean, for which Horden and Purcell have been rightly criticized. In other recent studies we see a stricter diachronic perspective, but what both approaches have in common is that connectivity and mobility are presented as the master narrative explaining the history and culture of the region. We find this in a more extreme way in Nayan Chanda's *Bound Together*, in which connectivity and mobility are identified as the story line of Homo sapiens over the last 60,000 years (Chanda, 2007). For Purcell, mobility is part of the human condition; as he stated in one of his earlier articles, "there is no real reason to assume that in human history the settled cultivator is the norm" (Purcell, 1990: 41). It may be questioned, however, whether integration and connectedness constitute a permanent state of being. It is not difficult to find periods of progressive or regressive tendencies in connectedness, and periods of expansion and contraction of Mediterranean culture and Mediterranean unity.[3] Such tendencies become visible especially in times of transition, such as the periods of the "rise and fall" of the Bronze Age palace societies. But there are also known cases of regions that chose not to connect, or maintained an ambivalent stance towards connecting with the Mediterranean. To give one example, during the second millennium BCE Egyptians imported goods from a number of coastal areas and islands in the Mediterranean basin, and possessed a fair amount of knowledge of some Mediterranean people and their lands and cultures. And although Egyptian ships sailed the Nile and the Red Sea, it seems that mostly Western Asian navigators and sailors were responsible for maintaining Egypt's intensive exchange network with the Mediterranean, which was sometimes referred to as "the great sea of Syria", indicating that it was regarded as an integral part of the Syrian rather than Egyptian

[3] Horden and Purcell (2000: 172) oppose this view, making a case for continuous interconnectivity during the early Medieval period and suggesting that thanks to the long-lasting tradition of cabotage something similar could be assumed for every period that counts as a dark age or period of low interconnectivity in Mediterranean history.

sphere. This lack of engagement with the Mediterranean for travelling, trading and fishing seems to have been the result of a long-lasting cultural practice (von Rüden, 2015, 37–42). Summing up, in studies of the *longue durée* of Mediterranean connectivity, fluctuations in connectivity and integration over time receive due attention, but what remains largely underexposed is the regional differentiality in connectivity within specific periods of connectedness. The inclusion of areas where disconnectedness prevailed or of different regional trajectories of connecting or disconnecting not only provides relief to the phenomenon of interconnectivity, but also helps us to prevent writing a master narrative in which "successfulness" becomes the leitmotif.

Secondly, with the depolarization of the substantivist–formalist debate, moderate substantivists in particular acknowledge that the ancient economy was more complex than Finley portrayed it. There was not one economic system in antiquity, but rather a plurality of micro-economies. In some periods and regions of the ancient world self-sufficiency prevailed, while in others something close to a market economy existed. In other words, the idea was embraced that the ancient economy was characterized by a situation of heterogeneous pluralism. Reckoning with heterogeneity and differentiality means that we also have to reckon with the possibility that not all groups within a society were connected in the same way. Taking into account the pluralism of the ancient economy, Paul Cartledge suggested that "perhaps one might approach them first by asking *whose* 'economy' or 'economies'?" (Cartledge, 2002: 13—original emphasis). In a similar vein, as students of ancient networks we may approach Mediterranean connectivity first by asking *whose* networks or *whose* connectedness are we studying?

This brings me to a next point: connectivity and politics. For substantivists, politics were the key to understanding the ancient economy (see e.g. Hasebroek, 1928). For Karl Polanyi and Moses Finley, the study of the ancient economy's embeddedness in politics, social relationships and external value systems was also a vehicle to critique the modern, disembedded economy (Morris, 1994). Politics do not play a very prominent role in the "New Mediterraneanism"—or at least not in a very visible way. For instance, Irad Malkin's "Small Greek World", is a world of expanding networks, without real centres and thus without power relationships (Malkin, 2011). There is a risk here of idealization, making the ancient world a good place where everybody was happily connected—somewhat reminiscent of the hopes and ideals prevailing in the early days of our own network and information society, when the so-called Utopians stressed the benefits of new information technologies leading to decentralization, democratization and freedom of choice.[4] The issue of politics and power structures was brought into the discussion by Ian Morris, who in the earlier cited article draws parallels with today's globalization. He points out that the emphasis that the connectedness model puts on fluidity, interconnection and openness betrays an input of ideas from our own, globalizing world. Drawing parallels

[4]Facebook's Mark Zuckerberg not only wrote a document entitled "Connectivity is a Human Right", but noted on more than one occasion (e.g. in Facebook's mission statement) that the social network wasn't originally designed to be a company, "It was built to accomplish a social mission" and "give people the power to build community and bring the world closer together".

with the modern globalization debate, he stresses that Mediterranean connectedness should be likewise approached not as a state but as a process. In analogy with the term "globalization", he suggests that "Mediterraneanization" describes this dynamic process better than the somewhat static "Mediterraneanism". Morris wishes to draw the globalization analogy even further: it provides a certain relevance to the study of the ancient Mediterranean for our own world, but it also induces us to ask questions similar to those that matter for our own world, for instance regarding both the positive and the negative effects of connectedness. Referring to Manuel Castells' classic trilogy *The information age: economy, society and culture* (1996, 1997, 1998), he argues that, just like globalization today, increasing connectedness in the ancient Mediterranean created winners and losers (Morris, 2003: 33, 40–44; see also Knapp, 2007: 38 on the relation between connectivity and power relations). But we may even go one step further. It needs no arguing that just because people or groups share a network, whether ancient or modern, it does not mean that they share the same interests. Different parties may wish to shape the infrastructure according to their own needs and, possibly conflicting, interests. Recent experiences with the manipulation of data and the monopolization of information networks may induce us to investigate whether also in antiquity connectedness and networks were subject to political manipulation to create or reinforce power relations. In this connection we may also draw inspiration from so-called mobility studies that have developed since the mid-2000s. One of the foci of interest is the entanglement of mobility with the production of hierarchies or, to put it more precisely, the role of power in the production of mobilities and the role of mobilities in the constitution of power (Creswell, 2010: 553; 2012: 650–651).

Happily Connected? A Case Study

In the last part of my contribution, I will illustrate some of these points, including the one on the political manipulation of networks and the link between connectedness and power relations. I will do this with the help of outcomes of a research project that I am conducting together with a group of PhD researchers (see n. 1). Taking the southern part of the island of Euboia in central Greece as a case study, the project's main aim is to give the Mediterranean interconnectivity model a firmer empirical basis and to critically examine some of its basic tenets. It departs from the observation that the connectedness model has led to a broadening of the scale of analysis, namely to supra-regional, Mediterranean perspectives with a strong emphasis on seaborne communications and mobility. In our project we want to also include developments in terrestrial communication systems and reintroduce into the discussion the local or regional connections, and analyse how these functioned in relation to wider Mediterranean interconnections. We have compiled a large database of legacy data, mainly from salvage excavations and surveys previously carried out in this region, supplemented with both new information that we have generated in the course of our project through a variety of remote sensing techniques, and data from our own targeted surveys. These pedestrian and drone surveys are carried out in particular areas and with specific research problems in mind, focusing especially on ancient road systems, harbour facilities and infrastructure related to the exploitation of natural resources (see e.g. Kooi et al., 2020). Spatial analyses are performed in a GIS environment using historical aerial photographs, aerial photographs taken at different altitudes, high-resolution satellite imagery, digital elevation maps, historic cartographic information and modern topographic maps. Another important source of information is our excavations at Karystos-Plakari investigating part of a Final Neolithic settlement and a sanctuary covering the eleventh to late fourteenth century BCE, as well as various aspects of the physical environment surrounding the site of Plakari (Crielaard, 2017; Crielaard & Songu, 2017 with references to preliminary reports; Crielaard et al., 2017).

Southern Euboia (or Karystia, as it was called in Antiquity) is an interesting region for the study of maritime and terrestrial interconnections and communications. This is, first of all, due to its geographical position (Fig. 10.1). The southern part of the island lies at a juncture of major maritime routes between the Cyclades and the Euboian Gulf region and is thus closely linked to both the Greek mainland and the Aegean archipelago and regions further away, such as coastal Anatolia (Crielaard, 2006; Papageorgiou, 2008: 10). Second, southern Euboia encompasses a variety of landscapes (coastal and alluvial plains, marshes and wetlands, well-watered foothills, and arid low and high mountain ranges in the hinterland) that are suitable for a range of sustenance activities, including fishing, agriculture, horticulture, stock breeding and transhumance. Moreover, it contains iron and marble deposits that were extensively exploited in Antiquity. The study area is confined on three sides by the sea, and on one by inhospitable mountain ranges, which means that in principle both seaborne and land-based communication was important. A third factor is the state of preservation of the region's archaeological record. The landscape has remained relatively untouched, although it has recently come under threat from the construction of summer houses and especially wind farms. After Antiquity, large parts were used only extensively, as surface surveys indicate (Keller, 1985: 230–235; Wickens et al., 2018: 32–34, 72–76; Kooi et al., 27) and, compared to other regions in Greece, modern tourism and land development have so far had limited effects on the landscape. As a result, archaeological sites and features, including ancient land routes, are well preserved. A large quantity and variety of find places dating from ca. 4000 BCE to the present day have been identified, thanks to excavations and, especially, regional surface surveys carried out over the last 40 years (see Crielaard et al., 2011–12: 88–93 for an overview of and references to the archaeological research carried out in the region; add Chidiroglou, 2012; Wickens et al., 2018).

This brief overview will highlight some aspects of the region's connectivity history during the second and especially the first millennium BCE. We start our overview in the Middle Bronze Age. The only inhabited site during this period is located on the hilltop site of Ayios Nikolaos Mylon, one of the foothills of Mount Ochi. It occupies a natural defensive position on top of a rocky ridge (ca. 250 masl) overlooking the Bay of Karystos. Although unexcavated, finds picked up during surveys clearly indicate that this was an important regional site. Within a possible defensive wall,

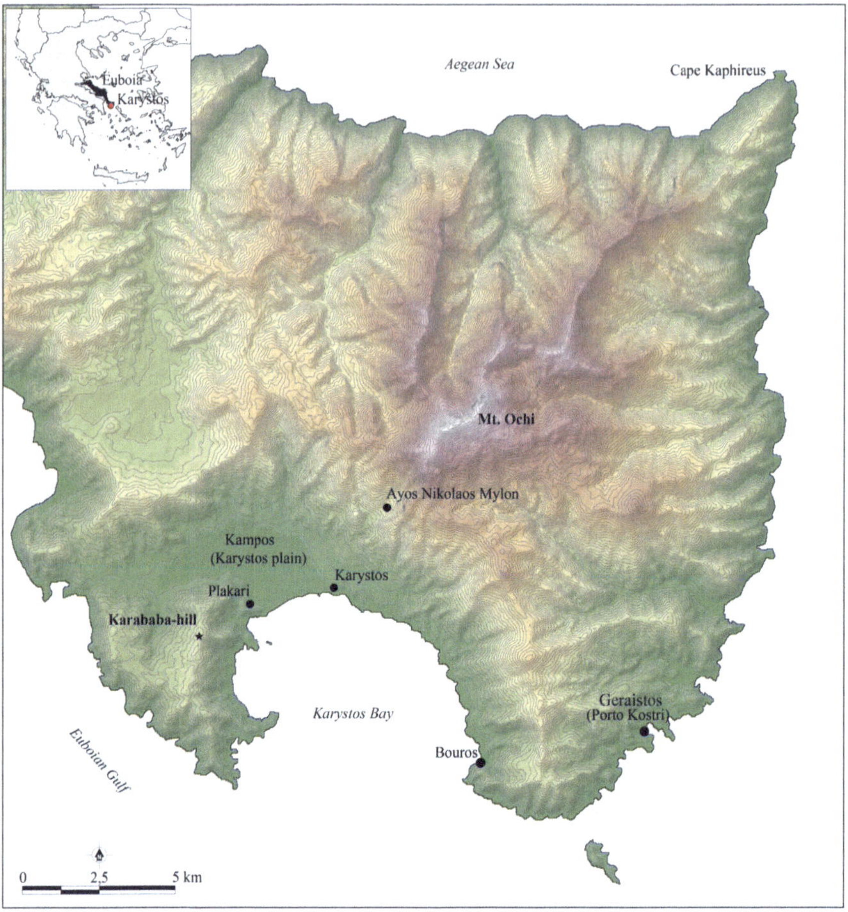

Fig. 10.1 Map of southern Euboia (Jaap Fokkema/Vrije Universiteit Amsterdam)

the remains of a number of buildings can be identified. Finds include pottery (local, central Euboian, Mainland and Cycladic wares), stone tools, some bronze objects, slag and a fragment of a bronze (copper?) ingot, suggesting that the site was used for storage and metalworking, among other things. Ayios Nikolaos Mylon continues to be occupied only during the first part of the Mycenaean period (Keller, 1985: 128–129, 276–278; Tankosić & Mathioudaki, 2011: 123–124, 127, 135 for the four LBA sherds from the site, broadly datable to late LH IIA to LH IIIA). On the whole, Karystia seems to be deserted during most of the palatial and post-palatial eras.[5] It follows patterns that in one way or another can also be observed in the Cyclades and elsewhere

[5]Theban Linear B documents mention a place called *ka-ru-to*, which has been identified with Karystos. However, given the extreme paucity of Mycenaean finds (and especially LH IIIB material), I suggest that this place must be located outside what was later known as Karystia (see Crielaard & Songu, 2017: 276–277; Crielaard, forthcoming, both with further refs.).

in Euboia. Jason Earle argues that the historically sudden disappearance of aspects of the material culture associated with the ideology and practices of palatial societies and the meaningful absence of imports from the Near East, indicate that during the Mycenaen palatial period the Mainland palaces excluded the Cyclades from the long-distance networks and the valuable resources circulating in these networks (Earle, 2012). Margaretha Kramer-Hajos, who studied the archaeology and socio-political situation in the Euboian Gulf region, concludes that the local elites of the region that had been up to date until the early Mycenaean period, seem to have lost all contact with the elite cultural norms during the LH IIIA2–IIIB period. The diminution of local power structures and the decline of sites in this period can be linked to a more general marginalization of the region, probably due to a reorientation of seaborne and land-based networks brought about by the palace of Thebes (Kramer-Hajos, 2017). We may say that the effects of this marginalization were even more dramatic for southern Euboia, which seems to have become deserted and probably remained uninhabited through much of the Late Bronze Age.

After a period of some three or four centuries with no traces of habitation, the earliest signs of the region's reoccupation come from the site of Plakari, which is located some 4 km west of the modern town of Karystos. Our excavations of a sanctuary on Plakari's hill top suggest that this cult place dates back to the late eleventh century BCE.[6] We may assume that this catered for a community that had settled lower down the hill. This must have been a pioneering community that had to set up a new infrastructure in the wilderness, so to speak, and almost immediately installed a cult place on the hill's summit—two activities that must have contributed significantly to community building and the creation of group identity. A finger ring and earring of gold, both chance finds dating to the early ninth century and with good parallels at Lefkandi, suggest that valuable items found their way to Plakari possibly from the central part of the island and certainly during a period when both gold and contacts were rare. After this kick start, the community was moderate in its outward orientation. Pottery and small finds indicate that it maintained contacts with Attica and central Euboia, but they are nothing of the kind that we find in contemporary Early Iron Age Lefkandi and Geometric Eretria. I have argued elsewhere that long-distance exchanges and colonization initiated by these central Euboian communities were closely connected to status competition; connectedness acted as a form of "symbolic capital", while imported valuables testified to the range of an individual's or family's network (Crielaard, 1996, in press). At Plakari we have only a small number of bronzes from Sicily and Macedonia that date to the seventh century (Crielaard, forthcoming, fig. 8), suggesting that southern Euboia was not much involved in the networks that in this period connected the Aegean to the eastern and central Mediterranean. Surveys show that during the Early Iron Age and Archaic period, habitation in southern Euboia was stable but barely expanding.

[6]The earliest metal finds are six symmetrical arched fibulae with twisted bow, three violin bow fibulae and three dress pins of bronze dating to the Sub-Mycenaean period (Crielaard, forthcoming, Fig. 10.3) The earliest identifiable pottery at the site is Early to Middle Protogeometric (see Charalambidou, 2017, 255–256).

When a large investment was made in overland communications, it happened within the religious and agricultural sphere in the form of the construction, probably during the late Archaic and Classical periods, of a road system connecting Plakari with a rural sanctuary on the fringes of a terraced agricultural area forming its main catchment area (Kooi et al., 2020). The picture that arises is that Plakari was an agrarian community focused on self-sufficiency rather than networking. In the later Archaic period, things started to change. Karystos began minting its own coins and sported an Olympian champion. Possibly in the sixth century it established an *oikos* or treasury in Apollo's sanctuary on the island of Delos, which was the hub in a cultic network encompassing much of the Archaic Aegean. This, however, did not last long, because as Christy Constatakopoulou in her *Dance of the islands* discusses, Athens took control over the common religious cults and festivals that united the participant states. These then became allies and, later, subjects, especially after Athens moved the treasury of the "Delian League" to the Acropolis (Constatakopoulou, 2007: 39–75).

But Karystos was going to suffer more at the hands of the Athenians. In 490 BCE, the polis had been besieged and its land ravaged by the Persians (Herodotus 6.99.2), but in the following decades it was again devastated, this time by the Greek anti-Persian coalition (480 BCE; Herodotus 8.112, 121.1) and by the Athenians (c. 476–469 BCE; Herodotus 9.105; Thucydides 1.98). This happened on the pretext that Karystos had been medizing, but the true reason was probably that for Athens' expansive policy an important polis at its front door was something it did not want to tolerate. The dearth of fifth century material found in the surveys and in the Plakari sanctuary suggests that this series of events seriously affected life in Karystia. It is probably no coincidence that we see an explosion of find places in the later 5th to early Hellenistic period, when Karystos first established good relations with Athens and later profited from the demise of Athens' regional hegemony. The surveys that we carried for our project show that the port town of Geraistos at today's Kastri on the east coast of southern Euboia (Fig. 10.2) started to flourish as a port of call on interregional shipping lanes. Its habitation consisted of domestic structures, farmhouses, potters' workshops producing transport amphorae, a number of iron production sites, and places for the storage and processing of agricultural products—probably olive oil and grain, and certainly honey. Harbour facilities were constructed and once again large-scale investments were made in the construction of a road network, but this time to connect the immediate hinterland and its production sites to the port of Geraistos.

To complete this brief overview of southern Euboia's connectivity history, I should like to point to a part of our study region that is of particular interest because of the *longue durée* of its state of "unconnectedness". To the northeast of ancient and modern Karystos lies a mountainous zone with Mt Ochi as the highest peak (ca. 1400 masl; see Fig. 10.1). High ridges, alternated with deep valleys and gorges, radiate from the Ochi massif towards the northern and eastern coasts. It is a monumental landscape that in almost every respect is larger than the human scale. The valleys are well watered, and terrace farming is possible on the steep slopes. The coasts generally consist of steep cliffs with only a small number of inlets, exposed to strong winds and currents. Kastri/Geraistos is the only protected deep-sea harbour on the southeast side of the island. The extreme north-eastern part is formed by the notorious

Fig. 10.2 Aerial photo of Kastri /ancient Geraistos (photo by Anke Stoker/SESLR-project)

Cape Kaphireus, which in ancient times was also called Xilophagos ("Timber eater") and in the Frankish and Venetian period Cavo d'Oro ("Gold cape"), because of the many shipwrecks that occurred here. The "Hollows of Euboia", where in 480 BCE the Persian fleet suffered heavy losses (Herodotus 8.13), are found here. According to the *Mediterranean Pilot* (IV, 1968, 210, 245) this part of the coast "consists principally of high precipitous rocks without shelter even for the smallest craft, nor scarcely a place where a boat can land" (Fig. 10.3). These characteristics of the land- and seascape make it a very inhospitable and difficult terrain to access by sea and to traverse over land. I give three examples from different periods that serve to show that isolation, alienation and marginalization characterize this region and its long-term history. In the Graeco-Roman world, it had earned a reputation as the archetypical place where people lived in isolation. For instance, the celebrated orator Dio Chrysostom (ca. 40–115 CE) in his *Seventh* or *Euboean Discourse* chose the area as the location where the I-figure shipwrecked and is taken care of by simple but honest people—hunters and herdsmen who live in the wilds of Euboia and almost never go to town (Lehmann et al., 2012). Our second example comes from the second half of the thirteenth century CE and relates to the story of Licario (or Ikarios, as Byzantine historians call him), a knight of humble origins from Karystos, son of a Venetian father and a local, Karystian mother. After he came into conflict with the Lombard triarchs in Negroponte (Chalkis), he fled to his home in the southern part of the island, where he took to a stronghold in the mountains, named Anemopylai ("Gates of the Wind"), which he fortified. The exact location of the place is disputed (see Kalamara, 2017: 545–546), but it must have been in the Cavo d'Oro area. Having

Fig. 10.3 Photo of coastal area near Cape Kaphireus (photo by Ruben Brugge/SESLR-project)

assembled some of the discontented elements in the island, he used this as an isolated but safe base for guerrilla-type raids and brigandage, first plundering the lands of his Lombard opponents and later conquering the entire island in the service of the Byzantine emperor as grand admiral (Setton, 1976: 425–428; Chapman, 1993: 112–113; Fine, 1994: 190). In the post-Medieval and modern period, finally, the area was inhabited by dispersed Greek- and Albanian-speaking communities. Because of the rugged terrain, some of the communities have developed a whistling language, *sfyria*, to communicate with each other. These places became connected to the modern world only after the mid-1980s when first electricity and somewhat later asphalt roads were introduced to the area. The area lies next to a busy shipping lane between the north-eastern Aegean and northwest Anatolia and the southern part of Greece, but the only link the local inhabitants had with these maritime networks was through scavenging the shores for lost cargo and driftwood from shipwrecked ships.

Concluding Remarks

The interconnectivity paradigm has led to a fundamentally different way of looking at Mediterranean, interregional interactions and Mediterranean history. In this paper I wanted to draw attention, however, to two aspects that tend to remain underexposed: regional differentiality in connectivity (including the possibility of certain areas experiencing prolonged periods of unconnectedness) and the socio-political manipulation of connectedness and networks to create or reinforce power relations.

The long-term history of southern Euboia shows that there were periods when this part of the Aegean was cut off from Mediterranean networks, and we may be certain that more cases like these can be found in any given period in the Mediterranean. We have also seen that there are areas or sub-regions that for various reasons tend towards "unconnectednesses", even during a substantial part of their history. This invites us to step a little back from a maximalist position in our views on Mediterranean connectivity and in the debate on the ancient economy. If we accept that risk management is an important feature of the Mediterranean agricultural economy (cf. Horden & Purcell, 2000: 175–230), we may say that connectivity was not always and everywhere a reliable or feasible strategy to deal with risks and uncertainty. In other words, self-sufficiency was not only an ideal to achieve, as Horden and Purcell believe, but also—under some conditions—a reliable means for survival.

Proponents of a connected Mediterranean attribute much importance to agency. In an article on insularity and island identity, Bernard Knapp acknowledges that insular resources and environments can be very real attributes of island life, but argues that insularity is also a social situation in the sense that it depends on what people make of it and take the sea as either a connector or separator (Knapp, 2007: 50). Horden and Purcell go one step further and claim that the geography of the Mediterranean incites its inhabitants to continually interact, attributing a considerable amount of agency to caboteurs. I have argued that there are good grounds to question ideas about free enterprise and the freedom of movement of goods, people and ideas (or the idea that isolation or connectnednes was a matter of choice) that underlie the notion of intense interactions between different Mediterranean micro-regions and of high Mediterranean interconnectivity and integration through the ages. Ship-building technology, the use of sea-going vessels, knowledge of the sea and navigation, and access to the circulation of goods are just a few factors that determined the measure of agency that people had. In addition to this, networks were not necessarily free and neutral means of interaction, but—as we just observed—were also subject to manipulation and power relations.

All this induces us to create more diverse, regional histories that take into account regional and temporal differentiality in connectnedness and integration, and the repercussions this had on local and regional economies. Archaeology and survey archaeology in particular have much to offer to such a regional approach.

References

Abulafia, D. (2011). *The Great Sea. A human history of the Mediterranean*. Oxford University Press.

Antoniadou, S., & Pace, A. (Eds.). (2007). *Mediterranean crossroads*. Pierides Foundation.

Arnaud, P. (2005). *Les routes de la navigation antique: itinéraires en Méditerranée*. Éditions Errance.

Arnaud, P. (2011). Ancient maritime trade and sailing routes in their administrative, legal and economic contexts. In A. Wilson and D. Robinson (Eds.), *Maritime archaeology and ancient trade in the Mediterranean* (pp. 59–78). Oxford Centre for Maritime Archaeology.

Ayers, B. (2016). *The German ocean: Medieval Europe around the North Sea*. Equinox.

Bailyn, B. (2005). *Atlantic history: concepts and contours*. Harvard University Press.

Benjamin, T. (2009). *The Atlantic world: Europeans, Africans, Indians and their shared history, 1400–1900*. Cambridge University Press.

Bentley, J. H. (1999). Sea and ocean basins as frameworks of historical analysis. *The Geographical Review, 89*, 215–224.

Berg, I. (2010). Re-capturing the sea: The past and future of 'island archaeology' in Greece. *Shima. The International Journal of Research into Island Cultures, 4*, 16–26.

Bernal, M. (1987–2006). *Black Athena: The Afroasiatic roots of Classical civilization, 1–3*, Vintage.

Bevan, A., & Conolly, J. (2013). *Mediterranean islands, fragile communities and persistent landscapes: Antikythera in long-term perspective*. Cambridge University Press.

Blake, E., & Knapp, A. B. (Eds.) (2005). *The archaeology of Mediterranean prehistory*. Wiley-Blackwell.

Boardman, J. (1998). *The Greeks overseas. Their early colonies and trade* (4th rev. ed.). Thames and Hudson.

Bodle, W. (2007). Atlantic history is the new 'New Social History'. *William and Mary Quarterly, 64*, 203–220.

Braudel, F. (1949). *La Méditerranée et le monde Méditerranéen à l'époque de Philippe II*. Librairie Armand Colin.

Bresson, A. (2016). *The making of the ancient Greek economy. Institutions, markets and growth in the city-states*. Princeton University Press.

Broodbank, C. (2000). *An island archaeology of the early Cyclades*. Cambridge University Press.

Broodbank, C. (2013). *The making of the Middle Sea: A history of the Mediterranean from the beginning to the emergence of the Classical world*. Thames and Hudson.

Burkert, W. (1992). *The Orientalizing revolution. Near Eastern influence on Greek culture in the early Archaic age* [original German version 1984]. Harvard University Press.

Burkert, W. (2004). *Babylon, Memphis, Persepolis. Eastern contexts of Greek culture*. Harvard University Press.

Cartledge, P. (2002). *The Greeks: A portrait of self and others*. Oxford University Press.

Castells, M. (Ed.). (2004). *The network society. A cross-cultural perspective*. Edward Elgar.

Champion, T. C. (Ed.). (1989). *Centre and periphery: Comparative studies in archaeology*. Routledge.

Chanda, N. (2007). *Bound together: How traders, preachers, adventurers, and warriors shaped globalization*. Yale University Press.

Chapman, W. P. (1993). *Karystos: city-state and country town*. Uptown Press.

Charalambidou, X. (2017). The pottery from the sacrificial refuse area in Plakari-Karystos: a first assessment. In Z. Tankosic, F. Mavridis, & M. Kosma (Eds.), *An island between two worlds: The archaeology of Euboea from prehistoric to Byzantine times*. Proceedings of international conference, Eretria, 12–14 July 2013, (pp. 253–274). Norwegian Institute at Athens.

Childe, G. (1925). *The dawn of European civilization*. A. A. Knopf.

Chidiroglou, M. (2012). *Η αρχαία Καρυστία. Συμβολή στην ιστορία και αρχαιολογία της περιοχής από τη Γεωμετρική έως και την Αυτοκρατορική εποχή* (unpublished PhD thesis, National and Kapodistrian University of Athens).

Constatakopoulou, C. (2007). *The dance of the islands: Insularity, networks, the Athenian empire, and the Aegean world*. Oxford University Press.

Cresswell, T. (2010). Mobilities I: Catching up. *Progress in Human Geography, 35*, 550–558.

Cresswell, T. (2012). Mobilities II: Still. *Progress in Human Geography, 36*, 645–653.

Crielaard, J. P. (1996). *The Euboeans overseas: Long-distance contacts and colonization as status activities in Early Iron Age Greece* (unpublished thesis, University of Amsterdam).

Crielaard, J. P. (1998). Surfing on the Mediterranean web: Cypriot long-distance communications during the eleventh and tenth centuries BC. In V. Karageorghis & N. Ch. Stampolidis (Eds.), *Proceedings of the international symposium 'Eastern Mediterranean: Cyprus-Dodecanese-Crete,*

16th-6th c. BC', Rethymnon, 1997 (pp. 187–206). Athens: University of Crete and A.G. Leventis Foundation.
Crielaard, J. P. (2006). *Basileis* at sea: Elites and external contacts in the Euboian Gulf region from the end of the Bronze Age to the beginning of the Iron Age. In S. Deger-Jalkotzy & I. S. Lemos (Eds.), *Ancient Greece: from the Mycenaean palaces to the age of Homer* (pp. 271–297). Edinburgh University Press.
Crielaard, J. P. (2017). The Early Iron Age sanctuary of Karystos-Plakari (southern Euboea) and its wider context. In A. Mazarakis Ainian et al. (Eds.), *Regional stories: Towards a new perception of the early Greek world. Acts of an international symposium in honour of Professor Jan Bouzek, Volos 18–21 June 2015* (pp. 127–144). University of Thessaly Press.
Crielaard, J. P. (forthcoming). Recent research at Karystos-Plakari: Cult, connectivity and networks in the 10th to 7th centuries BC. In T. E. Cinquantaquattro & M. D'Acunto (Eds.), *Euboica II. Pithekoussai and Euboea between East and West*. AION, Annali di Archeologia e Storia Antica, Università degli Studi di Napoli L'Orientale, n.s. 26, 2019.
Crielaard, J. P. (in press). Migration and mobility. In C. M. Antonaccio & J. B. Carter (Eds.), *Cambridge companion to the Greek Iron Age*. Cambridge University Press.
Crielaard, J. P., & Songu, F. (2017). Connectivity and insularity in first-millennium southern Euboia: The evidence from the sanctuary of Karystos–Plakari, In Z. Tankosic, F. Mavridis and M. Kosma (Eds.), *An island between two worlds: the archaeology of Euboea from prehistoric to Byzantine times. Proceedings of International Conference, Eretria, 12–14 July 2013* (pp. 275–290). Athens: Norwegian Institute at Athens.
Crielaard, J. P., Charalambidou, X., Chidiroglou, M., Groot, M., Kluiving, S., & Songu, F. (2017). The Plakari Archaeological Project. Preliminary report on the sixth field season (2015). *Pharos. Journal of the Netherlands Institute at Athens, 23–2,* 67–90.
Crielaard, J. P., Songu, F., Chidiroglou, M., & Kosma., M. (2011–12). The Plakari Archaeological Project. Project outline and preliminary report on the first field season. (2010). *Pharos. Journal of the Netherlands Institute at Athens, 18,* 83–106.
Cunliffe, B. (2001). *Facing the ocean: The Atlantic and its peoples 8000 BC–AD 1500*. Oxford University Press.
Cunliffe, B. (2008). *Europe between the oceans: Themes and variations: 9000 BC–AD 1000*. Yale University Press.
Cunliffe, B. (2017). *On the Ocean: The Mediterranean and the Atlantic from prehistory to AD 1500*. Oxford University Press.
Demand, N. H. (2011). *The Mediterranean context of early Greek history*. Wiley-Blackwell.
Douw, L. (2017). Reservations about an evolutionary approach to cross-border mobility. *International Review of Social History, 62,* 509–519.
Earle, J. (2012). A Cycladic perspective on Mycenaean long-distance exchanges. *Journal of Mediterranean Archaeology, 25,* 3–25.
Egerton, D. R. (2007). *The Atlantic world: A history, 1400–1888*. Harlan Davidson.
Fine, J. V. A. (1994). *The Late Medieval Balkans: A critical survey from the late twelfth century to the Ottoman conquest*. University of Michigan Press.
Harding, A. F. (2000). *European societies in the Bronze Age*. Cambridge University Press.
Harris, A. (Ed.). (2006). *Incipient globalization? Long-distance contacts in the sixth century*. BAR IS 1644. BAR Publishing.
Harris, W. V. (Ed.). (2005). *Rethinking the Mediterranean*. Oxford University Press.
Hasebroek, J. (1928). *Staat und Handel im alten Griechenland*. Verlag J.C.B. Mohr (P. Siebeck).
Hodos, T. (2006). *Local responses to colonization in the Iron Age Mediterranean*. Routledge.
Hodos, T. (Ed.). (2017). *Routledge handbook of archaeology and globalization*. Routledge.
Horden, P., & Purcell, N. (2000). *The corrupting sea: A study of Mediterranean history*. Blackwell.
Horden, P., & Purcell, N. (2019). *The boundless sea: writing Mediterranean history*. Routledge.
Iacono, F. (2019). *The archaeology of Late Bronze Age interaction and mobility at the gates of Europe: People, things and networks around the southern Adriatic Sea*. Bloomsbury Academic.
Jennings, J. (2011). *Globalizations and the ancient world*. Cambridge University Press.

Jordan, P. (2004). *North Sea saga*. Longman.
Kalamara, P. (2017). The settlements of the Middle and Late Byzantine period in Euboea. In Ž. Tankosić, F. Mavridis & M. Kosma (Eds.), *An island between two worlds: The archaeology of Euboea from prehistoric to Byzantine times. Proceedings of International Conference, Eretria, 12–14 July 2013* (pp. 537–558). Norwegian Institute at Athens.
Keller, D. R. (1985). *Archaeological survey in southern Euboea, Greece: A reconstruction of human activity from Neolithic times through the Byzantine period* (unpublished PhD thesis, Indiana University).
King, C. (2004). *The Black Sea: A history*. Oxford University Press.
Kistler, E. (2012). Glocal responses from Archaic Sicily. *Ancient West & East, 11*, 219–233.
Knapp, A. B. (2007). Insularity and island identity in the prehistoric Mediterranean. In S. Antoniadou & A. Pace (Eds.), *Mediterranean crossroads* (pp. 37–62). Pierides Foundation.
Knappett, C. (Ed.). (2013). *Network analysis in archaeology: New approaches to regional interaction*. Oxford University Press.
Knappett, C., Evans, T., & Rivers, R. (2011). The Theran eruption and Minoan palatial collapse: New interpretations gained from modelling the maritime network. *Antiquity, 85*, 1008–1023.
Kooi, S., Crielaard, J. P., & Brugge, R. (2020). Two sanctuaries, two *horos* inscriptions and a procession road of the Classical period in southern Euboia. Detection, reconstruction and interpretation. *Bulletin Antieke Beschaving, 95*, 1–46.
Kramer-Hajos, M. (2016). *Mycenaean Greece and the Aegean world: Palace and province in the Late Bronze Age*. Cambridge University Press.
Kramer-Hajos, M. (2017). Gaps in the record: The missing LH I-II and IIIB phases on Euboea. In Ž. Tankosić, F. Mavridis & M. Kosma (Eds.), *An island between two worlds: The archaeology of Euboea from prehistoric to Byzantine times. Proceedings of International Conference, Eretria, 12–14 July 2013* (pp. 159–170). Norwegian Institute at Athens.
Kristiansen, K. (1998). *Europe before history*. Cambridge University Press.
Kristiansen, K., & Larsson, T. B. (2005). The iconography of ruling elites: The Kivik burial and the origins of the Nordic Bronze Age. In K. Kristiansen & T. B. Larsson (Eds.), *The rise of Bronze Age society: Travels, transmissions and transformations* (pp. 186–212). Cambridge University Press.
Kümmel, C. (2001). *Frühe Weltsysteme: Zentrum und Peripherie-Modelle in der Archäologie*. Marie Leidorf.
LaBianca, O. S., & Scham, S. A. (2005). *Connectivity in antiquity: Globalization as long-term historical process*. Acumen Pub.
Land, I. (2007). Tidal waves: The new coastal history. *Journal of Social History, 40*, 731–743.
Lehmann, G. A., Engster, D., Gall, D., Goette, H. R., Herrmann-Otto, E., Heun, W., & Zehnpfennig, B. (2012). *Armut – Arbeit – Menschenwürde. Die Euböische Rede des Dion von Prusa*. SAPERE 19. Mohr Siebeck.
Malkin, I. (2011). *A small Greek world. Networks in the ancient Mediterranean*. Oxford University Press.
Maran, J. (2007). Seaborne contacts between the Aegean, the Balkans and the central Mediterranean in the 3rd millennium BC—The unfolding of the Mediterranean world. In I. Galanaki et al. (Eds.), *Between the Aegean and Baltic seas: Prehistory across borders. Proceedings of the international conference 'Bronze and Early Iron Age interconnections and contemporary developments between the Aegean and the regions of the Balkan peninsula, central and northern Europe', Zagreb, 2005*. Aegaeum 27, (pp. 3–12). Université de Liège, University of Textas at Austin.
Morris, I. (1994). Review article: The Athenian economy twenty years after *The Ancient Economy*. *Classical Philology, 89*, 351–366.
Morris, I. (2003). Mediterraneanization. *Mediterranean Historical Review, 18–2*, 30–55.
Morris, S. P. (1992). *Daidalos and the origins of Greek art*. Princeton University Press.
Papageorgiou, D. (2008). The marine environment and its influence on seafaring and maritime routes in the prehistoric Aegean. *European Journal of Archaeology, 11*, 199–222.

Pitts, M., & Versluys, M. (Eds.). (2015). *Globalisation and the Roman world. World history, connectivity and material culture*. Cambridge University Press.

Purcell, N. (1990). Mobility and the *polis*. In O. Murray & S. Price (Eds.), *The Greek city from Homer to Alexander* (pp. 29–58). Oxford University Press.

Rainbird, P. (2007). *The archaeology of islands*. Cambridge University Press.

Rönnby, J. (Ed.). (2003). *By the water: archaeological perspectives on human strategies around the Baltic Sea*. Sodertorns Hogskola.

Rowlands, M. J., Larsen, M. T., & Kristiansen, K. (Eds.). (1987). *Centre and periphery in the ancient world*. Cambridge University Press.

Setton, K. M. (1976). *The papacy and the Levant (1204–1571)* I: *The thirteenth and fourteenth centuries*. The American Philosophical Society.

Sherratt, A. (1993). What would a Bronze-Age world system look like? Relations between temperate Europe and the Mediterranean in later prehistory. *Journal of European Archaeology, 1*, 1–57.

Sherratt, A., & Sherratt, S. (1991). From luxuries to commodities: The nature of Mediterranean Bronze Age trading systems. In N. H. Gale (Ed.), *Bronze Age trade in the Mediterranean. Papers presented at the conference held at Rewley House, Oxford, 1989*. SIMA 90, (pp. 351–384). P. Åströms Förlag.

Sherratt, A., & Sherratt, S. (1993). The growth of the Mediterranean economy in the early first millennium BC. *World Archaeology, 24*, 361–378.

Sommer, M. (2004). Die Peripherie als Zentrum. Die Phöniker und der interkontinentale Fremdhandel im Weltsystem der Eisenzeit. In R. Röllinger & C. Ulf (Eds.), *Commerce and monetary systems in the ancient World. Means of transmission and cultural interaction. Proceedings of the fifth annual symposium of the Assyrian and Babylonian Intellectual Heritage Project, held at Innsbruck, Austria, 2002* (pp. 233–244). Franz Steiner Verlag.

Stein, G. (1998). World systems theory and alternative modes of interactions in the archaeology of culture contact. In J. G. Cusick (Ed.), *Studies in culture contact: Interaction, culture change, and archaeology* (pp. 225–232). Southern Illinois University Press.

Tabak, F. (2008). *The waning of the Mediterranean 1550–1870: A geohistorical approach*. Johns Hopkins University Press.

Tankosić, Ž., & Mathioudaki, I. (2011). The finds from the prehistoric site of Ayios Nikolaos Mylon, southern Euboea, Greece. *The Annual of the British School at Athens, 106*, 99–140.

Tartaron, T. F. (2013). *Maritime networks in the Mycenaean world*. Cambridge University Press.

Thornton, J. K. (2012). *A cultural history of the Atlantic world, 1250–1820*. Cambridge University Press.

Van de Noort, R. (2011). *North Sea archaeologies: A maritime biography, 10,000 BC–AD 1500*. Oxford University Press.

Van den Berg, K. (2018). *Keeping in touch in a changing world. Network dynamics and the connections between the Aegean and Italy during the Bronze Age—Iron Age transition (ca. 1250–1000 BC)*. Unpublished PhD thesis, VU University Amsterdam.

Van Dommelen, P., & Knapp, A. B. (Eds.). (2010). *Material connections in the ancient Mediterranean. Mobility, materiality and identity*. Routledge.

Vianello, A. (2008). Late Bronze Age Aegean trade routes in the western Mediterranean. In H. Whittaker (Ed.), *The Aegean Bronze Age in relation to the wider European context* (pp. 7–34). British Archaeological Reports.

Von Rüden, C. (2015). Making the way through the Sea. Experiencing Mediterranean seascapes in the second millennium B.C.E. In A. Lichtenberger & C. von Rüden (Eds.), *Multiple Mediterranean realities. Current approaches to spaces, resources, and connectivities* (pp. 31–65). Fink.

Wallerstein, I. (1974). *The modern world-system: Capitalist agriculture and the origins of the European world economy in the sixteenth century*. Academic Press.

West, M. L. (1997). *The east face of Helicon. West Asiatic elements in Greek poetry and myth*. Oxford University Press.

Wickens, J. M., Rotroff, S. I., Cullen, T., Talalay, L. E., Perlès, C., & McCoy, F. W. (2018). *Settlement and land use on the periphery: The Bouros-Kastri peninsula, southern Euboia*. Archaeopress.

Chapter 11
Aegean Transport Amphoras (Sixth to First Centuries BCE): Exploring Social Tension in a Path Dependency Model

Mark L. Lawall

Abstract Two aspects of the production of transport amphoras (shipping containers often for wine and oil) are considered in terms of path dependency and tensions within Greek society. Amphora shapes often align with broad geographic regions, but at times the shapes are more narrowly associated with a single polis. The geography of production is examined here in terms of the socially constructed pathways shaping amphora production. The practice of impressing names and images on amphoras before firing is often interpreted as a mechanism of civic fiscal management. Poleis often depended on their wealthier citizens for the management of complex and sometimes risky enterprises. Stability in the industry was thus achieved and yet changes to even the most complex stamping systems reveal potential tensions in the system.

Introductory Matters

This paper, like many in this volume, works to explain rather than simply describe an archaeologically observed phenomenon. Across the Mediterranean world in Classical Antiquity, many goods, but especially wine and olive oil, were packaged, shipped, and stored in two-handled clay jars, amphoras. This paper examines two facts about these amphoras: their differences in shape and their use of images, often on one or both handles, impressed into the clay before firing. As was the case in the version of this paper delivered at the conference in Vienna, the effort centers on a concept borrowed from Douglass North and elaborated upon within the broader field of New Institutional Economics (NIE): Path Dependency (North, 1990, esp. Chapter 11). Practices in a society will create "paths" of behavior which in turn constrain or encourage change. In something of a caricatured view, path dependency might start from a simple observable fact—the arrangement of keys on a typewriter or the width of a typical axle on a cart—as a seemingly simple prime mover, and then spin through the unforeseen, long-term impacts of that fact. The present, revised version

M. L. Lawall (✉)
Classics Department, University of Manitoba, Winnipeg, MB, Canada
e-mail: mark.lawall@umanitoba.ca

S. Gimatzidis and R. Jung (eds.), *The Critique of Archaeological Economy*,
Frontiers in Economic History,
https://doi.org/10.1007/978-3-030-72539-6_11

of this paper, however, treats those paths themselves as potential loci for cohesion or conflict. In other words, the social catalysts or impediments to economic change are themselves the dynamic products of tension or contradiction within society. Such scrutiny changes the tenor of the investigation. In a traditional approach to NIE, path dependency often implicitly portrays all participants as willingly, even unconsciously, acting in harmony within a complex social system. The process of seeking contradictions and potential loci of conflict along these paths forces the researcher to examine the roles of easily ignored groups within ancient society and to address issues that are not traditionally raised with respect to amphoras as archaeological evidence for ancient economies.

Amphoras

Before I introduce the main focus and argument of my paper, I should introduce briefly the material focus: Aegean transport amphoras. Even within mainstream Classical Archaeology, the understanding of Aegean amphoras pales compared either with fine painted pottery or with later Roman amphoras. Greek amphoras, like their later Roman counterparts, were the primary container for wine, olive oil, and other products in seaborne trade. They could be transported overland albeit at much greater cost, and they were often used for storage. But their design was clearly aimed to facilitate stacking on shipboard.

Research on Greek amphoras goes back to the sixteenth century (Badoud, 2015). From the beginning, particular interest was paid to the stamped impressions found on their handles. That focus on stamps quickly came to define the field of amphorology (Garlan, 2000): the study of stamps and, to a lesser extent amphora shapes, in terms of civic identity, the proper reading of each stamp, and the numbers of stamps of each type as found at each site.

As more typological research was carried out with more and more attention to production sites and fabrics, the one-to-one correspondence between city and amphora shape began to weaken (Lawall, 2011a). The meaning of amphora shapes, whether as simply a matter of regional style or a deliberate effort at branded marketing of goods using the shape of the vessel, became a point of debate in its own right. The same expansion of research made clear how uncommon and how varied amphora stamping really was. In addition, closer attention to papyrus documents listing goods carried in amphoras highlighted the fact that these were general purpose containers (Kruit & Worp, 2000). Shipwrecked cargoes, too, made clear the range of goods that might be shipped in any one amphora type (Carlson, 2003; Foley et al., 2012).

Indeed, the deeper one delves into Greek amphora studies, the more difficulties seem to arise. We cannot simply count stamps to get a sense of trade patterns (Empereur, 1982; Lawall, 2005); shapes cannot be equated easily to specific commodities (Bonifay, 2007; Lawall, 2011b; Panagou, 2016). And yet, that same increasingly complex picture also brings the advantage of revealing a much more diverse set of internal and external social relations mediated to one extent or another by these artifacts.

Amphoras and Socioeconomic Theory

Studies of Aegean transport amphoras of the late Archaic through Hellenistic periods rarely admit to a particular theoretical stance. Implicit assumptions of rational action underpin much of the scholarship: stamps certified capacity since no one would have trusted such handmade, clay vessels for commerce otherwise (Grace, 1949); shapes must have served to advertise the product of each unique polis as merchants vied for consumers (Koehler, 1996: 326); such branded jars helped to market the well-known wine or oil of the given city. Discussion of trade in earlier periods, particularly the late 8th- and early seventh-century "world of Homer", has placed considerable emphasis on the social embeddedness of the economy, trade, and exchange (Bravo, 1977; Mele, 1979; and with more emphasis on the profits of commerce, van Wees, 2009). Apart from the world of "untrustworthy Phoenicians", trade was a part-time business, and luxury goods moved as gifts among aristocrats. And yet, even in the rare instances where amphoras are mentioned in scholarship on Homeric economies, they are already associated with merchants, commerce, and advertising (Osborne, 2007: 285). By the late sixth century, once the Greek world was securely populated with "professional merchants" and widespread use of coinage, the social context of trade fades from the discussion. The evidence should speak for itself in a familiar language of economic rationality. From this period forward, amphoras are seen as standardized, branded, cargo containers serving the commercial needs of the monetized, developed Mediterranean economy.

Undeniably, there has been some debate over interpretive models. When the numbers of imported amphoras are too small, some scholars argue against a "trade" or "market" linking exporter and importer (Finkielsztejn, 2011). Many efforts at further interpretation may be dismissed as "modernist" (Badoud et al., 2012: 165). Somewhat ironically, the "straightforward" interpretation of all amphoras as branded containers of commodities—an explicitly modernist interpretation—stands largely immune to criticism. Even commentaries within the paradigm of NIE in the world of ancient economies pay no attention to such matters.

Path Dependency

Even so, NIE's attention to transaction costs does draw attention to archaeologically accessible variables such as marking practices, standardization, choices of shape, and so on. Equally important, and often ignored, is North's emphasis on path dependency in the study of economic development. Existing social, political, and economic conditions can either prevent or accelerate changes in economic systems.

The concept of path dependency involves what might be considered both social structure or social behavior as well as economics. In its most basic form, path dependency predicts that once started and successful, a given practice will tend to be followed and will tend to shape (often constrain) any further development. In economic terms, the risks of change from a successful path are too great; the costs of learning something entirely new are too high. From the perspective of economic geography, the location of a given business might attract related firms to the same location in order that they, too, might benefit from established routes of supply, shared knowledge, available labor, and so on (Fuchs & Shapira, 2005; Lagerholm & Malmberg, 2009; cf. Martin, 2012). Path dependency, however, need not impinge solely on what seem to be neatly economic practices. Terpstra's study (2013) of Roman commerce highlights the long-established emphasis on written law and the sunk costs of education that would dissuade actors from deviating from the social norms of behavior. Path dependency need not always have positive outcomes. Much of Jared Diamond's controversial analysis in *Collapse* depends on established social norms preventing societies from adapting to changing circumstances (Diamond, 2005; cf. Demenocal et al., 2005).

Cast in this way, path dependency is more than simply noting that the way things were done earlier strongly predicts how they will be done in the future. That in itself only defends a static view of economic practice that erases a need for economic history altogether; obviously, this is not the intended outcome. Instead, a wider socioeconomic view of path dependency encourages the search for social structures that affected and shaped economic systems and practices over time. At the same time, the changing economic systems might in turn reshape the paths themselves. We should be aware of casting past behavior solely in terms of agents maximizing profits within the rationality imposed by these path dependencies (cf. Halkos & Kyriazis, 2010: 261). Indeed, assumptions underlying the application of path dependence theory are very much at the forefront of debate in Economic Geography, where the theory has gained wide traction (e.g., Martin, 2012).

Studies of ancient Greek economies and society have shown relatively little interest in the concept of path dependency. There are some noteworthy exceptions. Halkos and Kyriazis (2010: 261) argue that continued Athenian investment in naval forces locked the Athenian economy onto an outward-looking, economically adventurous trajectory. Sparta in contrast, Ober notes (2015: 194), did not have a tradition of investment in naval power and so did not join the Athenian-led coalition against Persia in the early fifth century. More recently, Fleck and Hanssen (2018) note that those ancient Greek tyrannies that emerged from endogenous processes (i.e., those based on paths existing within the given polis) were more successful than those imposed from outside. A recent dissertation on Archaic maritime trade addresses path dependency in its opening theoretical overview and, in its conclusions, highlights the importance of pre-existing institutions (without explicitly invoking path dependency) (Salay, 2018: 66, 74, 82, 363–364).

Path dependency in these terms is largely descriptive, highlighting possibly unforeseen connections (e.g., Athens' naval build-up in the 480s BCE is connected with its long-term commercial interests stretching through the fourth century BCE). Path dependency, however, can be used more in line with the dialectical approach so accessibly described by Randall McGuire in his keynote address to the conference and in his earlier works (1992). Social structures, practices, organizations, and institutions contain within themselves the contradictions and tensions that encourage or prevent change. Paths in this sense are not simply "pre-existing conditions" but conditions that for some reason actively continue to exist, actively shape other paths, or actively prevent access to other paths. This paper explores certain aspects of the history of transport amphora use in the Greek world from this dialectical perspective on path dependency.

Amphora Shapes in a Social Critique

In turning now to the amphoras themselves, I will focus on the Aegean world of the late sixth through first centuries BCE. While it would be easy to consider this period one simply of professional merchants and markets, the situation is much more complex. This period includes major events in the political and economic history of the "Greek World": the arrival of Persian economic demands, then Athenian; the massive expansion of the Hellenistic world and the scale of its economic activity; the increasing integration of Roman and Greek economies in the later second and first centuries BCE. The economies of the Greek world did not remain static. Within this chronological framework, I will address two topics in particular: (1) amphora shape and (2) amphora stamps. While scholars agree that these two elements were important for the use of amphoras in antiquity, there is much debate as to the precise nature of that importance.

Path Dependency, Economic Geography of Amphora Production, and Amphora Shapes

An often-repeated concept regarding amphoras in the Greek world is that each jar indicated its place of origin through both its shape and, often, a stamp on the handle or neck. In this way, the jar advertised the goods of the region of production much like modern branded packaging. Implicit in this model is the modern idea that advertising and brand strength are natural and inevitable elements in economic competition. There are, however, important nuances that are often neglected in this characterization of Greek amphora production.

First, we should consider how and why shapes are shared among potters before assuming the goal of brand advertisement. Research on ceramic production from both ethnographic and archaeological perspectives has placed increasing emphasis on "communities of practice" and the cultural structure of learning the craft of pottery (e.g., Lave & Wenger, 1991; Wenger, 1998; Wendrich, 2012; Knappett & van der Leeuw, 2014). In such environments of active and communal production, similarities of form and decorative styles move from person to person and generation to generation. Clustering of potting workshops and kiln sites, as well-attested archaeologically, fits both the expectations raised by such active, shared learning processes and, to some extent, certain economic efficiencies. Clustered kiln sites reduce the footprint of risk from such pyrotechnics and reduce the travel costs for distributing clay and fuel. At the same time, some degree of spread over a landscape is needed both to avoid overburdening resources in terms of fuel and clay and to ease access to agricultural producers (wine, oil, and any other goods that might go into the jars). There is also a balance to be struck with the infrastructure for moving the filled amphoras to the ports if they are intended for wider distribution.

A patrilocal marriage system as existed in the Greek world might seem ill-suited to transferring style from place to place (cf. the movement of female potters through marriage as seen in much of the ethnographic literature). And yet, the Greek practice of equal inheritance to all sons, often resulting in the spatial dispersal of their households (even to the point of encouraging emigration), may have contributed to widespread communities of practice. Indeed, migrant potters are attested directly, as in the case of foreign names among Athenian fine ware potters and painters (often thought to be enslaved peoples) (Papadopoulos, 2009: 235), Athenian potters at Ephesos (Trinkl, 2013: 196–197) and a Jewish family of potters in Hellenistic Syron Kome in Egypt (*Berliner Griechische Urkunden* [*Ägyptische Urkunden aus den Kgl. Museen zu Berlin*] VI, 1282).

The potentially wide geographic extent of these communities of practice (here considered as equivalent to shape traditions in amphoras) is easily demonstrated through close typological studies of amphoras. Even as early as the 1950s, researchers recognized that not all jars that looked like those of a well-known producer were from that one site. Thus, Russian scholars distinguished Thasian amphoras from those labelled as "circle of Thasos" (Zeest, 1960). Since then, discoveries of kiln sites and closer studies of amphora fabrics and stamps make clear the long history of a broad regional style across the north Aegean from the Archaic through early Hellenistic periods. The same is true of the southeastern Aegean islands and the adjacent mainland. Smaller-scale regions of shared style may be noted around Lesbos and Aeolis as well as Chios and the adjacent mainland (Lawall, 2011a, 2017).

Considerations of path dependency related to transmission of knowledge, mobility of craftsmen, and sunk costs related to location of workshops all go far to explain the widespread phenomenon of regional styles among Aegean amphora producers. Even the slightest shifts in this model—particularly in terms of limiting the mobility of craftsmen or increasing the benefits that might accrue from proximity to reliable agricultural and shipping infrastructure—could narrow the spread of a regional style into a very localized style, limited perhaps to the territory of only one polis.

The Social Cost of Large-Scale Agriculture and Narrowed Communities of Practice

This explanation of localized style and its coexistence with regional styles of amphoras is of fundamental importance. Narrowly localized styles might appear to us, viewing the ancient world through a modern lens, as a case of brand marketing (e.g., Twede, 2002: 189–193; Rauh et al., 2013: 157–158; cf. Lawall, 2011a: 45). We know that ancient amphoras could be (but not always were) referred to by a geographical title (Rhodian, Thasian, etc., see Kruit & Worp, 2000). And, in some cases, the stamps that appear on the jars make direct reference to the city of origin. But there is a substantive difference between features given to an artifact through the course of its production that are *intended* to serve those roles of economic brands, on the one hand; and the same features arising from the course of production *without any intentions* of facilitating trade in the ways recognized through brand-based marketing, on the other.

Many different variables affect whether we see a wide geographic spread of a given amphora shape or a narrow concentration of that shape: freedom of movements of potters, sunk costs of establishing production sites, necessary scale of amphora production, scale of production of goods to fill the amphoras, proximity to producers of goods to be packaged, proximity to ports for export, available social/economic infrastructure for exports, levels of demand for amphora-borne goods. Many of these variables are intimately related. Those persons with the socioeconomic capital to create large-scale farms or amalgamate the production of smaller farms might well have the "international" contacts to facilitate transfers of substantial quantities of surplus goods in amphoras. As land is converted from small-scale, diversified production for local needs to large scale, homogenous production of "cash crops", other groups within the local population might be forced or encouraged to expand into crafts or other activities that serve these elite landowners. Scattered, small-scale amphora production—sharing shapes over a wide area—would be forced to coalesce into larger workshops serving larger farms. Emigration of potters might be restricted as local demand for their wares increases; increasingly complex mechanisms may be needed to manage new scales of production and distribution of the jars. Quantitative change leads to qualitative change (McGuire, 1992: 97; Ollman, 2014: 371).

We should be wary of expecting or assuming inevitable stability in this seemingly "natural" progression in scale and concomitant increase in complexity (on scalar stress and complexity, see Johnson, 1982). As Paynter observed:

> Inequality became an increasingly prominent aspect of complex society [with complexity emerging as a response to scalar stress], and problems arose from the efforts to maintain

> it. Neoevolutionary theory, however, never deemed these problems a significant source of cultural change. (1989: 374)

The internal social tensions are not hard to imagine. Access to land and its potential to offer autarchic subsistence would be cut off. With arable land and other raw materials increasingly serving production for exportable surplus under elite control, options for the livelihoods of others would change. While some new service occupations might be created, other past practices would no longer be available. Movement over the landscape would be restricted, and, with that restriction, opportunities for new social connections and new sources of wealth would become limited. Tensions need not be limited only to the gap between elites and nonelites. Elite competition for control of surplus products and for networks of trade or exchange could have been a further locus of instability. Such competition might occur within or among multiple communities of elites, and this competition might be manifest in any number of social, political, and economic fora.

Even so, such limitations both on opportunities and on access to resources for some and such competition for the fruits of labor and exchange for others do not appear to have resulted in widespread conflict and social instability. Why not? Can we even be sure that such an impression of socioeconomic stability is correct? The next section of this paper addresses this issue of social stability or instability.

A brief summary of the discussion so far: I have treated amphora shapes, shared over wider or narrower geographic regions, as manifestations of communities of practice. As certain communities shrank in geographical extent, the uniqueness of the shape could be interpreted as an advertisement for the commodities of the resulting narrower region. Such a market-oriented function of amphora shapes may have resulted from the forces creating narrow correlations between shape and place, but it would be a mistake to assume this was the goal without considering the potential social change that led to this point. In the next section, I consider the phenomenon of amphora stamping, not as a means of commodity advertising or even quality assurance, but as a practice emerging at times out of a web of path dependencies that may help explain this apparent social stability. From here it will be possible to seek evidence for tension and conflict underlying what appears to be a complex, but stable, system.

Amphora Stamps, Complexity, and Social (In)Stability

A textbook view of the interaction between ancient Greek social complexity, primarily focused on governance, and social stability may be summarized as follows. With the rise of landed wealth and oligarchic government following the collapse of the Bronze Age palaces, Greece struggled through a period of tension among elites, most notably manifest in the rise and fall of "tyrants", conventionally defined as rulers operating outside the traditional constitutional structures. Whether through the work of such tyrants or through the work of "lawgivers" tensions between rich and poor were alleviated through legal reforms and redistribution of wealth, in some cases through emigration to "colonies". Concepts of *isonomia* (equality before the law) and *demokratia* (rule by the people) emerge as guiding principles in Greek society and governance, admittedly with a strongly Athenocentric perspective. While such principles in no way removed the gap between rich and poor, many different steps were taken to bond the *polis* community together despite such differences (and again most of our evidence comes from Athens). Wealth or even popularity was not an impediment to political office when such positions were assigned simply by lot. Judicial matters were in the hands of massive citizen juries, and such duty was a source of (very modest) income. The wealthy were given many opportunities to contribute visibly to the collective needs of the community. In some cases, foreign elites were given extensive and very public local honors for similar favors to the *polis*. Commentary on social complexity and instability in ancient Greece tends to focus on the interactions among competing elites and the tension between the interests of the family and the interests of the state. Particularly once democracy was established in Athens at the end of the sixth century BCE, interactions between rich and poor, large and small landowners, are rarely considered.

The use of stamps in the developing complexity of amphora production and trade can be viewed against this more general social backdrop in two ways. First, the development of the institutions relevant to amphora stamps can be set easily into the stability-maintaining paths widely recognized in Classical and Hellenistic *poleis*. And yet, second, these same institutions may be viewed as placing the *polis* in a middle role (in the sense of managing the production of workers for the owners of those products, the wealthy landowners) maintaining a social stability for the benefit of the wealthy. Hints of lingering tensions underlying the institutions related to amphora stamping may be seen in both the changes to stamping practices themselves, change within different communities of practice, and even in historical events that are connected with the amphora trade.

Amphora Stamps and Social Stability

Some general background is needed to understand how amphora stamps might fit into the broader structure of Classical and Hellenistic Greek society. The practice of marking amphoras with an image or name impressed in the clay prior to firing dates back to the earliest production of post-Bronze Age Greek shipping containers. Only in the decades around 400 BCE, do we start to see complex stamping systems providing one name, conventionally labelled by modern scholars as the fabricant, another indicating the annual magistrate or priest, and the ethnic identifier (Balabanov et al., 2016; Tzochev, 2016; Garlan, 1999). This pattern of amphora stamping then continued with some variation through the end of the second century BCE.

The purpose of such stamping has dominated amphora-related debate throughout the life of the field. There are four main camps in the discussion: (1) those who see in the stamps a reference to some civic process of taxation (Grace, 1934; Garlan,

2013; Rauh et al., 2013: 150–151; Badoud, 2019), (2) those who see a guarantee of capacity or other quality of the jar (Finkielsztejn, 2006, 2012; Grace, 1949), (3) those who see some sort of reference to private ownership (cf. Garlan, 2013, 2019), and (4) those who argue for the stamps' relationship to a system of managing the commerce in amphoras (Palaczyk, 2016, 2017). Reference to a private system now has few adherents; the role of certification comes in and out of scholarly favor; some role in civic taxation is currently the more dominant of the four.

The debate tends to hinge on the inherent characteristics of the stamps themselves (Garlan, 2000, 2013). Stamps were often as poorly legible in antiquity as they are now; they cannot have played a consistent or detailed role for distant consumers. Despite their permanence, stamps were most meaningful at the time and place they were applied (a buyer at the Pontic site of Olbia, for example, would have no way of complaining to the persons named on a Thasian or Rhodian amphora stamp even if the names were legible). Even at the peak of their use in a given city, stamps were never applied to every jar, so the act of stamping one jar had to matter for other jars left unstamped. Stamps were applied before firing making measurement and certification of the jars problematic. In cities that used these fairly complex stamping systems, the degree of coordination required to design and distribute the annually changing stamps' dies renders especially problematic the idea of the private initiative behind these systems.

A fundamental difficulty is that we do not know the job description of the fabricant. In rare instances, titles identify the fabricant as *keramarch* and *ergasteriarch* (Garlan, 2013; Panagou, 2010). In some, but not all, cases each Thasian workshop assemblage is dominated by only one or two fabricants, such as Skymnos at Chioni, Lysikles at Limenaria, or the likely fatherson pair of Aristagoras and Demalkes at Kalonero. And yet, the Molos workshop, while dominated by Pylades, offers a scatter of other names; and the Keramidi workshop attests at least six fabricants with substantial numbers of stamps (Garlan, 2004–2005). A similar situation may be present, later, near Knidos, where an area roughly 900 by 300 m yielded deposits attesting ten different fabricants (Empereur et al., 1999). Known pairings of Thasian fabricants and eponyms indicate that fabricants could maintain their position for multiple years and even decades; the same is true for Rhodes, Knidos, Sinope and elsewhere (Garlan, 1999; Cankardeş-Şenol, 2015–2017; Grace, 1985; Garlan, 2004). Later Thasian stamps, after around 332 BCE, replaced the actual name of the fabricant with a system of images, one for each fabricant, which then changed from year to year (Tzochev, 2016). From such terminology and patterns of practice, the most common interpretation of fabricant has been workshop owner or maker's name (Debidour, 1998), but fabricants have also been interpreted as owners of estates that used or even owned the nearby workshops, managers of amphora distribution, or those individuals who may have overseen the workshops and paid the required taxes from their profits (Badoud, 2019; Garlan, 1998, 2013).

By way of exploring the role or roles of fabricants, I start from a basic point: Amphora production has many "moving parts". There were many different elements that needed to be coordinated and financed, from procurement of raw materials on a large scale, to potting and drying, to firing and stockpiling in anticipation of the vintage or oil pressing or other agricultural processes (Lawall, 2005; Palaczyk, 2016, 2017). In other instances of multi-part enterprises with substantial costs, at least some Greek poleis turned to their wealthier citizens (and non-citizens in rare cases) to provide the finances: the construction, upkeep, and manning of a trireme (Gabrielsen, 1994; Jordan, 2001), a dramatic production (Wilson, 2000), cultivation of sacred land, or the operation of a mine (Crosby, 1950; Lalonde et al., 1991; Shipton, 2000). In some cases, such liturgical services brought little more than renown and thanks in return. In other cases, the harder the laborers worked and the less was spent on supporting their labor, the greater the profit for the lessee. And whether in the case of sacred land or mines, leases could continue for decades.

Amphora stamps may have been part of some sort of accounting mechanism in this process of coordinating production and initial distribution of the jars. Given the inconsistencies of their application and given at least some ancient Greek penchant for memorializing such elite support for their cities, the stamps may have served no greater purpose than to offer the occasional reminder of who was insuring the smooth operation of the city's shipping container supply. Stamps would also offer a permanent record that a person did fulfill their duty; that degree of accounting as provided by the stamps at the very least can be assumed. We need not expect each jar to be certified as "tax paid" in the sense that modern liquor bottles must display a tax sticker. But enough jars were marked to make clear that the duties of the fabricant—whether tax collection somehow related to the amphoras or broader matters of amphora management—had been fulfilled. Then as now, the stamps offered proxy evidence that a complex system existed.

A further feature of these "fabricants" is that their civic status seems to have varied from place to place and over time. While some fabricant names (e.g., those of the stamps of Chios) correlate closely with names on inscriptions and hence presumably higher status citizens; in other cases, the names of women or foreigners appear as fabricants (García Sánchez, 2008; Badoud, 2019; Badoud & Dana, 2019).

In this sense, fabricant stamping uses the established path of enlisting and then commemorating (presumably wealthy) individuals to manage a new organizational challenge. Earlier stamping practices of the sixth and fifth centuries need not be manifestations of this same path nor can we assume they addressed the same problem. Among earlier stamps, abbreviations for ethnic labels and civic-themed images are fairly common (though not exclusively), but there are also isolated letters without a clear point of reference (Lawall, Forthcoming). Particularly in the case of references to the polis in these earlier stamps, we may be seeing the start of "the state" taking on some sort of managerial role (Garlan, 2013); even enigmatic letter stamps or other markings may indicate the same thing, but any certainty in this regard is elusive. In turning next to examining potential social tensions inherent to the socioeconomic systems attested by the amphora stamps, it is sufficient to take the ca. 400 BCE emergence of fabricant stamping as our starting point.

Amphora Stamps and Instability

Up to this point, I have characterized the need for management of the amphora production and distribution system as a matter of an organizational challenge needing a response. The civic response of arranging for or recognizing some commemorated role for fabricants may appear as simply a benign, even benevolent resolution to an otherwise crisis-laden situation of "scalar stress". The state, looked at in this way, is providing an organizational layer to alleviate conflicts and confusion that might arise simply from the increased scale of production and export of amphora-borne goods. The roots of such conflicts, however, might not be limited to the numbers of jars to be filled, the number of potters having to share one kiln site, or the number of ships needed to export the season's production.

Potential loci of conflict become clearer when one considers the admittedly vague term fabricant in the framework of the dialectic. A person cannot be a fabricant without that role (whatever it may be in specific terms) being assigned by or at least recognized by the city to serve, somehow, in the administration of amphora use benefitting the elite landowners. At the same time, the existence of the fabricant presupposes those being managed in some way by that position—to some extent the potters creating the amphoras and agricultural workers producing the goods to fill them. In this sense, the civic apparatus personified by the fabricant exists as something of a Marxist "middle class" (McGuire, 1993: 103). If the "normal" material trace of this three-way definition is the amphora stamp with the name of the fabricant, the eponym, and the ethnic (name or image), then changes or deviations from this normal approach might hint at social tensions that are worth further exploration.

Changes to such systems are relatively common but tend to be viewed as matters for classification rather than social history. Thus, over the third quarter of the fourth century BCE, Thasian amphora stamps downplayed the importance of the fabricant by replacing the names with annually changing symbols. The change did not occur at one specific point, and recent work has highlighted the problems of thinking about Thasian amphora stamps as "old style" (with fabricant names) and "new style" (fabricant symbols) (Tzochev, 2016). And yet, selection and coordination of this new system are recognized as putting a greater burden on the polis itself. For whatever reason, this added effort was deemed more appealing than naming fabricants. The ethnic remained. *Kudos* to the city; the fabricant disappeared into anonymity.

The Pontic city of Chersonesos, initially provided the fabricant's name as only a small monogram or name in small letters, but eventually that is dropped and the magistrate's (*astynomos*) name stands alone (Kac, 1994). The name of the city never appeared. Another Pontic center, Sinope, gave prominent place to both the *astynomos* and the fabricant name, even providing patronymics in some cases to clarify identity with greater precision. Here, too, the ethnic is never spelled out but is sometimes indicated by an image echoing Sinopean coin types (Garlan, 2004).

For much of the Hellenistic period, especially the later third and second centuries BCE, Rhodes and Knidos provided the names of fabricants, magistrates/priests, and some indication of ethnic identity on their amphora stamps with great consistency. By the mid first century BCE, however, both cities shifted to a very rudimentary stamping system of an image (sometimes of ethnic significance, but in the case Knidos just a palm branch) or monogram (for Rhodes, Finkielsztejn, 2000; for Knidos, Jefremow, 1995).

Such changes in stamping behavior could be viewed as simple administrative changes that were not indicative of deeper social difficulty. On the other hand, if a city such as Thasos considered it necessary to commemorate fabricants in their roles for the first two generations of amphora stamping, then a deliberate removal of those names—particularly to replace the names with a system requiring even more oversight—is difficult to see as simply neutral. At the same time, we need not assume (as scholars have argued in the past) that such a change could only come about through the arrival of some external political force (Macedon in the case of Thasos, see Grace, 1949: 182). Unfortunately, it is difficult to propose specific explanations underlying the changes apparent in the stamping systems. The value in thinking about fabricant stamps as part of a three-way relationship (elite landowners—fabricant—workers) is that changes in "the material culture" of fabricant now become warning signs encouraging us to explore both the civic or political history surrounding the period of change and the evidence for labor and production at the same time. The context of civic history is often more readily available than that of labor history, but increased attention to the archaeology of rural industry (especially amphora production, oil and wine production) and farm sites should prove useful once we know when and where to be seeking data.

Conclusion

This paper has attempted to meld together two different, yet not entirely distinct, models for interpreting economic change. Path dependency in its simplest form predicts that pre-existing practices will impede or otherwise shape any future change. Much of the work in this area treats economic systems as built on standard assumptions of efficiency and maximization, and as systems working (or not working) as harmonious, homogenous entities. A key element of Marxist theory is the importance of context; here, too, pre-existing elements in a system shape its future. The models differ in their assumptions about the harmony and homogeneity of society, but the process of bringing them together has highlighted important features and potential research questions.

I began by characterizing amphora production in terms of communities of practice. This view of craft production should, inherently, encourage the reproduction of traditions and pursuit of established paths. By considering opposing forces such as free movement versus geographically restricted labor, or self-sufficiency versus surplus production, observable changes in the geography of amphora production become more complex, perhaps more sinister in a way, than simply a deviation from pre-existing practice. Changing scale of production and export of amphora-borne goods seems to be significantly correlated with such changes in the geography of amphora shapes. In this sense, a deviation from a path draws attention to tensions rather than harmonies within society. Ancient Greek society is often portrayed as striving toward equality under the law (for citizens) and an ideology of cohesion and unity. While the existence of wealth in the hands of the elite was never denied, it was harnessed for the public good. On the one hand, the emergence of amphora stamping systems naming "fabricants" might be interpreted, benignly, as evidence for a polis following the established path of harnessing elite resources for the management of a complex industry. Alternatively, the appearance, modification, and even disappearance of "fabricant stamping" may be related to tensions among a triad of groups: the workers producing and filling the amphoras; the civic government potentially benefitting from the operation of the amphora trade; and the elite profiting from participation in the amphora trade.

Much of the scholarship related to amphora shapes and stamps has been descriptive in nature, or at best attempting to assign the purpose of amphora stamping to a particular function in ancient Greek society. The other papers in this volume establish a context that should challenge archaeologists of Classical and Hellenistic Greek economies to seek ways of illuminating ancient internal relations beyond the polis ideology of harmony and equality that ancient and many modern sources offer us.

References

Badoud, N. (2015). *Le temps de Rhodes. Une chronologie des inscriptions de la cité fondée sur l'étude de ses inscriptions*. Vestigia 63. C.H. Beck.

Badoud, N. (2019). Ce qu'étaient les timbres amphoriques grecs: Genre et statut dans l'industrie céramique rhodienne. In A. Marangou & N. Badoud (Eds.), *Analyse et exploitation des timbres amphoriques grecs* (pp. 195–209). Presses Universitaires de Rennes.

Badoud, N., & Dana, D. (2019). L'onomastique des fabricants d'amphores rhodiennes. In A. Marangou & N. Badoud (Eds.), *Analyse et exploitation des timbres amphoriques grecs* (pp. 173–193). Presses Universitaires de Rennes.

Badoud, N., Dupont, P., Garlan, Y., & Marangou-Lerat, A. (2012). Bulletin Archéologique: Amphores et timbres amphoriques (2007–2012). *Revue des Études Grecques, 125,* 159–271.

Balabanov, P., Garlan, Y., & Avram, A. (2016). *Les timbres amphoriques grecs d'Heraclée Pontique et de quelques autres centres de production recueillis dans l'établissement de Kostadin Tchechma près de Debelt (Bulgarie) (première moitié du IVe siècle av. J.-C.).* Pontica 48–49, Supplement 4. Muzeul de Istorie Naţională şi Arheologie Constanţa.

Bonifay, M. (2007). Que transportaient donc les amphores africaines? In E. Papi (Ed.), *Supplying Rome and the empire: The proceedings of an international seminar held at Siena-Certosa di Pontignano on May 2–4 2004, on Rome, the provinces, production, and distribution* (pp. 8–31). Journal of Roman Archaeology Supplement 69. Portsmouth, Rhode Island.

Bravo, B. (1977). Remarques sur les assises sociales, les formes d'organisation et la terminologie du commerce maritime grec a l'époque archaïque. *Dialogues d'Histoire Ancienne, 3,* 1–59.

Cankardeş-Şenol, G. (2015–2017). *Lexicon of eponym dies on Rhodian amphora stamps, vols. 1–4.* Études Alexandrines 39. Centre d'Études Alexandrines.

Carlson, D. N. (2003). The classical Greek shipwreck at Tektaş Burnu Turkey. *American Journal of Archaeology, 107,* 581–600.

Crosby, M. (1950). The leases of the Laureion mines. *Hesperia, 19,* 189–297.

Debidour, M. (1998). La tutelle de la cite sur la production des amphores à Thasos à la lumière d'un exemple: le 'groupe au rhyton.' *Topoi, 8,* 591–606.

Demenocal, P. B., Cook, E., Demeritt, D., Hornborg, A., Kirch, P., McElreath, R., & Tainter, J. (2005). Perspectives on Diamond's *Collapse: How societies choose to fail or succeed. Current Anthropology, 46*(supplement), S91–S99.

Diamond, J. (2005). *Collapse: How societies choose to fail or succeed.* Viking.

Empereur, J.-Y. (1982). Les anses d'amphores timbrées et les amphores: Aspects quantitatifs. *Bulletin de Correspondence Hellénique, 106,* 219–233.

Empereur, J.-Y., Hesse, A., & Tuna, N. (1999). Les ateliers d'amphores de Datça, Péninsule de Cnide. In Y. Garlan (Ed.), *Production et commerce des amphores anciennes en Mer Noire. Colloque international organisé à Istanbul, 25–28 mai 1994* (pp. 105–115). Publications de l'Université de Provence.

Finkielsztejn, G. (2000). Chronologie et diffusion des dernières amphores timbrées rhodiennes: étude préliminaire. *Rei cretariae romanae fautorum acta, 36,* 407–415.

Finkielsztejn, G. (2006). Production et commerce des amphores hellénistiques: recipients, timbrage et métrologie. In R. Descat (Ed.), *Approches de l'économie hellénistique,* Entretiens d'archéologie et d'histoire 7 (pp. 17–34). Musée archéologique de Saint-Bertrand-de-Comminges and De Boccard.

Finkielsztejn, G. (2011). Black Sea amphora stamps found in the southern Levant: Most probably not a trade. In C. Tzochev, T. Stoyanov, & A. Bozkova (Eds.), *PATABS II. Production and trade of amphorae in the Black Sea: Acts of the international round table held at Kiten, Nessebar and Sredetz, September 26–30, 2007* (pp. 55–61). Bulgarian Academy of Sciences, National Archaeological Institute with Museum and St. Kliment Ohridski University of Sofia.

Finkielsztejn, G. (2012). Réflexions additionnelles sur le marquage des instruments et récipients à l'époque hellénistique. In K. Konuk (Ed.), *Stephanèphoros. De l'économie antique à l'Asie Mineure. Hommages à Raymond Descat* (pp. 77–84). Ausonius Éditions.

Fleck, R. K., & Hanssen, F. A. (2018). Path dependence and transitions from tyranny to democracy: Evidence from ancient Greece. *Constitutional Political Economy, 29,* 371–388. https://doi.org/10.1007/s10602-018-9268-z.

Foley, B. P., Hansson, M. C., Kourkoumelis, D. P., & Theodoulou, T. A. (2012). Aspects of ancient Greek trade re-evaluated with amphora DNA evidence. *Journal of Archaeological Science, 39,* 389–398. https://doi.org/10.1016/j.jas.2011.09.025.

Fuchs, G., & Shapira, P. (Eds.). (2005). *Rethinking regional innovation and change: Path dependency or regional breakthrough,* Economics of Science, Technology and Innovation 30. Springer.

Gabrielsen, V. (1994). *Financing the Athenian fleet: Public taxation and social relations.* Johns Hopkins University Press.

García Sánchez, M. (2008). Les femmes et les amphores: épigraphie amphorique rhodienne et histoire de la femme dans le monde hellénistique. *Bulletin de Correspondance Hellénique, 132,* 285–310.

Garlan, Y. (1998). Les fabricants d'amphores. *Topoi, 8,* 581–590.

Garlan, Y. (1999). *Les timbres amphoriques de Thasos. 1 Timbres protothasiens et thasiens anciens,* Études thasiennes 18. École française d'Athènes and De Boccard.

Garlan, Y. (2000). *Amphores et timbres amphoriques grecs. Entre erudition et idéologie.* De Boccard.

Garlan, Y. (2004). *Les timbres céramiques sinopéens sur amphores et sur tuiles trouvés à Sinope. Présentation et catalogue,* Varia Anatolica 16. Institut français d'études anatoliennes G. Dumezil and De Boccard.

Garlan, Y. (2004–2005). En visitant et revisitant les ateliers amphoriques de Thasos. *Bulletin de Correspondance Hellénique, 128–129,* 269–329.

Garlan, Y. (2013). Les timbres amphoriques en Grèce ancienne. Nouvelles questions. Nouvelles méthodes Nouveaux résultats. *Journal des Savants, 2013,* 203–270.

Garlan, Y. (2019). Le timbrage amphorique grec a-t-il été une initiative privée? L'exemple 'héracléote.' In A. Marangou & N. Badoud (Eds.), *Analyse et exploitation des timbres amphoriques grecs* (pp. 123–128). Presses Universitaires de Rennes.

Grace, V. R. (1934). Stamped amphora handles found in 1931–1932. *Hesperia, 3,* 197–310.

Grace, V. R. (1949). Standard pottery containers of the Greek world. In *Commemorative studies in honor of Theodore Leslie Shear, Hesperia,* Supplement 8 (pp. 175–189). American School of Classical Studies at Athens.

Grace, V. R. (1985). The Middle Stoa dated by amphora stamps. *Hesperia, 54,* 1–54.

Halkos, G. E., & Kyriazis, N. C. (2010). The Athenian economy in the age of Demosthenes: Path dependence and change. *European Journal of Law and Economics, 29,* 255–277. https://doi.org/10.1007/s10657-009-9120-z.

Jefremow, N. (1995). *Die Amphorenstempel des hellenistischen Knidos,* Quellen und Forschungen zur antiken Welt 19. Tuduv.

Johnson, G. (1982). Organizational structure and scalar stress. In C. Renfrew, M. J. Rowlands, & B. A. Segraves (Eds.), *Theory and explanation in archaeology: The Southampton conference* (pp. 389–421). Academic Press.

Jordan, B. (2001). Metic Trierarchs. *The Ancient History Bulletin, 15,* 131–134.

Kac, V. I. (1994). *Keramičeskie klejma Chersonesa Tavričeskogo. Katalog-opredelitel.* Izd. Saratovskogo universiteta.

Knappett, C., & van der Leeuw, S. (2014). A developmental approach to ancient innovation: The potter's wheel in the Bronze Age east Mediterranean. *Pragmatics & Cognition, 22,* 64–92. https://doi.org/10.1075/pc.22.1.04kna.

Koehler, C. G. (1996). Wine amphoras in ancient Greek trade. In P. E. McGovern, S. J. Fleming, & S. H. Katz (Eds.), *The origins and ancient history of wine* (pp. 323–337). Routledge.

Kruit, N., & Worp, K. A. (2000). Geographical jar names: Towards a multi-disciplinary approach. *Archiv für Papyrusforschung und verwandte Gebiete, 46,* 65–146.

Lagerholm, M., & Malmberg, A. (2009). Path dependence in economic geography. In L. Magnusson & J. Ottosson (Eds.), *The evolution of path dependence, new horizons in institutional and evolutionary economics* (pp. 87–107). Edward Elgar.

Lalonde, G. V., Langdon, M. K., & Walbank, M. B. (1991). *Inscriptions: Horoi, poletai records, leases of public land,* The Athenian Agora 19. American School of Classical Studies at Athens.

Lave, J., & Wenger, E. (1991). *Situated learning: Legitimate peripheral participation.* Cambridge University Press.

Lawall, M. L. (2005). Amphoras and Hellenistic economies: Addressing the (over) emphasis on stamped amphora handles. In Z. H. Archibald, J. K. Davies, & V. Gabrielsen (Eds.), *Making, moving, and managing: The new world of ancient economies, 323–31 BC* (pp. 188–232). Oxbow.

Lawall, M. L. (2011a). Imitative amphoras in the Greek world. *Marburger Beiträge zur Antiken Handels-, Wirtschafts- und Sozialgeschichte, 28,* 45–88.

Lawall, M. L. (2011b). Socio-economic conditions and the contents of amphorae. In C. Tzochev, T. Stoyanov, & A. Bozkova (Eds.), *PATABS II. Production and trade of amphorae in the Black Sea. Acts of the international round table held at Kiten, Nessebar and Sredetz, September 26–30, 2007* (pp. 23–33). Bulgarian Academy of Sciences, National Archaeological Institute with Museum and St. Kliment Ohridski University of Sofia.

Lawall, M. L. (2017). Regional styles of transport amphora production in the Archaic Aegean. In S. Handberg & A. Gadolou (Eds.), *Material Koinai in the Greek Iron Age and Archaic Period. Acts of an International Conference at the Danish Institute at Athens, 30 January – 1 February 2015.* Monographs of the Danish Institute at Athens 22 (pp. 289–311). Aarhus University Press and the Danish Institute at Athens.

Lawall, M. L. (Forthcoming). Markings on Greek transport amphoras, 8th through 1st centuries BC. In W. Broekaert, A. Delattre, E. Dupraz, & M. J. Estarán Tolosa (Eds.), *Epigraphy on ceramics.* Droz editions.

Martin, R. (2012). (Re)placing path dependence: A response to the debate. *International Journal of Urban and Regional Research, 36,* 179–192. https://doi.org/10.1111/j.1468-2427.2011.01091.x.

McGuire, R. H. (1992). *A marxist archaeology*. Academic Press.
McGuire, R. H. (1993). Archaeology and marxism. *Archaeological Method and Theory, 5,* 101–157.
Mele, A. (1979). *Il commercio greco arcaico: Prexis ed emporie*. Institut français de Naples.
North, D. C. (1990). *Institutions, institutional change, and economic performances*. Cambridge University Press.
Ober, J. (2015). *The rise and fall of classical Greece*. Princeton University Press.
Ollman, B. (2014). Historical archaeology, dialectical marxism, and 'C.F.U.G studies.' *International Journal of Historical Archaeology, 18,* 361–373. https://doi.org/10.1007/s10761-014-0262-5.
Osborne, R. (2007). Archaic Greece. In W. Scheidel, I. Morris, & R. Saller (Eds.), *The Cambridge economic history of the Greco-Roman world* (pp. 277–301). Cambridge University Press.
Palaczyk, M. (2016). Major innovations in the Rhodian Wine-Trade after 200 BC?—Rhodian Stamps from Monte Iato in West Sicilian context. In S. Japp & P. Kögler (Eds.), *Traditions and innovations: Tracking the development of pottery from the late classical to the early imperial periods*. Proceedings of the 1st Conference of IARPotHP, Berlin, 7–10 November 2013 (pp. 123–134). Phoibos.
Palaczyk, M. (2017). Gibt es Verbreitungsmuster der rhodischen 'Fabrikantenstempel'? In L. Cappuccini, C. Leypold, & M. Mohr (Eds.), *Fragmenta Mediterranea. Contatti, tradizioni e innovazioni in Grecia, Magna Grecia, Etruria e Roma*. Studi in onore de Christoph Reusser (pp. 231–240). All'Insegna del Giglio s.a.s.
Panagou, T. M. (2010). *Η σφράγιση των αρχαίων ελληνικών εμπορικών αμφορέων. Κέντρα παραγωγής και συνθετική αξιολόγηση*. Ph.D. thesis, University of Athens.
Panagou, T. M. (2016). Transport amphoras and their contents. In M. Yiannopoulou & C. Kallini (Eds.), *ἠχάδιν II. Τιμητικός τόμος για τη Στέλλα Δρούγου* (pp. 312–334). Ekdose tou tameiou archaiologikon poron kai apallotrioseon.
Papadopoulos, J. K. (2009). The relocation of potters and the dissemination of style: Athens, Corinth, Ambrakia and the Agrinion Group. In J. H. Oakley & O. Palagia (Eds.), *Athenian Potters and Painters II* (pp. 232–240). Oxbow Books.
Paynter, R. (1989). The archaeology of equality and inequality. *Annual Review of Anthropology, 18,* 369–399.
Rauh, N. K., Autret, C., & Lund, J. (2013). Amphora design and marketing in antiquity. In M. Frass (Ed.), *Kauf, Konsum und Märkte. Wirtschaftswelten im Fokus – Von der römischen Antike bis zur Gegenwart*, Philippika 59 (pp. 145–181). Harrassowitz Verlag.
Salay, P. W. (2018). *The more things change: Economic institutions and maritime trade in the Archaic Western Mediterranean*, Ph.D. thesis, University of Southern California, Los Angeles.
Shipton, K. (2000). *Leasing and lending: The cash economy in fourth-century Athens*, Bulletin of the Institute of Classical Studies, Supplement 74. Institute of Classical Studies.
Terpstra, T. T. (2013). *Trade communities in the Roman world: A micro-economic and institutional perspective*, Columbia Studies in the Classical Tradition 37. Brill.
Trinkl, E. (2013). Classical black-glazed imports to western Asia Minor. In A. Tsingarida & D. Viviers (Eds.), *Pottery markets in the Ancient Greek World (8th – 1st centuries B.C.). Proceedings of the international symposium held at the Université libre de Bruxelles 19–21 June 2008* (pp. 189–202). CReA-Patrimoine.
Twede, D. (2002). The packaging technology and science of ancient transport amphoras. *Packaging Technology and Science, 15,* 181–195. https://doi.org/10.1002/pts.597.
Tzochev, C. (2016). *The amphora stamps from Thasos*, The Athenian Agora 37. The American School of Classical Studies at Athens.
van Wees, H. (2009). The economy. In K. A. Raaflaub & H. van Wees (Eds.), *A companion to Archaic Greece* (pp. 444–467). Blackwells Publishing.
Wendrich, W. (Ed.). (2012). *Archaeology and apprenticeship: Body knowledge, identity, and communities of practice*. The University of Arizona Press.
Wenger, E. (1998). *Communities of practice: Learning, meaning and identity*. Cambridge University Press.

Wilson, P. (2000). *The Athenian institution of the Khoregia: The chorus, the city, and the stage.* Cambridge University Press.
Zeest, I. (1960). *Keramičeskaja tara Bospora*, Materialy i issledovanija po archeologii SSSR 83. Izd. Akademii Nauk SSSR.

Chapter 12
Modelling Trade in Athenian Pottery in the Archaic and Classical Period

Robin Osborne

Abstract This paper explores the nature of the distribution of Greek painted pottery and argues on the basis of the distinctive features of this distribution that various possible types of trade and exchange can be ruled out. In particular, it establishes the importance of the middleman's knowledge of the market to the distribution pattern, but argues that if we are to understand change over time then we have to allow that the painters of the pots were in the end responsible for the nature and range of imagery available for sale.

"Human agency is socio-historically restricted, which means that individuals can become active social performers, yet under the restriction of certain conditions". So Stefanos Gimatzidis and Reinhard Jung in their initial description of what they were hoping to do in this conference, before setting out the aim of the conference as "not to test the theoretical models under scrutiny, but rather to present evidence against the rationalization of past economic behavior according to the rules of modern markets".

This is not a paper that presents significant new evidence; I am interested in what the evidence that we have already to hand enables us to say, and in establishing the conditions which any claims about past economic behaviour need to satisfy. The pattern which Gimatzidis and Jung noted, whereby "In the first half of the twentieth century, cultural historical approaches projected modern economic models into the past through a rather formalist perspective; processual archaeology attempted to quantify these relations; finally, post-processual critique emphasized the role of the individual in shaping ancient economic patterns", certainly applies to the study of trade in Greek pottery. Robert Cook's classic 1959 paper established the small scale of the Athenian pot "industry", and David Gill (1991) was still primarily concerned to deny that pottery was an important item of trade in its own right. Work since the 1990s has been particularly concerned with establishing individual patterns and emphasising the different ways in which different potters manipulated the market

---

R. Osborne (✉)
King's College, Cambridge, United Kingdom
e-mail: ro225@cam.ac.uk

S. Gimatzidis and R. Jung (eds.), *The Critique of Archaeological Economy*, Frontiers in Economic History,
https://doi.org/10.1007/978-3-030-72539-6_12

(most obviously through adapting the shape of products to conform to models with which the market was already familiar, in the case of the Nikosthenes workshop (Tosto, 1999), or the ways in which particular iconographies were sought out by particular places (again primarily with regard to the question of Etruscan taste for particular themes)). These recent studies have left us with a lot of evidence, but what, in economic terms, does that evidence amount to?

This paper is primarily concerned with patterns in the spatial and chronological distribution of (largely Athenian) pottery across the Mediterranean and the Black Sea. But it is important first of all to establish something of the total quantity. The recent work of Philip Sapirstein is important here. Sapirstein has argued that Beazley's attributions produce an implausibly large number of painters to whom few pots can be attributed. He suggests that in the first half of the fifth century, when Attic vase painting was at its height, there were just over 40 potter-painters and around 30 specialist painters, and that between them they produced around 50,000 pots a year (of which between 0.5 and 1.00% have survived [Sapirstein, 2013, 2014]). Sapirstein's estimates more or less halve Robert Cook's calculations as to numbers of painters, and keep the scale of the industry in Athens small. But what I want to emphasise is less the number of potters, painters and workshops than the number of pots in question. Athenian fine pottery was produced and consumed in large quantities, and the chances that the patterns we can see emerging are the products of differential survival are extremely slim. For all that we have lost a great deal of invaluable information in losing the findspots of so many pots, our data remain robust.

Pottery is vital for our understanding of the economy for three reasons: it survives better than anything else—it is not perishable; it cannot be repurposed easily (as metals can be by melting down); and it is produced in sufficiently varied forms and with sufficiently varied decoration that those engaged in transporting it and/or those buying it face repeated choices. Some, but not all, of those choices relate to function, and some, but not all, of the functional choices relate to culturally chosen rather than practically imposed affordances. Any economic modelling needs to answer the question, who made what choices and for what reasons? If some sectors of the economy were driven by need alone, this sector of the economy was not.

What are the patterns of pottery distribution that any economic model needs to take into account? (cf. Langridge-Noti, 2013).

Uncontroversial are the claims that not every shape of pot nor every potter/painter is represented at every place to which Athenian pots get sent. So we can not only show that some potters/painters were more popular in some places than others, but that different shapes, even among the works of a single potter/painter, are found in different places. Somehow or other the market discriminates, and arguably from at least 600 onwards for Athenian pottery, between potters/painters and between shapes (so already Osborne, 1996).

More controversial, but I think widely accepted, in at least general terms, what ends up where is not independent of quality: the market discriminates according to quality (cf. Moore, 1997). The lowest quality Athenian pots do not end up in Etruria—the distribution of works by the Pithos painter, whose low-quality works primarily go east, is telling here: Beazley records pieces from Athens (11), Gela (6),

Adria (3), "Italy" (1), Olynthos (1), Vrastina Kalyvia near Thessaloniki (2), Rhitsona (1), Corinth (1), Perachora (1), Rheneia (1), Chios (1), Kameiros (4), "Rhodes" (1), Marion (1), Tell-en Nasbeh (1), Al Mina (10), Tel Jemmeh (1), Tell Abu Hawam (1) (Beazley, 1963: 139–142).

Most controversial is the question of whether the market discriminates according to the scenes painted on pots. Some scholars maintain that some myths and some non-mythological scenes were particularly desired in some places, and that there were regional or more local preferences for particular scenes that significantly affected supply and demand. There are three reasons why this issue has proved controversial and hard to resolve. First, that whereas shape is relatively easily established, and even painters' hands can be clear from relatively small fragments, iconography is harder to establish from fragments. Second, although shapes come in a wide range, that range is nothing to the variety of iconographies; many scenes occur just a handful of times, and given the high proportion of pots that survive without provenance, it is very common for the sample of surviving examples of a particular scene which have a secure provenance to be too small to draw conclusions from. Third, although the relationship is not direct, shape and iconography are not independent variables—some scenes occur only on particular shapes of pot. Add to all these the practical problem that no complete collection of material ordered by iconography is available (Beazley's lists, and hence the Beazley archive, are list of pots that Beazley considered that he could attribute to the hands of particular painters or workshops).

That it was possible for someone to order specific pots, that is pots of a specific shape and/or specific iconography is not to be doubted (cf. Webster, 1972: 42–62). One clear case is provided by the series of uniquely shaped white-ground cups with unique iconography attributed to Sotades and the Sotades painter found in an Athenian grave. The iconography of these scenes is linked to death and rebirth and it, along with the delicate and shape of the cups, points strongly to the pots having been made and decorated for inclusion in this burial—perhaps even ordered in advance by the deceased (Burn, 1985; Hoffmann, 1997). A different sort of case, and one that is very hard fully to understand, is represented by the Pronomos Painter's name vase, a volute crater found in Ruvo, decorated with a unique scene of a satyr chorus "off stage", in which the actors are given "real" names and featuring the known auletes Pronomos of Thebes (Taplin & Wiles, 2010). How this pot came to end up in Ruvo is a mystery, but that it was made to order cannot be doubted. Whatever in the end, and I shall return to the issue, we think about the case of the Etruscans (cf. Osborne, 2001), the model we have of trade in Athenian pottery has to allow for the possibility of specific orders.

In general, indeed, the most important conclusion that must be drawn from the data is the most basic one: no model of exchange in archaic and classical Greece that would produce random distribution of the works of painters and random distribution of pottery shapes can be supported. So we can dismiss a situation where both the middlemen of the exchange, the distributors, acquired pottery indiscriminately and also the end-point of the exchange, the consumers of pottery, acquired pottery indiscriminately. Discrimination is certainly being exercised, whether by the distributors or by the consumers or both, and that discrimination extends certainly to shape and quality, and plausibly both to decoration and to painter.

We can go at least a step further than this: any model where there are discriminating consumers but not discriminating distributors is implausible. Are we to think that distributors travelled with a random sample every time, that the consumers always picked out the same items, and that the distributor every time went back with the same items unsold, yet picked up more similar items on the next occasion? Short of our finding that there were some accept-all consumers at the end of some putative trading routes, who always took whatever the distributor had left, we have to believe that distributors did not repeatedly take random selections of pots. How fast and how accurately they predicted the preferences of the consumers they served we cannot tell, but the existence of the patterns we have guarantees that there was indeed a process of matching going on, and that this was done at least in part by the distributors.

But on what criteria was discrimination happening? Some of the discrimination is relatively crude. Because shape and function are closely related, distributors who had some idea of what use pots were being put to would have some idea of what shapes of pot might be in demand. So in the archaic period, one way of reading the material from Tocra in Libya, where the sanctuary of Demeter turned out to have a very high proportion of plates, is that merchants who knew that pots were required as dedications made sure that they had plates handy. So too the funerary custom at Spina of including in the grave a krater and drinking vessels to form a symposium set (Langridge-Noti, 2013) will have encouraged distributors to ensure that they had such symposium sets for sale.

Discrimination at this level might be consistent with a range of models. Although it continues to be popular to imagine an early Iron Age world in which the spread of knowledge about the world is very limited, there are strong reasons—above all the spread of the alphabet, but also the differential use of orientalising motifs—for thinking that communication was already lively by the eighth century BCE. I have argued elsewhere that the marked regional and local patterns of the eighth century are a product of knowledge, and of conscious local discrimination, not a product of ignorance (Osborne, 2018b). The more familiar we think that individuals across the Greek world were with what else was happening in the central Mediterranean, the less we have to invoke highly specialist distributors.

Precisely what sort of knowledge was required in order to meet the different demands of different markets for pottery? At least issues such as whether one is dealing with a Greek community whose religious practices are closely comparable to one's own are likely to have been unproblematic to establish. Indeed, if we take Herodotos as our example of the sorts of things that those who move around the Greek world notice, the particular gods who are primarily worshipped would be likely to be known—whether this was a community where Demeter was a major deity or one where Apollo was, for instance. Herodotos' curiosity about burial customs operates only on the most general level, but few who had spent time in a community can have been unaware of funerary practices, and the basic determinants of what and how much pottery might be consumed in burials were easily observed—whether they cremated, or inhumed; whether they used sarcophagi or cist graves; whether there was a funerary banquet.

It is indeed to be noted that "windfall" profits for merchants are spoken of only in relation to being blown outside the Pillars of Herakles (Herodotus 4.152 of Kolaios making a massive profit from ending up at Tartessos). Equally, novelties might be widely distributed initially and then catch on only in some places, or in none. Shefton suggested that black and coral-red cups were intended specifically to recall the gold or silver gilt work of luxury vessels, and it is unsurprising, if this is the case, that such fake-luxury ceramics proved widely attractive, from Cyprus to Ampurias, even if they did not then catch on in a big way (see Padgett, 2009: 227).

If we reckon that there was enough movement of individuals around the central Mediterranean to ensure that those living there were widely knowledgeable about that world, and if we are dealing with discrimination merely at the level of what sorts of pottery gets deposited in graves or dedicated in temples or used in households, then we need presuppose relatively little specialisation on the part of distributors. Those planning a cargo for a specific region would be able to find enough general knowledge of that region and particular knowledge about the different settlements in that region to judge the pots to ship that would have best chances of selling. The prejudice of excavations towards those sites likely to be most discriminating—sanctuaries and cemeteries—makes it likely that we over-estimate the degree of discrimination to some extent. Were we to have sufficient domestic excavations we might find the domestic assemblages showing a distinctly wider and more variable range, as homes absorbed pots not suitable for sanctuary or grave. But at the same time, it was the practices of dedication and deposition in graves that were the largest pottery consumers, taking pottery immediately out of circulation, the most public, and the most governed by custom; hence targeting pot use in these contexts was arguably easier than targeting the markets for domestic pottery.

Crucial to the question of whether merchants demanded specialist knowledge of the places with which they traded is the issue of exactly how fine the discrimination between markets was. Here Michael Shanks' work on Corinthian pots is particularly striking. He found (1999: Fig. 4.5) that while around 30% of friezes on earlier Corinthian pots (from the 7th century) in mainland and Aegean cemeteries contained people, none of the friezes in "colonial and Italian" cemeteries did so, and only about 10% of friezes on vessels from sanctuaries did so. By contrast, there were no birds on friezes from mainland and Aegean cemeteries, but around 15% of friezes from sanctuaries and from "colonial and Italian" cemeteries show birds (Shanks, 1999: Fig. 4.6). Comparably, among later Corinthian friezes from mainland, and from "colonial and Italian" cemeteries a negligible number are made up of ornament, but some 20% of friezes from sanctuaries are made up of ornament. It seems unlikely that even those who noticed what sort of pot was deposited or dedicated would have consciously registered what the pot showed, and knowledge of local and use-specific taste of this sort can hardly have been common. In this case, some very specific information seems to be moving down the line, and must be moving between people who have a direct interest in the production, exchange and consumption of pottery.

The same conclusion emerges from the fine distinctions between different Etruscan markets apparent in, for instance, their consumption of products of the Nikosthenic workshop. Cerveteri is the findspot of all Nikosthenic black-figure amphoras of known provenance found in Italy (one was found on the Athenian acropolis) but otherwise, the only Nikosthenic pot found at Cerveteri is a red-figure pyxis. From Vulci, on the other hand, come 12 Nikosthenic cups, three olpai and two phialai. Only three other Nikosthenic pots of known provenance come from Etruria (two from Tarquinia and one from Orvieto). All Nikosthenic skyphoi of known provenance come from the Athenian acropolis (Tosto, 1999: 201 and Appendices B and C; cf. Reusser, 2002). The absence of amphoras from Vulci and of cups from Cerveteri is so striking that it cannot be a matter of chance. It is made more striking by the fact that cups from other Attic workshops appear in Cerveteri in cemetery, sanctuary and domestic contexs, and amphoras of other workshops in Vulci at least in cemetery contexts (Reusser, 2002). This looks to be a case where the discovery by a particular trader that a particular market is differentially keen on a particular shape of pot leads to their taking only pots of that shape to that market.

In the case of discrimination by shape, it is not hard to imagine that any regular exchange links between an Etruscan city and Athens could lead to widespread knowledge that some places were simply not interested in pots of a particular shape. But it is harder to imagine it to have been general knowledge that Vulci liked amphoras but not Nikosthenic amphoras, or that Cervetri liked cups but not Nikosthenic cups. It is harder still to imagine that Italian sanctuaries articulated their interest in vessels decorated with ornament in such a way that this became general knowledge, or that "colonial and Italian" cemeteries had a stated policy of avoiding friezes with people on earlier Corinthian pottery—particularly when that prejudice disappears in later Corinthian pottery.

In this last case, we must believe either (1) that merchants persistently found themselves not selling particular pots, observed what it was about these pots that made them unattractive, and gave up supplying them, until that knowledge died and when another merchant came along with the full range of scenes the market decided to purchase what it had previously avoided; or (2) that merchants did not observe what the market was and was not buying, kept trying to sell the same sorts of pots, and that after many years of having to take the figured part of their stock away again unsold, eventually found themselves selling figure scenes after all; or (3) that it so happened that the merchants from whom colonial and Italian sanctuaries were buying happened for many years to frequent only those workshops of Corinthian pottery that did not specialise in figures. Given that the pattern persists over some time and that it is unlikely that all such cemeteries were served by the same merchants, one of the former explanations seems preferable.

Not all who carried Greek pottery to consumers outside Greece will have been equally knowledgeable, and the more discriminating the consumers, the more lack of knowledge among the sellers will have reduced the proportion of the stock carried that was sold, and so undermined the profits to be made. There was an incentive for merchants to finding out whether it was worth carrying a particular shape of pottery to a particular place. There was therefore an incentive to establishing regular exchange over relying on serendipity. Such regular exchange will have allowed for, and is a necessary prerequisite for, orders, whether for particular pots with singular decoration or writing or simply for particular sorts of pot. But such regular exchange is also likely to have been conservative, with every cargo tending to replicate the last cargo. Such regular exchange may indeed effectively impose the tastes of the shipper upon the consumers; a seller who has decided, perhaps on the basis of an initial experience of difficulty selling particular pots in a particular place, that a particular set of items sells well (or does not sell at all) at a particular place may well produce a dominance (or a complete absence) of those items in that place, whether or not the consumers there would really limit their purchases in those ways, given a chance.

The strength of the patterns might be thought to show that consumers did have strong preferences. But they might equally, as in the last scenario discussed, suggest that there was little competition among suppliers. In a situation where one shipper has decided to offer only the narrow set of items that, in their experience, sells, but where other shippers arrive with no idea about the preferences of that market or with discrepant views of the market, then unless the first shipper has got the preferences dead right, the second shipper will manage to sell a wide range of forms, and the assemblage will lose its strongly discriminating features.

The data we have on the distribution of Corinthian and Athenian pottery alike during the seventh, sixth and fifth centuries require that general knowledge of who wanted what was widely shared across the societies of at least the central Mediterranean and the Black Sea. But the data also require that some involved in moving goods around had very particular knowledge about local demand, knowledge that certainly involved what shapes of pot were being used for what purpose, and what quality of pottery was required, but which may have included knowledge of what sorts of decoration were preferred in particular situations. We can think of this knowledge as acquired by trial and error, by market survey or by sharing in the life of the consumer society for long enough to absorb a sense of what those consumers expected. To differentiate between these models we need a better sense of the rhythms and timing of exchange in this world, but at least for the core central Mediterranean world we can exclude some extreme models:

i. down the line trade: a shipper dumps a cargo at a port and the goods trickle down to other markets;
ii. tramping: a shipper goes on from place to place, dropping off whatever can be sold at a particular location (We might wonder whether import and export taxes discouraged this anyway: did a merchant have to pay import tax on everything he put on sale? and did he then have to pay export tax on what he failed to sell and took with him to the next port?).
iii. windfalls: relying on arriving at a place with goods so unusual that they can be sold for a great profit, and not expecting ever to return again (Homer's Phoenicians)
iv. retail chain stores: everywhere there are branches of essentially the same retail outlet selling the same lines.

The seller may not have directly known the consumer, in the way that Finley and his fellow-travellers once assumed, but the seller exercised a significant amount of local knowledge. Exchange can be reckoned to have involved a high degree of knowledge, the advantage of which was a low degree of wastage.

But where does the producer—the potter, and more particularly the painter—come in this story? How far was what was produced influenced by what merchants came back and ordered? Here the data point in different directions. In as far as there are pots that are individually commissioned, the production and the product were entirely determined by the customer. That applies too to some specialist pots. For instance, Panathenaic amphoras go on being produced, and produced in what came to be an obsolete technique, because of the specific demand for these items to satisfy a particular market. Production of the krateriskoi particularly associated with sanctuaries of Artemis in Attica may be another instance where both shape and decoration were entirely determined by a specialist market, and the producer was entirely reactive, if not to individual commissions then to the existence of this particular market niche. But how far is this to be generalised?

Two features of Athenian pottery production demand consideration here. One is the resistance to repetition (see Osborne, 2018a: 36–40; cf. also Stissi, 2014). Although there are a small number of pots that appear to replicate other pots exactly, the proportion of such repeated images in the whole Attic vase production is vanishingly small. We might explain this in two different ways. One explanation would be that very large numbers of pots were made to order, and those orders were specific enough to demand constant iconographic innovation by painters, even within a single theme. But this explanation is hardly plausible. There are many scenes that can be described in essentially the same terms ("athlete standing scraping himself with a strigil; boundary stone of gymnasium behind him"; "soldier takes helmet from a women facing him"), yet visually these scenes are distinct. It would simply not have been possible for a customer who was not actually in the workshop at the moment the pot was painted to determine the exact appearance and ensure that this soldier taking his helmet was different from other soldiers taking their helmets. We are therefore left with the other explanation, that the painter determined the nature of the scene, and that variation is a consequence of technique—there were no advantages to reproducing identical scenes for an able artist—and no one who was not an able artist would survive long in the business (Beazley [1963: 1353–1354] ascribed only 22 pots, all from Spina, to the artist whom he named "the Worst Painter").

The question, however, is how far this painterly initiative went. Did it extend only to the precise disposition of figures on a pot, or did it apply, in general, to the subject? Important here is the evidence for change over time. As I have recently sought to show (Osborne, 2018a), there was a sea-change in the iconographic content of scenes on Athenian red-figure pottery between early red-figure pots of the years down to the Persian Wars and classical red-figure pots of the middle of the fifth century. This sea-change did not so much involve whole areas of imagery going out of, or coming into fashion, though there was some of that—most notoriously scenes of explicit sexual activity are very largely limited to early red-figure pots and absent from classical red-figure pottery—rather, it involved a different, and more restricted range of imagery featuring on classical than on earlier red-figure pottery. Essentially early red-figure pots are more interested in quirky individual scenes, more interested in competition, and more interested in people doing things, often doing things to other people. Classical red-figure pots are more interested in people contemplating doing things, or contemplating having done things—warriors caught at the last moment before they leave the house to go to war, athletes caught scraping themselves down after athletics or standing with jumping weights in their hand receiving a talking to before they go jump; they are more interested also in how people relate to one another.

The relevance of this change of iconography to the question of the nature of the pottery trade rests with the fact that the change of iconography is a general one. That is, this is not a matter of individual scenes becoming more or less popular, something that might result from a scene initially being painted to the order of a customer, or a middleman, and then "catching on", in the way that Exekias' scene of Achilles and Aias dicing seems to have "caught on" in the latter half of the sixth century (whatever motivated Exekias to choose that scene in the first place). Rather, this is a matter of the taste for action and competition being replaced by a taste for contemplation and collaboration—even in the case of types of action where in real-life competition and action continued to be manifested, as they must have been in both warfare and athletics. Did such a general change stem from changing customer tastes, or from the changing tastes of the producers?

Our answer to that question is going to depend on the homogeneity of the world which consumed Athenian pottery. If we think that essentially the whole Mediterranean world, or at least the Mediterranean world that was in touch with Greece, constituted a single co-ordinated community, with shared values and tastes, then we can imagine the change of imagery to be a consequence of the changing tastes of consumers. "Something in the air" will have persuaded the whole community of the Mediterranean that was in touch with Greece to think less competitively and more contemplatively in the middle of the fifth century than in the previous generations. And, given that not all the world that was in touch with Greece had been threatened by Persian or Phoenician attack, that "something in the air" cannot have been the "barbarian wars" repulsed in 480 and 479 BCE.

Such homogeneity in the Mediterranean world that was in touch with Greece is, however, implausible. There are many ways in which life in Etruria in the fifth century BCE was distinct from the life of Greek cities in these years, just as there are many ways in which it had been distinctive in the sixth century. The imagery that we find in Etruscan tombs reinforces this point, since the iconography of painted tombs is highly distinctive, for all that it shares motifs and techniques with the Greek world. And if the Mediterranean world that was in touch with Greece was not homogenous, and was not all demanding the same changes to the selection of scenes on painted pottery at the same time, then the impetus for change must have come either from the artists, or alternatively, but less plausibly, from one particular set of customers (with the artists assuming that changes which they found themselves asked for by some of their customers would go down well also with other customers).

The quantity of Athenian pottery found in Etruria declines over the course of the fifth century. There may be all sorts of reasons for that decline, many of them to do with what was happening in Etruria itself. But that decline certainly allows for the possibility that the changes in the sorts of scenes that were painted on Athenian pottery may not have been changes that the Etruscans found altogether attractive. Just as earlier, in the sixth century, what was on offer from Corinthian potters seems to have been found steadily less attractive than what was on offer from Athenian potters, so too, in the course of the later fifth century, what came to be on offer from potters and painters in southern Italy came to be more attractive locally than what was on offer from Athens.

If we are correct to reckon that those engaged in the pottery trade knew a lot about their markets, and chose the pots that they traded to fit with what they knew those markets liked, then we have also to recognise that they could only exercise that knowledge upon a body of material that Athenian potters and painters had produced or were willing to produce. That is, the merchant's choice was limited by decisions made by the potter and painter. Merchants could hint about certain shapes being favoured, or indeed press for certain sorts of scenes to be painted, but it was the painters' changing tastes that determined the limits of the available stock. The painters' tastes may well have been shared by, indeed shaped by, the community of which they themselves were part—something suggested by the way in which sculpture produced across the Greek world, and indeed the wall paintings of which non-Athenians were the most famous exponents, were marked by similar changes in iconographic choice. But for all that Nikosthenes, at the end of the sixth century, tried producing specifically Etruscan-shaped pots for the Etruscan market, no painter of pots in the middle of the fifth century stuck to the old iconographic choices that had sold so well there. If merchants tried to persuade them to do so, they simply failed: painters could be persuaded to paint particular subjects, but not to paint those subjects in a particular way.

There are arguably big historical conclusions lurking in these changing patterns of pottery consumption. That the Etruscans in the sixth century voraciously consumed the particular view of the world pedalled by Athenian black-figure and early red-figure artists (Osborne, 2001) says something about the extent to which the competitive culture centred on male performance and the drinking of alcohol was shared across the Mediterranean. That classical Athenian red-figure pottery was less voraciously consumed says something about the limits to the extent to which classical Greek culture was shared outside the Greek-speaking world—one might note here the degree to which the popularity of classical Athenian pottery and the popularity of Greek theatre coincided (on theatre see Bosher, 2012).

There are also conclusions for the way in which we model trade. If we are to rule out down-the-line trade, tramping, windfalls, and chain stores, we are also to rule out a market shaped by producer reaction to customer surveys. Trade depended upon the knowledge possessed and used by the middleman, who selected from available goods to match, as best he could, the known preferences of those to whom he sold. This was effectively a world of specialist stores, which stocked what they considered their market to want. But they could only stock what the manufacturers chose to make. And when it came to figured pottery, too much was bound up in the nature of the figurative decoration for anything to be possible. For the scenes on pots carried a world view, not in the sense that they showed everything that went on in the world, but in the sense that they carried a way of seeing what went on in the world, a way of seeing that was actually highly selective. Painters arguably simply could not see in the middle of the fifth century what they had been able to see at the end of the sixth century. Just as the only way for a late fifth-century poet to write Homeric epic or Aeschylean tragedy was as parody (cf. Aristophanes' *Frogs*), so "archaizing" scenes on Panathenaic amphoras come to seem parodic. Arguably, successful marketing depended not merely on merchants who selected wisely but upon the ability of the painted pottery that was on sale to persuade those to whom it was offered to share its way of seeing the world. As in the modern world, not all changes of fashion in clothing are found persuasive by all markets, so in antiquity, there was a limit to how immediately persuasive the vision of the world offered at a particular point by Athenian pot-painters proved to be. The image, as well as the potter, painter, merchant and consumer, must be allowed some agency in this story.

References

Beazley, J. D. (1963). *Attic Red-Figure Vase-Painters*. Second edition. Oxford Clarendon Press

Bosher, K. (2012). *Greek theatre outside Athens: Drama in Greek Sicily and South Italy*. Cambridge University Press.

Burn, L. M. (1985). Honey pots: Three white-ground cups by the Sotades Painter. *Antike Kunst, 28*, 93–105.

Cook, R. M. (1959). Die Bedeutung der bemalten Keramik für den griechischen Handel. *Jahrbuch des Deutschen Archäologischen Instituts, 74*, 114–123.

Gill, D. W. J. (1991). Pots and trade: Spacefillers or objets d'art? *Journal of Hellenic Studies, 111*, 29–47.

Hoffmann, H. (1997). *Sotades: Symbols of immortality on Greek vases*. Clarendon Press.

Langridge-Noti, E. (2013). Consuming iconographies. In A. Tsingarida & D. Viviers (Eds.), *Pottery markets in the Ancient Greek world (8th–1st Centuries B.C.)* (pp. 61–72). CReA-Patrimoine.

Moore, M. B. (1997). Attic red-figure painters and the Athenian agora. In J. H. Oakley, W. D. E. Coulson, & O. Palagia (Eds.), *Athenian potters and painters* (pp. 469–472). Oxbow Books.

Osborne, R. G. (1996). Pots, trade and the archaic Greek economy. *Antiquity, 70*(267), 31–44.

Osborne, R. G. (2001). Why did Athenian pots appeal to the Etruscans? *World Archaeology, 33*(2), 277–295.

Osborne, R. G. (2018a). *The transformation of Athens: Painted pottery and the creation of classical Greece*. Princeton University Press.

Osborne, R. G. (2018b). A world of choice: Taking archaic Greek diversity seriously. In C. Draycott, R. Raja, K. Welch, & W. Wootton (Eds.), *Visual histories of the classical world: Essays in honour of R. R. R. Smith* (pp. 5–14). Brepols.

Padgett, M. J. (2009). Attic imports at Marion: Preliminary results of the Princeton University archaeological expedition to Polis Chrysochous, Cyprus. In J. H. Oakley & O. Palagia (Eds.), *Athenian potters and painters II* (pp. 220–231). Oxbow Books.

Reusser, C. (2002). *Vasen für Etrurien: Verbreitung und Funktionen attischer Keramik im Etrurien des 6. und 5: Jahrhunderts vor Christus*. Akanthus.

Sapirstein, P. (2013). Painters, potters, and the scale of the Attic vase-painting industry. *American Journal of Archaeology, 117*, 493–510.
Sapirstein, P. (2014). Demography and productivity in the ancient Athenian pottery industry. In J. H. Oakley (Ed.), *Athenian potters and painters III* (pp. 175–186). Oxbow Books.
Shanks, M. (1999). *Art and the early Greek state: An interpretive archaeology*. Cambridge University Press.
Stissi, V. (2014). Standardization and Greek pottery, a broad view from far above. In A. Kotsonas (Ed.), *Understanding standardization and variation in Mediterranean ceramics mid 2nd to late 1st millennium BC* (pp. 115–131). Peeters.
Taplin, O., & Wiles, R. (2010). *The Pronomos vase in context*. Oxford University Press.
Tosto, V. (1999). *The black-figure pottery signed ΝΙΚΟΣΘΕΝΕΣΕΠΟΙΕΣΕΝ*. Allard Pierson.
Webster, T. B. L. (1972). *Potter and patron in classical Athens*. Methuen.

The manufacturer's authorised representative in the EU is Springer Nature Customer Service Centre GmbH, Europaplatz 3, 69115 Heidelberg, Germany. If you have any concerns regarding our products, please contact ProductSafety@springernature.com

Printed and bound by CPI Group (UK) Ltd, Croydon, CR0 4YY
30/09/2026
02225692-0002